SUICIDE RESEARCH: SELECTED READINGS

Volume 9

November 2012 – April 2013

E. Barker, A-M. Snider, S. McPhedran and D. De Leo

Australian Institute for Suicide Research and Prevention

Griffith UNIVERSITY

WHO Collaborating Centre for
Research and Training in Suicide Prevention

National Centre of Excellence in Suicide Prevention

First published in 2013
Australian Academic Press
32 Jeays Street
Bowen Hills Qld 4006
Australia
www.australianacademicpress.com.au

ISBN: 9781922117182

Book and cover design by Maria Biaggini — The Letter Tree.

Contents

Foreword vii

Acknowledgments viii

Introduction

Context 1

Methodology 2

Key articles

Almeida et al, 2012. Factors associated with suicidal thoughts in a large community study of older adults 8

Atkins Whitmer et al, 2012. Analysis of the cost effectiveness of a suicide barrier on the Golden Gate Bridge 10

Bartik et al, 2013. Adolescent survivors after suicide: Australian young people's bereavement narratives 13

Biddle et al, 2013. Qualitative interviewing with vulnerable populations: Individuals' experiences of participating in suicide and self-harm based research 15

Bilén et al, 2013. Can repetition of deliberate self-harm be predicted? A prospective multicenter study validating clinical decision rules 17

Bolton et al, 2013. Parents bereaved by offspring suicide: A population-based longitudinal case-control study 19

Carter et al, 2013. Postcards from the EDge: 5-year outcomes of a randomised controlled trial for hospital-treated self-poisoning 22

Cash et al, 2013. Adolescent suicide statements on MySpace.............. 24

Cebrià et al, 2013. Effectiveness of a telephone management programme for patients discharged from an emergency department after a suicide attempt: Controlled study in a Spanish population 26

Chapple et al, 2013. How people bereaved by suicide perceive newspaper reporting: Qualitative study 29

Cho et al, 2013. Age and gender differences in medical care utilization prior to suicide 31

Cox et al, 2013. Interventions to reduce suicides at suicide hotspots: A systematic review 33

De Leo et al, 2013. Has the suicide rate risen with the 2011 Queensland floods? 35

Desmarais et al, 2012. Pilot implementation and preliminary evaluation of START: AV assessments in secure juvenile correctional facilities 37

Fässberg et al, 2013. Suicidal feelings in the twilight of life: A cross-sectional population-based study of 97-year-olds 39

Hawton et al, 2013. Long term effect of reduced pack sizes of paracetamol on poisoning deaths and liver transplant activity in England and Wales: Interrupted time series analyses 41

Hegerl et al, 2013. One followed by many?- Long-term effects of a celebrity suicide on the number of suicidal acts on the German railway net 43

Horowitz et al, 2013. Ask suicide-screening questions to everyone in medical settings: The asQ'em quality improvement project 45

Kleiman et al, 2013. Social support as a protective factor in suicide: Findings from two nationally representative samples.............................. 47

Laukkanen et al, 2013. Adolescent self-cutting elsewhere than on the arms reveals more serious psychiatric symptoms 49

Luke et al, 2013. Suicide ideation and attempt in a community cohort of urban Aboriginal youth: A cross-sectional study...................... 51

Mark et al, 2013. Suicidal ideation, risk factors, and communication with parents: An HBSC study on school children in Estonia, Lithuania, and Luxembourg.. 53

Matsubayashi et al, 2013. Natural disasters and suicide: Evidence from Japan.. 55

Nock et al, 2013. Prevalence, correlates, and treatment of lifetime suicidal behavior among adolescents: Results from the national comorbidity survey replication adolescent supplement 57

Nordentoft et al, 2013. Excess mortality, causes of death and life expectancy in 270,770 patients with recent onset of mental disorders in Denmark, Finland and Sweden 59

O'Dwyer et al, 2013. Suicidal ideation in family carers of people with dementia: A pilot study 61

Pan et al, 2012. Effectiveness of a nationwide aftercare program for suicide attempters 63

Pisani et al, 2012. Emotion regulation difficulties, youth-adult relationships, and suicide attempts among high school students in underserved communities 65

Richard-Devantoy et al, 2013. Altered explicit recognition of facial disgust associated with predisposition to suicidal behavior but not depression 67

Rosmarin et al, 2013. A test of faith in God and treatment: The relationship of belief in God to psychiatric treatment outcomes 69

Wiktorsson et al, 2013. Neuroticism and extroversion in suicide attempters aged 75 and above and a general population comparison group 71

Recommended readings 73

Citation list
  Fatal suicidal behaviour:
      Epidemiology 118
      Risk and protective factors 129
      Prevention 140
      Postvention and bereavement 147
  Non-fatal suicidal behaviour:
      Epidemiology 148
      Risk and protective factors 159
      Prevention 186
      Care and support 187
  Case reports 196
  Miscellaneous...203

Foreword

This volume contains quotations from internationally peer-reviewed suicide research published during the semester November 2012 – April 2013; it is the ninth of a series produced biannually by our Institute with the aim of assisting the Commonwealth Department of Health and Ageing in being constantly updated on new evidences from the scientific community. Compared to previous volumes, an increased number of examined materials have to be referred. In fact, during the current semester, the number of articles scrutinised has been the highest yet, with a progression that testifies a remarkably growing interest from scholars for the field of suicide research (718 articles for the first, 757 for the second, 892 for the third, 1,121 for the fourth, 1,276 for the fifth, 1,472 for the sixth, 1,515 for the seventh, 1,743 for the eighth and 1,751 in the present volume).

As usual, the initial section of the volume collects a number of publications that could have particular relevance for the Australian people in terms of potential applicability. These publications are accompanied by a short comment from us, and an explanation of the motives that justify why we have considered of interest the implementation of studies' findings in the Australian context. An introductory part provides the rationale and the methodology followed in the identification of papers.

The central part of the volume represents a selection of research articles of particular significance; their abstracts are reported *in extenso*, underlining our invitation at reading those papers in full text: they represent a remarkable advancement of suicide research knowledge.

The last section reports all items retrievable from major electronic databases. We have catalogued them on the basis of their prevailing reference to fatal and non-fatal suicidal behaviours, with various sub-headings (e.g. epidemiology, risk factors, etc). The deriving list guarantees a level of completeness superior to any individual system; it can constitute a useful tool for all those interested in a quick update of what most recently published on the topic.

Our intent was to make suicide research more approachable to non-specialists, and in the meantime provide an opportunity for a *vademecum* of quotations credible also at the professional level. A compilation such as the one that we provide here is not easily obtainable from usual sources and can save a considerable amount of time to readers. We believe that our effort in this direction may be an appropriate interpretation of one of the technical support roles to the Government that the new status of National Centre of Excellence in Suicide Prevention — which has deeply honoured our commitment —entails for us.

The significant growth of our centre, the Australian Institute for Suicide Research and Prevention, and its influential function, both nationally and internationally, in the fight against suicide, could not happen without the constant support of Queensland Health and Griffith University. We hope that our passionate dedication to the cause of suicide prevention may compensate their continuing trust in our work.

Diego De Leo, DSc
Director, Australian Institute for Suicide Research and Prevention

Acknowledgments

This report has been produced by the Australian Institute for Suicide Research and Prevention, WHO Collaborating Centre for Research and Training in Suicide Prevention and National Centre of Excellence in Suicide Prevention. The assistance of the Commonwealth Department of Health and Ageing in the funding of this report is gratefully acknowledged.

Introduction

Context

Suicide places a substantial burden on individuals, communities and society in terms of emotional, economic and health care costs. In Australia, about 2000 people die from suicide every year, a death rate well in excess of transport-related mortality. At the time of preparing this volume, the latest available statistics released by the Australian Bureau of Statistics[1] indicated that, in 2009, 2,132 deaths by suicide were registered in Australia, representing an age-standardized rate of 9.6 per 100,000.

Further, a study on mortality in Australia for the years 1997–2001 found that suicide was the leading cause of avoidable mortality in the 25–44 year age group, for both males (29.5%) and females (16.7%), while in the age group 15–24 suicide accounted for almost a third of deaths due to avoidable mortality[2]. In 2003, self-inflicted injuries were responsible for 27% of the total injury burden in Australia, leading to an estimated 49,379 years of life lost (YLL) due to premature mortality, with the greatest burdens observed in men aged 25–64[3].

Despite the estimated mortality, the prevalence of suicide and self-harming behaviour in particular remains difficult to gauge due to the often secretive nature of these acts. Indeed, ABS has acknowledged the difficulties in obtaining reliable data for suicides in the past few years[4, 5]. Without a clear understanding of the scope of suicidal behaviours and the range of interventions available, the opportunity to implement effective initiatives is reduced. Further, it is important that suicide prevention policies are developed on the foundation of evidence-based empirical research, especially as the quality and validly of the available information may be misleading or inaccurate. Additionally, the social and economic impact of suicide underlines the importance of appropriate research-based prevention strategies, addressing not only significant direct costs on health system and lost productivity, but also the emotional suffering for families and communities.

The Australian Institute for Suicide Research and Prevention (AISRAP) has, through the years, gained an international reputation as one of the leading research institutions in the field of suicide prevention. The most important recognition came via the designation as a World Health Organization (WHO) Collaborating Centre in 2005. In 2008, the Commonwealth Department of Health and Ageing (DoHA) appointed AISRAP as the National Centre of Excellence in Suicide Prevention. This latter recognition awards not only many years of high-quality research, but also of fruitful cooperation between the Institute and several different governmental agencies. The new role given to AISRAP will translate into an even deeper commitment to the cause of suicide prevention amongst community members of Australia.

As part of this initiative, AISRAP is committed to the creation of a databank of the recent scientific literature documenting the nature and extent of suicidal and self-harming behavior and recommended practices in preventing and responding to these behaviors. The key output for the project is a critical bi-annual review of the national and international literature outlining recent advances and promising developments in research in suicide prevention, particularly where this can help to inform national activities. This task is not aimed at providing a critique of new researches, but rather at drawing attention to investigations that may have particular relevance to the Australian context. In doing so, we are committed to a user-friendly language, in order to render research outcomes and their interpretation accessible also to a non-expert audience.

In summary, these reviews serve three primary purposes:

1. To inform future State and Commonwealth suicide prevention policies;
2. To assist in the improvement of existing initiatives, and the development of new and innovative Australian projects for the prevention of suicidal and self-harming behaviors within the context of the Living is for Everyone (LIFE) Framework (2008);
3. To provide directions for Australian research priorities in suicidology.

The review is presented in three sections. The first contains a selection of the best articles published in the last six months internationally. For each article identified by us (see the method of chosing articles described below), the original abstract is accompanied by a brief comment explaining why we thought the study was providing an important contribution to research and why we considered its possible applicability to Australia. The second section presents the abstracts of the most relevant literature — following our criteria - collected between November 2012 and April 2013; while the final section presents a list of citations of all literature published over this time-period.

Methodology

The literature search was conducted in four phases.

Phase 1

Phase 1 consisted of weekly searches of the academic literature performed from November 2012 to April 2013. To ensure thorough coverage of the available published research, the literature was sourced using several scientific electronic databases including: Pubmed, Proquest, Scopus, Safetylit and Web of Science, using the following key words: *suicide, suicidal, self-harm, self-injury and parasuicide.*

Results from the weekly searches were downloaded and combined into one database (deleting duplicates).

Specific inclusion criteria for Phase 1 included:

- Timeliness: the article was published (either electronically or in hard-copy) between November 2012 and April 2013.
- Relevance: the article explicitly referred to fatal and/or non-fatal suicidal behaviour and related issues and/or interventions directly targeted at preventing/treating these behaviours.

• The article was written in English.

Articles about euthanasia, assisted suicide, suicide terrorist attacks, and/or book reviews, abstracts and conference presentations were excluded.

Also, articles that have been published in electronic versions (ahead of print) and therefore included in the previous volume (Volumes 1 to 8 of *Suicide Research: Selected Readings*) were excluded to avoid duplication.

Phase 2

Following an initial reading of the abstracts (retrieved in Phase 1), the list of articles was refined down to the most relevant literature. In Phase 2 articles were only included if they were published in an international, peer-reviewed journal.

In Phase 2, articles were excluded when they:

• were not particularly instructive or original
• were of a descriptive nature (e.g. a case-report)
• consisted of historical/philosophical content
• were a description of surgical reconstruction/treatment of self-inflicted injuries
• concerned biological and/or genetic interpretations of suicidal behaviour, the results of which could not be easily adoptable in the context of the LIFE Framework.

In order to minimise the potential for biased evaluations, two researchers working independently read through the full text of all articles selected to create a list of most relevant papers. This process was then duplicated by a third researcher for any articles on which consensus could not be reached.

The strength and quality of the research evidence was evaluated, based on the *Critical Appraisal Skills Programme (CASP) Appraisal Tools* published by the Public Health Resource Unit, England (2006). These tools, publically available online, consist of checklists for critically appraising systematic reviews, randomized controlled trials (RCT), qualitative research, economic evaluation studies, cohort studies, diagnostic test studies and case control studies.

Phase 3

One of the aims of this review was to identify research that is both evidence-based and of potential relevance to the Australian context. Thus, the final stage of applied methodology focused on research conducted in countries with populations or health systems sufficiently comparable to Australia. Only articles in which the full-text was available were considered. It is important to note that failure of an article to be selected for inclusion in Phase 3 does not entail any negative judgment on its 'objective' quality.

Specific inclusion criteria for Phase 3 included:

• applicability to Australia
• the paper met all criteria for scientificity (i.e., the methodology was considered sound)
• the paper represented a particularly compelling addition to the literature, which would be likely to stimulate suicide prevention initiatives and research

- inevitably, an important aspect was the importance of the journal in which the paper was published (because of the high standards that have to be met in order to obtain publication in that specific journal); priority was given to papers published in high impact factor journals
- particular attention has been paid to widen the literature horizon to include socio-logical and anthropological research that may have particular relevance to the Australian context.

After a thorough reading of these articles ('Key articles' for the considered timeframe), a written comment was produced for each article detailing:

- methodological strengths and weaknesses (e.g., sample size, validity of measurement instruments, appropriateness of analysis performed)
- practical implications of the research results to the Australian context
- suggestions for integrating research findings within the domains of the LIFE framework suicide prevention activities.

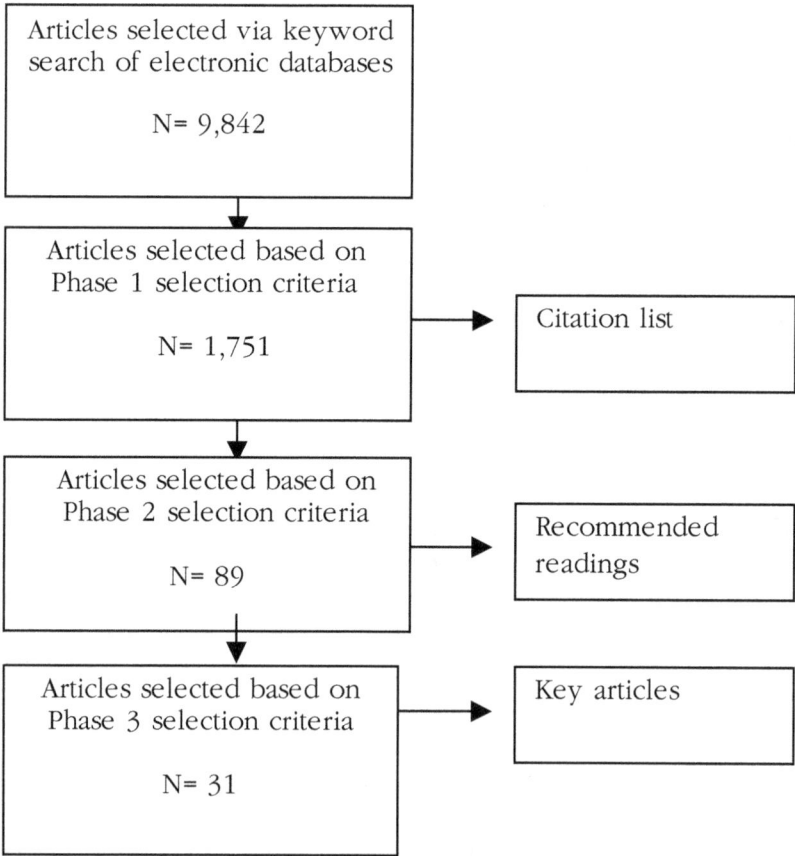

Figure 1 Flowchart of process.

Phase 4

In the final phase of the search procedure all articles were divided into the following classifications:

- *Fatal suicidal behaviour* (epidemiology, risk and protective factors, prevention, postvention and bereavement)

- *Non-fatal suicidal/self-harming behaviours* (epidemiology, risk and protective factors, prevention, care and support)

- *Case reports* include reports of fatal and non-fatal suicidal behaviours

- *Miscellaneous* includes all research articles that could not be classified into any other category.

Allocation to these categories was not always straightforward, and where papers spanned more than one area, consensus of the research team determined which domain the article would be placed in. Within each section of the report (i.e., Key articles, Recommended readings, Citation list) articles are presented in alphabetical order by author.

Endnotes

1   Australian Bureau of Statistics (2011). *Causes of Death, Australia, 2009, Suicides.* Cat. No. 3303.0. ABS: Canberra.

2   Page A, Tobias M, Glover J, Wright C, Hetzel D, Fisher E (2006). *Australian and New Zealand Atlas of avoidable mortality.* Public Health Information Development Unit, University of Adelaide: Adelaide.

3   Begg S, Vos T, Barker B, Stevenson C, Stanley L, Lopez A (2007). *The burden of disease and injury in Australia 2003.* Australian Institute for Health and Welfare, Canberra.

4   Australian Bureau of Statistics (2009). *Causes of Death, Australia, 2007,* Technical Note 1, Cat. No. 3303.0. ABS: Canberra.

5   Australian Bureau of Statistics (2009c). *Causes of Death, Australia, 2007, Explanatory Notes.* Cat. No. 3303.0. ABS: Canberra.

Key Articles

Factors associated with suicidal thoughts in a large community study of older adults

Almeida OP, Draper B, Snowdon J, Lautenschlager NT, Pirkis J, Byrne G, Sim M, Stocks N, Flicker L, Pfaff JJ (Australia)

British Journal of Psychiatry 201, 466-472, 2012

Background: Thoughts about death and self-harm in old age have been commonly associated with the presence of depression, but other risk factors may also be important.

Aims: To determine the independent association between suicidal ideation in later life and demographic, lifestyle, socioeconomic, psychiatric and medical factors.

Method: A cross-sectional study was conducted of a community derived sample of 21 290 adults aged 60-101 years enrolled from Australian primary care practices. We considered that participants endorsing any of the four items of the Depressive Symptom Inventory — Suicidality Subscale were experiencing suicidal thoughts. We used standard procedures to collect demographic, lifestyle, psychosocial and clinical data. Anxiety and depressive symptoms were assessed with the Hospital Anxiety and Depression Scale.

Results: The 2-week prevalence of suicidal ideation was 4.8%. Male gender, higher education, current smoking, living alone, poor social support, no religious practice, financial strain, childhood physical abuse, history of suicide in the family, past depression, current anxiety, depression or comorbid anxiety and depression, past suicide attempt, pain, poor self perceived health and current use of antidepressants were independently associated with suicidal ideation. Poor social support was associated with a population attributable fraction of 38.0%, followed by history of depression (23.6%), concurrent anxiety and depression (19.7%), prevalent anxiety (15.1%), pain (13.7%) and no religious practice (11.4%).

Conclusions: Prevalent and past mood disorders seem to be valid targets for indicated interventions designed to reduce suicidal thoughts and behaviour. However, our data indicate that social disconnectedness and stress account for a larger proportion of cases than mood disorders. Should these associations prove to be causal, then interventions that succeeded in addressing these issues would contribute the most to reducing suicidal ideation and, possibly, suicidal behaviour in later life.

Declaration of interest: None.

Comment

Main findings: While often hidden or disguised, suicidal thoughts are shown to precede suicide in older adults and the elderly[1]. In an effort to address this, suicide prevention strategies for older populations have mainly focused on detecting and managing depression and anxiety. Although depression and anxiety are correlated with suicidal thoughts, collaborative care strategies aimed at reducing the severity of depression and the prevalence of suicidal ideation in older populations have reported only moderate success in decreasing suicide. In addition to psychiatric and clinical factors, this study explored independent socio-demographic and lifestyle factors that predicted suicidal ideation in older adults in Australia. Significant predictors of suicidal ideation included living alone, poor social support, financial stress, physical abuse during childhood, suicide in the family, but also pain, use of anti-depressants, anxiety and depression and past suicide attempt. Older adults with suicidal ideation were more likely to be educated non-religious males. These results were derived from an Australian cross-sectional study where a questionnaire was sent to all participants over 60 years old in primary care practices located in New South Wales, Queensland, South Australia, Victoria, and Western Australia. A total of 21 290 questionnaires were returned out of the 35 099 that were tracked. To date this is the most in-depth study to explore the demographic, lifestyle, socioeconomic and clinical factors associated with older persons' suicidal ideation.

Implications: This large community-based Australian study has important implications to suicide prevention in older populations, who have shown high suicide rates, especially males aged 75 years and over (25.2 per 100 000 compared to the total age-standardised male rate of 16.3 in 2010 preliminary data)[2]. As indicated by the authors, while many of the older adults who experienced suicidal ideation had a history of anxiety or depression and a past suicide attempt; social factors, such as poor perceived social support and living alone, were also independently associated with suicidal ideation. Consequently, focusing older population suicide prevention strategies on mood disorders may have only limited impact on the overall prevalence of suicide ideation. Providing more social support for older populations by telephone support and befriending, could contribute to the reduction of high suicide rates of older people in Australia[3]. Also, gender-specific interventions for older populations need to be considered as men are less likely to seek help and may prefer interventions programs that emphasize problem solving, rather than expressing emotions or building new relationships[4].

Furthermore, this study highlights the importance of independent social factors and emphasises that future research must address the prevalence of suicidal ideation by targeting people with symptoms of risk, including mental factors as well as demographic, lifestyle and socioeconomic characteristics.

Endnotes

1. Scocco P, De Leo D (2002). One-year prevalence of death thoughts, suicide ideation and behaviours in an elderly population. *International Journal of Geriatric Psychiatry* 17, 842-846.
2. Australian Bureau of Statistics (2001-2010). *Suicide in Australia: Suicide summary statistics, Australia, (2001-2010)*. Canberra: ABS.
3. De Leo D, Dello Buono M, Dwyer J (2002). Suicide among the elderly: The long-term impact of a telephone support and assessment intervention in northern Italy. *British Journal of Psychiatry* 181, 226-229.
4. Lapierre S, Erlangsen A, Waern M, De Leo D, Oyama H, Scocco P, Gallo J, Szanto K, Conwell Y, Draper B, Quinnett P (2011). A systematic review of elderly suicide prevention programs. *Crisis* 32, 88-98.

Analysis of the cost effectiveness of a suicide barrier on the Golden Gate Bridge

Atkins Whitmer D, Woods DL (USA)

Crisis 34, 98-106, 2013

Background: The Golden Gate Bridge (GGB) is a well-known "suicide magnet" and the site of approximately 30 suicides per year. Recently, a suicide barrier was approved to prevent further suicides.

Aims: To estimate the cost-effectiveness of the proposed suicide barrier, we compared the proposed costs of the barrier over a 20-year period ($51.6 million) to estimated reductions in mortality.

Method: We reviewed San Francisco and Golden Gate Bridge suicides over a 70-year period (1936-2006). We assumed that all suicides prevented by the barrier would attempt suicide with alternative methods and estimated the mortality reduction based on the difference in lethality between GGB jumps and other suicide methods. Cost/benefit analyses utilized estimates of value of statistical life (VSL) used in highway projects.

Results: GGB suicides occur at a rate of approximately 30 per year, with a lethality of 98%. Jumping from other structures has an average lethality of 47%. Assuming that unsuccessful suicides eventually committed suicide at previously reported (12-13%) rates, approximately 286 lives would be saved over a 20-year period at an average cost/life of approximately $180,419 i.e., roughly 6% of US Department of Transportation minimal VSL estimate ($3.2 million).

Conclusions: Cost-benefit analysis suggests that a suicide barrier on the GGB would result in a highly cost-effective reduction in suicide mortality in the San Francisco Bay Area.

Comment

Main findings: Within the past decade jumping has become the most lethal method of suicide in San Francisco, increasing from 4-11 cases per year in the 1940s-1960s, to 30 per year in the 2000s. In particular, the lethality of jumping from the Golden Gate Bridge is extremely high (98%) compared to other methods of suicide, making this a site more lethal than firearms (95%) in San Francisco and Marin County. Previous attempts to prevent suicides include a foot patrol on the Golden Gate Bridge which began in 1966, and the installation of a crisis telephone in 1980, had limited effect and the number of Golden Gate Bridge deaths continued to increase.

The current paper examines from an economic perspective, the cost of barriers on the Golden Gate Bridge in terms of the number of lives that would be saved and the value of these lives. The authors make a number of assumptions. Central to these is the value to be placed on the saving of a life. Most would readily agree that human life is priceless, but to provide a rational analysis of the problem the authors resort to a widely used concept in economics, that of the value of a statistical life (VSL)[1,2]. This is an estimate of the dollar cost of a fatality and is used in economic analysis in public health and transport engineering, among other disciplines. The lower bound estimate used by the US Office of Transportation, based on wages and salaries forgone by a person's death, is $3.2 million. A second assumption is that the rate of suicide by jumping from the bridge would continue into the future (20 years for the purposes of the analysis) at its present figure if barriers were not erected. A third assumption has to do with the likely outcome for those persons who are prevented from jumping from the bridge, if barriers were erected. Here the authors expect potential substitution of the method and they consider the lethality of other suicide attempts in the area (43.4%). Based on past research they further assume that 12-13% of people who attempted suicide would still take their own lives in a 20 year period. With these assumptions and estimates in place the authors run the analysis for a 20 year period and find that 286 lives would be saved, which in terms of the construction and maintenance costs mentioned earlier means a cost per life saved of $180,419. This represents less than 6% of the lower bound estimate of the VSL and would thus suggest a considerable benefit. Not considered, however, are alternative uses of the $51.6 million and the return on this, such as reducing fatalities through improving highways.

Implications: Erecting barriers where suicide by jumping poses a threat has proved to be an effective deterrent in a number of studies[3]. A natural experiment in Auckland where barriers were erected on the Grafton Bridge, then removed because of community concern, and once again erected demonstrated a reduction of suicide by jumping to zero as a consequence of the barriers[4]. Erecting barriers is however controversial, with objections being raised on aesthetic grounds (e.g., changing the form of an icon such as the Golden Gate Bridge) and on economic grounds (e.g., the cost of construction and ongoing maintenance, which in the case of the Golden Gate bridge was estimated in 2009 at $50 million initially and $79,000 per year of operation).

Exercises of the sort that the authors have undertaken can be criticised and no doubt this one will as part of the process of ongoing scientific review. However, the paper does provide a thoughtful analysis of one of the primary objections to erecting barriers, a well-attested method for reducing suicide by jumping, on the Golden Gate Bridge. Generalisation of the authors' methods and argument to other sites known for a high incidence of suicide by jumping needs to proceed cautiously. Rates and estimates depend on a careful examination of the site to which the generalisation is to be made (e.g., VSL is not a constant but varies with such factors as income, age, and country). The aesthetic argument of course remains, but economic arguments can have a persuasive effect on those who make decisions about erecting barriers on bridges.

The recent decision by the Brisbane City Council to erect suicide prevention barriers at the historical landmark Story Bridge, is a positive initiative to help prevent suicides.

Endnotes

1. Access Economics (2008). *The health of nations: the value of a statistical life. Report to the Office of the Australian Safety and Compensation Council, Department of Education, Employment and Workplace Relations.* Canberra: Author. Retrieved 29 January 2013 from http://www.safeworkaustralia.gov.au/sites/swa/about/publications/pages/rr200807valueofastatisticallife.

2. Ashenfelter O (2006). Measuring *the value of a statistical life: Problems and prospects.* Working Paper 11916. National Bureau of Economic Research, Cambridge, MA. Retrieved 29 January 2013 from http://www.nber.org/papers/w11916

3. Bennewith O, Nowers M, Gunnell D (2007). Effect of barriers on the Clifton suspension bridge, England, on local patterns of suicide: Implications for prevention. *British Journal of Psychiatry* 190, 266-267.

4. Beautrais AL, Gibb SJ, Fergusson DM, Horwood LJ, Larkin GL. (2009). Removing bridge barriers stimulates suicides: An unfortunate natural experiment. *Australian and New Zealand Journal of Psychiatry* 43, 495-497.

Adolescent survivors after suicide: Australian young people's bereavement narratives

Bartik W, Maple M, Edwards H, Kiernan M (Australia)

Crisis. Published online: 28 January 2013. doi: 10.1027/0227-5910/a000185, 2013

Background: While the research literature exploring suicide bereavement has expanded in recent years, this has been primarily quantitative and has focused more on the bereavement experience of parents and siblings. The bereavement experience of young people affected through the suicide death of a friend remains under-conceptualized and not well understood.

Aims: To develop an understanding of the experiences of young people bereaved by the suicide of a friend.

Method: Ten young people participated in a pilot study with in-depth interviews to explore their suicide bereavement experiences. Narrative inquiry methodology was utilized to analyze the qualitative data.

Results: The findings indicated multiple grief experiences caused by suicide. Four themes reported are meaning making, feeling guilt, risky coping behavior, and relating to friends following suicide loss.

Conclusions: Implications include the need for increased awareness that friends of young people who die by suicide may have significant health and well-being challenges associated with bereavement, and that friends in these circumstances may not readily present at services for assistance.

Comment

Main findings: Using qualitative methods, this study sought to explore how young Australians, aged 12-24 years, experienced the loss of loved one to suicide. A total of 10 participants (8 female, 2 male) with the average age of 24 took part in the in-depth, narrative format interviews. In all, the group had experienced 24 suicide deaths — 22 being friends, and 2 family members — and of the 24 deaths, five participants had experienced the same suicide death. Furthermore, of these five, they had experienced another 14 unrelated suicide deaths, including one sibling. The authors acknowledge the amount of bereavement within these five participants' lives leaves this group highly exposed to intense trauma. Only one participant had experienced one death by suicide. There emerged four relevant themes in the young people's bereavement experience: meaning making, feeling guilty, risky coping behaviour and relating to friends. The themes suggest that although participants made an effort to search for meaning in their suicide-bereavement experiences, they typically were unable to find this, and could not understand why their friend had not been able to confide in them prior to death. Participants also felt guilt about not having 'done more' for their friend, and about not having recognised that their friend was considering suicide. Many of the participants struggled to incorporate the absence of their loved one into their lives. Also, several of the participants engaged in risk taking behaviour (such as drug and alcohol use) to seek comfort as well as avoid the emotions that arose as a result of their loved one's suicide. Although risk taking behaviour is thought to be normal during adolescence it seemed that bereaved young persons' behaviours were 'more extreme' and 'potentially harder to control' by their own standards. Finally, participants reported that they experienced difficulties relating to friends following bereavement, with some participants reporting longer-term impacts on future friendships and their capacity to trust those relationships. However, the findings from this study may not be typical, given the small sample size and their level of exposure to deaths by suicide.

Implications: Engaging with social networks is critical to a young person's growth, and can potentially offer protection against suicide. However, the themes in this paper suggest that some bereaved young people may become more isolated, reducing their circle of friends and struggling with trust in relationships after the loss of their loved one; and some young people find it very difficult to make meaning out of suicide-bereavement experiences. Policies geared towards helping young people bereaved through the loss of their loved one to suicide should take these qualitative findings into account, and consider the possible benefits of having accessible and appropriately qualified counsellors work specifically with young bereaved people in Australia, across a range of settings (work, school, university, etc). Aside from supporting them through the process of trying to establish meaning, and feeling guilt, a key aspect of working with bereaved young people may be helping them regain trust in relationships, as many of these young participants struggled to do so after the loss of their loved one to suicide.

Qualitative interviewing with vulnerable populations: Individuals' experiences of participating in suicide and self-harm based research

Biddle L, Cooper J, Owen-Smith A, Klineberg E, Bennewith O, Hawton K, Kapur N, Donovan J, Gunnell D (UK, Australia)

Journal of Affective Disorders 145, 356-362, 2013

Background: Concern exists that involving vulnerable individuals as participants in research into suicide and self-harm may cause distress and increase suicidal feelings. Actual understanding of participants' experiences is however limited, especially in relation to in-depth qualitative research.

Methods: Data were collected from four separate studies focused on self-harm or suicide. These included people with varying levels of past distress, including some who had made nearly lethal suicide attempts. Each involved semi-structured qualitative interviewing. Participants (n=63) were asked to complete a visual analogue scale measuring current emotional state before and after their interview and then comment on how they had experienced the interview, reflecting on any score change.

Results: Most participants experienced a change in well-being. Between 50% and 70% across studies reported improvement, many describing the cathartic value of talking. A much smaller group in each study (18-27%) reported lowering of mood as they were reminded of difficult times or forced to focus on current issues. However, most anticipated that their distress would be transient and it was outweighed by a desire to contribute to research. An increase in distress did not therefore necessarily indicate a negative experience.

Limitations: There was no follow-up so the long-term effects of participation are unknown. Scores and post interview reflections were collected from participants by the researcher who had conducted the interview, which may have inhibited reporting of negative effects.

Conclusions: These findings suggest individuals are more likely to derive benefit from participation than experience harm. Overprotective gate-keeping could prevent some individuals from gaining these benefits.

Comment

Main findings: Suicide research is imperative for further understanding and preventing suicidal behaviours. Although various safeguards have been suggested in order to reduce the chances of potential harm to suicide research participants[1], concerns remain over the effects of research participation on the well-being of already vulnerable individuals (for example, persons who have a history of suicidal behaviour). However, the majority of previous research has failed to demonstrate negative outcomes, with some suggestions that the participatory experience may be a positive, therapeutic one[2]. Using data collected from four previous UK studies, all evaluating self-harm and/or suicidal behaviours through the use of semi-structured one-on-one interviews, the current paper analysed emotional well-being of participants before and after research participation. The majority of participants (between five and seven out of every 10 people, across the four studies) reported that their emotional state improved after the experience. Approximately one fifth of participants felt worse after the interview, while 21% of participants over the four studies did not experience any change to their emotional state. While some participants experienced a degree of distress during the interview process, not all of these individuals reported negative emotional outcomes on completion, with some actually reporting an improvement in emotional wellbeing. Despite the various strengths of the current study, the authors point to a major gap in the research; the need for further studies evaluating the long-term effect of suicide research on participants.

Implications: This paper provides support for the use of qualitative methods in suicide prevention research. The majority of previous research has focused on the effect on participants completing survey questionnaires or structured interviews. This paper built on current literature by analysing semi-structured interview participants and including a qualitative reflection on the interview process, which was not presented in previous studies.

Currently, a lack of understanding and an overestimation of the negative effects of participation in suicide research may result in an overprotective stance from ethical committees, subsequently impeding suicide research[2]. However, this study — although certainly not definitive — nonetheless suggests that participation in suicide research may be beneficial for many individuals (including those who may be considered vulnerable), and that the possibility of experiencing distress during participation should not necessarily be equated with the likelihood of experiencing a negative emotional outcome from participation.

Although the majority of participants reported positive, or no, changes to their emotional wellbeing, a small number of participants did experience negative emotions following participation. This emphasises the importance of following guidelines for safe practice, including monitoring participant well-being, using interviewers with sufficient skills and training and providing options for follow-up care when required[1].

Endnotes

1. Lakeman R, Fitzgerald M (2009). The ethics of suicide research. The views of ethics committee members. *Crisis* 30, 13-19.
2. Cukrowicz K, Smith P, Poindexter E (2010). The effect of participating in suicide research: Does participating in a research protocol on suicide and psychiatric symptoms increase suicide ideation and attempts? *Suicide and Life-Threatening Behavior* 40, 535-543.

Can repetition of deliberate self-harm be predicted?
A prospective multicenter study validating clinical decision rules

Bilén K, Ponzer S, Ottosson C, Castrén M, Owe-Larsson B, Ekdahl K, Pettersson H (Sweden)
Journal of Affective Disorders. Published online: 28 February 2013. doi: 10.1016/j.jad.2013.01.037, 2013

Background: Clinical decision rules have been developed to help identify patients at high risk of repeating deliberate self-harm actions. The objective of this study was to prospectively validate the clinical decision rules', Södersjukhuset Self-Harm Rule and Manchester Self-Harm Rule, ability to predict repetition of deliberate self-harm (DSH).

Methods: A consecutive series of 325 patients attending two large emergency departments in Stockholm, Sweden due to DSH were included and followed for six months. Predictive factors were collected from hospital charts at the emergency department. A nationwide register-based follow-up of new DSH within six months was used. We calculated the sensitivity and specificity to evaluate the different decision rules' ability to identify repetition of DSH. Main outcome measure repeated DSH within six months.

Results: The cumulative incidence for patients repeating within six months was 24.6% (95% CI: 19.9-29.3). Application of Södersjukhuset Self-Harm Rule yielded a sensitivity of 89% (95%CI: 79.2-94.4) and a specificity of 11% (95%CI: 7.9-16.2). Application of Manchester Self-Harm Rule to our material yielded a sensitivity of 94% (95%CI: 85.4-97.7) and a specificity of 18% (95%CI: 13.8-23.9).

Limitations: If data regarding predictive factors were missing it was not possible to investigate this further and in the statistical analysis missing data was classified as no. This would imply that the predicted risks may be underestimated.

Conclusion: Clinical decision rules could be used as a compliment providing important additional information regarding risk of repetition in an ED setting when focusing on high sensitivity.

Comment

Main findings: Deliberate self-harm (DSH) is a well known risk factor for suicide. High repetition rates among individuals who deliberately self-harm have also been documented[1], which can put a considerable strain on ED units. In an effort to improve the ability to differentiate between DSH patients at high risk of suicide and those at lower risk, and to provide appropriate care for DSH patients, this study sought to distinguish individuals most likely to engage in repetitious DSH behaviour using a clinical decision rule sheet. This included factors from two well known tools to predict DSH repetition — the Manchester Self-Harm Rule (MSHR) and Södersjukhuset Self-Harm Rule (SoS-4). Participants consisted of all patients over the age of 18 years who attended the EDs of Södersjukhuset and Karolinska University Hospitals due to DSH. The final study population consisted of 325 patients. The authors of this paper were in a unique position to link data from both hospitals with all residents included in the Swedish National Registry using the individual's personal identification number given at birth or upon receiving residency in Sweden. Linking was done to predict subsequent suicide after DSH and test whether or not the SoS-4 and MSHR have the ability to predict repetition of DSH. High risk patients were detected using the MSHR's four clinical correlates: history of self harm, previous psychiatric treatment, benzodiazepine used in the attempt, current psychiatric treatment, and the SoS-4, which checked five correlates: gender, antidepressant treatment, any history of self-harm, admission to a psychiatric clinic and current psychiatric treatment. The study shows that both the SoS-4 and MSHR correctly identify patients with a high risk of repeating their DSH actions, however, the SoS-4 did not perform as well as the MSHR.

Implications: All individuals who display DSH behaviours should be offered psychological intervention specifically designed for people who self-harm. However, this may not always be possible, due to lack of availability, budget shortfalls, or other reasons. The current study examines a potentially useful method through which 'higher risk' patients may be identified and prioritised for urgent intervention. Although well validated clinical rules for predicting repetition of DSH are still in their infancy, the current results suggest that decision tools based around the correlates found in the SoS-4 and the MSHR may offer a useful complement for existing assessment practices and may assist in referring patients to the most appropriate forms of support. The use of such tools may also help clinicians establish a better understanding of patients who may potentially repeat acts of DSH in the near future.

Endnote

1. Lilley R, Owens D, Horrocks J, House A, Noble R, Bergen H, Hawton K, Casey D, Simkin S, Murphy E, Cooper J, Kapur N (2008). Hospital care and repetition following self-harm: Multicentre comparison of self-poisoning and self-injury. *British Journal of Psychiatry* 192, 440–445.

Parents bereaved by offspring suicide: A population-based longitudinal case-control study

Bolton JM, Au W, Leslie WD, Martens PJ, Enns MW, Roos LL, Katz LY, Wilcox HC, Erlangsen A, Chateau D, Walld R, Spiwak R, Seguin M, Shear K, Sareen J (Canada)

Archives of General Psychiatry. Published online: 10 December 2012. doi: 10.1001/jamapsychiatry.2013.275, 2012

Context: Suicide bereavement remains understudied and poorly understood.

Objectives: To examine outcomes of parents bereaved by the suicide death of their offspring and to compare these with both nonbereaved parent controls and parents who had offspring die in a motor vehicle crash (MVC).

Design: Population-based case-control study. Suicide-bereaved parents were compared with nonbereaved matched control parents in the general population (n = 1415) and with MVC-bereaved parents (n = 1132) on the rates of physician-diagnosed mental and physical disorders, social factors, and treatment use in the 2 years after death of the offspring. Adjusted relative rates (ARRs) were generated by generalized estimating equation models and adjusted for confounding factors.

Setting: Manitoba, Canada.

Participants: All identifiable parents who had an offspring die by suicide between 1996 and 2007 (n = 1415).

Main Outcome Measures: Mental and physical disorders, social factors, and treatment use.

Results: Suicide bereavement was associated with an increased rate of depression (ARR, 2.14; 95% CI, 1.88-2.43), anxiety disorders (ARR, 1.41; 95% CI, 1.24-1.60), and marital breakup (ARR, 1.18; 95% CI, 1.13-1.23) in the 2 years after the suicide of an offspring, as compared with the 2 years prior to the death. Suicide-bereaved and MVC-bereaved parents had very few differences on predeath to postdeath outcomes. Depression rate increases were greater for MVC-bereaved parents (19.9%) compared with suicide-bereaved parents (15.9%; P = .005), whereas suicide-bereaved parents had higher rate increases of hospitalization for mental illness (P = .049). Suicide-bereaved parents were more likely than their MVC-bereaved counterparts to have depression (ARR, 1.30; 95% CI, 1.06-1.61), physical disorders (ARR, 1.32; 95% CI, 1.19-1.45), and low income (ARR, 1.34; 95% CI, 1.18-1.51) before their offspring's death.

Conclusions: Suicide bereavement is associated with adverse mental health and social outcomes. These consequences appear similar to those associated with MVC bereavement. Parents who lose offspring to suicide appear to be a vulnerable group even prior to their offspring's death.

Comment

Main findings: The grief after the loss of a loved one has been linked to increased risk of physical and mental health problems, as well as an increased risk of mortality[1]. Certain factors may influence the severity of adverse reactions, with close relatives such as a child, spouse or parent, being more likely to develop ongoing mental problems than those experiencing grief over the loss of a more distant relative or friend[2]. Although there are similarities between different types of grief, individuals bereaved by suicide more frequently experience shame, responsibility and rejection[3] induced by the social stigma[4].

Despite these suggestions, findings in this area are inconclusive, with a systematic literature review finding no significant differences between the general mental health, depression, PTSD symptoms, anxiety and suicidal behaviours of those experiencing grief over a suicide to other causes of death[5]. The current study compared the grief reactions of parents bereaved by the suicide of an offspring to those bereaved by the death of a child in a motor vehicle crash (MVC), hypothesising that suicide bereavement outcomes would not differ significantly from outcomes related to MVC.

This Canadian population-based case-control study used Generalized Estimating Equation (GEE) models to compare the mental health, physical health, social factors and health service use of parents bereaved by suicide, to parents bereaved by MVC and to matched non-bereaved control parents. In the two year period following the suicide of a child, suicide-bereaved parents had more than double the rates of diagnosed depression than they did in the two year period before the loss. Anxiety disorders and overall mental disorders also increased by 40% and 60% respectively. The loss of an offspring to suicide appeared to be linked to marital breakdown, with single marital status increasing by 18%. The incidence of cancer, diabetes and physician visits for mental and physical illnesses also increased significantly. Outcomes for MVC-bereaved participants were generally similar to those of suicide-bereaved parents, except for experiencing greater increases in the development of depression and less hospitalisation for mental illness following the death. When compared to non-bereaved matched control parents, suicide-bereaved parents experienced more alcohol use disorders, diagnosed depression, anxiety disorders, and overall mental disorders and were more likely to be single and have low income both before, and after the child's death, indicating that quite often these parents were already experiencing mental health and social problems before the loss. The presence of depression before the suicide of the child in many cases may explain why the increase in depression was greater in MVC-bereaved parents.

Implications: Mixed findings in this area to date have resulted in suicide bereavement being rather poorly understood. Past studies have been plagued by small samples of participants often recruited from bereavement groups or obituary notices, raising the possibility of sampling bias. The current study was the first known population-based study evaluating the grief outcomes of parents experiencing the loss of a child to suicide. The results of the study suggest that suicide-bereaved individuals often experience a number of negative outcomes after the loss and are in need of support. In Australia, the community-based StandBy Response Service aims to reduce adverse outcomes after the loss of a loved one to suicide by providing 24-hour crisis support in 10 locations around the country[6]. Additional research in this area may potentially aid in the further development of services for these individuals.

From a suicide prevention perspective, the finding of negative health and social factors in suicide-bereaved parents even before the death of the child may contribute to the understanding and prevention of youth suicide. Results suggest that further research may be warranted, which considers whether addressing these parental factors early on, may have the ability to reduce offspring suicide.

Endnotes

1. Stroebe M, Schut H, Stroebe W (2007). Health outcomes of bereavement. *Lancet* 370, 1960-1973.

2. Mitchell AM, Sakraida TJ, Kim Y, Bullian L, Chiappetta L (2009). Depression, anxiety and quality of life in suicide survivors: A comparison of close and distant relationships. *Archives of Psychiatric Nursing* 23, 2-10.

3. Bailey SE, Keal MJ, Dunham K (1999). Survivors of suicide do grieve differently: Empirical support for a common sense proposition. *Suicide and Life-Threatening Behaviour* 29, 256-271.

4. Ellenbogen S, Gratton F (2001). Do they suffer more? Reflections on research comparing suicide survivors to other survivors. *Suicide and Life-Threatening Behaviour* 31, 83-90.

5. Sveen CA, Walby FA (2008). Suicide survivors mental health and grief reactions: A systematic review of controlled studies. *Suicide and Life-Threatening Behavior* 38, 13-29.

6. Webpage of United Synergies: StandBy Response Service. Retrieved 25 January 2013 from http://www.unitedsynergies.com.au/index.php?option=com_content&view=article&id=40&I temid=40

Postcards from the EDge: 5-year outcomes of a randomised controlled trial for hospital-treated self-poisoning

Carter GL, Clover K, Whyte IM, Dawson AH, D'Este C (Australia)

British Journal of Psychiatry. Published online: 21 March 2013. doi: 10.1192/bjp.bp.112.112664, 2013

Background: Repetition of hospital-treated self-poisoning and admission to psychiatric hospital are both common in individuals who self-poison.

Aims: To evaluate efficacy of postcard intervention after 5 years.

Method: A randomised controlled trial of individuals who have self-poisoned: postcard intervention (eight in 12 months) plus treatment as usual v. treatment as usual. Our primary outcomes were self-poisoning admissions and psychiatric admissions (proportions and event rates).

Results: There was no difference between groups for any repeat-episode self-poisoning admission (intervention group: 24.9%, 95% CI 20.6-29.5; control group: 27.2%, 95% CI 22.8-31.8) but there was a significant reduction in event rates (incidence risk ratio (IRR) = 0.54, 95% CI 0.37-0.81), saving 306 bed days. There was no difference for any psychiatric admission (intervention group: 38.1%, 95% CI 33.1-43.2; control group: 35.5%, 95% CI 30.8-40.5) but there was a significant reduction in event rates (IRR = 0.66, 95% CI 0.47-0.91), saving 2565 bed days.

Conclusions: A postcard intervention halved self-poisoning events and reduced psychiatric admissions by a third after 5 years. Substantial savings occurred in general hospital and psychiatric hospital bed days.

Comment

Main findings: Self-poisoning is one of the most common methods of self-harm to require hospital bed use in Australia[1,2], and identifying ways to reduce repeated self-poisoning has the potential to reduce both completed suicides and health system resource use. This study tested whether or not sending 'postcards' was an effective intervention method for reducing the number of hospital-treated patients for repeat self-poisoning over five years (a four year follow-up, after a one year intervention). The sample consisted of all the individuals over the age of 16 years who had presented to the Hunter Area Toxicology service in Newcastle, New South Wales from 1998 to 2001, as well as individuals who presented elsewhere in the greater Newcastle and Hunter Valley area. All consenting individuals were randomised into two separate groups – control or intervention. This resulted in 394 control and 378 intervention participants. Individuals in the intervention group received 'postcards' (in a sealed envelope) in months 1, 2, 3, 4, 6, 8, 10, and 12 after hospital discharge.

After five years, there was no significant difference between groups in the proportion of participants with repeat self-poisoning (control: 27.2%; intervention: 24.9%). However, in terms of the actual number of repeat admissions to the general hospital, there were 484 repeat self-poisonings in the control group and 252 in the intervention group, a difference of 232 readmissions. This is thought to have saved 306 days of hospital beds. Separate analysis on demographics showed the treatment was effective for women but not men. Regarding episodes of admission to a psychiatric hospital, there were 771 admissions in the control group and 447 in the intervention, with a total of 6008 bed days in the control group and 3443 beds in the intervention group, resulting in a difference of 2565 days. The findings suggest that the 'postcards' intervention was effective in reducing the number of repeat self-poisoning episodes per individual for general hospital treated groups (by nearly 50%), however, this mostly benefitted women. Within psychiatric hospitals the reduction of episodes was around one third, and was not significant for any gender.

Implications: Post-discharge from hospital after an episode of self-harm with suicidal intent is known as an acute window of time where follow-up contact is greatly needed to support at-risk individuals. In addition, facilitating connections with suitable care services, over time, is an important aspect of care provision for persons at risk of suicide. 'Postcards' are a low cost option for hospitals that may not have the resources to undertake more intensive follow-up (such as telephone calls or face-to-face visits). Although the authors did not perform a cost-benefit analysis, they concluded that the reductions in number of admissions in both general and psychiatric hospitals were 'clinically significant', as they reduced the number of bed days utilised by self-poisoning patients. Although not a replacement for ongoing engagement with appropriate care, Australian hospitals may consider using 'postcards' as a means of potentially reducing the number of repetitions of self poisoning and as a way of staying in touch with, and making patients feel cared for, after they leave the hospital.

Endnotes

1. McGrath J (1989). A survey of deliberate self-poisoning. *Medical Journal of Australia* 150, 317-322.
2. Tovell A, McKenna K, Bradley C, Pointer S (2012). *Hospital separations due to injury and poisoning, Australia 2009-2010.* Injury research and statistics series No. 69. Cat. No. INJCAT 145. Canberra: AIHW.

Adolescent suicide statements on MySpace

Cash SJ, Thelwall M, Peck SN, Ferrell JZ, Bridge JA (USA, UK)

Cyberpsychology, Behavior, and Social Networking 16, 166-174, 2013

The use of social networking sites (SNSs) has proliferated throughout the last several years for all populations, but especially adolescents. Media reports have also identified several instances in which adolescents broadcast their suicidal behaviors via the Internet and/or SNSs. Despite the increase in the usage of SNSs, there has been little research conducted on how adolescents use SNSs to communicate these behaviors. The objective of this study was to explore the ways in which adolescents use MySpace to comment on their suicidal thoughts and intentions. Content analysis was used to identify suicidal statements from public profiles on MySpace. The original sample consisted of 1,038 comments, made by young people ages 13-24 years old. The final sample resulted in 64 comments, where *Potential Suicidality* was identified. Through content analysis, the following subthemes (within the *Potential Suicidality* theme) were found: *Relationships, Mental Health, Substance Use/Abuse, Method of Suicide,* and *Statements without Context.* Examples and discussion for each subtheme are identified. The comments referenced a significant amount of hopelessness, despair, and desperation. This study provides support that adolescents use public Web sites to display comments about their suicidal thoughts, behaviors, and possible intentions. Future research is warranted to explore the relationship between at-risk behaviors and suicidality as expressed on SNSs.

Comment

Main findings: Social networking sites (SNSs), such as MySpace, are a place where anyone with internet access can create an online community by communicating through personalised profiles. Since MySpace was introduced in 2003 it has become particularly popular among young people, and this paper examined if MySpace could be used to detect suicidal behaviour among young (13-24 years old) users. This was done using a complex process of data selection to source suicide-related comments/phrases, posted on MySpace profiles. Initially, there were 1,038 suicide-related comments identified. Three phases of removal were then used to exclude comments that were not judged to represent 'serious' suicidality (for example, comments that referred to someone else's suicidality, or comments that were obvious hyperbole), resulting in a total of 64 comments considered to represent 'serious' potential suicidality. The authors then attempted to link context, such as relationship break-up or mental health to these comments, and found that 51.6% of the comments had no context. The remaining comments with context mostly pertained to statements regarding relationship problems ('break-ups') and family relationship problems (42.2% of comments), and only 6.3% of the contextualised suicide statements discussed mental health issues. Overall, the findings in this paper add support to the theory young people may communicate suicidal thoughts and intentions online, possibly as a way of seeking help and support.

Implications: Following the tragedy of a joint suicide pact posted by two teenage girls in Melbourne (Australia), MySpace launched a partnership with the Inspire Foundation, to put up banners on the website to direct potentially suicidal visitors to national helplines[1,2]. Whether or not these banners have been effective in directing at-risk individuals to appropriate help, or have had any influence on suicide completions, is unknown. There is a clear need for further investigation of ways in which social media, and new technology more generally, may be able to be used effectively to assist young people at risk of suicide.

When considering the context of the potential suicidality comments identified in the current study, a low percentage dealt directly with mental health. While this may reflect low levels of self-identification of mental health issues among young people, it may also indicate that factors such as family and inter-personal relationship problems require heightened focus within suicide prevention programs aimed at young people. Regarding young people's online communication of suicidality, and ways in which technology may be used within a suicide prevention framework, there may be value in establishing partnerships between SNSs and youth-oriented family and personal relationship support services, rather than focusing primarily on youth mental health.

Endnotes

1. Tiong-Thye G, Yen-Pei H (2009). Monitoring youth depression in risk in Web 2.0. *VINE* 39, 192-202.
2. Aspen Education Group (2007). MySpace joins forces with Inspire Foundation. Message posted to http://www.4troubledteens.com/blog/2007/05/myspace-joins-forces-with-inspire.html.

Effectiveness of a telephone management programme for patients discharged from an emergency department after a suicide attempt: Controlled study in a Spanish population

Cebrià AI, Parra I, Pàmias M, Escayola A, García-Parés G, Puntí J, Laredo A, Vallès V, Cavero M, Oliva JC, Hegerl U, Pérez-Solà V, Palao DJ (Spain)

Journal of Affective Disorders. Published online: 6 December 2012. doi: 10.1016/j.jad.2012.11.016, 2012

Objective: To determine the effectiveness over one year of a specific telephone management programme on patients discharged from an emergency department (ED) after a suicide attempt. We hypothesized that the programme will reduce the percentage of patients re-attempting suicide and delay the time between attempts.

Design: A multicentre, case-control, population-based study. The effect of the 1-year intervention on the main outcome measures was evaluated with respect to a 1-year baseline period and a control group.

Setting: Two hospitals with distinct catchment areas in Catalonia (Spain).

Participants: A total of 991 patients discharged from the ED of either hospital after a suicide attempt during the baseline year and the intervention year.

Intervention: The intervention was carried out on patients discharged from the ED for attempted suicide (Sabadell). It consisted of a systematic, one-year telephone follow-up programme: after 1 week, thereafter at 1, 3, 6, 9 and 12-month intervals, to assess the risk of suicide and increasing adherence to treatment. The population in the control group (Terrassa) received treatment as usual after discharge, without additional telephone management.

Main Outcome Measures: Time elapsed between initial suicide attempt and subsequent one, and changes in the annual rate of patients who reattempted suicide in the year of the intervention and the preceding one.

Results: The telephone management programme delayed suicide reattempts in the intervention group compared to the baseline year (mean time in days to first reattempt, year 2008 = 346.47, sd = 4.65; mean time in days to first reattempt, year 2007 = 316.46, sd = 7.18; P<0.0005; χ^2 = 12.1, df = 1) and compared to the control population during the same period (mean time in days to first reattempt, treatment period = 346.47, sd = 4.65; mean time in days to first reattempt, pre-treatment period = 300.36, sd = 10.67; P<0.0005; χ^2 = 16.8, df = 1). The intervention reduced the rate of patients who reattempted suicide in the experimental population compared to the previous year (Intervention 6% (16/296) v Baseline 14% (39/285) difference 8%, 95% confidence interval 2% to 12%) and to the control population (Intervention 6% (16/296) v Control 14% (31/218) difference 8%, -13% to -2%)

Limitations: One of the main obstacles was the difficulty to contact all patients within the established deadlines. Another limitation of our study was that patients under the age of 18 underwent an intensive intervention in the day hospital, although their number was very small (13/319 in 2008) and did not significantly influence the results. But the main limitation of our study was that it was performed within the EAAD project. This project includes a comprehensive multi-level intervention practically in the same experimental area and aimed at an early diagnosis and treatment of depression, which is the main psychiatric disorder associated with suicide.

Conclusion: A telephone management programme for patients discharged from an ED after a suicide attempted would be a useful strategy in delaying further suicide attempts and in reducing the rate of reattempts, which is known as the highest risk factor for suicide completion.

Comment

Main findings: The aim of the current study was to analyse the effectiveness of a one-year telephone management program on patients discharged from two Spanish EDs after presenting with a suicide attempt. The days between first suicide attempt and repetition of suicidal behavior, and the percentage of patients who reattempted during the one year program was compared to a baseline period from the year before and to a control group from the same period who received treatment as usual during admission but did not participate in the telephone management program after discharge. The program began on the day after discharge, with follow up calls being made after 1 week, 1 month, 3 months, 6 months, 9 months and 12 months. Patients were also visited face-to-face by a psychiatrist within one week of discharge. Participants in the program experienced significantly longer delays between the initial attempt and reattempts when compared to the baseline year and the control group. The proportion of patients in the program who reattempted suicide was also significantly smaller than the control group and the baseline from the previous year. No significant differences were found between the control groups in the year before and during program implementation.

Implications: The hospital Emergency Department (ED) is the first point of contact for many individuals who have attempted suicide, with an Australian study showing that the majority (44%) of suicidal individuals who had only sought help from one source had approached a hospital over mental health professionals (26.3%) and General Practitioners (20.3%)[1]. In Australia between the years 2010-2011 there were 31,507 separations (episodes of care for admitted patients) from public hospitals due to self-harm and 796 from private hospitals[2]. Ongoing care after presentation to an ED is imperative, as a history of suicide attempts is a strong predictor of further attempts as well as subsequent death by suicide[3]. Currently, it is unclear which follow up services may provide the most effective care of suicidal individuals after leaving hospital, with a number of previous studies on telephone management programs retrieving negative results due to program shortfalls. The program analysed in the current study achieved more positive outcomes, possibly due to earlier commencement of follow-up calls and more frequent contact with patients. Results suggest that carefully implemented telephone-management programs may have potential to reduce further suicidal behaviours, at least in the short term.

There is a need for further studies analysing the effect of such programs over a longer period of time to give an indication of whether these interventions may aid in a long term reduction of suicide attempts or completed suicides. It may be that longer periods of follow up care are required for certain high-risk individuals.

Endnotes

1. Milner A, De Leo D (2010). Who seeks treatment where? Suicidal behaviours and health care. *Journal of Nervous and Mental Disease* 198, 412-419.

2. Australian Institute for Health and Welfare. 2012. *Australian hospital statistics 2010-11.* Canberra: AIHW.

3. Christiansen E, Jensen BF (2007). Risk of repitition of suicide attempt, suicide or all deaths after an epidsode of attempted suicide. A register-based survival analysis. *Australian & New Zealand Journal of Psychiatry* 41, 257-265.

How people bereaved by suicide perceive newspaper reporting: Qualitative study

Chapple A, Ziebland S, Simkin S, Hawton K (UK)

British Journal of Psychiatry. Published online: 7 February 2013. doi: 10.1192/bjp. bp.112.114116, 2013

Background: People bereaved by suicide are often reported to be distressed by media reporting. Current media guidelines for reporting suicide focus especially on prevention of copycat behaviour.

Aims: To explore bereaved individuals' experiences of media reporting after suicide and to examine their priorities in relation to media guidelines.

Method: In-depth interviews with 40 people bereaved by suicide, with qualitative analysis. Review of four guidelines.

Results: There is a difference of emphasis between guidance for the press that aims to prevent copycat suicides (especially avoidance of details such as method used) and the perspectives of bereaved people (who prioritise sympathetic and accurate reporting, sometimes including details of the death and images of the person who died). We found that bereaved relatives were sometimes keen to talk to the press. Those who were upset by the press focused on careless reporting, misquoting and speculation that gave an inaccurate impression of the death.

Conclusions: The Leveson enquiry has drawn attention to the damage that can be caused by irresponsible journalism. Guidelines written to prevent 'copycat' suicides are important, but so are the needs of bereaved relatives. Because accuracy matters greatly to the bereaved, families should be able to work with an intermediary such as a police press officer to prepare a statement for the press to minimise the risk of misrepresentation.

Declaration of interest: None.

Comment

Main findings: The majority of research into suicide and the media concerns 'copycat' behaviour. This study using in-depth interviews was one of the first to examine the experiences and needs of suicide survivors in relation to media involvement, their interactions with journalists, and media reporting of deaths. From a sample of 40 suicide survivors, just under half did not mention any interaction with the media, while four had been too young to remember a media reporting. Of those who did remember, accurate reporting was often cited as an important aspect of their satisfaction or dissatisfaction with the press. Those who were dissatisfied with the press, and in particular the behaviour of journalists, felt 'hounded' by journalists whom they described as 'unsympathetic'. Importantly, satisfaction for the suicide survivors was related, mainly, to the accuracy of the report. Even minor inaccuracies, such as spelling the deceased's name wrong, caused distress for relatives and friends. Although some suicide survivors had significant issues with journalists, interactions with the press were not always negative; some interviewees mentioned that it was important to communicate what has happened, had a strong urge to do so, and felt that journalists had done a good job reporting their loved one's death.

Implications: Around the world, where guidelines exist for journalists on reporting a suicide, these guidelines — while not uniform — are often written to prevent 'copycat' suicides and reduce sensationalism[1]. Even though Australia's media guideline, Reporting suicide and mental illness[2] (provided by the Mindframe National Media Initiative), is an informative document for media professionals, it primarily highlights 'safe' ways to report suicide such as the use of suicide statistics and minimising the specifics of method. Although this guideline goes into significant detail, it contains relatively little information about ways in which journalists can avoid causing distress to bereaved families and friends. However, results from the current study show that while media reporting of an individual's suicide can in some instances be of help to survivors, it can also be very distressing if it is not done carefully and correctly. This suggests a need to consider incorporating into media guidelines more detailed recommendations about avoiding distress, such as attention to accuracy in even the smallest details, as well as the possible use of intermediaries between the bereaved and the media.

Endnotes

1. Kõlves K (2012). The facts about safe reporting of suicide. Published 14 September 2012. The Conversation. Retrieved 14 February 2013 from http://theconversation.edu.au/the-facts-about-safe-reporting-of-suicide-9501

2. Mindframe National Media Initiative (2011). Reporting suicide and mental illness. Commonwealth of Australia 2011. Retrieved from http://www.mindframemedia.info/__data/assets/pdf_file/0018/5139/Media-Book-col.pdf

Age and gender differences in medical care utilization prior to suicide

Cho J, Kang DR, Moon KT, Suh M, Ha KH, Kim C, Suh I, Shin DC, Jung SH (Korea)
Journal of Affective Disorders 146, 181-188, 2013

Background: Analysis of temporal patterns of medical care utilization prior to suicide may aid in developing suicide prevention programs. The aim of this study was to investigate age and gender differences in temporal patterns of medical care utilization during 1 year prior to suicide.

Methods: Medical care utilization data of all suicide completers in the Republic of Korea whose death occurred in 2004 (7903 men and 3620 women) was used. Differences among the quarters in medical expenditures and number of medical care visits were analyzed using a repeated measures analysis. Total medical expenditures were compared to those of age- and gender-matched controls by multiple logistic regression analysis.

Results: Among suicides, 84% (81% in men, 91% in women) contacted medical care in the year prior to suicide. In 10-39 year-old women, the number of medical care visits for gastrointestinal disease increased significantly during the final 3 months prior to suicide. All suicide completers showed that the number of medical care visits for psychiatric disorders increased significantly during the final 3 months with the exception of 10-19 year age group. Total medical expenditures during the year prior to suicide were elevated significantly and associated significantly with suicide risk (OR, 1.20; 95% CI, 1.19-1.21).

Limitations: Inaccuracies in the underlying disease and death statistics data may have led to misclassification bias.

Conclusions: Medical care utilization increased as the date of suicide approached. There are age and gender differences in medical care utilization in the year prior to suicide.

Comment

Main findings: Research suggests that in some Western countries, around a third of depressed patients take their own lives within 12 months of seeking psychiatric help[1]. Although cultural factors can influence help-seeking behaviour, little is known about the psychiatric and general medical care seeking habits of those who take their own lives, outside Western countries. Using historical medical care data of all suicides in Korea (7903 men and 3620 women), that occurred in 2004, this study found that for both sexes and all ages above 19 years, over 80 percent of individuals who died by suicide had contact with a medical service at least once in the year before death. Of medical contacts by people who took their own lives, 25 percent were for a psychiatric disorder. The number of medical care visits for psychiatric disorders significantly increased in the three months prior to death by suicide, with women more often than men sourcing psychiatric care. After adjusting for age, gender, residence and socioeconomic status, statistical analysis also revealed that low socioeconomic status was associated with increased suicide risk.

Implications: Several approaches for suicide prevention initiatives were proposed by the authors of this paper regarding age, gender and culture-based strategies. Considering Australia's multicultural society, it is important to understand how cultural factors may relate to help-seeking behaviour. This Korean study shows some similarities with patterns of medical care contact and help-seeking behaviour that have been found in Australian studies, for example, that a number of individuals who die by suicide have contact with medical services for a physical condition prior to death[2], and that women are more likely than men to seek help for various physical and psychiatric disorders[3]. However, levels of contact with medical care for psychiatric conditions prior to suicide were lower in Korea, relative to Western countries. This may indicate the influence of different cultural understandings about risk factors for suicide, as well as culturally-grounded differences in patterns of help-seeking behaviour prior to death by suicide. To ensure that Australian suicide prevention efforts are culturally appropriate and properly targeted, it is important to incorporate these considerations into the design and implementation of suicide prevention programs. It is also important to recognise the role that general practitioners can play in identifying and assisting persons at risk of suicide, even if those individuals present for physical, rather than psychiatric, conditions.

Endnotes

1. Hunt IM, Kapur N, Robinson J, Shaw J, Flynn S, Bailey H, Meehan J, Bickley H, Parsons R, Burns J, Amos T, Appleby L (2006). Suicide within 12 months of mental health service contact in different age and diagnostic groups: National clinical survey. *British Journal of Psychiatry* 188, 135-142.
2. Milner A, De Leo D (2010). Who seeks treatment where? Suicidal behaviours and health care: Evidence from a community survey. *Journal of Nervous & Mental Disease* 198, 412-419.
3. Judd F, Komiti A, Jackson H (2008). How does being female assist help-seeking for mental health problems? *Australian and New Zealand Journal of Psychiatry* 42, 24-29.

Interventions to reduce suicides at suicide hotspots: A systematic review

Cox GR, Owens C, Robinson J, Nicholas A, Lockley A, Williamson M, Cheung YTD, Pirkis J (Australia, UK)
BMC Public Health 13, 214, 2013

Background: 'Suicide hotspots' include tall structures (for example, bridges and cliffs), railway tracks, and isolated locations (for example, rural car parks) which offer direct means for suicide or seclusion that prevents intervention.

Methods: We searched Medline for studies that could inform the following question: 'What interventions are available to reduce suicides at hotspots, and are they effective?'

Results: There are four main approaches: (a) restricting access to means (through installation of physical barriers); (b) encouraging help-seeking (by placement of signs and telephones); (c) increasing the likelihood of intervention by a third party (through surveillance and staff training); and (d) encouraging responsible media reporting of suicide (through guidelines for journalists). There is relatively strong evidence that reducing access to means can avert suicides at hotspots without substitution effects. The evidence is weaker for the other approaches, although they show promise.

Conclusions: More well-designed intervention studies are needed to strengthen this evidence base.

Comment

Main findings: Studies were included in the review if they described an intervention relating to a known suicide hotspot, evaluated it using at least a before-and-after design, and used suicide as the outcome. This extensive search identified 14 relevant studies at 13 different locations worldwide. After reviewing these papers, the authors concluded there are four main approaches to suicide hotspots interventions: restriction of access, encouraging help-seeking behaviour, increasing the chances of intervention by a third party and encouraging responsible media reporting of suicide. Of these interventions, the most effective method was restricting access to means, mostly through installation of barriers at jumping sites. The nine studies that document this indicate that once barriers were put in place, the number of suicides at those locations reduced. In one particular study, where the barriers were removed, there was an increase in the number of suicides[1]. Eight of those studies attempted to determine whether there were increases in suicides at alternative sites; seven found that the number of suicides at other sites remained the same, or in some instances decreased. However, there were several limitations in this systematic review; for instance, the authors were concerned about the lack of randomised controlled trials, regarding evidence of intervention effectiveness. Also, there may be 'publication biases' whereby positive findings about particular interventions are more likely to appear in print than negative findings, and the terms 'hotspot,' 'intervention' and 'effectiveness' may be interpreted differently by research groups.

Implications: Of the four main approaches to suicide hotpot intervention there has been considerable debate over the cost-effectiveness of barriers at jumping sites, as well as disagreement over whether barriers at a particular site (or sites) are likely to lead to the reduction of overall suicide figures. One of the main arguments against the erection of barriers is that those who are unable to take their own lives at one site will use another site or another method of suicide. A current gap in knowledge is whether restricting access to suicide hotspots saves *individual* lives. Although it is possible to assess changes in suicide rates by particular methods for populations (such as the Australian population overall, or men, or young people), it is far more difficult to show this at the individual level, and to do so would require information about the numbers of people who were restricted from accessing a particular suicide hotspot who did, and did not, die by some other method of suicide. In addition, when thinking about the range of different available intervention methods, it is important to consider there is very limited research on the effectiveness of methods such as encouraging help-seeking methods, increasing the chance of intervention by third party and encouraging responsible media reporting of suicide at certain locations.

Endnote

1. Beautrais A (2007). Suicide by jumping: A review of research and prevention strategies. *Crisis* 28, 58-63.

Has the suicide rate risen with the 2011 Queensland floods?

De Leo D, Too LS, Kõlves K, Milner A, Ide N (Australia)
Journal of Loss and Trauma 18, 170-178, 2013

This study compared the prevalence and characteristics of suicides following the January 2011 Queensland floods to the 11 years prior (for the period January–June) for two severely affected locations: Ipswich and Toowoomba. Findings showed no significant increase in suicide rates during the 6 months after the floods. This may be explained by the elevated level of social support and care available in this period, which protected residents against risk factors for suicide. Nonetheless, the floods may have a delayed effect on suicide mortality. This highlights the importance of continued monitoring of suicidal behaviors and providing support to the people affected.

Comment

Main findings: In January 2011, several regions of Queensland were affected by extreme flash flooding, in what has been described as the worst natural disaster to hit the state in the last 30 years[1]. Previous research has suggested that individuals who fall victim to natural disasters may experience suicidal ideation or attempts shortly after the event[2]. However, a recent review of 42 papers examining the relationship between natural disasters and fatal and non-fatal suicidal behaviours worldwide has indicated that non-fatal suicidal behaviour may decrease in the period following the event and increase sometime after the event, due to diminishing availability of support from the community and mental health care professionals over time[3]. The review further indicates that the increase in suicidal behaviour over time may be impacted by other life factors such as mental disorders, property damage and economic problems[3]. Findings regarding fatal suicidal behaviour were much less consistent, with studies showing mixed results[3].

The current study evaluated the impact of the 2011 floods on suicide rates in Ipswich and Toowoomba, after a coronial inquest suggested that rates may increase in the areas most affected by the floods. The study compared rates in the six months after the floods, to the same six month period (January-June) in 2000-2010. Suicide cases in these areas were identified using the Queensland Suicide Register (QSR), and crude suicide rates were calculated using estimated population data from the Australian Bureau of Statistics[4]. Results of the current paper suggested that fatal suicidal behaviour did not increase in the six months following the event. For Toowoomba in particular, suicide rates decreased following the floods. While no suicide cases in Ipswich in 2011 mentioned the floods as a significant stressor preceding the death, one suicide case from Toowoomba did mention the floods as a possible contributing factor, however, this case also involved other negative life factors such as financial problems, depression and unemployment.

Implications: Much of the current research analysing the impact of natural disasters on suicidal behaviours has been conducted overseas, with earthquakes being the most frequently studied disaster[3]. While events such as earthquakes are rare in Australia, Australia is regularly affected by a number of other natural disasters, including floods, and the current study has built on existing literature by providing an analysis which is more relevant to the Australian context. Previous studies involving fatal suicidal behaviour have retrieved mixed results. The current study lends support to the idea that fatal suicidal behaviours may decrease following a natural disaster, in a similar fashion to the decline consistently witnessed in non-fatal suicidal behaviours. However, more research is required in this area before a clear pattern over a longer period can be identified.

Research has suggested that suicidal behaviour may increase in the years following a natural disaster. As noted by the authors of the current study, to prevent a similar increase following the 2011 Queensland floods, it is imperative that continued mental health care and community support is made available to those individuals affected by the floods, particularly those who may be experiencing other life stressors such as mental illness or financial difficulties.

Endnotes

1. Queensland Government (2011). *Operation Queenslander: The state community, economic and environmental recovery and reconstruction plan.* Retrieved 9 January 2012 from http://www.qldreconstruction.org.au/state-plan

2. Chuang HL , Huang WC (2007). A re-examination of the suicide rates in Taiwan. *Social Indicators Research* 83, 465-485.

3. Kõlves K, Kõlves KE, De Leo D (2012). Natural disasters and suicidal behaviours: A systematic literature review. *Journal of Affective Disorders.* Published online: 20 August 2012. doi: 10.1016/j.jad.2012.07.037.

4. Australian Bureau of Statistics (2000-2010). *Population by aeg and sex, regions of Australia.* Canberra: Australian Bureau of Statistics.

Pilot implementation and preliminary evaluation of START: AV assessments in secure juvenile correctional facilities

Desmarais SL, Sellers BG, Viljoen JL, Cruise KR, Nicholls TL, Dvoskin JA (USA)
International Journal of Forensic Mental Health 11, 150-164, 2012

The Short-Term Assessment of Risk and Treatability: Adolescent Version (START:AV) is a new structured professional judgment guide for assessing short-term risks in adolescents. The scheme may be distinguished from other youth risk assessment and treatment planning instruments by its inclusion of 23 dynamic factors that are each rated for both vulnerability and strength. In addition, START:AV is also unique in that it focuses on multiple adverse outcomes-namely, violence, self-harm, suicide, unauthorized leave, substance abuse, self-neglect, victimization, and general offending-over the short-term (i.e., weeks to months) rather than long-term (i.e., years). This article describes a pilot implementation and preliminary evaluation of START:AV in three secure juvenile correctional facilities in the southern United States. Specifically, we examined the descriptive characteristics and psychometric properties of START:AV assessments completed by 21 case managers on 291 adolescent offenders (250 boys and 41 girls) at the time of admission. Results provide preliminary support for the feasibility of completing START:AV assessments as part of routine practice. Findings also highlight differences in the characteristics of START:AV assessments for boys and girls and differential associations between the eight START:AV risk domains. Though results are promising, further research is needed to establish the reliability and validity of START:AV assessments completed in the field.

Comment

Main findings: Youths in juvenile correctional facilities are at an increased risk for a number of adverse outcomes including substance abuse and psychiatric disorders[1]. Substance abuse and psychiatric disorders have in turn been linked to higher risk of attempted suicide in juvenile corrections populations[2] and the identification of risk and protective factors on intake to corrective facilities is imperative to prevent the development of suicidal behaviours. The current study presented the pilot implementation and evaluation of the Short-Term Assessment of Risk and Treatability: Adolescent Version (START: AV) guide in three juvenile correctional facilities in the United States. The START: AV aims to provide a comprehensive evaluation of the short-term risks for adverse outcomes including suicide, self-harm and substance use, as well as violence, unauthorized leave and self-neglect. START: AV consists of 23 items ranging from questions on social skills and support, mental and emotional states, attitudes and plans, to the youths parenting/home environment. Assessments were completed by the case managers of 291 adolescent offenders, and the feasibility, reliability and integrity of START: AV assessments were analysed. The authors found support for the feasibility of the guide, with the information required to complete the START: AV being readily available in United States juvenile correctional facilities. When comparing results between boys and girls, a number of important differences were apparent, with girls rated as being at higher risk than boys on a number of outcomes, including self-harm and suicide. It was not possible to say whether these represented true differences in risk between boys and girls, or whether they were a reflection of assessor or instrument bias.

Implications: As at the 30th of June 2008, there were a total of 841 juveniles between the ages 10 to 17 in detention centres in Australia[3]. Suicide and self-harming behaviour can be a significant problem within the juvenile correctional environment, with a previous study into the suicidal and self-harming behaviour of incarcerated youth in a correctional facility in the United States reporting that 12.4% of incarcerated youths had a past suicide attempt and 30% had engaged in self-harming behaviour while incarcerated[4]. Despite this, a number of current risk assessment measures focus predominately on risk of violence and reoffending, with less attention on other important outcomes including suicide and self-harming behaviours.

The START: AV is one of the few instruments to include the identification of protective as well as risk factors in incarcerated youths. It is also in the minority of risk assessment measures which assess risk in incarcerated youths as opposed to youths who are serving probation or other community-based sentences. Despite some limitations, such as a small number of girls in the sample, the current study suggests that the START: AV holds potential for the assessment of short-term risk in youth in juvenile detention centres. This may aid in the development of suicide prevention practices for this population.

Endnotes

1. Desai RA, Goulet JL, Robbins J, Chapman JF, Migdole SJ, Hoge MA (2006). Mental health care in juvenile detention facilities: A review. *Journal of the American Academy of Psychiatry and the Law Online* 34, 204-214.
2. Wasserman GA, McReynolds LS (2006). Suicide risk at juvenile justice intake. *Suicide and Life-Threatening Behavior* 36, 239-249.
3. Richards K (2011). *Trends in juvenile detention in Australia.* No. 416. Canberra: Australian Institute of Criminology.
4. Penn JV, Esposito CL, Schaeffer LE, Fritz GK, Spirito A (2003). Suicide attempts and self-mutilative behaviour in a juvenile correctional facility. *Journal of the American Academy of Child and Adolescent Psychiatry* 42, 762.

Suicidal feelings in the twilight of life: A cross-sectional population-based study of 97-year-olds

Fässberg MM, Östling S, Börjesson-Hanson A, Skoog I, Wærn M (Sweden)

BMJ Open 3. Published online: 1 February 2013. doi: 10.1136/bmjopen-2012-002260, 2013

Objective: To examine the occurrence of past month suicidal feelings in extreme old age. Further, to identify factors associated with such feelings.

Design: Cross-sectional population-based study.

Setting: Gothenburg, Sweden.

Participants: 269 adults (197 women, 72 men) without dementia born in 1901-1909 who participated in a psychiatric examination.

Main outcome measures: Death thoughts and suicidal feelings. The latter were rated in accordance with the Paykel questions (life not worth living, death wishes, thoughts of taking own life, seriously considered taking own life, attempted suicide) during the past month.

Results: One quarter of the sample (26.7%) reported that they thought about their own death at least once a month. Past month thoughts that life was not worth living were acknowledged by 7.9% of the total sample, death wishes by 10.5% and thoughts of taking life by 3.8%. Few had serious thoughts of taking own life (0.8%) and none had attempted suicide. In all, 11.5% acknowledged some level of suicidal feelings. Most (77.4%) of those who reported such feelings fulfilled criteria for neither major nor minor depression. Neither poor perceived health nor disability (hearing, vision and motor function) was associated with suicidal feelings. Problematic sleep and deficient social contacts were also related to suicidal feelings after adjustment for depression.

Conclusions: Suicidal feelings may occur outside the context of depression and disability in this age group. Results can inform clinicians who care for persons who reach extreme old age.

Comment

Main findings: Little is known about the phenomena of suicidal ideation and behaviour in extreme old age (ages 95 and older). The unique participants of this study were part of a wider program called the 'Gothenburg 95+ Study', which covers aspects of mental health in those who reached the age of 97 in between the years 1998-2007, in Gothenburg, Sweden. Participants were identified through the Swedish Population Register, with 911 people eligible for inclusion. Just over half of these (64.9%) agreed to participate, and after those who had a diagnosis of dementia were excluded, the total number of participants was 269. Participants completed a number of assessments through home visits. These covered aspects such as suicidal thoughts, sleep satisfaction, cardio-health, hearing impairment, motor skills, cognitive function, religiosity, and social factors. Findings showed that although around one quarter of the total population thought about their own death at least monthly, a smaller proportion — just over one in 10 — had suicidal feelings. Initial data analysis associated several factors with suicidal feelings, such as dissatisfaction with sleep, trouble initiating sleep, aches and pains, having never had a spouse, not having children, and depression. Interestingly, although depression was more commonly found among those with suicidal feelings than those without suicidal feelings (22.6% vs. 6.3%), the vast majority — more than three quarters — of participants who reported suicidal feelings did not have depression. Also, participants with suicidal feelings were more likely to report spending too little time with children, friends and acquaintances, and neighbours, and experienced higher levels of loneliness. After adjusting for differences in sex and depression, only sleep difficulties, too little time spent with friends and acquaintances, and too little time spent with neighbours continued to be associated with suicidal feelings.

Implications: Although occurrences of suicidal feelings were relatively infrequent in this extremely elderly sample, it appears that sleep difficulties and insufficient perceived levels of certain types of social contact may have an important relationship with suicidal ideation in this group of people. While the current study was based on a small sample size and was not able to establish causal relationships, it is nonetheless reasonable to suggest that comfort, rest, and reducing perceived social isolation could in turn assist in reducing suicidal feelings among the very elderly.

Increasing social connectedness and quality time spent with others may be challenging among this age group, especially in instances where people may have outlived close friends or other peers. However, efforts to create enjoyable and accessible social activities and opportunities — coupled with practical measures such as transport assistance — may provide wellbeing benefits for the extremely elderly[1].

This paper is also important in evidencing the presence of suicidal ideation in absence of depression.

Endnote

1. Nichols DR (2010). Leisure activities and health: Conversations with isolated seniors. *Revue phén EPS/PHEnex Journal* 2, 1-7.

Long term effect of reduced pack sizes of paracetamol on poisoning deaths and liver transplant activity in England and Wales: Interrupted time series analyses

Hawton K, Bergen H, Simkin S, Dodd S, Pocock P, Bernal W, Gunnell D, Kapur N (UK)

British Medical Journal 346, f403, 2013

Objective: To assess the long term effect of United Kingdom legislation introduced in September 1998 to restrict pack sizes of paracetamol on deaths from paracetamol poisoning and liver unit activity.

Design: Interrupted time series analyses to assess mean quarterly changes from October 1998 to the end of 2009 relative to projected deaths without the legislation based on pre-legislation trends.

Setting: Mortality (1993-2009) and liver unit activity (1995-2009) in England and Wales, using information from the Office for National Statistics and NHS Blood and Transplant, respectively.

Participants: Residents of England and Wales.

Main Outcome Measures: Suicide, deaths of undetermined intent, and accidental poisoning deaths involving single drug ingestion of paracetamol and paracetamol compounds in people aged 10 years and over, and liver unit registrations and transplantations for paracetamol induced hepatotoxicity.

Results: Compared with the pre-legislation level, following the legislation there was an estimated average reduction of 17 (95% confidence interval -25 to -9) deaths per quarter in England and Wales involving paracetamol alone (with or without alcohol) that received suicide or undetermined verdicts. This decrease represented a 43% reduction or an estimated 765 fewer deaths over the 11 1/4; years after the legislation. A similar effect was found when accidental poisoning deaths were included, and when a conservative method of analysis was used. This decrease was largely unaltered after controlling for a non-significant reduction in deaths involving other methods of poisoning and also suicides by all methods. There was a 61% reduction in registrations for liver transplantation for paracetamol induced hepatotoxicity (-11 (-20 to -1) registrations per quarter). But no reduction was seen in actual transplantations (-3 (-12 to 6)), nor in registrations after a conservative method of analysis was used.

Conclusions: UK legislation to reduce pack sizes of paracetamol was followed by significant reductions in deaths due to paracetamol overdose, with some indication of fewer registrations for transplantation at liver units during the 11 years after the legislation. The continuing toll of deaths suggests, however, that further preventive measures should be sought.

Comment

Main findings: In 1998, the United Kingdom government introduced legislation limiting the pack sizes of paracetamol sold in pharmacies to 32 tablets and to 16 tablets per pack for non-pharmacy sales, in an attempt to reduce suicides, accidental deaths and liver damage caused by paracetamol overdose[1]. This study analysed the effectiveness of this legislation on paracetamol related overdoses, using Mortality data from England and Wales between 1993 and 2009 and hospital registrations for liver transplants between 1995 and 2009. For the purpose of this study, undetermined deaths (open cases) were included with suicides, and only those deaths involving paracetamol alone, or paracetamol mixed with alcohol in people over 10 years old were analysed. Between 1993 and 2009, 6-10% of all poisoning deaths in individuals over 10 were due to paracetamol overdose. When compared to the expected number of deaths based on the pre legislation period, paracetamol related deaths by suicide and open verdict reduced significantly after implementation by an average of 17 per quarter, with an overall decrease of 43% or 765 fewer deaths than expected. The reduction was still significant when considering paracetamol induced deaths by accidental poisoning. As well as a decrease in deaths, registrations for liver transplants due to paracetamol use were reduced by 61% or 482 fewer registrations after implementation. The number of completed liver transplants after the 1998 legislation saw a reduction; however this reduction was not significant.

Implications: Paracetamol is one of the most frequently used drugs in intentional overdoses worldwide[2] and is the main pharmaceutical agent resulting in calls to Australian poisons information centres[3]. The current UK study indicates that measures such as limiting pack sizes may have the ability to reduce the number of intentional paracetamol related overdoses. Meanwhile the most recent research in Australia suggests that paracetamol related hospital presentations have been increasing, with one study finding an 85% increase over the 4 year study period[4]. Results of the current study indicate that adopting similar legislation in Australia may warrant consideration to reverse this trend. However, it is clear given the relative lack of Australian studies on this topic, that more research into the occurrence of intentional paracetamol-related overdoses in Australian adults is required.

Previous studies analysing the effect of the current legislation in England and Wales, and similar legislation in Scotland, have returned mixed results. This paper filled a gap in the research by presenting a much needed longer term analysis of the effect of the legislation in England and Wales.

Endnotes

1. Committee on Safety of Medicines. Paracetamol and aspirin. *Current Problems in Pharmacovigilance* 23, 9.
2. Gunnell D, Murray V, Hawton K (2000). Use of paracetamol (acetaminophen) for suicide and nonfatal poisoning: Worldwide patterns of use and misuse. *Suicide and Life-Threatening Behavior* 30, 313-326.
3. Daly F, Fountain JS, Murray L, Graudins A, Buckley NA (2008). Guidelines for the management of paracetamol poisoning in Australia and New Zealand – Explanation and elaboration. *Medical Journal of Australia* 188, 296-301.
4. Ayonrinde OT, Phelps GJ, Hurley JC, Ayonrinde OA (2005). Paracetamol overdose and hepatotoxicity at a regional Australian hospital: A 4-year experience. *Internal Medicine Journal* 35, 655-660.

One followed by many? — Long-term effects of a celebrity suicide on the number of suicidal acts on the German railway net

Hegerl U, Koburger N, Rummel-Kluge C, Gravert C, Walden M, Mergl R (Germany)
Journal of Affective Disorders 146, 39-44, 2013

Background: Following the railway suicide of Robert Enke, a famous German football goal keeper, short-term copycat effects have been found. Main aims of the present study were to analyze long-term effects of this incidence and to compare them with overall national suicide data, as well as to investigate possible "anniversary effects".

Methods: For long-term effects, the number of railway suicidal acts in the two years before and after Robert Enke's suicide (10th November 2009) were compared. For anniversary effects, the corresponding 2-week-periods in 2009, 2010 and 2011 were analyzed. Incidence ratios with 95% confidence intervals were computed.

Results: Compared to the two years before Enke's suicide the incidence ratio of the number of railway suicidal acts in the 2-year-period following this event increased by 18.8% (95% confidence interval (CI)=11.0-27.1%; p<0.001). The median number of suicidal acts per day increased from 2 to 3 (p<0.001). This effect remains significant after excluding short-term 2-week effects of Enke's suicide. An anniversary effect was not present. The increase of fatal railway suicides between 2007 and 2010 (25%) was significantly different from that for the total number of suicides in Germany (6.6%) (p<0.0001).

Limitations: Due to missing data, analyses regarding gender were limited and regarding age not feasible.

Conclusions: Long-term effects of Enke's suicide on railway suicidal acts in Germany in the sense of copycat behavior are probable as this increase cannot be explained by corresponding changes of the total number of suicides in Germany.

Comment

Main findings: The "Werther-effect", an increase in suicidal behaviour by the same method, has been witnessed following the extensive media reporting of suicide events such as the suicide deaths of celebrities[1] and the portrayal of fictional suicides[2]. The current study aimed to test the long-term effect of media reporting of the suicide death of a famous German football player on copycat events. The possibility of an anniversary effect in the days surrounding the date of the incident in the following years was also investigated. The long term-effect of the celebrity death was analysed by comparing completed suicides and non-fatal suicide attempts on the German railway system in the two-year period following the celebrity suicide with the two-year period before the celebrity suicide. The total number of suicide acts (fatal and non-fatal) in both men and women increased significantly from 1681 in the two years before the event, to 1997 in the two years following. Completed suicides increased from 1418 in the two years before the event, to 1767 in the two years following. The increase in fatal railway suicides could not be explained by a general increase in suicide rates. The anniversary reaction was analysed by looking at the frequency of railway suicide acts two weeks before, and two weeks after the day of the celebrity suicide in the two years following the event. No anniversary reaction was identified, with no significant increase in rail-related suicidal behaviour surrounding the first or second anniversary of the event, despite another peak in media reporting around these times. The findings of the current study suggest the presence of a "Werther-effect" with an increase in suicide in the initial period following the reporting of the suicide event, as well as a sustained increase over the longer-term.

Implications: Suicide by collision with a train is a highly lethal means of suicide, comprising 1.96% of suicides in Queensland between 1990 and 2004, with an average of 11 suicide deaths per year[3]. The lethality of this method, along with the potential serious impacts on third parties such as train drivers and onlookers[4] have resulted in considerable research focusing on rail related suicides and strategies for prevention. The current paper supports previous suggestions that reducing the media coverage of rail-related suicide events may have the potential to prevent copycat events[5]. Findings emphasise the importance of media guidelines such as the Australian Federal Government's MindFrame National Media Initiative encouraging careful media reporting of suicides[6].

The majority of past research in this area has evaluated the effect of media reporting of suicides in the initial days and weeks surrounding the incident. This paper filled a gap in the current literature by providing an analysis of the long-term effect of such events on both fatal and non-fatal suicidal acts.

Endnotes

1. Stack S (2005). Suicide in the media: A quantitative review of studies based on non-fictional stories. *Suicide and Life-Threatening Behavior* 35, 121-133.
2. Pirkis J, Blood WR (2001). Suicide and the media: Part II: Portrayal in fictional media. *Crisis* 22, 155-162.
3. De Leo D, Krysinska K (2008). Suicidal behaviour by train collision in Queensland, 1990-2004. *The Australian and New Zealand Journal of Psychiatry* 42, 772-779.
4. Lukaschek K, Baumert J, Ladwig KH (2011). Behaviour patterns preceding a railway suicide: Explorative study of German federal police officers' experiences. *BMC Public Health* 11, 620.
5. Etzersdorfer E, Sonneck G (1998). Preventing suicide by influencing mass-media reporting. The Viennese experience 1980-1996. *Archives of Suicide Research* 4, 67.
6. Commonwealth of Australia (2011). *Suicide and mental illness in the media: A Mindframe resource for the mental health and suicide prevention sectors.* Canberra: Commonwealth of Australia.

Ask suicide-screening questions to everyone in medical settings: The asQ'em quality improvement project

Horowitz LM, Snyder D, Ludi E, Rosenstein DL, Kohn-Godbout J, Lee L, Cartledge T, Farrar A, Pao M (USA)

Psychosomatics. Published online: 8 February 2013. doi: 10.1016/j.psym.2013.01.002, 2013

Background: Suicide in hospital settings is a frequently reported sentinel event to the Joint Commission (JC). Since 1995, over 1,000 inpatient deaths by suicide have been reported to the JC; 25% occurred in non-behavioral health settings. Lack of proper "assessment" was the leading root cause for 80% of hospital suicides. This paper describes the "Ask Suicide-Screening Questions to Everyone in Medical Settings (asQ'em)" Quality Improvement Project. We aimed to pilot a suicide screening tool and determine feasibility of screening in terms of prevalence, impact on unit workflow, impact on mental health resources, and patient/nurse acceptance.

Methods: We piloted the asQ'em two-item screening instrument that assesses suicidal thoughts and behaviors, designed specifically for nurses to administer to medical patients. Educational in-services were conducted. A convenience sample of adult patients, 18 years or older, from three selected inpatient units in the National Institutes of Health Clinical Center, participated.

Results: A total of 331 patients were screened; 13 (4%) patients screened "positive" for suicide risk and received further evaluation. No patient had acute suicidal thoughts or required an observational monitor. Screening took approximately 2 minutes; 87% of patients reported feeling comfortable with screening; 81% of patients, 75% of nurses, and 100% of social workers agreed that all patients in hospitals should be screened for suicide risk.

Discussion: Nurses can feasibly screen hospitalized medical/surgical patients for suicide risk with a two-item screening instrument. Patients, nurses, and social workers rated their experience of screening as positive and supported the idea of universal suicide screening in the hospital.

Comment

Main findings: Within the United States, inadequate assessment of suicide risk in hospital settings outside of behavioural health (for instance, oncology units) was a major contributor to hospital suicide deaths between 1995 and 2012[1]. In an effort to address this, a two-item tool – asQ'em –was created for general hospital nurses to screen patients for suicide risk at inpatient medical/surgical units. The first question asks: "In the past month have you had thoughts about suicide?" The second: "Have you ever made a suicide attempt?" If the patient answered yes to either question, a follow up question was asked: "Are you having thoughts of suicide right now?" These questions were chosen as they are predictive of suicide, and markers of emotional distress that may warrant further intervention. Eligible patients were selected from a convenience sample of individuals enrolled in medical/surgical clinical research trials at the National Institute of Health Clinical Centre, in Bethesda, Maryland. Data collection occurred over two phases (January 8-12, and April 23-June 18, 2012) in the cancer unit and infectious diseases unit, resulting in 331 patients for screening. Patients were excluded if they were cognitively impaired or unable to speak English fluently.

The feasibility of asQ'em was tested in four domains: prevalence, impact on unit workflow, patient/nurse acceptance and the impact of the tool on mental health resources. The authors concluded that nurses can feasibly screen hospitalised medical/surgical patients for suicide risk with a two-item scale. Data analysis showed that only 4% of the patients screened positive for suicide risk. For patients who screened positive, the time of screening averaged five minutes - a considerably low impact on workflow. Patients were quite accepting of the tool, with over three quarters (79%) of the patients rating their experience as positive, and 85% of the patients reporting they were glad the hospital was asking about suicide. Interestingly, nurses rated themselves as less comfortable with administering the test than did the patients. Nurses also underrated patients' comfort with answering the screening questions (0.35 points less than the patients rated themselves). Initially, the nurses implementing the screening tool felt uncomfortable asking the questions and described feeling that "it's too personal (to ask)", however, their discomfort decreased over time.

Implications: Given increasing recognition of links between physical illness and suicide risk, there is a need to improve detection of potential suicidality within the context of physical health settings. Overall the participants in this study seemed to be "glad" that the NIH clinical centre was asking about suicidal thoughts, which suggests that brief screening tools can feasibly be applied in general medical settings, by nurses, without distressing patients. In addition, there is no evidence that asking questions about suicide is likely to present a risk to patients or to 'put the idea into their heads'[2]. Although very few patients in the current study (4%) reported having suicidal thoughts, tools such asQ'em could nonetheless lead to potentially useful data about suicide risk within physical, rather than mental, healthcare settings, as well as facilitate better care. However, it is important to consider that while the findings about this tool are promising, it has not been widely validated on an adult medical population.

Endnotes

1. The Joint Commission (1995-2012): *Sentinel Event Type – Event type by year.* Retrieved April 23 2013 from http://www.jointcommission.org/assets/1/18/Event_Year_1995_1Q2012.pdf.

2. Headspace (2009). *Myth buster: Suicidal ideation.* Retrieved April 23 2013 from www.headspace.org.au.

Social support as a protective factor in suicide: Findings from two nationally representative samples

Kleiman EM, Liu RT (USA)

Journal of Affective Disorders. Published online: 4 March 2013. doi: 10.1016/j.jad.2013.01.033, 2013

Background: Suicide is a problem of worldwide concern and research on possible protective factors is needed. We explored the role of social support as one such factor. Specifically, we hypothesized that increased social support would be associated with decreased likelihood of a lifetime suicide attempt in two nationally representative samples as well as a high-risk subsample.

Methods: We analyzed the relationship between social support and lifetime history of a suicide attempt, controlling for a variety of related psychopathology and demographic variables, in the National Comorbidity Study Replication (NCS-R), a United States sample and the Adult Psychiatric Morbidity Study (APMS), an English sample.

Results: Results indicate that social support is associated with decreased likelihood of a lifetime suicide attempt controlling for a variety of related predictors in both the full US sample (OR = 0.68, p<.001) and the full English sample (OR = 0.93, p<.01).

Limitations: The cross-sectional data do not allow true cause and effect analyses.

Conclusions: Our findings suggest social support is associated with decreased likelihood of a lifetime suicide attempt. Social support is a highly modifiable factor that can be used to improve existing suicide prevention programs worldwide.

Comment

Main findings: In an effort to examine social support as a protective/resiliency factor against suicide, the authors sourced two large datasets: The National Comorbidity Study Replication — a nationally representative sample from the United States from the years 2001-2003, and the 2007 Adult Psychiatric Morbidly Survey —— a nationally representative English sample from October 2006 — December 2007. This was done to establish whether or not findings from the United States could be replicated in an English population sample. Both studies used interview-based surveys which collected information about variables known for their links to increased suicide risk, such as psychiatric history, parental divorce and the death of a parent. The surveys also asked whether participants had ever attempted suicide, whether they had engaged in help seeking behaviour, and captured participants' perceived levels of support from family and friends. Logistic regression using the nationally representative US sample, and controlling for demographic, psychiatric history, family background, and help-seeking behaviour variables showed that higher likelihood of a lifetime suicide attempt was associated with lower age, lower education and female gender. Greater social support was associated with lower likelihood of a lifetime suicide attempt. Results from the UK also showed that lower age and female gender predicted greater likelihood of a lifetime suicide attempt, while greater social support was associated with lower likelihood of a lifetime suicide attempt. Therefore, the authors provided evidence that, to a degree, there is 'universality' in the association between social support and suicide attempts between the US and UK, in that greater social support was associated with lower likelihood of a lifetime suicide attempt in both countries.

Implications: Within suicide research, risk factors are widely explored, while less is known about protective/resiliency factors such as social support. The authors of this study sought to understand if social support could predict the likelihood of a lifetime suicide attempt and whether or not any connection between social support and likelihood of a suicide attempt was culturally specific to the USA. In doing so, they also confirmed many similar risk factors between the USA and UK — such as major depression, dysthymias, bipolar I/II/subthreshold, generalised anxiety disorder, and other psychiatric conditions. Considering the Australian context, there has been substantial research on these risk factors, producing similar results, however there is substantially less research on protective factors, including social support. From studies that include variables related to social support within Australia, there is evidence that compromised social support, in the form of lack of supportive parental relationships, increases the likelihood of suicide in young people[1]. Further research using longitudinal data is needed to understand whether or not social support is consistently able to predict the likelihood of suicidal behaviour in different groups of people (for example, those from different age groups or cultural backgrounds) within Australia, and what types of social support may be the most important in terms of protection against suicide.

Endnote

1. Beautrais, A (2001). Risk factors for suicide and attempted suicide among young people. *Australian and New Zealand Journal of Psychiatry* 34, 420-436.

Adolescent self-cutting elsewhere than on the arms reveals more serious psychiatric symptoms

Laukkanen E, Rissanen ML, Tolmunen T, Kylmä J, Hintikka J (Finland)

European Child & Adolescent Psychiatry. Published online: 20 February 2013. doi: 10.1007/s00787-013-0390-1, 2013

Self-cutting as a form of self-harm is a common and multifaceted phenomenon among adolescents. The aim of this study was to investigate whether the location of self-cutting (arms or other areas of the body) could help to assess the severity of the underlying psychiatric problems. A sample of adolescents who reported self-cutting (n = 440) was drawn from a large sample of community adolescents (n = 4,019). The majority of self-cutting adolescents, 296 (67.2 %), reported cutting only the upper arms, while 144 (32.8 %) also cut other parts of the body. The data included a structured self-rating questionnaire, questions about self-cutting, the Youth Self-Report (YSR) for adolescents aged 11-18 years, the Beck Depression Inventory, the Toronto Alexithymia Scale and the Adolescent Disso-ciative Experience Scale (A-DES). The results indicate that self-cutting on other parts of body than the arms was associated with female gender, a wide range of emotional and dissociative symptoms and suicidal ideation. In logistic regression analysis, the most pronounced association between self-cutting on other places than the arms was found with YSR subscales withdrawn/depressed, social prob-lems and thought problems, and dissociation (A-DES). We conclude that self-cutting adolescents, mostly girls, with wounds elsewhere than on the arms present with the most serious psychiatric symptoms. It is important to perform a careful physical examination when an adolescent has unexplained wounds or scars on the arms or on other parts of the body. These adolescents also need a caring and con-scientious psychiatric examination and possible psychiatric treatment.

Comment

Main findings: The first symptoms of more severe developmental and psychiatric problems may appear in adolescence, and some of these problems may manifest in attempts to 'manipulate the body' through self-injury (for example, cutting of the arms and/or other parts of the body). This study sought to understand if there is a difference in psychiatric symptoms and suicidal ideation, depending where on the body adolescents cut themselves. From an eligible sample of 6,421 students aged 13-18 years living in Kuopio, Finland (of which 98% inhabitants are Cau-casians), 4,214 students participated (a 65.6% response). Participants completed questionnaires covering depression, social functioning, emotional awareness, interpersonal relationships, frequency of dissociative experiences, suicidal ideation, and self-cutting. Results showed that 440 students reported self-cutting, with 393 of them being girls (89.3%). Among the 440 students who reported self-cutting, 296 cut only on the arms, while 144 cut on other parts of the body. Girls were more likely than boys to cut on other parts of the body than the arms (34.9% vs. 10.7% respectively), but the small number of boys in the study rendered it not possible to further analyse gender differences. Cutting behaviour usually started around age 15 (mean age 15.8, SD 1.4 years). Those who cut themselves on more than one part of the body were more likely to have planned in advance to do so, than those who only cut on the arms (32.6% vs. 12.5%). The group who cut on other parts of the body also more commonly 'idealised' death as part of their self-harming behaviour, than those who self-cut on the arms alone (31.9% vs. 16.5%). Both groups (self-cutting on the arms alone, and other parts of the body) had more mental symptoms and substance abuse than their age and sex matched 'non-cutting' controls. Suicidal thoughts were more common among those who cut on other parts of the body than those who cut only on the arms (65.0% vs. 42.2% respectively), as were later suicide attempts (12.9% vs. 3.5% respectively). Self-cutting on the arms was typically characterised as a 'cry for help,' while cutting other parts of the body was more likely to be associated with relief from mental distress and self-punishment.

Implications: It can be difficult for parents, teachers and other school staff such as counsellors or nurses to offer help to self-cutting adolescents, as knowledge about this behaviour is limited, and there are few interventions for self-cutting that have been carefully evaluated. A useful implication from this study is that self-cutting should be regarded as a request for help and/or an indicator of mental distress — not as a form of manipulative behaviour[1] — as many of the self-cutting students in this study were also suffering from suicidal thoughts and other psychiatric symptoms. Therefore, regarding school-based assistance, it may be helpful to educate teachers and other staff how to respectfully approach and ask questions of a student if that student seems to have cutting scars on their arms or any other part of their body, and to have pathways to provide further assistance/referrals for that student. Young people themselves have suggested a number of strategies for the prevention of self-harm including: listening to young people's problems (especially young women), giving them confidence, and being there for them and not letting them down[2]. Also, it is important to consider this is a Finnish example of students, where nearly the entire population is Caucasian; an Australian study may generate different results, due in part to cultural differences[3].

Endnotes

1. Walsh BW (2006). *Treating self-injury: A practical guide.* New York, NY: Guilford Press.
2. Fortune S, Sinclair J, Hawton K (2008). Adolescents' views on preventing self-harm: A large community study. *Social Psychiatry and Psychiatric Epidemiology* 43, 96-104.
3. Farrelly T, Francis K (2009). Definitions of suicide and self-harm behaviour in an Australian Aboriginal Community. *Suicide and Life-Threatening Behavior* 39, 182-189.

Suicide ideation and attempt in a community cohort of urban Aboriginal youth: A cross-sectional study

Luke JN, Anderson IP, Gee GJ, Thorpe R, Rowley KG, Reilly RE, Thorpe A, Stewart PJ (Australia)
Crisis. Published online: 28 January 2013. doi: 10.1027/0227-5910/a000187, 2013

Background: There has been increasing attention over the last decade on the issue of indigenous youth suicide. A number of studies have documented the high prevalence of suicide behavior and mortality in Australia and internationally. However, no studies have focused on documenting the correlates of suicide behavior for indigenous youth in Australia.

Aims: To examine the prevalence of suicide ideation and attempt and the associated factors for a community[1] cohort of Koori[2] (Aboriginal) youth.

Method: Data were obtained from the Victorian Aboriginal Health Service (VAHS) Young People's Project (YPP), a community initiated cross-sectional data set. In 1997/1998, self-reported data were collected for 172 Koori youth aged 12-26 years living in Melbourne, Australia. The data were analyzed to assess the prevalence of current suicide ideation and lifetime suicide attempt. Principal components analysis (PCA) was used to identify closely associated social, emotional, behavioral, and cultural variables at baseline and Cox regression modeling was then used to identify associations between PCA components and suicide ideation and attempt.

Results: Ideation and attempt were reported at 23.3% and 24.4%, respectively. PCA yielded five components: (1) emotional distress, (2) social distress A, (3) social distress B, (4) cultural connection, (5) behavioral. All were positively and independently associated with suicide ideation and attempt, while cultural connection showed a negative association.

Conclusions: Suicide ideation and attempt were common in this cross-section of indigenous youth with an unfavorable profile for the emotional, social, cultural, and behavioral factors.

Comment

Main findings: Aboriginal and Torres Strait Islander youth in Australia are at an increased risk for suicide; with a recent Queensland paper finding Aboriginal and Torres Strait Islanders aged 15-24 were four times more likely to die by suicide than other Australians in the same age group[1]. The current paper used the Victorian Aboriginal Health Service (VAHS) Young People's Project (YPP) data, obtained through a self-report survey administered by trained peer interviewers to 172 Aboriginal and Torres Strait Islander people between the ages of 12 and 26. Results of the survey indicated that 23.3% of youth (n = 40) had experienced suicidal ideation in the 2 weeks before participation. Further, 24.4% of youth (n = 42) had attempted suicide at least once in their lifetime. Suicidal ideation was more often reported in older youth aged 17-21 than those aged 16 years or younger, and its presence was associated with a number of negative experiences including depression, anger, boredom, loneliness, anxiety, sexual abuse, low self-esteem, history of suicide attempts by family or friends in the last year, homosexuality/bisexuality, intravenous drug use and racial discrimination. Engaging in social activities such as spending time with family and friends appears to offer protection against suicidal ideation. Similar to ideation, suicide attempts were more common in the older age groups with only 4.7% of attempters being aged 16 years or younger. Negative experiences associated with suicide attempts were similar to those reported for suicidal ideation, however attempters were significantly more likely to experience physical abuse, parental separation, being raised by people other than parents, unemployment, time in youth training, smoking and marijuana use. Low self-esteem, having an adult to talk to, homosexuality/bisexuality and visiting and spending time with family were not associated with suicide attempts. However, spending time with friends and participating in sports appeared to act as protective factors against lifetime suicide attempts.

Implications: Suicide in Aboriginal and Torres Strait Islander youth is a major problem in Australia. Although the high incidence of suicide in this group has been consistently documented, there is currently a lack of clear understanding of reasons for the increased risk. Through analysing the association between a number of life experiences and the presence of recent suicidal ideation or lifetime suicide attempts in Aboriginal and Torres Strait Islander youth, the current paper identified a number of possible risk and protective factors for these behaviours.

Results of the paper suggest that for this population group, there are a number of factors other than depression and mental illness which are associated with suicidal behaviour. The authors suggest that it may be useful to take a broader approach to screening for suicide risk in Aboriginal and Torres Strait Islander youth, including other social, cultural and behavioural risk factors. The finding that spending time with friends and involvement in sport may act as protective factors supports the implementation of suicide prevention programs, such as the Alive and Kicking Goals! program in Western Australia, encouraging social connectedness through participation in team sports and using linkages with sports teams as a way to reach out to young people[2].

Endnotes

1. De Leo D, Sveticic J, Milner A (2011). Suicide in Indigenous people in Queensland, Australia: Trends and methods, 1994-2007. *Australian and New Zealand Journal of Psychiatry* 45, 532-538.
2. Tighe J, McKay K (2012). Alive and Kicking Goals!: Preliminary findings from a Kimberly suicide prevention program. *Advances in Mental Health* 10, 240-245.

Suicidal ideation, risk factors, and communication with parents: An HBSC study on school children in Estonia, Lithuania, and Luxembourg

Mark L, Samm A, Tooding L-M, Sisask M, Aasvee K, Zaborskis A, Zemaitiene N, Värnik A
(Estonia, Lithuania)
Crisis 34, 3-12, 2013

Background: Suicide is a leading cause of death among youth. In the year 2002, Lithuania had the 2nd, Luxembourg the 5th, and Estonia the 9th highest suicide rates among 15- to 19-year-olds across 90 countries worldwide. Suicidal ideation is a significant precursor to suicide.

Aims: To report on the prevalence of and associations between suicidal ideation, smoking, alcohol consumption, physical fighting, bullying, and communication with parents among 15-year-old school children.

Methods: The survey analyzes data from the 2005/2006 HBSC study from Estonia, Lithuania, and Luxembourg (N = 4,954). The risk factors were calculated through multinomial logistic regression analyses.

Results: The overall prevalence of suicidal ideation in the preceding year was 17%. Suicidal thoughts were associated with communication difficulties with parents (OR from 2.0 to 4.6) and other risk factors, especially multiple risks (OR for 4-5 concurrent risk factors from 4.5 to 13.6). Parent-child communication had a significant mediating effect by decreasing the odds for suicidality and multiple risks.

Limitations: The prevalence estimates were obtained by self-reports. The causal relationships need further investigation.

Conclusion: The risk factors studied, particularly multiple risks, were associated with higher odds for suicidal ideation. Good parent-child communication is a significant resource for decreasing suicidal ideation among adolescents.

Comment

Main findings: A number of factors leading to increased risk of suicidal ideation and behaviour in adolescents have been identified in previous literature. These factors include stressful life events, drug and alcohol use, sexual activity, unstable family environments and low levels of parental monitoring[1]. The current study used 2005/2006 data from The Health Behavior in School-Aged Children (HBSC) study from Estonia, Lithuania and Luxembourg; three countries with high adolescent suicide rates[2], to evaluate the relationship between smoking, alcohol use, fighting, bullying and parental communication on suicidal ideation. Overall, 810 of the 4,954 participants (16.7%) had experienced suicidal thoughts in the previous 12 months. Results indicated that females experienced suicidal ideation more often than males. The number of youths engaging in risky behaviour varied significantly between the three countries; however, overall, adolescents who had tried smoking or engaged in regular smoking, had participated in drinking or getting drunk, and were involved in physical fights or bullying as either victim or perpetrator were more likely to report suicidal ideation than their peers. Those with multiple risk factors were at an even greater risk. Adolescents with good parental relationships with adequate communication experienced fewer risk factors and less suicidal ideation, while those experiencing difficult parental relationships with poor communication were more likely to experience suicidal thoughts.

Implications: Suicide is the leading cause of death in young Australian males aged between 15 and 19 years, comprising approximately one quarter of deaths in this age group[3]. Considering suicidal ideation is a major predictor of subsequent death by suicide[4], it is imperative to understand the risk factors for suicidal thoughts in adolescents. The current study supports previous findings that there may be a number of clear risk factors for suicidal ideation and behaviour in young people. Perhaps most important from a preventative perspective is the finding that effective parent-child communication may act as a protective factor against suicidal ideation, which may prove useful when working with families of suicidal adolescents or with families of young people displaying behavioural problems.

Although promising, the current study was limited to Estonia, Lithuania and Luxembourg and found significant differences between these countries on a number of variables. These findings suggest that studies on adolescents in other countries may not be transferrable to the Australian context, and it is important that similar research is conducted in Australia.

Endnotes

1. King RA, Schwab-Stone M, Flisher AJ, Greenwald S, Kramer RA, Goodman SH, Lahey BB, Shaffer D, Gould M (2001). Psychosocial and risk behaviour correlates of youth suicide attempts and suicidal ideation. *Journal of the American Academy of Child and Adolescent Psychiatry* 40, 837-846.

2. Wasserman D, Cheng Q, Jiang GX (2005). Global suicide rates among young people aged 15-19. *World Psychiatry* 4, 114-120.

3. Australian Bureau of Statistics (2013). *Causes of death, Australia, 2011.* Cat. No. 3303.0. Canberra: ABS.

4. Nock MK, Borges G, Bromet EJ, Alonso J, Angermeyer M, Beautrais A, Bruffaerts R, Chiu WT, de Girolamo G, Gluzman S, de Graaf R, Gureje O, Haro JM, Huang Y, Karam E, Kessler RC, Lepine JP, Levinson D, Medina-Mora ME, Ono Y, Posada-Villa J, Williams D (2008). Cross national prevalence and risk factors for suicidal ideation, plans and attempts. *British Journal of Psychiatry* 192, 98-105

Natural disasters and suicide: Evidence from Japan

Matsubayashi T, Sawada Y, Ueda M (USA, Japan)

Social Science and Medicine 82, 126-133, 2013

Previous research shows no consensus as to whether and how natural disasters affect suicide rates in their aftermath. Using prefecture-level panel data of natural disasters and suicide in Japan between 1982 and 2010, we estimate both contemporaneous and lagged effects of natural disasters on the suicide rates of various demographic groups. We find that when the damage caused by natural disasters is extremely large, as in the case of the Great Hanshin-Awaji Earthquake in 1995, suicide rates tend to increase in the immediate aftermath of the disaster and several years later. However, when the damage by natural disasters is less severe, suicide rates tend to decrease after the disasters, especially one or two years later. Thus, natural disasters affect the suicide rates of affected populations in a complicated way, depending on the severity of damages as well as on how many years have passed since the disaster. We also find that the effects of natural disasters on suicide rates vary considerably across demographic groups, which suggests that some population subgroups are more vulnerable to the impact of natural disasters than others. We then test the possibility that natural disasters enhance people's willingness to help others in society, an effect that may work as a protective factor against disaster victims' suicidal risks. We find that natural disasters increase the level of social ties in affected communities, which may mitigate some of the adverse consequence of natural disasters, resulting in a decline in suicide rates. Our findings also indicate that when natural disasters are highly destructive and disruptive, such protective features of social connectedness are unlikely to be enough to compensate for the severe negative impact of disasters on health outcomes.

Comment

Main findings: Worldwide, the occurrence of natural disasters has increased in recent years[1]. These disasters often result in negative mental and financial impacts on survivors, potentially acting as risk factors for suicidal behaviour[2]. This paper analysed the short and long-term effects of natural disasters on suicides in Japan from 1982-2010, as well as possible protective factors after these events. Overall, working-age men and elderly women were most at risk for suicidal behaviours; however, the results indicated that the outcomes of natural disasters might depend on the severity of the disaster (measured in this case by the number of victims and the damage caused to the affected area). Severe disasters with the most damage and loss of life were accompanied by an initial increase in suicides, then a decrease in the one or two years following the disaster, with another increase in the years after that. On the other hand, less severe disasters only witnessed a decrease, particularly in the two years following the event. The paper considered the social connectedness which often occurs after a natural disaster as a possible protective factor and explanation for this decrease in suicides. Social connectedness was measured by the number of people donating blood during different time periods.

It was found that the number of people giving blood decreased in the initial period after a natural disaster, but increased again in the two year period following the disaster. The severity of damages from natural disasters was positively associated with blood donations for five years after the event which authors suggest may be indicative of long lasting community support.

Implications: Existing papers analysing the effects of natural disasters on suicidal behaviours have often suffered from methodological shortcomings and have resulted in contradictory findings. Studies such as the current Japanese paper are imperative for a clearer understanding of risk in the time surrounding these events. The current findings suggest that effects of natural disasters may depend on the severity of the disaster and that certain age groups and sexes may be at increased risk around these times, possibly warranting targeted suicide prevention efforts.

Australia has experienced a number of serious natural disasters in the past including floods, bushfires and cyclones. Most recently, in Queensland, the 2011 floods had devastating effects with the most serious repercussions being felt in Ipswich and Toowoomba. A recent paper has indicated that suicide rates did not significantly increase in these areas during the six months following the floods[3]. The results of the current paper suggest that even in the absence of an initial increase in suicides there is a need for continuing social support and availability of mental health services for the people affected to prevent an increase in the following years.

Endnotes

1. Centre for Research on the Epidemiology of Disasters (2012). *The EM-DAT: The international disaster database.* Retrieved 17 April 2013 from http://www.emdat.be/.
2. Kõlves K, Kõlves KE, De Leo D (2013). Natural disasters and suicidal behaviours: A systematic literature review. *Journal of Affective Disorders* 146, 1-14.
3. De Leo D, Too LS, Kõlves K, Milner A, Ide N (2012). Has the suicide rate risen with the 2011 Queensland Floods? *Journal of Loss and Trauma* 18, 170-178.

Prevalence, correlates, and treatment of lifetime suicidal behavior among adolescents: Results from the national comorbidity survey replication adolescent supplement

Nock MK, Green JG, Hwang I, McLaughlin KA, Sampson NA, Zaslavsky AM, Kessler RC (USA)
JAMA Psychiatry 70, 300-310, 2013

Context: Although suicide is the third leading cause of death among US adolescents, little is known about the prevalence, correlates, or treatment of its immediate precursors, adolescent suicidal behaviors (ie, suicide ideation, plans, and attempts).

Objectives: To estimate the lifetime prevalence of suicidal behaviors among US adolescents and the associations of retrospectively reported, temporally primary DSM-IV disorders with the subsequent onset of suicidal behaviors.

Design: Dual-frame national sample of adolescents from the National Comorbidity Survey Replication Adolescent Supplement.

Setting: Face-to-face household interviews with adolescents and questionnaires for parents.

Participants: A total of 6483 adolescents 13 to 18 years of age and their parents.

Main Outcome Measures: Lifetime suicide ideation, plans, and attempts.

Results: The estimated lifetime prevalences of suicide ideation, plans, and attempts among the respondents are 12.1%, 4.0%, and 4.1%, respectively. The vast majority of adolescents with these behaviors meet lifetime criteria for at least one DSM-IV mental disorder assessed in the survey. Most temporally primary (based on retrospective age-of-onset reports) fear/anger, distress, disruptive behavior, and substance disorders significantly predict elevated odds of subsequent suicidal behaviors in bivariate models. The most consistently significant associations of these disorders are with suicide ideation, although a number of disorders are also predictors of plans and both planned and unplanned attempts among ideators. Most suicidal adolescents (>80%) receive some form of mental health treatment. In most cases (>55%), treatment starts prior to onset of suicidal behaviors but fails to prevent these behaviors from occurring.

Conclusions: Suicidal behaviors are common among US adolescents, with rates that approach those of adults. The vast majority of youth with suicidal behaviors have preexisting mental disorders. The disorders most powerfully predicting ideation, though, are different from those most powerfully predicting conditional transitions from ideation to plans and attempts. These differences suggest that distinct prediction and prevention strategies are needed for ideation, plans among ideators, planned attempts, and unplanned attempts.

Comment

Main findings: Suicidal ideation, plans and attempts are known precursors to reoccurring suicidal behaviour and eventual death by suicide[1]. Another major risk factor for suicide and suicidal behaviour is mental illness[2]. The current US paper used face-to-face household interviews with 6483 adolescents aged between 13 and 18 and their parents to analyse the lifetime prevalence of suicidal behaviours and the relationships with mental disorders among adolescents. Overall, 12.1% of adolescent participants had experienced suicidal ideation at some time during their lives, while 4% had made suicidal plans and 4.1% had made a previous suicide attempt. Out of the 12.1% of participants who had experienced suicidal ideation, 33.4% had later developed a suicide plan and 33.9% had attempted suicide, with almost nine out of 10 (88.4%) of those attempts occurring within one year of making the plans. The development of suicidal ideation was less than 1% before the age of ten, increasing substantially between 12 and 17 years of age. The presence of suicide plans and attempts was similarly low until the age of 12 (less than 1%) but increasing between ages of 12 and 17. Out of all adolescents reporting suicidal ideation in their lifetime, 89.3% had at least one diagnosable mental disorder in their lifetime, while 96.1% of suicide attempters met the criteria for a mental disorder, most commonly Major Depressive Disorder. The vast majority of adolescents (80.2% of ideators, 87.5% of planners and 94.2% of attempters) had received some form of treatment, most commonly from a mental health expert, followed by treatment by school-based services and General Practitioners. However, despite around half to three quarters (55.3%-73.2%) of adolescents across categories receiving mental health treatment before suicidal behaviour emerged, this treatment was unable to prevent the behaviour from occurring.

Implications: As the authors note, many papers focusing on the lifetime prevalence of suicidal behaviour in adolescents have suffered from poor generalisability due to small sample sizes. The current paper used a large nationally representative sample to provide an indication of the prevalence and course of suicidal behaviours in adolescents, information which is important when considering the identification of suicidal adolescents and effective suicide prevention practices for those at risk.

This paper gives some important insights into the treatment of suicidal adolescents with mental disorders in the US. The finding that the majority of suicidal adolescents had been seen by a mental health expert is promising. However, there is some indication that this treatment may not be as effective as it could be at preventing the onset of suicidal behaviours. This highlights the importance of better understanding what factors may contribute to the development of mental disorders and/or suicidal behaviours in adolescents. A similar large scale study in Australia may provide essential information about the background, trajectories, and treatment of suicidal adolescents in Australia.

Endnotes

1. Nock MK, Borges G, Bromet EJ, Alonso J, Angermeyer M, Beautrais A, Bruffaerts R, Chiu WT, de Girolamo G, Gluzman S, de Graaf R, Gureje O, Haro JM, Huang Y, Karam E, Kessler RC, Lepine JP, Levinson D, Medina-Mora ME, Ono Y, Posada-Villa J, Williams D (2008). Cross national prevalence and risk factors for suicidal ideation, plans and attempts. *British Journal of Psychiatry* 192, 98-105.
2. Hawton K, van Heeringen K (2009). Suicide. *Lancet* 373, 1372-1381.

Excess mortality, causes of death and life expectancy in 270,770 patients with recent onset of mental disorders in Denmark, Finland and Sweden

Nordentoft M, Wahlbeck K, Hällgren J, Westman J, Ösby U, Alinaghizadeh H, Gissler M, Laursen TM (Denmark, Sweden, Finland)

PLoS ONE 8, e55176-e55176, 2013

Background: Excess mortality among patients with severe mental disorders has not previously been investigated in detail in large complete national populations.

Objective: To investigate the excess mortality in different diagnostic categories due to suicide and other external causes of death, and due to specific causes in connection with diseases and medical conditions.

Methods: In longitudinal national psychiatric case registers from Denmark, Finland, and Sweden, a cohort of 270,770 recent-onset patients, who at least once during the period 2000 to 2006 were admitted due to a psychiatric disorder, were followed until death or the end of 2006. They were followed for 912,279 person years, and 28,088 deaths were analyzed. Life expectancy and standardized cause-specific mortality rates were estimated in each diagnostic group in all three countries.

Results: The life expectancy was generally approximately 15 years shorter for women and 20 years shorter for men, compared to the general population. Mortality due to diseases and medical conditions was increased two- to three-fold, while excess mortality from external causes ranged from three- to 77-fold. Mortality due to diseases and medical conditions was generally lowest in patients with affective disorders and highest in patients with substance abuse and personality disorders, while mortality due to suicide was highest in patients with affective disorders and personality disorders, and mortality due to other external causes was highest in patients with substance abuse.

Conclusions: These alarming figures call for action in order to prevent the high mortality.

Comment

Main findings: Individuals suffering from mental illness are at an increased risk of premature mortality, not only by suicide but also by other external causes and natural causes such as illness and disease[1]. Previous research has found that people with mental disorders die an average of 8.2 years earlier than the general population[2]. Nordentoft and collegues followed 270,770 recent onset patients from national psychiatric case registers from Denmark, Finland and Sweden who were admitted at least once during 2000-2006 for treatment of a psychiatric illness. Patients with a primary diagnosis of any schizophrenia spectrum disorder, affective disorder, substance abuse or personality disorder were included in the sample, while those with an intellectual disability or dementia were excluded. Overall, participants with any mental disorder were found to have a decreased life expectancy of at least 10 years, with the shortest overall life expectancy witnessed in those with substance abuse disorders, and the highest life expectancy in those with affective disorders. Different mental illnesses were associated with different causes of death, with substance abuse disorders, schizophrenia and personality disorders more often associated with death by natural causes and affective and personality disorders more often associated with death by suicide. Substance abuse disorders were most often related to other external causes of death, particularly accidents (traffic accidents, accidental overdoses etc.). The first year after discharge was found to present the greatest risk of mortality by either natural or external causes.

Implications: The current study has expanded on previous research by using a large sample obtained through population-based register data. At the time of publication, this was the first paper to provide such an analysis across several different countries. The results emphasise the importance of considering mental illness and post-hospitalisation care when developing and implementing suicide prevention strategies. The fact that the risk of death was highest in the first year after discharge suggests that follow up care for both mental and physical health is imperative during this period.

There is a need for further exploration of why mental disorders appear to substantially increase the risk of death by natural causes, including studies that control for the influence of socioeconomic factors on both mental and physical health outcomes[3] Some research has suggested that inequalities in healthcare systems — such as the separation of mental health services from other health services and stigma associated with mental illness — have led to individuals with mental illness not being properly diagnosed with, or receiving substandard treatment for, physical illnesses[4]. Measures should be developed to improve diagnosis, monitoring and treatment of physical medical conditions within the context of psychiatric illness, and to aid in overall positive lifestyle changes after individuals have been released from psychiatric care.

Endnotes

1. Laursen TM, Munk-Olsen T, Nordentoft M, Mortensen PB (2007). Increased mortality among patients admitted with major psychiatric disorders: A register-based study comparing mortality in unipolar depressive disorder, bipolar affective disorder, schizoaffective disorder and schizophrenia. *Journal of Clinical Psychiatry* 68, 899-907.

2. Druss BG, Zhao L, Von Esenwein S, Morrato EH, Marcus SC (2011). Understanding excess mortality in persons with mental illness: 17-year follow up of a nationally representative U.S. survey. *Medical Care* 49, 599-604.

3. Australian Inssitute of Health and Welfare (2010). *Australia's health, 2010.* Cat. no. AUS 122. Canberra: AIHW.

4. Lawrence D, Kisely S (2010). Inequalities in healthcare provision for people with severe mental illness. *Journal of Psychopharmacology* 24, 61-68.

Suicidal ideation in family carers of people with dementia: A pilot study

O'Dwyer ST, Moyle W, Zimmer-Gembeck M, De Leo D (Australia)
International Journal of Geriatric Psychiatry. Published online: 4 March 2013. doi: 10.1002/gps.3941, 2013

Objective: The objective of this pilot study was to gather preliminary evidence on suicidal ideation in family carers of people with dementia.

Methods: An online, cross-sectional survey was conducted with 120 family carers, the majority of whom were located in Australia and USA. The survey included measures of suicidality, self-efficacy, physical health, depression, hopelessness, anxiety, optimism, caregiver burden, coping strategies and social support.

Results: Twenty-six percent of carers had contemplated suicide more than once in the previous year. Only half of these had ever told someone they might commit suicide and almost 30% said they were likely to attempt suicide in the future. Carers who had contemplated suicide had poorer mental health, lower self-efficacy for community support service use and greater use of dysfunctional coping strategies than those who had not. In a logistic regression, only depression predicted the presence of suicidal thoughts.

Conclusions: A significant number of people might contemplate suicide while caring for a family member with dementia. Although more research is required to confirm this finding, there are clear implications for policy and clinical practice in terms of identifying and supporting carers who are already contemplating suicide.

Comment

Main findings: Caring for people with dementia can have negative impacts on the mental health and overall wellbeing of carers[1]. A number of factors may influence the level of stress felt by carers including the severity of impairment of the person they are caring for, the number of tasks performed, the number of hours spent in the role each week and the relationship to the person they are caring for[1]. The current paper had three main aims; to gather evidence of the occurrence of suicidal ideation in family dementia carers, to analyse the differences between the health and wellbeing of suicidal and non-suicidal family carers, and to identify risk factors which may precede suicidality in this group. The study included 120 participants recruited from online carer discussion boards of Australian, US and UK organisations, who each completed an online survey. Around one quarter (26%) of participants had experienced thoughts of suicide more than once in the 12 months before completing the survey. Only 16 of these participants (50%) had ever told someone that they had contemplated suicide, despite one third (n=9) considering themselves likely to attempt suicide in the future. A number of differences were present between suicidal and non-suicidal carers, with the suicidal group being more likely to report more behavioural and psychological problems in the person they were caring for, more severe reactions to these problems, and lower levels of optimism. Furthermore, the suicidal carers had less self-efficacy with regards to access of community support services, were less satisfied with the level of social support which they did receive and were more likely to experience feelings of hopelessness, depression, anxiety and high levels of burden. When a logistic regression was performed, depression was the only variable which significantly increased the risk of suicidal ideation.

Implications: Research has previously indicated that carers who spend the highest number of hours in the role each week[1] and care for a family member, particularly a spouse[2] are most likely to experience severe negative effects. In Australia, most dementia sufferers in the community are cared for by a member of their family, with a quarter of these carers providing at least 40 hours of care per week[3].

While past research has previously looked at the effects on the mental health and general wellbeing of carers, the current paper was the first to specifically focus on suicidal ideation in family carers. Considering the levels of suicidal ideation observed in this study , it is important that mental health professionals work to develop screening tools and suicide prevention programs to identify and assist family carers who may be at risk of suicide.

Endnotes

1. Sörensen S, Duberstein P, Gill D, Pinquart M (2006). Dementia care: Mental health effects, intervention strategies, and clinical implications. *The Lancet Neurology* 5, 961-973.

2. Pinquart M, Sorensen S (2003). Differences between carers and noncaregivers in psychological health and physical health: A meta-analysis. *Psychology and Aging* 18, 250-267.

3. Access Economics (2009). *Making Choices: Future Dementia Care – Projects, Problems and Preferences.* Canberra: Alzheimer's Australia.

Effectiveness of a nationwide aftercare program for suicide attempters

Pan Y-J, Chang W-H, Lee M-B, Chen C-H, Liao S-C, Caine ED (UK,Taiwan,USA)

Psychological Medicine. Published online: 22 October 2012. doi:10.1017/S0033291712002425, 2012

Background: The effectiveness of large-scale interventions to prevent suicide among persons who previously attempted suicide remains to be determined. The National Suicide Surveillance System (NSSS), launched in Taiwan in 2006, is a structured nationwide intervention program for people who survived their suicide attempts. This naturalistic study examined its effectiveness using data from the first 3 years of its operation.

Methods: Effectiveness of the NSSS aftercare services was examined using a logistic/proportional odds mixture model, with eventual suicide as the outcome of interest. As well, we examined time until death for those who died and factors associated with eventual suicide.

Results: Receipt of aftercare services was associated with reduced risk for subsequent suicide; for service recipients who eventually killed themselves, there was a prolonged duration between the index and fatal attempts. Elderly attempters were particularly prone to a shorter duration between the index and fatal attempts. Male gender, the lethality potential of the index attempt, and a history of having had a mental disorder also were associated with higher risk.

Conclusions: The structured aftercare program of the NSSS appears to decrease suicides and to delay time to death for those who remained susceptible to suicide.

Comment

Main findings: Taiwan has linked a national-level registry with a national aftercare program that includes counselling, psycho-education and follow-up contacts for individuals who have survived a suicide attempt. From 2006-2008 Taiwan registered 50805 survivors of suicide attempts, aged 15 years and older. Each survivor was initially contacted either through phone or in person within three days of the suicide attempt, with a subsequent minimum of two contacts per month for at least three months. The frequency of contact varied over time, depending on an individual's level of risk detected at the most recent contact. An individual at high risk would be referred to intensive psychiatric treatment. For moderate risk, contact was once or twice per week, with psychotherapy or counselling offered if needed. For low risk, contact would occur twice per month. Results indicated that aftercare decreased subsequent deaths by suicide in individuals who had made a suicide attempt. There was a 63.5% decreased risk of death by suicide for those who were willing to participate in the aftercare program. Those who did not initially want to participate in the program showed a smaller decrease in subsequent risk of death by suicide (22.5%), however this may be related to the patients' pessimism towards the aftercare program or determination to end their own life. In cases where death by suicide occurred, aftercare was associated with a longer time period between a suicide attempt and death.

Implications: A past suicide attempt is one of the strongest predictors of subsequent death by suicide. This study shows that an aftercare program can help those individuals who are considered at risk of taking their own lives. Other studies have been limited in their ability to draw conclusions about the role of aftercare in terms of saving lives, partly because of a lack of linkages between data on suicide attempts, participation in aftercare, and suicide completions. Although registries for suicide attempts — whether national or state-based — are difficult to implement, a suicide attempt registry system in Australia may assist to efficiently connect individuals who are at high risk of suicide with appropriate aftercare programs, and potentially reduce the occurrence of individuals being lost to follow-up. Also, a registry program could provide a clearer picture of at risk populations in various parts of Australia.

There have been relatively few Australian studies of what types of aftercare are likely to be most effective in reducing deaths by suicide among people who have previously made a suicide attempt. However, based on the current study's findings, a regimen of ongoing personal contact between healthcare professionals and individuals who have attempted suicide, with contact frequency based on level of risk, could reasonably be expected to help reduce the number of subsequent deaths by suicide[1,2].

Endnotes

1. Carter GL, Clover K, Whyte IM, Dawson AH, D'Este C (2005). Postcards from the EDge project: Randomised controlled trial of an intervention using postcards to reduce repetition of hospital treated deliberate self poisoning. *British Medical Journal* 331, 805.
2. Aoun S (1999). Deliberate self-harm in rural Western Australia: Results of an intervention study. *Australian and New Zealand Journal of Mental Health Nursing* 8, 65-73.

Emotion regulation difficulties, youth-adult relationships, and suicide attempts among high school students in underserved communities

Pisani AR, Wyman PA, Petrova M, Schmeelk-Cone K, Goldston DB, Xia Y, Gould MS (USA)
Journal of Youth and Adolescence. Published online: 18 December 2012. doi: 10.1007/s10964-012-9884-2, 2012

To develop and refine interventions to prevent youth suicide, knowledge is needed about specific processes that reduce risk at a population level. Using a cross-sectional design, the present study tested hypotheses regarding associations between self-reported suicide attempts, emotion regulation difficulties, and positive youth-adult relationships among 7,978 high-school students (48.6% male, 49.9% female) in 30 high schools from predominantly rural, low-income communities. 683 students (8.6%) reported a past-year suicide attempt. Emotion regulation difficulties and a lack of trusted adults at home and school were associated with increased risk for making a past-year suicide attempt, above and beyond the effects of depressive symptoms and demographic factors. The association between emotion regulation difficulties and suicide attempts was modestly lower among students who perceived themselves as having higher levels of trusted adults in the family, consistent with a protective effect. Having a trusted adult in the community (outside of school and family) was associated with fewer suicide attempts in models that controlled only for demographic covariates, but not when taking symptoms of depression into account. These findings point to adolescent emotion regulation and relationships with trusted adults as complementary targets for suicide prevention that merit further intervention studies. Reaching these targets in a broad population of adolescents will require new delivery systems and "option rich" (OR) intervention designs.

Comment

Main findings: Although reducing youth suicidal behaviour has been a national priority in the US for over a decade, US youth suicide rates have remained high. In an effort to target more vulnerable areas, such as rural communities, thirty high schools were selected based on being underserved (based on country mental health departments or school administrators describing barriers to mental health services among a high proportion of students), or self identified need for suicide prevention intervention. Adolescent perceptions of open, honest safe communication with adults were measured in three domains of life: parents and family, school and community.

Among young people, lack of emotional clarity and limited emotion regulation strategies were both associated with depressive symptoms and suicide attempts. However, when controlling for differences in emotion regulation and depressive symptoms, this study showed that a positive relationship with one or more family adults moderated the relationship between emotion regulation problems and suicide attempts. That is, students who reported having a trusting and safe connection to parent's or other adults in the family were less likely to have attempted suicide in the past year, even when depressive symptoms, demographic factors, and emotion regulation were taken into account. Caring and trustworthy adults at school was also associated with reduced likelihood of a suicide attempt, when other factors were controlled for. However, having trusted adults in the community more generally was not associated with lower suicide attempts once depressive symptoms were considered.

Implications: In the past, Australia has implemented several national efforts to address barriers that may prevent young people from obtaining help when they feel suicidal; however, it is unclear as to whether these programs specifically had a significant effect on the reduction of youth suicide rates observed in the early 2000s[1]. While emotion regulation may contribute to the development of other risk factors for suicide, such as depression[2], this study emphasises that young people's perception of trustworthy and safe adults in both their family and school environments may moderate their suicidal behaviour, once emotion regulation and depressive symptoms are taken into account. In the future, it may be helpful to focus on ways to strengthen child-parent relationships and encourage communities to facilitate trusting and safe relationships between young people and adults within school settings. Programs that aim to educate young people about emotion regulation skills may also be beneficial.

Endnotes

1. Page A, Taylor R, Gunnell D, Carter G, Morrell S, Martian G (2011). Effectiveness of Australian youth suicide prevention initiatives. *The British Journal of Psychiatry* 199, 423-429.
2. Joormann J, Gotlib J (2010). Emotion regulation in depression: Relation to cognitive inhibition. *Cognition & Emotion* 24, 281-298.

Altered explicit recognition of facial disgust associated with predisposition to suicidal behavior but not depression

Richard-Devantoy S, Guillaume S, Olié E, Courtet P, Jollant F (Canada, France)
Journal of Affective Disorders. Published online: 13 March 2013. doi: 10.1016/j.jad.2013.01.049, 2013

Background: Suicidal acts result from a complex interplay between vulnerability factors, such as reduced social and cognitive abilities, social stressors. To our knowledge nothing is known about the explicit recognition of others' facial emotions, a major component of social interactions, in patients at long-term risk for suicide.

Methods: Thirty-five non-depressed patients with a history of a serious suicide attempt and mood disorders were compared with 31 patients with a history of mood disorders but no personal history of suicidal acts, and with 37 healthy controls with no personal history of mood disorders or suicide attempts. The explicit recognition of six facial emotions (anger, disgust, fear, sadness, happiness, and neutral) was assessed.

Results: Suicide attempters made significantly more errors in the explicit recognition of disgust, relative to the other groups, with no differences between the control groups or for the other emotions examined. Semantic verbal fluency and verbal working memory performances were also reduced in suicide attempters relative to the other two groups but could not explain the facial recognition deficits.

Limitations: Our results need replication with a larger sample size. Most patients were medicated.

Conclusions: Explicit recognition of disgust appears to be specifically altered in relation to vulnerability to suicide but not to depression. Reduced ability to recognize some social emotions may impair the patient's capacity to adequately interact with his own social environment, potentially increasing the risk of interpersonal conflict, negative emotions and suicidal crisis. Improving cognitive and social skills may be a target for future individual suicide prevention.

Comment

Main findings: While people experience a range of negative life events, most will not engage in suicidal behaviour as a result. Research into the neuropsychological risks for suicide has suggested that particular neurocognitive dysfunctions such as higher attention to negative emotional stimuli, impaired decision-making and problem-solving skills and a lack of verbal fluency may make some individuals more vulnerable to experiencing a suicidal crisis when faced with negative circumstances[1]. The current study, conducted at the Montpellier University Hospital in France, hypothesised that patients with a history of a serious suicide attempt and mood disorders would be less able to identify angry facial expressions on a computer screen compared to patients with a history of mood disorders but without a history of a suicidal act and healthy controls who were neither depressed nor suicidal. Furthermore, it was expected that all patients (suicidal and non-suicidal) would have more difficulty than healthy controls in identifying happy or neutral facial expressions. Participants also took part in a number of neuropsychological assessments including tests of verbal IQ, attention, verbal working memory and phonemic and semantic verbal fluency. Compared to the other two groups, suicidal participants scored significantly worse on the tests of working memory and semantic verbal fluency and made significantly more mistakes in recognising the portrayal of disgust in facial expressions. The suicidal group was also less accurate than healthy controls in identifying expressions of fear. No other significant differences were found between groups in identification of the remaining emotions. There were no significant differences in emotion recognition between the healthy control group and the non-suicidal depressed patients, suggesting the differences observed for suicidal patients were associated with suicidal behaviour rather than the presence/absence of depression.

Implications: The ability to recognise different emotions through facial expressions has been used in the past as a measure of social skill competency[2]. The current study built on this previous research, by exploring differences in social skills between suicide attempters and non-suicidal individuals. The finding that suicide attempters were less competent at recognising certain negative facial expressions may be indicative of difficulty responding appropriately in adverse social situations, which may in turn be associated with increased vulnerability to suicidal behaviours.

Findings such as these are important to further increasing the ability to identify individuals who may be more vulnerable to suicidal behaviour when faced with particular negative life experiences.

Endnotes

1. Jollant F, Lawrence NL, Olié E, Guillaume S, Courtet P (2011). The suicidal mind and brain: A review of neuropsychological and neuroimaging studies. *The World Journal of Biological Psychiatry* 12, 319-339.
2. Kennedy DP, Adolphs R (2012). The social brain in psychiatric and neurological disorders. *Trends in Cognitive Sciences* 16, 559-572.

A test of faith in God and treatment: The relationship of belief in God to psychiatric treatment outcomes

Rosmarin DH, Bigda-Peyton JS, Kertz SJ, Smith N, Rauch SL, Björgvinsson T (USA)

Journal of Affective Disorders 146, 441-446.

Background: Belief in God is very common and tied to mental health/illness in the general population, yet its relevance to psychiatric patients has not been adequately studied. We examined relationships between belief in God and treatment outcomes, and identified mediating mechanisms.

Methods: We conducted a prospective study with n = 159 patients in a day-treatment program at an academic psychiatric hospital. Belief in God, treatment credibility/expectancy, emotion regulation and congregational support were assessed prior to treatment. Primary outcomes were treatment response as well as degree of reduction in depression over treatment. Secondary outcomes were improvements in psychological well-being and reduction in self-harm.

Results: Belief in God was significantly higher among treatment responders than non-responders $F(1,114) = 4.81$, $p<.05$. Higher levels of belief were also associated with greater reductions in depression ($r = .21$, $p<.05$) and self-harm ($r = .24$, $p<.01$), and greater improvements in psychological well-being ($r = .19$, $p<.05$) over course of treatment. Belief remained correlated with changes in depression and self-harm after controlling for age and gender. Perceived treatment credibility/expectancy, but not emotional regulation or community support, mediated relationships between belief in God and reductions in depression. No variables mediated relationships to other outcomes. Religious affiliation was also associated with treatment credibility/expectancy but not treatment outcomes.

Conclusions: Belief in God, but not religious affiliation, was associated with better treatment outcomes. With respect to depression, this relationship was mediated by belief in the credibility of treatment and expectations for treatment gains.

Comment

Main findings: Very few studies have examined the relationship between belief in God and the effectiveness of psychiatric treatment with patient samples. This is one of the first studies to do so, using a population sample of 159 patients from an academic psychiatric hospital in Belmont, Massachusetts (USA). Before being treated patients were assessed on their belief in God, congregational support, emotional regulation, perceived treatment credibility and expectations about the outcomes of their treatment. Results showed that belief in God was associated with greater perceived treatment credibility and reduction in depression. Belief is God was also associated with increases in psychological well-being and a reduction in self harm. In terms of identifying with a church, religious affiliation was not associated with greater likelihood of treatment response. Although this study was limited to just one location, it nonetheless suggests a potential interaction between spirituality and psychiatric treatment outcomes.

Implications: In this study, belief in God was highlighted as important positive mediator for the patient's belief in the credibility of their psychiatric treatment and expected treatment outcomes. Although spirituality may not play a central role in modern Australian life (compared to the United States, where 93% of the population have belief in God or a higher power), census findings show that 69% of Australians believe in a higher power (Australian Bureau of Statistics, 2010)[1]. Several Australian studies have explored the relationship between depression and spirituality; however, there is a lack of research on the mediating effects of spirituality, the patient's belief in the credibility of treatment and treatment outcomes[2]. In the future, Australian mental health care programs may benefit from greater understanding of Australian spirituality, as this American study's findings indicate that spirituality can be associated with improved outcomes in psychiatric treatment. Australian psychiatric care may also consider incorporating secular programs that nurture hope and optimism (as these attributes may represent alternative mediators to spirituality). It may be helpful for policy-makers to examine ways of strengthening social and cultural factors that can assist in developing and promoting these attributes.

Endnotes

1. Australian Bureau of Statistics (2010). *Year book Australia, 2009-2010.* Canberra: ABS. Retrieved from http://www.abs.gov.au/ausstats/abs@.nsf/mf/1301.0
2. Bennet K, Shepherd J (2012). Depression in Australian Women: The varied roles of spirituality and social support. *Journal of Health Psychology* 18, 429-438.

Neuroticism and extroversion in suicide attempters aged 75 and above and a general population comparison group

Wiktorsson S, Berg AI, Billstedt E, Duberstein PR, Marlow T, Skoog I, Waern M (Sweden, USA)

Aging and Mental Health 17, 479-488, 2013

Personality traits have been shown to influence suicidal behaviour but the literature on '*older*' elderly is sparse. The aim was to compare neuroticism and extroversion in hospitalized suicide attempters aged 75 and above and a general population comparison group. Seventy-two hospitalized suicide attempters (mean age 81 years) were interviewed. Comparison subjects were drawn from participants in population studies on health and ageing. Participants completed the Eysenck Personality Inventory (EPI) and symptoms of depression were rated with the Montgomery-Asberg Depression Rating Scale (MADRS). Depression diagnoses were made in accordance with Diagnostic and Statistical Manual of Mental Disorders, fourth edition. Attempters scored higher on the neuroticism scale than comparison subjects (mean = 9.9 vs. 7.6, t = 3.74, df = 358, p < 0.001) and lower on the extroversion scale (mean = 10.8 vs. 12.0; t = -2.76, df = 358, p = 0.006). While these differences did not remain after adjustment for major depression, attempters with minor depression were less neurotic than comparison subjects with this diagnosis (mean = 6.6 vs. 11.1, t = -3.35, df = 63, p = 0.001) and a negative association with neuroticism remained in a multivariate model. In conclusion cases scored higher on neuroticism and lower on extroversion compared to comparison subjects. The finding that attempters with minor depression were *less* neurotic than comparison subjects with this diagnosis was unexpected and needs to be examined in larger samples.

Comment

Main findings: Findings of past studies have suggested that high levels of neuroticism may be associated with increased risk of depression and suicidal behaviour[1]. The current paper focused specifically on neuroticism in older suicide attempters aged 75 years and above, predicting that suicidal individuals would show higher levels of neuroticism and lower levels of extroversion than the non-suicidal population comparison group. Seventy-two suicidal participants with a mean age of 81.4 years were recruited from emergency departments of five Swedish hospitals over a three-year recruitment period. The comparison group comprised of 288 non-suicidal individuals who were currently participating in other ongoing studies. As hypothesised, both men and women suicide attempters showed higher levels of neuroticism, with women also showing lower levels of extraversion. When major depression was included in the analysis, neither neuroticism nor extraversion remained associated with suicide attempts, with major depression instead being the main predictor. Surprisingly, suicidal individuals with minor depression had lower levels of neuroticism when compared to non-suicidal participants with minor depression. When looking only at the group with previous suicide attempts, a history of psychiatric treatment was associated with lower levels of extraversion, loneliness was associated with increased neuroticism and lower extraversion, and major depression and feelings of hopelessness were related to higher levels of neuroticism.

Implications: From 2005-2007 in Queensland, males aged 75 years and older died by suicide at a rate of 29.16 deaths per 100,000[2] men. Previous research has evaluated the association between different personality traits and suicidal behaviours; however, few papers have included a specific focus on older individuals. Given many countries, including Australia, have an ageing population, this is a notable limitation in knowledge and impedes the ability to develop effective, evidence-based interventions. This paper filled a gap in the research, being the first to focus on personality traits of suicidal attempters aged 75 years and older. Results indicate that older suicidal individuals appear to have similar personality traits to the younger individuals included in previous studies, suggesting that suicide in elderly populations should not be attributed solely to functional decline or other negative aspects of old age.

The finding that neuroticism was lower in suicidal participants with minor depression than non-suicidal attempters was unforeseen and could not be explained in the current study. Future research with larger sample sizes may be required to explore this further.

Endnotes

1. Chioqueta AP, Stiles TC (2005). Personality traits and the development of depression, hopelessness and suicide ideation. *Personality and Individual Differences* 38, 1283-1291.
2. De Leo D, Sveticic J (2011). *Suicide in Queensland 2005-2007: Mortality rates and related data.* Brisbane: Australian Institute for Suicide Research and Prevention.

Recommended Readings

Correlates of proximal premeditation among recently hospitalized suicide attempters

Bagge CL, Littlefield AK, Lee H-J (USA)
Journal of Affective Disorders. Published online: 16 March 2013. doi: 10.1016/j.jad.2013.02.004, 2013

Background: Different conceptualizations of an impulsive suicide attempt (ISA) have not been studied systematically and there is no standard assessment of an ISA. This lack of clarity hinders the advancement of suicidological research and knowledge. The aim of the current study was to examine clinical correlates of different facets of an ISA (reduced proximal contemplation, planning, and decision to act) across divergent methodologies.

Methods: Participants included 212 recent suicide attempters presenting to a Level 1 trauma hospital. The Suicide Intent Scale and the Timeline Follow-Back Interview for suicide attempts were used to assess different facets of an ISA and their associations with other attempt characteristics, and proximal and distal clinical correlates.

Results: A large percentage of patients had an ISA using facets of varying severity (ranging from 42% [contemplation] to 85% [decision]). Multivariate analyses revealed unique associations between a particular ISA facet and the following: hopelessness and depressive symptoms (contemplation), subjective expectation of fatality (planning), and acute negative life events (decision).

Limitations: Validated self-report screening measures were used to assess current psychopathology and future studies should include structured interviews to assess diagnostic features.

Conclusions: Our results suggest that a fine-grained approach is needed for furthering our understanding of the ISA construct. In light of the current findings, ISA should be seriously considered given clinicians' task of determining whether a particular patient is at imminent risk for suicide.

Peer response to messages of distress: Do sex and content matter?

Barton AL, Hirsch JK, Lovejoy MC (USA)
Crisis. Published online: 28 November 2012. doi: 10.1027/0227-5910/a000169, 2012

Background: Suicidal young adults often confide their distress to peers. It is unclear, however, what types of assistance a friend may offer in response to various symptoms of distress as well as whether the sex of either individual affects responses.

Aims: We examined open-ended responses to e-mail vignettes from a fictitious friend exhibiting depressed, irritable, or overtly suicidal communications.

Method: College student participants (n = 106) read e-mail messages from a fictitious friend, to which they composed a reply. Replies were coded to reflect the presence/absence of mention of professional help, problem-oriented (personal) help, and social support.

Results: Problem-oriented help was offered the most across conditions; professional help was offered least in response to depressed or irritable vignettes. Women were more likely to offer any type of help than men. Patterns of help-giving and sex differences in help-giving varied by condition.

Conclusions: Results indicate students' preferences for solving peer problems personally rather than professionally. Campus prevention and intervention efforts should focus on enhancing students' peer support and referral skills.

Suicidal behavior among delinquent former child welfare clients

Björkenstam C, Björkenstam E, Ljung R, Vinnerljung B, Tuvblad C (Sweden, USA)

European Child and Adolescent Psychiatry. Published online: 8 January 2013.doi: 10.1007/s00787-012-0372-8, 2013

Child welfare clients represent a high-risk group for delinquency and adult criminality, but also for future suicidal behavior. We examine associations between delinquency and suicidal behavior in a national child welfare population. This register-based cohort study is based on data for all Swedish former child welfare clients born between 1972 and 1981 that experienced interventions before their adolescent years. We followed 27,228 individuals from age 20 years until 31 December 2006. Juvenile delinquency was defined as being convicted of at least one crime between age 15 and 19. The risk of suicidal behavior was calculated as incidence rate ratios (IRRs). Fifteen percent of the women and 40 % of the men had at least one conviction between the age 15 and 19. The adjusted risk of suicidal behavior among women with five or more convictions was 3.5 (95 % CI 2.0-6.2); corresponding IRR for men was 3.9 (95 % CI 3.1-4.9). Child welfare experience-specifically of out-of-home care-in combination with delinquency is a potent risk factor for suicidal behavior among young adults. However, we cannot exclude that some of this association is an epiphenomenon of uncontrolled confounders, such as impulsivity or severity of psychiatric disease. Despite this caveat, results should be disseminated to practitioners in the health and correction services.

Predicting impulsive self-injurious behavior in a sample of adult women

Black EB, Mildred H (Australia)

Journal of Nervous and Mental Disease 201, 72-75, 2013

The current research used a prospective design to evaluate whether there is a progression between these different types of self-injurious behaviors (SIB) over time. Support was found for a progression from compulsive SIB (including hair pulling, nail-biting, skin picking, scratching, and preventing wounds from healing) to impulsive SIB (including cutting, burning, carving, pin sticking, and punching) in a group of adult women (N = 106). Other factors hypothesized to be linked to this outcome were disordered eating, age, and personality facets of impulsivity (specifically, urgency and lack of perseverance). Of these variables, only urgency positively predicted impulsive SIB at the study's conclusion. These findings are discussed, limitations of the study are noted, and directions for future research are outlined.

Lithium in the public water supply and suicide mortality in Texas

Blüml V, Regier MD, Hlavin G, Rockett IRH, König F, Vyssoki B, Bschor T, Kapusta ND (Austria, USA, Germany)

Journal of Psychiatric Research. Published online: 9 January 2013. doi: 10.1016/j.jpsychires.2012.12.002, 2013

There is increasing evidence from ecological studies that lithium levels in drinking water are inversely associated with suicide mortality. Previous studies of this association were criticized for using inadequate statistical methods and neglecting socioeconomic confounders. This study evaluated the association between lithium levels in the public water supply and county-based suicide rates in Texas. A state-wide sample of 3123 lithium measurements in the public water supply was examined relative to suicide rates in 226 Texas counties. Linear and Poisson regression models were adjusted for socioeconomic factors in estimating the association. Lithium levels in the public water supply were negatively associated with suicide rates in most statistical analyses. The findings provide confirmatory evidence that higher lithium levels in the public drinking water are associated with lower suicide rates. This association needs clarification through examination of possible neurobiological effects of low natural lithium doses.

Misclassification of suicide deaths: Examining the psychiatric history of overdose decedents

Bohnert ASB, McCarthy JF, Ignacio RV, Ilgen MA, Eisenberg A, Blow FC (USA)

Injury Prevention. Published online: 15 January 2013. doi: 10.1136/injuryprev-2012-040631, 2013

Objectives: The intent of a death from overdose can be difficult to determine. The goal of this study was to examine the association of psychiatric diagnoses among overdose deaths ruled by a medical examiner as intentional, unintentional and indeterminate intent.

Methods: All Veterans Health Administration patients in Fiscal Year 1999 (n=3 291 891) were followed through Fiscal Year 2006. We tested the relative strength of association between psychiatric disorders among types of overdoses (categorised by intent) using multinomial models, adjusted for age, sex, Veterans Affairs priority status and Charlson comorbidity scores. Data were from National Death Index records and patient medical records.

Results: Substance use disorders (SUD) had a stronger association with indeterminate intent overdoses than intentional overdoses (adjusted OR (AOR)=1.80, 95% CI 1.47 to 2.22). SUDs also had a stronger association with unintentional overdoses than intentional (AOR=1.48, 95% CI 1.27 to 1.72), but the reverse was true for all other psychiatric disorders (except post-traumatic stress disorder).

Conclusions: Overdoses ruled indeterminate may be misclassified suicide deaths and are important to suicide surveillance and prevention efforts. Additionally, overdose deaths not classified as suicides may include some cases due to suicidal-like thinking without overt suicidal intent.

An organisational response to an increase in suicides: A case study

Burke W, Colmer D, Johnson N, Leigh J, Key B, Parker C (UK)

Journal of Public Mental Health 11, 98-105, 2012

Purpose: This paper seeks to describe the development of a real time suicide alert system and to identify how, as a result, organisations were able to respond in a timely way to an increasing trend in suicides within the County Durham and Darlington area.

Design/Methodology/Approach: Between October 2008 and August 2009 an unprecedented concentration of
suicides occurred in County Durham, North East England. As a result, an independent review of these deaths was conducted in 2009/2010. Recommendations from the review were implemented and included the development of a real time suicide alert system.

Findings: Following implementation of the real time suicide alert system in autumn 2010 a further significant concentration of cases was immediately identified. A total of 24 deaths were identified between September and December 2010. There was a wide geographical spread across County Durham and Darlington.

The case profiles revealed a number of risk factors including recent bereavement, relationship difficulties and financial problems. In addition sleeplessness, low mood and problems associated with housing were also identified. Men under the age of 50 years accounted for over 63 per cent of the cases. An organisational response in County Durham and Darlington was triggered by the information provided via the real time alert. The response was framed by the case profiles, evidence from the literature and lessons learned from other areas in the UK that had also experienced an escalation of suicide cases. In January 2011 there were no further potential suicides in County Durham and Darlington and the three-month rolling average number of suicides returned to below expected limits, and this remains the case as of December 2011. No direct correlation between the work of the response team across County Durham and Darlington and rate of suicides resuming within normal limits can be claimed, indeed many of the initiatives are still being evaluated but the organisation now has much better control over the ability to respond, characterised by timely evidence based interventions and improved partnership working.

Practical Implications: The development of a local real time suicide alert system can reduce the delay in the reporting of potential suicides and can identify trends; it can also provide the basis for a timely organisational response.

Originality/Value: This paper describes an innovative multiagency approach to the problem of delay in the notification of suicides. This will be of interest to commissioners and providers who may want to develop similar systems so that they can immediately identify an escalation of deaths due to suicide and respond in timely manner.

Sexual minority-related victimization as a mediator of mental health disparities in sexual minority youth: A longitudinal analysis

Burton CM, Marshal MP, Chisolm DJ, Sucato GS, Friedman MS (USA)
Journal of Youth and Adolescence 42, 394-402, 2013

Sexual minority youth (youth who are attracted to the same sex or endorse a gay/lesbian/bisexual identity) report significantly higher rates of depression and suicidality than heterosexual youth. The minority stress hypothesis contends that the stigma and discrimination experienced by sexual minority youth create a hostile social environment that can lead to chronic stress and mental health problems. The present study used longitudinal mediation models to directly test sexual minority-specific victimization as a potential explanatory mechanism of the mental health disparities of sexual minority youth. One hundred ninety-seven adolescents (14-19 years old; 70 % female; 29 % sexual minority) completed measures of sexual minority-specific victimization, depressive symptoms, and suicidality at two time points 6 months apart. Compared to heterosexual youth, sexual minority youth reported higher levels of sexual minority-specific victimization, depressive symptoms, and suicidality. Sexual minority-specific victimization significantly mediated the effect of sexual minority status on depressive symptoms and suicidality. The results support the minority stress hypothesis that targeted harassment and victimization are partly responsible for the higher levels of depressive symptoms and suicidality found in sexual minority youth. This research lends support to public policy initiatives that reduce bullying and hate crimes because reducing victimization can have a significant impact on the health and well-being of sexual minority youth.

Police suicide: Prevalence, risk, and protective factors

Chae MH, Boyle DJ (USA)
Policing 36, 91-118, 2013

Purpose: The purpose of this paper is to explore risk and protective factors associated with suicidal ideation among law enforcement personnel.

Design/Methodology/Approach: The methodology employed is based on the "Best Evidence Synthesis" approach, whereby researchers systematically examine and integrate the most empirically sound available research on the topic under investigation.

Findings: Results of studies showed that the interaction of multiple risk factors had a cumulative effect in increasing the risk for suicidal ideation. In total, five prominent aspects of policing were associated with risk for suicidal ideation: organizational stress; critical incident trauma; shift work; relationship problems; and alcohol use and abuse. Studies also indicated that protective factors and preventative measures had stress-buffering effects which decreased the impact of police stressors.

Research limitations/Implications: The model is limited because few studies have employed methodologically-sound research designs to test risk and protective factors related to police suicide. This conceptual overview may facilitate theory development and provide directions for future research.

Practical implications: Law enforcement agencies which implement programs that assist police personnel in developing active coping styles, identify and access available social support systems, as well as utilize community-based services may decrease risk for suicidal ideation. This review provides practical applications for law enforcement training, education, and program development.

Originality/Value: The paper represents the most recent review of risk and protective factors related to suicidal ideation among police personnel. This integration of research provides police practitioners with an evidence-based ecological framework that can be applied universally in police management settings.

Systematic meta-analysis of the risk factors for deliberate self-harm before and after treatment for first-episode psychosis

Challis S, Nielssen O, Harris A, Large M (Australia)

Acta Psychiatria Scandinavia. Published online: 9 January 2013. doi: 10.1111/acps.12074, 2013

Objective: Attempted suicide and deliberate self-injury can occur before or after presentation with a first-episode of psychosis. The aim of the study is to identify the factors associated with suicide attempts or deliberate self-injury before and after treatment for first-episode psychosis.

Method: A systematic review and meta-analysis of controlled studies of factors associated with either suicide attempts or deliberate self-injury, referred to here as deliberate self-harm (DSH).

Results: The pooled proportion of patients who reported DSH prior to treatment for first-episode psychosis was 18.4% (95% Confidence Interval (CI) 14.4-23.3, N = 18 studies, I(2) = 93.8). The pooled proportion of patients with DSH during the period of untreated psychosis was 9.8%, (95% CI 6.7-14.2, N = 5 studies, I(2) = 58.9). The pooled proportion of patients committing DSH during periods of follow up of between 1 and 7 years was 11.4%, (95% CI, 8.3-15.5, N = 13 studies, I(2) = 89.2). Categorical factors associated with an increased risk of DSH were a prior history of DSH (OR = 3.94), expressed suicide ideation (OR = 2.34), greater insight (OR = 1.64), alcohol abuse (OR = 1.68) and substance use (OR = 1.46). Continuous variables associated with an increased risk of DSH were younger age of onset (Standardized Mean Difference (SMD) = -0.28), younger age at first treatment (SMD = -0.18), depressed mood (SMD = 0.49) and the duration of untreated psychosis (SMD = 0.20). Depressed mood and substance use were associated with DSH both before and after treatment, negative symptoms were associated with DSH after treatment but not before treatment. Positive symptoms and social and global functioning were not associated with DSH. Younger age and the duration of untreated psychosis were associated with DSH before treatment but not after treatment.

Conclusion: Earlier treatment of first-episode psychosis and successful treatment of depression and substance use could prevent some episodes of DSH and might reduce suicide mortality in early psychosis.

Suicide by burning barbecue charcoal in England

Chen Y-Y, Bennewith O, Hawton K, Simkin S, Cooper J, Kapur N, Gunnell D (Taiwan, UK)

Journal of Public Health. Published online: 23 November 2012. doi: 10.1093/pubmed/fds095, 2012

Background: Suicide by carbon monoxide poisoning from burning barbecue charcoal has become a common method of suicide in several Asian countries over the last 15 years. The characteristics of people using this method in Western countries have received little attention.

Method: We reviewed the inquest reports of 12 English Coroners (11% of all Coroners) to identify charcoal-burning suicides. We compared socio-demographic and clinical characteristics of suicide by charcoal burning occurring between 2005 and 2007 with suicides using other methods in 2005.

Results: Eleven charcoal-burning suicides were identified; people using this method were younger (mean age 33.4 versus 44.8 years, P = 0.02), and more likely to be unemployed (70.0 versus 30.1%, P = 0.01) and unmarried (100 versus 70%, P = 0.04) than those using other methods. Charcoal-burning suicides had higher levels of contact with psychiatric services (80.0 versus 59.1%) and previous self-harm (63.6 versus 53.0%) compared with suicides using other methods, but these differences did not reach conventional levels of statistical significance. Over one-third of people dying by charcoal burning obtained information on this method from the Internet.

Conclusions: Working with media, including Internet Service Providers, and close monitoring of changes in the incidence of suicide using this method might help prevent an epidemic of charcoal-burning suicides such as that seen in some Asian countries.

The impact of media reporting on the emergence of charcoal burning suicide in Taiwan

Chen Y-Y, Chen F, Gunnell D, Yip PSF (Taiwan, Australia, UK, Hong Kong)

PLoS ONE. Published online: 30 January 2013. doi: 10.1371/journal.pone.0055000, 2013

We investigated the association of the intensity of newspaper reporting of charcoal burning suicide with the incidence of such deaths in Taiwan during 1998-2002. A counting process approach was used to estimate the incidence of suicides and intensity of news reporting. Conditional Poisson generalized linear autoregressive models were performed to assess the association of the intensity of newspaper reporting of charcoal burning and non-charcoal burning suicides with the actual number of charcoal burning and non-charcoal burning suicides the following day. We found that increases in the reporting of charcoal burning suicide were associated with increases in the incidence of charcoal burning suicide on the following day, with each reported charcoal burning news item being associated with a 16% increase in next day charcoal burning suicide (p<.0001). However, the reporting of other methods of suicide was not related to their incidence. We conclude that extensive media reporting of charcoal burning suicides appears to have contributed to the rapid rise in the incidence of the novel method in Taiwan during the initial stage of the suicide epidemic. Regulating media reporting of novel suicide methods may prevent an epidemic spread of such new methods.

Application of scan statistics to detect suicide clusters in Australia

Cheung YTD, Spittal MJ, Williamson MK, Tung SJ, Pirkis J (Australia, China)
PLoS ONE 8, e54168, 2013

Background: Suicide clustering occurs when multiple suicide incidents take place in a small area or/and within a short period of time. In spite of the multi-national research attention and particular efforts in preparing guidelines for tackling suicide clusters, the broader picture of epidemiology of suicide clustering remains unclear. This study aimed to develop techniques in using scan statistics to detect clusters, with the detection of suicide clusters in Australia as example.

Methods and Findings: Scan statistics was applied to detect clusters among suicides occurring between 2004 and 2008. Manipulation of parameter settings and change of area for scan statistics were performed to remedy shortcomings in existing methods. In total, 243 suicides out of 10,176 (2.4%) were identified as belonging to 15 suicide clusters. These clusters were mainly located in the Northern Territory, the northern part of Western Australia, and the northern part of Queensland. Among the 15 clusters, 4 (26.7%) were detected by both national and state cluster detections, 8 (53.3%) were only detected by the state cluster detection, and 3 (20%) were only detected by the national cluster detection.

Conclusions: These findings illustrate that the majority of spatial-temporal clusters of suicide were located in the inland northern areas, with socio-economic deprivation and higher proportions of indigenous people. Discrepancies between national and state/territory cluster detection by scan statistics were due to the contrast of the underlying suicide rates across states/territories. Performing both small-area and large-area analyses, and applying multiple parameter settings may yield the maximum benefits for exploring clusters.

Non-suicidal self-injury and suicidal behavior: Prevalence, co-occurrence, and correlates of suicide among adolescents in Hong Kong

Cheung YTD, Wong PWC, Lee AM, Lam TH, Fan YSS, Yip PSF (Hong Kong)
Social Psychiatry and Psychiatric Epidemiology. Published online: 22 December 2012. doi: 10.1007/s00127-012-0640-4, 2012

Background: Despite increasing concern over the prevalence of non-suicidal self-injury (NSSI) among adolescents, there is debate about its classification as a stand-alone psychiatric diagnosis. This study investigated the patterns, co-occurrence, and correlates of NSSI and other suicidal behaviors among a representative community sample of in-school adolescents.

Methods: A cross-sectional survey of 2,317 adolescents was conducted. Participants were asked to self-report NSSI, suicidal ideation, suicide attempt, and psychosocial conditions over the past 12 months. Logistic regression and cumulative logit modeling analyses were conducted to investigate the different and similar correlates among these self-harm behaviors.

Results: The age-standardized prevalence rates of NSSI among male and female adolescents were estimated to be 13.4 and 19.7 %, respectively, compared with 11.1 and 10.1 % for male and female suicide attempt. Only a small proportion engaged in NSSI exclusively in the past year. NSSI by burning or reckless and risky behaviors, frequent drinking, and sexual experience were associated with increasing severity level of suicidal behaviors among individuals with NSSI.

Conclusions: NSSI is prevalent among in-school adolescents in Hong Kong. However, it co-occurs with suicidal ideation and suicide attempt. High lethality of NSSI, frequent drinking habit, and lifetime sexual experience are suggested to be indicators for screening potential suicide attempters among those having NSSI.

The great recession, jobs and social crises: Policies matter

Chowdhury A, Islam I, Lee D (Thailand, Switzerland, USA)
International Journal of Social Economics 40, 220-245, 2013

Purpose: The purpose of the paper is to review the social consequences of the Great Recession of 2008-2009. In particular, it looks at impacts on the world of work - unemployment, informal and vulnerable employment, working poor and youth unemployment, and on public health - hunger and malnutrition, suicides, domestic violence and child abuse. In all fronts, the Great Recession had serious adverse impacts and morphed into a global social crisis. The situation is made worse due to obsessions with fiscal consolidation in the midst of tepid and uncertain recovery. The paper argues that policies matter and advocates for strengthening social protection and continued stimulus in order to ensure robust recovery.

Design/Methodology/Approach: The paper is a general review and it draws on the findings of the United Nations flagship publication, Report of the World Social Situation 2011. It is an analytical narrative of impacts of on-going economic crisis.

Findings: The paper finds a worsening employment situation - rise in unemployment, informal and vulnerable employment, youth unemployment, and working poverty. It also finds adverse public health impacts in terms of rise in malnutrition and hunger, suicide rates, domestic violence and child abuse. Finally the paper finds that policies matters in mitigating worst impacts as well as sustaining recovery.

Research limitations/Implications: The findings are tentative as the social impacts of economic crisis become obvious after a long time lag.

Originality/Value: The paper argues that policies matter and advocates for strengthening social protection and continued stimulus in order to ensure robust recovery.

Neurobiology of suicide: Do biomarkers exist?

Costanza A, D'Orta I, Perroud N, Burkhardt S, Malafosse A, Mangin P, La Harpe R (Switzerland)
International Journal of Legal Medicine. Published online: 22 February 2013. doi: 10.1007/s00414-013-0835-6, 2013

Clinical risk factors have a low predictive value on suicide. This may explain the increasing interest in potential neurobiological correlates and specific heritable markers of suicide vulnerability. This review aims to present the current neurobiological findings that have been shown to be implicated in suicide completers and to discuss how postmortem studies may be useful in characterizing these individuals. Data on the role of the main neurobiological systems in suicidality, such as the neurotransmitter families, hypothalamic-pituitary-adrenal axis, neurotrophic factors, and polyamines, are exposed at the different biochemical, genetic, and epigenetic levels. Some neuroanatomic and neuropathological aspects as well as their in vivo morphological and functional neuroimaging correlates are also described. Except for the serotoninergic system, particularly with respect to the polymorphism of the gene coding for the serotonin transporter (5-HTTLPR) and brain-derived neurotrophic factor, data did not converge to produce a univocal consensus. The possible limitations of currently published studies are discussed, as well as the scope for long-term prospective studies.

Mapping the evidence of prevention and intervention studies for suicidal and self-harming behaviors in young people

De Silva S, Parker A, Purcell R, Callahan P, Liu P, Hetrick S (Australia)
Crisis. Published online: 15 March 2013. doi: 10.1027/0227-5910/a000190, 2013

Background: Suicide and self-harm (SSH) in young people is a major cause of disability-adjusted life years. Effective interventions are of critical importance to reducing the mortality and morbidity associated with SSH.
Aims: To investigate the extent and nature of research on interventions to prevent and treat SSH in young people using evidence mapping.
Method: A systematic search for SSH intervention studies was conducted (participant mean age between 6-25 years). The studies were restricted to high-quality evidence in the form of systematic reviews, meta-analyses, and controlled trials.
Results: Thirty-eight controlled studies and six systematic reviews met the study inclusion criteria. The majority (n = 32) involved psychological interventions. Few studies (n = 9) involved treating young people with recognized mental disorders or substance abuse (n = 1) which also addressed SSH.
Conclusion: The map was restricted to RCTs, CCTs, systematic reviews, and meta-analyses, and thus might have neglected important information from other study designs. The effectiveness of interventions within the trials was not evaluated. The evidence base for SSH interventions in young people is not well established, which hampers best-practice efforts in this area. Promising interventions that need further research include school-based prevention programs with a skills training

component, individual CBT interventions, interpersonal psychotherapy, and attachment-based family therapy. Gaps in the research exist in evaluations of interventions for SSH in young people with identifiable psychopathology, particularly substance use disorder, and research that classifies participants on the basis of their suicidal intent.

Age-related response to redeemed antidepressants measured by completed suicide in older adults: A nationwide cohort study

Erlangsen A, Conwell Y (USA)

American Journal of Geriatric Psychiatry. Published online: 6 February 2013 doi: 10.1016/j.jagp.2012.08.008, 2013

Objective: To examine if the suicide rate of older adults prescribed antidepressants varies with age and to assess the proportion of older adults who died by suicide that had recently been prescribed antidepressants.

Methods: A population-based cohort study using a nationwide linkage of individual-level records was conducted on all persons aged 50+ living in Denmark during 1996-2006 (1,215,524 men and 1,343,568 women). Suicide rates by treatment status were calculated using data on all antidepressant prescriptions redeemed at pharmacies.

Results: Individual-level data covered 9,354,620 and 10,720,639 person-years for men and women, respectively. Men aged 50-59 who received antidepressants had a mean suicide rate of 185 (95% confidence interval [CI]: 160-211) per 100,000, whereas for those aged 80+ the rate was 119 (95% CI: 91-146). For women, the corresponding values were 82 (95% CI: 70-94) and 28 (95% CI: 20-35). Logistic regression showed a 2% and 3% decline in the rate for men and women, respectively, considered in treatment with antidepressants, with each additional year of age. An opposite trend was found for persons not in treatment. Fewer persons aged 80+ dying by suicide had received antidepressant prescriptions during the last months of life than younger persons.

Conclusion: An age-dependent decline in suicide rate for antidepressant recipients was identified. One reason could be that older adults respond better to antidepressants than younger age groups. Still, the increasing gap with age between estimated prevalence of depression and antidepressant prescription rate in persons dying by suicide underscores the need for assessment of depression in the oldest old.

Suicide and unintentional injury mortality among homeless people: A Danish nationwide register-based cohort study

Feodor Nilsson S, Hjorthøj CR, Erlangsen A, Nordentoft M (Denmark)

European Journal of Public Health. Published online: 12 March 2013. doi: 10.1093/eurpub/ckt025, 2013

Background: Homeless people have elevated mortality, especially due to external causes. We aimed to examine suicide and unintentional injury mortality levels and identify predictors in the homeless population.

Methods: A nationwide, register-based cohort study of homeless people aged 16 years and older was carried out using the Danish Homeless Register, 1999-2008.

Results: In all, 32 010 homeless people (70.5% men) were observed. For men, the mortality rate was 174.4 [95% confidence interval (CI) = 150.6-198.1] per 100 000 person-years for suicide and 463.3 (95% CI = 424.6-502.0) for unintentional injury. For women, the corresponding rates were 111.4 (95% CI = 81.7-141.1) for suicide and 241.4 (95% CI = 197.6-285.1) for unintentional injury. Schizophrenia spectrum, affective, personality and substance use disorders were strongly associated with increased risk of suicide; the highest risk estimates were found for schizophrenia spectrum disorders among both men [hazard ratio (HR) = 3.1, 95% CI = 2.0-4.9] and women (HR = 15.5, 95% CI = 4.5-54.0). Alcohol and drug use disorders were predictors of death by unintentional injury for both men and women, whereas schizophrenia spectrum disorders and personality disorders were only significant predictors among men; the highest risk estimates were found for drug use disorders among men (HR = 2.2, 95% CI = 1.8-2.8) and women (HR = 3.1, 95% CI = 1.8-5.4). A history of psychiatric admission and emergency room contact were predictors for dying by suicide and unintentional injury.

Conclusion: People in the homeless shelter population with a history of a psychiatric disorder constitute a high-risk group regarding the elevated suicide and unintentional injury mortality.

Firearm legislation and firearm-related fatalities in the United States

Fleegler EW, Lee LK, Monuteaux MC, Hemenway D, Mannix R (USA)

JAMA International Medicine. Published online: 6 March 2013. doi: doi:10.1001/jamainternmed.2013.1286, 2013

Importance: Over 30,000 people die annually in the United States from injuries caused by firearms. Although most firearm laws are enacted by states, whether the laws are associated with rates of firearm deaths is uncertain.

Objective: To evaluate whether more firearm laws in a state are associated with fewer firearm fatalities.

Design: Using an ecological and cross-sectional method, we retrospectively analyzed all firearm-related deaths reported to the Centers for Disease Control and Prevention Web-based Injury Statistics Query and Reporting System from 2007 through 2010. We used state-level firearm legislation across 5 categories of laws to create a "legislative strength score," and measured the association of the score with state mortality rates using a clustered Poisson regression. States were divided into quartiles based on their score.

Setting: Fifty US states.

Participants: Populations of all US states.

Main Outcome Measures: The outcome measures were state-level firearm-related fatalities per 100 000 individuals per year overall, for suicide, and for homicide. In various models, we controlled for age, sex, race/ethnicity, poverty, unemployment, college education, population density, nonfirearm violence-related deaths, and household firearm ownership.

Results: Over the 4-year study period, there were 121 084 firearm fatalities. The average state-based firearm fatality rates varied from a high of 17.9 (Louisiana) to a low of 2.9 (Hawaii) per 100 000 individuals per year. Annual firearm legislative strength scores ranged from 0 (Utah) to 24 (Massachusetts) of 28 possible points. States in the highest quartile of legislative strength (scores of $>/ = 9$) had a lower overall firearm fatality rate than those in the lowest quartile (scores of $</ = 2$) (absolute rate difference, 6.64 deaths/100 000/y; age-adjusted incident rate ratio [IRR], 0.58; 95% CI, 0.37-0.92). Compared with the quartile of states with the fewest laws, the quartile with the most laws had a lower firearm suicide rate (absolute rate difference, 6.25 deaths/100 000/y; IRR, 0.63; 95% CI, 0.48-0.83) and a lower firearm homicide rate (absolute rate difference, 0.40 deaths/100 000/y; IRR, 0.60; 95% CI, 0.38-0.95).

Conclusions and Relevance: A higher number of firearm laws in a state are associated with a lower rate of firearm fatalities in the state, overall and for suicides and homicides individually. As our study could not determine cause-and-effect relationships, further studies are necessary to define the nature of this association.

Self-mutilation induced by psychotropic substances: A systematic review

Gahr M, Plener PL, Kölle MA, Freudenmann RW, Schönfeldt-Lecuona C (Germany)
Psychiatry Research 200, 977-983, 2012

Self-mutilation (SM) not only occurs among patients with schizophrenia, personality disorders or transsexuality but also as a phenomenon induced by psychotropic substances (PS). We intended to find characteristics of patients at risk to perform SM induced by PS (SMIPS), frequent PS within this phenomenon and typical presentations of SMIPS. A systematic review of the literature (including Medline, the Cochrane Database of Systematic Reviews, the Cochrane Central Register of Controlled Trials and Scopus) was conducted. On October 2011 we identified 26 cases (23 publications) of SM related to PS. Majority of patients (85%) was male, mean age was 30 years (median 41 years). Seventy-three percent of patients developed SM subsequent to the use of one PS, 27% presented SM after the use of more than one PS. Alcohol (25%), hallucinogens (25%) and amphetamines (22%) were found most frequently among the reported substances. Major impairment was present in 80%. Our findings suggest male sex, young age, a previous history of abuse of PS and the current use of alcohol, hallucinogens or amphetamines to favour SMIPS.

Iowa gambling task performance in currently depressed suicide attempters

Gorlyn M, Keilp JG, Oquendo MA, Burke AK, John Mann J (USA)
Psychiatry Research. Published online: 13 March 2013. doi: 10.1016/j.psychres.2013.01.030, 2013

Deficits in decision-making using the Iowa Gambling Task (IGT) have been found in past suicide attempters, but primarily euthymic and/or medicated patients. This study compared IGT performance among medication-free, currently depressed patients (unipolar and bipolar) with (n=26) and without (n=46) a past history of suicide attempt, and healthy volunteers (n=42). Attempter status, in a sample whose attempts were predominantly non-violent, was not associated with impaired IGT performance even when accounting for sex, mood disorder type, and comorbid Borderline Personality Disorder. A non-significant trend towards poorer performance was found in a small subgroup of past attempters who had used a violent method, consistent with prior studies. Suicide intent and ideation were unrelated to IGT scores. There were no consistent associations between IGT performance and ratings of impulsiveness (Barratt Impulsiveness Scale (BIS)), hostility (Buss-Durkee Hostility Inventory (BDHI)) or aggression (Brown-Goodwin Aggression Inventory (BGAI)). Results suggest that decision-making impairment is related to specific subtypes of suicidal behavior, but may not be universally sensitive to suicide risk in all types of attempters, especially those using non-violent means. Psychometric and conceptual issues surrounding the IGT also appear to affect its utility as a general marker of suicidal behavior risk.

Self-injury in teenagers who lost a parent to cancer: A nationwide, population-based, long-term follow-up

Grenklo TB, Kreicbergs U, Hauksdóttir A, Valdimarsdóttir UA, Nyberg T, Steineck G, Fürst CJ (Sweden)

JAMA Pediatrics 167, 133-140, 2013

Objective: To investigate the risk of self-injury in parentally cancer-bereaved youth compared with their nonbereaved peers.

Design: Population-based study of cancer-bereaved youth and a random sample of matched population controls.

Setting: Sweden in 2009 and 2010.

Participants: A total of 952 youth (74.8%) confirmed to be eligible for the study returned the questionnaire: 622 (73.1%) of 851 eligible young adults who lost a parent to cancer between the ages of 13 and 16 years, in 2000 to 2003, and 330 (78.4%) of 451 nonbereaved peers.

Main Exposure: Cancer bereavement or nonbreavement during the teenage years.

Main Outcome Measures: Unadjusted and adjusted odds ratios (ORs) of self-injury after January 1, 2000.

Results: Among cancer-bereaved youth, 120 (19.5%) reported self-injury compared with 35 (10.6%) of their nonbereaved peers, yielding an OR of 2.0 (95% CI, 1.4-3.0). After controlling for potential confounding factors in childhood (eg, having engaged in self-destructive behavior, having been bullied, having been sexually or physically abused, having no one to share joys and sorrows with, and sex), the adjusted OR was 2.3 (95% CI, 1.4-3.7). The OR for suicide attempts was 1.6 (95% CI, 0.8-3.0).

Conclusions: One-fifth of cancer-bereaved youth reported self-injury, representing twice the odds for selfinjury in their nonbereaved peers, regardless of any of the adjustments we made. Raised awareness on a broad basis in health care and allied disciplines would enable identification and support provision to this vulnerable group.

Time trends in coroners' use of different verdicts for possible suicides and their impact on officially reported incidence of suicide in England: 1990-2005

Gunnell D, Bennewith O, Simkin S, Cooper J, Klineberg E, Rodway C, Sutton L, Steeg S, Wells C, Hawton K, Kapur N (UK)

Psychological Medicine. Published online: 1 November 2012. doi: 10.1017/S0033291712002401, 2012

Background: Official suicide statistics for England are based on deaths given suicide verdicts and most cases given an open verdict following a coroner's inquest. Previous research indicates that some deaths given accidental verdicts are considered to be suicides by clinicians. Changes in coroners' use of different verdicts may bias suicide trend estimates. We investigated whether suicide trends may be over- or underestimated when they are based on deaths given suicide and open verdicts.

Method: Possible suicides assessed by 12 English coroners in 1990/91, 1998 and 2005 and assigned open, accident/misadventure or narrative verdicts were rated by three experienced suicide researchers according to the likelihood that they were suicides. Details of all suicide verdicts given by these coroners were also recorded.

Results: In 1990/91, 72.0% of researcher-defined suicides received a suicide verdict from the coroner, this decreased to 65.4% in 2005 (p trend < 0.01); equivalent figures for combined suicide and open verdicts were 95.4% (1990/91) and 86.7% (2005). Researcher-defined suicides with a verdict of accident/misadventure doubled over that period, from 4.6% to 9.1% (p < 0.01). Narrative verdict cases rose from zero in 1990/91 to 25 in 2005 (4.2% of researcher-defined suicides that year). In 1998 and 2005, 50.0% of the medicine poisoning deaths given accidental/misadventure verdicts were rated as suicide by the researchers.

Conclusions: Between 1990/91 and 2005, the proportion of researcher-defined suicides given a suicide verdict by coroners decreased, largely due to an increased use of accident/misadventure verdicts, particularly for deaths involving poisoning. Consideration should be given to the inclusion of 'accidental' deaths by poisoning with medicines in the statistics available for monitoring suicides rates..

Developing social capital in implementing a complex intervention: A process evaluation of the early implementation of a suicide prevention intervention in four European countries

Harris FM, Maxwell M, O Connor RC, Coyne J, Arensman E, Szekely A, Gusmäo R, Coffey C, Costa S, Cserháti Z, Koburger N, Van Audenhove C, McDaid D, Maloney J, Värnik P, Hegerl U
(UK, USA, Germany, Belgium, Estonia, Hungary)

BMC Public Health 13, 158, 2013

Background: Variation in the implementation of complex multilevel interventions can impact on their delivery and outcomes. Few suicide prevention interventions, especially multilevel interventions, have included evaluation of both the process of implementation as well as outcomes. Such evaluation is essential for the replication of interventions, for interpreting and understanding outcomes, and for improving implementation science. This paper reports on a process evaluation of the early implementation stage of an optimised suicide prevention programme (OSPI-Europe) implemented in four European countries.

Methods: The process analysis was conducted within the framework of a realist evaluation methodology, and involved case studies of the process of implementation in four European countries. Datasets include: repeated questionnaires to track progress of implementation including delivery of individual activities and their intensity; serial interviews and focus groups with stakeholder groups; and detailed observations at OSPI implementation team meetings.

Results: Analysis of local contexts in each of the four countries revealed that the advisory group was a key mechanism that had a substantial impact on the ease of implementation of OSPI interventions, particularly on their ability to recruit to training interventions. However, simply recruiting representatives of key organisations into an advisory group is not sufficient to achieve impact on the delivery of interventions. In order to maximise the potential of high level 'gatekeepers', it is necessary to first transform them into OSPI stakeholders. Motivations for OSPI participation as a stakeholder included: personal affinity with the shared goals and target groups within OSPI; the complementary and participatory nature of OSPI that adds value to pre-existing suicide prevention initiatives; and reciprocal reward for participants through access to the extended network capacity that organisations could accrue for themselves and their organisations from participation in OSPI.

Conclusions: Exploring the role of advisory groups and the meaning of participation for these participants revealed some key areas for best practice in implementation: careful planning of the composition of the advisory group to access target groups; the importance of establishing common goals; the importance of acknowledging and complementing existing experience and activity; and facilitating an equivalence of benefit from network participation.

The role of exposure to self-injury among peers in predicting later self-injury

Hasking P, Andrews T, Martin G(Australia)

Journal of Youth and Adolescence. Published online: 24 February 2013. doi: 10.1007/s10964-013-9931-7, 2013

While researchers are beginning to reach consensus around key psychological correlates of non-suicidal self-injury (NSSI), comparatively less work has been done investigating the role and influence of peers. Given evidence that engagement in this behavior may be susceptible to peer influence, especially during the early stages of its course, the current study prospectively explored whether knowing a friend who self-injures is associated with the onset, severity, and subsequent engagement in NSSI. The moderating roles of adverse life events, substance use and previous suicidal behavior in this relationship also were explored. Self-report data were collected from 1,973 school-based adolescents (aged 12-18 years; 72 % female) at two time points, 1 year apart. Knowing a friend who self-injured, negative life events, psychological distress and thoughts of NSSI differentiated those who self-injured from those who did not, and also predicted the onset of NSSI within the study period. Further, adverse life events and previous thoughts of NSSI moderated the relationship between exposure to NSSI in peers and engaging in NSSI at Time 2. However, the effect of having a friend who self-injures was not related to the severity of NSSI. Having a friend who self-injures appears to be a risk factor for self-injury among youth who are experiencing high levels of distress. Implications of these findings are discussed.

Risk factors for suicide in individuals with depression: A systematic review

Hawton K, Casanas ICC, Haw C, Saunders K (UK)

Journal of Affective Disorders 147, 17-28, 2013

Background: Depression is the most common psychiatric disorder in people who die by suicide. Awareness of risk factors for suicide in depression is important for clinicians.

Methods: In a systematic review of the international literature we identified cohort and case-control studies of people with depression in which suicide was an outcome, and conducted meta-analyses of potential risk factors.

Results: Nineteen studies (28 publications) were included. Factors significantly associated with suicide were: male gender (OR=1.76, 95% CI=1.08-2.86), family history of psychiatric disorder (OR=1.41, 95% CI=1.00-1.97), previous attempted suicide (OR=4.84, 95% CI=3.26-7.20), more severe depression (OR=2.20, 95% CI=1.05-4.60), hopelessness (OR=2.20, 95% CI=1.49-3.23) and comorbid disorders, including anxiety (OR=1.59, 95% CI=1.03-2.45) and misuse of alcohol and drugs (OR=2.17, 95% CI=1.77-2.66).

Limitations: There were fewer studies than suspected. Interdependence between risk factors could not be examined.

Conclusions: The factors identified should be included in clinical assessment of risk in depressed patients. Further large-scale studies are required to identify other relevant factors.

Ask suicide-screening questions (ASQ) a brief instrument for the pediatric emergency department

Horowitz LM, Bridge JA, Teach SJ, Ballard E, Klima J, Rosenstein DL, Wharff EA, Ginnis K, Cannon E, Joshi P, Pao M (USA)

Archives of Pediatrics & Adolescent Medicine 166, 1170-1176, 2012

Objective: To develop a brief screening instrument to assess the risk for suicide in pediatric emergency department patients.

Design: A prospective, cross-sectional instrument-development study evaluated 17 candidate screening questions assessing suicide risk in young patients. The Suicidal Ideation Questionnaire served as the criterion standard.

Setting: Three urban, pediatric emergency departments associated with tertiary care teaching hospitals. Participants: A convenience sample of 524 patients aged 10 to 21 years who presented with either medical/surgical or psychiatric chief concerns to the emergency department between September 10, 2008, and January 5, 2011. Main Exposures: Participants answered 17 candidate questions followed by the Suicidal Ideation Questionnaire.

Main Outcome Measures: Sensitivity, specificity, predictive values, likelihood ratios, and area under the receiver operating characteristic curves of the best-fitting combinations of screening questions for detecting elevated risk for suicide.

Results: A total of 524 patients were screened (344 medical/surgical and 180 psychiatric). Fourteen of the medical/surgical patients (4%) and 84 of the psychiatric patients (47%) were at elevated suicide risk on the Suicidal Ideation Questionnaire. Of the 17 candidate questions, the best-fitting model comprised 4 questions assessing current thoughts of being better off dead, current wish to die, current suicidal ideation, and past suicide attempt. This model had a sensitivity of 96.9% (95% CI, 91.3-99.4), specificity of 87.6% (95% CI, 84.0-90.5), and negative predictive values of 99.7% (95% CI, 98.2-99.9) for medical/surgical patients and 96.9% (95% CI, 89.3-99.6) for psychiatric patients.

Conclusions: A 4-question screening instrument, the Ask Suicide-Screening Questions (ASQ), with high sensitivity and negative predictive value, can identify the risk for suicide in patients presenting to pediatric emergency departments.

The impact of social contagion on non-suicidal self-injury: A review of the literature

Jarvi S, Jackson B, Swenson L, Crawford H (USA)

Archives of Suicide Research 17, 1-19, 2013

In this review, we explore social contagion as an understudied risk factor for non-suicidal self-injury (NSSI) among adolescents and young adults, populations with a high prevalence of NSSI. We review empirical studies reporting data on prevalence and risk factors that, through social contagion, may influence the transmission of NSSI. Findings in this literature are consistent with social modeling/learning of NSSI increasing risk of initial engagement in NSSI among individuals with certain individual and/or psychiatric characteristics. Preliminary research suggests iatrogenic effects of social contagion of NSSI through primary prevention are not likely. Thus, social contagion factors may warrant considerable empirical attention. Intervention efforts may be enhanced, and social contagion reduced, by implementation of psychoeducation and awareness about NSSI in schools, colleges, and treatment programs.

Melancholic features and hostility are associated with suicidality risk in Asian patients with major depressive disorder

Jeon HJ, Peng D, Chua HC, Srisurapanont M, Fava M, Bae JN, Man Chang S, Hong JP (South Korea, China, Singapore, Thailand)

Journal of Affective Disorders. Published online: 13 February 2013. doi:.10.1016/j.jad.2013.01.001, 2013

Background: Suicide rates are higher in East-Asians than other populations, and especially high in Koreans. However, little is known about suicidality risk and melancholic features in Asian patients with major depressive disorder (MDD). *Method:* Drug-free MDD outpatients were included from 13 centers across five ethnicities consisting of Chinese (n = 290), Korean (n = 101), Thai (n = 102), Indian (n = 27), and Malay (n = 27). All were interviewed using the Mini-International Neuropsychiatric Interview (M.I.N.I.), the Montgomery-Åsberg Depression Rating Scale (MADRS), and the Symptoms Checklist 90-Revised (SCL-90-R). *Results:* Of 547 subjects, 177 MDD patients showed melancholic features (32.4%). These melancholic MDD patients revealed significantly higher suicidality risk (p<0.0001), hostility (p = 0.037), and severity of depression (p<0.0001) than those MDD patients without melancholic features. Suicidality risk was significantly higher in MDD with melancholic features than those without in subjects with lower hostility, whereas it showed no difference in higher hostility. Adjusted odds ratios of melancholic features and hostility for moderate to high suicidality risk were 1.79 (95% CI = 1.15-2.79) and 2.45 (95% CI = 1.37-4.38), after adjusting for age, sex, education years, and depression severity. Post-hoc analyses showed that suicidality risk was higher in Korean and Chinese than that of Thai, Indian and Malay in MDD subjects with melancholic features, although depression severity showed no significant differences among the ethnicities.

Conclusions: Suicidality risk is associated with both melancholic features and hostility and it shows cross-ethnic differences in Asian MDD patients, independent of depression severity.

The association between anxiety disorders and suicidal behaviors: A systematic review and meta-analysis

Kanwar A, Malik S, Prokop LJ, Sim LA, Feldstein D, Wang Z, Murad MH (USA)
Depression and Anxiety. Published online: 13 February 2013. doi: 10.1002/da.22074, 2013

Background: Although anxiety has been proposed to be a potentially modifiable risk factor for suicide, research examining the relationship between anxiety and suicidal behaviors has demonstrated mixed results. Therefore, we aimed at testing the hypothesis that anxiety disorders are associated with suicidal behaviors and evaluate the magnitude and quality of supporting evidence.

Methods: A systematic literature search of multiple databases was conducted from database inception through August 2011. Two investigators independently reviewed and determined the eligibility and quality of the studies based upon a priori established inclusion criteria. The outcomes of interest were suicidal ideations, suicide attempts, completed suicides, and a composite outcome of any suicidal behaviors. We pooled odds ratios from the included studies using random effects models.

Results: Forty-two observational studies were included. The studies had variable methodological quality due to inconsistent adjustment of confounders. Compared to those without anxiety, patients with anxiety were more likely to have suicidal ideations (OR = 2.89, 95% CI: 2.09, 4.00), attempted suicides (OR = 2.47, 95% CI: 1.96, 3.10), completed suicides (OR = 3.34, 95% CI: 2.13, 5.25), or have any suicidal behaviors (OR = 2.85, 95% CI: 2.35, 3.46). The increase in the risk of suicide was demonstrated for each subtype of anxiety except obsessive-compulsive disorder (OCD). The quality of this evidence is considered low to moderate due to heterogeneity and methodological limitations.

Conclusions: This systematic review and meta-analysis provides evidence that the rates of suicides are higher in patients with any type of anxiety disorders excluding OCD.

Utilized social support and self-esteem mediate the relationship between perceived social support and suicide ideation a test of a multiple mediator model

Kleiman EM, Riskind JH (USA)
Crisis 34, 42-49, 2013

Background: While perceived social support has received considerable research as a protective factor for suicide ideation, little attention has been given to the mechanisms that mediate its effects.

Aims: We integrated two theoretical models, Joiner's (2005) interpersonal theory of suicide and Leary's (Leary, Tambor, Terdal, & Downs, 1995) sociometer theory of self-esteem to investigate two hypothesized mechanisms, utilization of social support and self-esteem. Specifically, we hypothesized that individuals must utilize the social support they perceive that would result in increased self-esteem, which in turn buffers them from suicide ideation.

Method: Participants were 172 college students who completed measures of social support, self-esteem, and suicide ideation.

Results: Tests of simple mediation indicate that utilization of social support and self-esteem may each individually help to mediate the perceived social support/suicide ideation relationship. Additionally, a test of multiple mediators using bootstrapping supported the hypothesized multiple-mediator model.

Limitations: The use of a cross-sectional design limited our ability to find true cause-and-effect relationships.

Conclusion: Results suggested that utilized social support and self-esteem both operate as individual moderators in the social support/self-esteem relationship. Results further suggested, in a comprehensive model, that perceived social support buffers suicide ideation through utilization of social support and increases in self-esteem.

Association of suicide rates, gun ownership, conservatism and individual suicide risk

Kposowa AJ (USA)
Social Psychiatry and Psychiatric Epidemiology. Published online: 28 February 2013. doi: 10.1007/s00127-013-0664-4, 2013

Objectives: The purpose of the study was to examine the association of suicide rates, firearm ownership, political conservatism, religious integration at the state level, and individual suicide risk. Social structural and social learning and social integration theories were theoretical frameworks employed. It was hypothesized that higher suicide rates, higher state firearm availability, and state conservatism elevate individual suicide risk.

Method: Data were pooled from the Multiple Cause of Death Files. Multilevel logistic regression models were fitted to all deaths occurring in 2000 through 2004 by suicide.

Results: The state suicide rate significantly elevated individual suicide risk (AOR = 1.042, CI = 1.037, 1.046). Firearm availability at the state level was associated with significantly higher odds of individual suicide (AOR = 1.004, CI = 1.003, 1.006). State political conservatism elevated the odds of individual suicides (AOR = 1.005, CI = 1.003, 1.007), while church membership at the state level reduced individual odds of suicide (AOR = 0.995, CI = 0.993, 0.996). The results held even after controlling for socioeconomic and demographic variables at the individual level.

Conclusion: It was concluded that the observed association between individual suicide odds and national suicide rates, and firearm ownership cannot be discounted. Future research ought to focus on integrating individual level data and contextual variables when testing for the impact of firearm ownership. Support was found for social learning and social integration theories.

Back so soon: Rapid re-presentations to the emergency department following intentional self-harm

Kuehl S, Nelson K, Collings S (New Zealand)

New Zealand Medical Journal 125, 70-79, 2012

Aim: To describe the number, characteristics and management of patients who presented to an emergency department (ED) with intentional self-harm and then re-presented for any reason within 1 week, over a 1-year period.

Method: A retrospective records review from one New Zealand ED over 12 months.

Results: Of the 120 patients who attended the ED more than once with intentional self-harm, 48 re-presented on 73 occasions within 7 days of the index presentation. Of the re-presentations, 55% occurred within 1 day. Mental health assessments by emergency department staff were minimal; challenging incidents occurred in 40% of presentations; and there was an increase in the inpatient admission rate for second presentations.

Conclusion: We identified a small group of patients who rapidly re-present to the ED following intentional self-harm. The reasons behind those re-presentations could include limited mental health assessments in ED and inadequate follow-up on discharge. System improvements in the ED including better collaboration with mental health services could improve how services address the needs of patients who present with intentional self-harm and reduce costs.

Time to hospitalization for suicide attempt by the timing of parental suicide during offspring early development

Kuramoto SJ, Runeson B, Stuart EA, Lichtenstein P, Wilcox HC (Sweden)

Archives of General Psychiatry 70, 149-157, 2013

Context: Previous studies have suggested that children who experience parental suicide at earlier ages are at higher risk of future hospitalization for suicide attempt. However, how the trajectories of risk differ by offspring age at the time of parental suicide is currently unknown.

Objective: To study time at risk to suicide attempt hospitalization among offspring of suicide decedents as compared with offspring of unintentional injury decedents by their developmental period at the time of parental death.

Design: Population-based retrospective cohort study.

Setting: Sweden.

Participants: Twenty-six thousand ninety-six offspring who experienced parental suicide and 32 395 offspring of unintentional injury decedents prior to age 25 years between the years 1973 and 2003.

Main Outcome Measure: Parametric survival analysis was used to model the time to hospitalization for suicide attempt among offspring who lost a parent during early childhood (0-5 years old), later childhood (6-12 years old), adolescence (13-17 years old), and young adulthood (18-24 years old).

Results: The risk in offspring who lost a parent to suicide or an unintentional injury during childhood surpassed the other age groups' risk approximately 5 years after the origin and, for the youngest group, continued to rise over decades. Offspring who lost a parent during adolescence or young adulthood were at greatest risk within 1 to 2 years after parental death, and risk declined over time. Offspring who lost a parent to suicide in childhood and young adulthood had earlier onset of hospitalization for suicide attempt compared with offspring who lost a parent to an unintentional injury.

Conclusions: The hospitalization risk for suicide attempt in offspring who lost a parent during their childhood is different from those who lost a parent later in development. The results suggest critical windows for careful monitoring and intervention for suicide attempt risk, especially 1 to 2 years after parental death for the older age groups and over decades for childhood survivors of parental death.

Cyber bullying and physical bullying in adolescent suicide: The role of violent behavior and substance use

Litwiller BJ, Brausch AM (USA)

Journal of Youth and Adolescence 42, 675-684, 2013

The impact of bullying in all forms on the mental health and safety of adolescents is of particular interest, especially in the wake of new methods of bullying that victimize youths through technology. The current study examined the relationship between victimization from both physical and cyber bullying and adolescent suicidal behavior. Violent behavior, substance use, and unsafe sexual behavior were tested as mediators between two forms of bullying, cyber and physical, and suicidal behavior. Data were taken from a large risk-behavior screening study with a sample of 4,693 public high school students (mean age = 16.11, 47 % female). The study's findings showed that both physical bullying and cyber bullying associated with substance use, violent behavior, unsafe sexual behavior, and suicidal behavior. Substance use, violent behavior, and unsafe sexual behavior also all associated with suicidal behavior. Substance use and violent behavior partially mediated the relationship between both forms of bullying and suicidal behavior. The comparable amount of variance in suicidal behavior accounted for by both cyber bullying and physical bullying underscores the important of further cyber bullying research. The direct association of each risk behavior with suicidal behavior also underscores the importance of reducing risk behaviors. Moreover, the role of violence and substance use as mediating behaviors offers an explanation of how risk behaviors can increase an adolescent's likelihood of suicidal behavior through habituation to physical pain and psychological anxiety.

A one-year observational study of all hospitalized and fatal acute poisonings in Oslo: Epidemiology, intention and follow-up

Lund C, Teige B, Drottning P, Stiksrud B, Rui TO, Lyngra M, Ekeberg Ø, Jacobsen D, Hovda KE (Norway)

BMC Public Health 20, 49, 2012

Background: Up to date information on poisoning trends is important. This study reports the epidemiology of all hospitalized acute poisonings in Oslo, including mortality, follow-up referrals, and whether the introduction of over-the-counter sales of paracetamol outside pharmacies had an impact on the frequency of poisonings.

Methods: All acute poisonings of adults ($> = 16$ years) treated at the five hospitals in Oslo from April 2008 to April 2009 were included consecutively in an observational cross-sectional multicentre study. A standardized form was completed by the treating physician, which covered the study aims. All deaths by poisoning in and outside hospitals were registered at the Institute of Forensic Medicine.

Results: There were 1065 hospital admissions of 912 individuals; 460 (50 %) were male, and the median age was 36 years. The annual incidence was 2.0 per 1000. The most frequent toxic agents were ethanol (18 %), benzodiazepines (15 %), paracetamol (11 %), and opioids (11 %). Physicians classified 46 % as possible or definite suicide attempts, 37 % as accidental overdoses with substances of abuse (AOSA), and 16 % as other accidents. Twenty-four per cent were discharged without any follow-up and the no follow-up odds were highest for AOSA. There were 117 deaths (eight in hospital), of which 75 % were males, and the median age was 41 years. Thus, the annual mortality rate was 25 per 100 000 and the in-hospital mortality was 0.8 %. Opioids were the most frequent cause of death.

Conclusions: The incidence of hospitalized acute poisonings in Oslo was similar to that in 2003 and there was an equal sex distribution. Compared with a study performed in Oslo in 2003, there has been an increase in poisonings with a suicidal intention. The in-hospital mortality was low and nine out of ten deaths occurred outside hospitals. Opioids were the leading cause of death, so preventive measures should be encouraged among substance abusers. The number of poisonings caused by paracetamol remained unchanged after the introduction of over-the-counter sales outside pharmacies and there were no deaths, so over-the-counter sales may be considered safe.

Applying the Anderson-Darling test to suicide clusters

Mackenzie DW (USA)

Crisis. Published online: 15 March 2013. doi: 10.1027/0227-5910/a000197, 2013

Background: Suicide clusters at Cornell University and the Massachusetts Institute of Technology (MIT) prompted popular and expert speculation of suicide contagion. However, some clustering is to be expected in any random process.

Aim: This work tested whether suicide clusters at these two universities differed significantly from those expected under a homogeneous Poisson process, in which suicides occur randomly and independently of one another.

Method: Suicide dates were collected for MIT and Cornell for 1990-2012. The Anderson-Darling statistic was used to test the goodness-of-fit of the intervals between suicides to distribution expected under the Poisson process.

Results: Suicides at MIT were consistent with the homogeneous Poisson process, while those at Cornell showed clustering inconsistent with such a process (p = .05).

Conclusions: The Anderson-Darling test provides a statistically powerful means to identify suicide clustering in small samples. Practitioners can use this method to test for clustering in relevant communities. The difference in clustering behavior between the two institutions suggests that more institutions should be studied to determine the prevalence of suicide clustering in universities and its causes.

Gender and racial differences for suicide attempters and ideators in a high-risk community corrections population

McCullumsmith CB, Clark CB, Perkins A, Fife J, Cropsey KL (USA)

Crisis 34, 50-62, 2013

Background: Community corrections populations are a high-risk group who carry multiple suicide risk factors.

Aims: To identify factors correlated with historical suicide attempts and ideation among African-American men, African-American women, White men, and White women in a community corrections population.

Method: Self-report data from 18,753 enrollees in community corrections were analyzed. Multinomial logistic regression analyses were conducted to determine associations between historical suicidal ideation and attempts among the four demographic groups.

Results: Participants with historical suicide attempts tended to be younger, White, female, be taking psychotropic medication, have a history of physical or sexual abuse, and meet criteria for dependence on alcohol, amphetamines, cocaine, opioids, or sedatives. Five variables were commonly associated with suicide attempts for all four race/gender groups: younger age, being on disability or retirement, taking psychotropic medication, history of sexual or physical abuse, and cocaine dependence. Other demographic variables had race or gender specificities as risk factors for suicide attempts.

Conclusions: Participants had high rates of historical suicide attempts with unique correlates differentiating attempters from ideators among different racial and gender groups. Cocaine dependence was universal predictor of suicide attempts, while other substance dependencies show specific racial and gender profiles associated with suicide attempts.

Decisions to initiate involuntary commitment: The role of intensive community services and other factors

McGarvey EL, Leon-Verdin M, Wanchek TN, Bonnie RJ (USA)

Psychiatric Services 64, 120-126, 2013

Objective: This study examined the predictors of actions to initiate involuntary commitment of individuals experiencing a mental health crisis.

Methods: Emergency services clinicians throughout Virginia completed a questionnaire following each face-to-face evaluation of individuals experiencing a mental health crisis. Over a one-month period in 2007, a total of 2,624 adults were evaluated. Logistic hierarchical multiple regression was used to analyze the relationship between demographic, clinical, and service-related variables and outcomes of the emergency evaluations.

Results: Several factors predicted 84% of the actions taken to initiate involuntary commitment. These included unavailability of alternatives to hospitalization, such as temporary housing or residential crisis stabilization; evaluation of the client in a hospital emergency room or police station or while in police custody; current enrollment in treatment; and clinical factors related to the commitment criteria, including risk of self-harm or harm to others, acuity and severity of the crisis, and current drug abuse or dependence.

Conclusions: A lack of intensive community-based treatment and support in lieu of hospitalization accounted for a significant portion of variance in actions to initiate involuntary commitment. Comprehensive community services and supports for individuals experiencing mental health crises may reduce the rate of involuntary hospitalization. There is a need to enrich intensive community mental health services and supports and to evaluate the impact of these enhancements on the frequency of involuntary mental health interventions.

Depression and suicide ideation in late adolescence and early adulthood are an outcome of child hunger

McIntyre L, Williams JVA, Lavorato DH, Patten S (Canada)
Journal of Affective Disorders. Published online: 29 December 2012. doi: 10.1016/j.jad.2012.11.029, 2012

Background: Child hunger represents an adverse experience that could contribute to mental health problems in later life. The objectives of this study were to: (1) examine the long-term effects of the reported experience of child hunger on late adolescence and young adult mental health outcomes; and (2) model the independent contribution of the child hunger experience to these long-term mental health outcomes in consideration of other experiences of child disadvantage.

Methods: Using logistic regression, we analyzed data from the Canadian National Longitudinal Survey of Children and Youth covering 1994 through 2008/2009, with data on hunger and other exposures drawn from NLSCY Cycle 1 (1994) through Cycle 7 (2006/2007) and mental health data drawn from Cycle 8 (2008/2009). Our main mental health outcome was a composite measure of depression and suicidal ideation.

Results: The prevalence of child hunger was 5.7% (95% CI 5.0-6.4). Child hunger was a robust predictor of depression and suicidal ideation [crude OR = 2.9 (95% CI 1.4-5.8)] even after adjustment for potential confounding variables, OR = 2.3 (95% CI 1.2-4.3).

Limitations: A single question was used to assess child hunger, which itself is a rare extreme manifestation of food insecurity; thus, the spectrum of child food insecurity was not examined, and the rarity of hunger constrained statistical power.

Conclusions: Child hunger appears to be a modifiable risk factor for depression and related suicide ideation in late adolescence and early adulthood, therefore prevention through the detection of such children and remedy of their circumstances may be an avenue to improve adult mental health.

Intimate partner abuse and suicidality: A systematic review

McLaughlin J, O'Carroll RE, O'Connor RC (UK)

Clinical Psychology Review 32, 677-689, 2012

Research has demonstrated an association between intimate partner abuse and suicidality, presenting a serious mental health issue. However, studies have differed widely in the samples and methods employed, and in the depth of the investigation. Given the level of heterogeneity in the literature, this systematic review examines, for the first time, the nature of the relationship between intimate partner abuse and suicidality. The three main psychological and medical databases (PsychInfo 1887-March 2011; Medline, 1966-March 2011; Web of Knowledge 1981-March 2011) were searched. Thirty-seven papers on the topic of intimate partner abuse and suicidality were found. With only one exception, all of the studies found a strong and consistent association between intimate partner abuse and suicidality. Significantly, this relationship held irrespective of study design, sample and measurement of abuse and suicidality, thus demonstrating a consistently strong relationship between intimate partner abuse and suicidality. This review highlights that intimate partner abuse is a significant risk factor for suicidal thoughts and behaviours, which has important clinical implications.

Positron emission tomography quantification of serotonin transporter in suicide attempters with major depressive disorder

Miller JM, Hesselgrave N, Ogden RT, Sullivan GM, Oquendo MA, Mann JJ, Parsey RV (USA)

Biological Psychiatry. Published online: 1 March 2013. doi: 10.1016/j.biopsych.2013.01.024, 2013

Background: Several lines of evidence implicate abnormal serotonergic function in suicidal behavior and completed suicide, including low serotonin transporter binding in postmortem studies of completed suicide. We have also reported low in vivo serotonin transporter binding in major depressive disorder (MDD) during a major depressive episode using positron emission tomography (PET) with [11C]McN5652. We quantified regional brain serotonin transporter binding in vivo in depressed suicide attempters, depressed nonattempters, and healthy controls using PET and a superior radiotracer, [11C]DASB.

Methods: Fifty-one subjects with DSM-IV current MDD, 15 of whom were past suicide attempters, and 32 healthy control subjects underwent PET scanning with [11C]DASB to quantify in vivo regional brain serotonin transporter binding. Metabolite-corrected arterial input functions and plasma free-fraction were acquired to improve quantification.

Results: Depressed suicide attempters had lower serotonin transporter binding in midbrain compared with depressed nonattempters (p = .031) and control subjects (p = .0093). There was no difference in serotonin transporter binding comparing all depressed subjects with healthy control subjects considering six a priori regions of interest simultaneously (p = .41).

Conclusions: Low midbrain serotonin transporter binding appears to be related to the pathophysiology of suicidal behavior rather than of major depressive disorder. This is consistent with postmortem work showing low midbrain serotonin transporter binding capacity in depressed suicides and may partially explain discrepant in vivo findings quantifying serotonin transporter in depression. Future studies should investigate midbrain serotonin transporter binding as a predictor of suicidal behavior in MDD and determine the cause of low binding.

Helping elderly patients to avoid suicide: A review of case reports from a national veteran's affairs database

Mills PD, Watts BV, Huh TJW, Boar S, Kemp J (USA)
Journal of Nervous and Mental Disease 201, 12-16, 2013

This study examines the health system factors associated with completed suicide among veterans older than 65 years. All root cause analysis reports of suicides that occurred between 2008 and 2010 in the Veterans Health Administration were reviewed; of those, 46 reports were for those 65 years or older. The average age in the sample was 76.96 years; all were men. Method of suicide, stressors, previous attempts, root causes, and action plans designed to address the root causes are reported. Based on these results, recommendations are made for the assessment and treatment of suicide in elderly men.

The impact of media reports on the 2008 outbreak of hydrogen sulfide suicides in Japan

Nakamura M, Yasunaga H, Toda A, Sugihara T, Imamura T (Japan)
International Journal of Psychiatry in Medicine 44, 133-140, 2012

Objective: Japan experienced a nationwide outbreak of hydrogen sulfide suicides (HSS) between April and May 2008. The annual number of HSS skyrocketed from 19 in 2007 to 1,056 in 2008. However, the factors affecting this enormous increase remain unknown. The present study aimed to examine the effect of media coverage of the incidents on the subsequent epidemic of HSS.

Method: We collected time series data from the 1st week of February to the last week of September 2008 (34 weeks), including the number of HSS (St), the number of articles on HSS published in the five major newspapers (N t), and the number of Internet searches with the keyword "hydrogen sulfide suicide" (Gt). The generalized method of moments was applied to model the concurrent effects of Nt and G t on St.

Results: The increase in the number of newspaper articles significantly induced the increase in HSS (coefficient, 0.84; 95% confidence interval (CI), 0.28-5.3), while the number of Internet searches did not significantly affect the number of HSS (coefficient, -0.75; 95%CI, -19.3-0.45).

Conclusions: Exposure to information on HSS from newspaper articles could have directly affected the subsequent increase in the number of suicides. On the other hand, the number of the Internet searches did not have a direct influence on HSS.

Attitudes towards suicidal behaviour in outpatient clinics among mental health professionals in Oslo

Norheim AB, Grimholt TK, Ekeberg O (Norway)

BMC Psychiatry 13, 90, 2013

Background: To investigate attitudes of professionals working in mental health care outpatient clinics in Child and Adolescent Psychiatry (CAP) (for children and adolescents aged 0—18 years) and District Psychiatric Centres (DPC) (for adults aged 18—67 years).

Methods: Professionals in four outpatient units in Oslo were enrolled (n = 229: 77%). The Understanding of Suicidal Patient scale (USP) (11 = positive to 55 = negative) and Attitudes Towards Suicide questionnaire (ATTS) (1 = totally disagree to 5 = totally agree) were used to assess professionals' attitudes. Questions explored competence, religion, experiences of and views on suicidal behaviour and its treatment.

Results: All the professionals indicated positive attitudes (USP 18.7) and endorsed the view that suicide was preventable (ATTS 4.3). Professionals who had received supervision or were specialists had attitudes that were more positive. Professionals in CAP were less satisfied with available treatment. Psychiatric disorders were considered the most common cause of suicidal behaviour, and psychotherapy the most appropriate form of treatment. The professionals confirmed that patients with other disorders of comparable severity are followed up more systematically.

Conclusions: The professionals showed positive attitudes with minor differences between CAP and DPC.

Factors that distinguish college students with depressive symptoms with and without suicidal thoughts

Nyer M, Holt DJ, Pedrelli P, Fava M, Ameral V, Cassiello CF, Nock MK, Ross M, Hutchinson D, Farabaugh A (USA)

Annals of Clinical Psychiatry 25, 41-49, 2013

Background: Suicide among college students is a significant public health concern. Although suicidality is linked to depression, not all depressed college students experience suicidal ideation (SI). The primary aim of this study was to determine potential factors that may distinguish college students with depressive symptoms with and without SI.

Methods: A total of 287 undergraduate college students with substantial depressive symptoms (Beck Depression Inventory [BDI] total score >13) with and without SI were compared across psychiatric and functional outcome variables. Independent sample t tests were conducted for each outcome variable using the suicide item of the BDI as a dichotomous (ie, zero vs nonzero score) grouping variable.

Results: Relative to students with substantial depressive symptoms without SI, those with SI were more symptomatic overall, having significantly higher levels of depressive symptoms, hopelessness, and anxiety. However, contrary to our expectations, nonsuicidal and suicidal students did not differ on measures of everyday functioning (ie, cognitive and physical functioning and grade point average).

Conclusions: Our findings suggest that SI among college students is associated with increased subjective distress but may not adversely impact physical or cognitive functioning or academic performance.

Differential patterns of activity and functional connectivity in emotion processing neural circuitry to angry and happy faces in adolescents with and without suicide attempt

Pan La, Hassel S, Segreti Am, Nau Sa, Brent Da, Phillips Ml (Canada, USA, UK)
Psychological Medicine. Published online: 9 January 2013. doi: 10.1017/S0033291712002966, 2013

Background: Neural substrates of emotion dysregulation in adolescent suicide attempters remain unexamined.

Method: We used functional magnetic resonance imaging to measure neural activity to neutral, mild or intense (i.e. 0%, 50% or 100% intensity) emotion face morphs in two separate emotion-processing runs (angry and happy) in three adolescent groups: (1) history of suicide attempt and depression (ATT, n = 14); (2) history of depression alone (NAT, n = 15); and (3) healthy controls (HC, n = 15). Post-hoc analyses were conducted on interactions from 3 group × 3 condition (intensities) whole-brain analyses (p < 0.05, corrected) for each emotion run.

Results: To 50% intensity angry faces, ATT showed significantly greater activity than NAT in anterior cingulate gyral-dorsolateral prefrontal cortical attentional control circuitry, primary sensory and temporal cortices; and significantly greater activity than HC in the primary sensory cortex, while NAT had significantly lower activity than HC in the anterior cingulate gyrus and ventromedial prefrontal cortex. To neutral faces during the angry emotion-processing run, ATT had significantly lower activity than NAT in the fusiform gyrus. ATT also showed significantly lower activity than HC to 100% intensity happy faces in the primary sensory cortex, and to neutral faces in the happy run in the anterior cingulate and left medial frontal gyri (all p < 0.006, corrected). Psychophysiological interaction analyses revealed significantly reduced anterior cingulate gyral-insula functional connectivity to 50% intensity angry faces in ATT v. NAT or HC.

Conclusions: Elevated activity in attention control circuitry, and reduced anterior cingulate gyral-insula functional connectivity, to 50% intensity angry faces in ATT than other groups suggest that ATT may show inefficient recruitment of attentional control neural circuitry when regulating attention to mild intensity angry faces, which may represent a potential biological marker for suicide risk.

Does the level of education influence completed suicide? A nationwide register study

Pompili M, Vichi M, Qin P, Innamorati M, De Leo D, Girardi P (Italy)

Journal of Affective Disorders. Published online: 26 September 2012. doi: 10.1016/j.jad.2012.08.046, 2012

Objective: To evaluate whether education attainment was associated with completed suicide, a topic only marginally investigated in the literature.

Methods: Data for the years between 2006 and 2008 were extracted from the Italian Mortality Database to include all deaths by suicide and natural causes and to obtain information on their education attainment.

Results: We found significant differences in education attainment between suicide victims and individuals deceased by natural causes, stratified by sex and broken down by age bands. Of both males and females from 15 to 64 years old, suicide victims were significantly more often to have a higher education attainment compared with the same sex and age counterparts died from natural causes. Persons with higher school attainment, compared with those with a maximum primary school degree, had significantly increased odds ratios of dying from a suicide rather than a natural cause. For persons aged 65-74 years or above, however, the differences were not so much obvious. These observations remained almost the same after adjustment for marital status, region of residence and age.

Conclusions: Individual with higher educational achievement may be more prone to suicide risk when facing failures, public shame, and high premorbid functioning.

Family history of suicide and exposure to interpersonal violence in childhood predict suicide in male suicide attempters

Rajalin M, Hirvikoski T, Jokinen J (Sweden)

Journal of Affective Disorders. Published online: 25 December 2012. doi: 10.1016/j.jad.2012.11.055, 2012

Background: Family studies, including twin and adoption designs, have shown familial transmission of suicidal behaviors. Early environmental risk factors have an important role in the etiology of suicidal behavior. The aim of the present study was to assess the impact of family history of suicide and childhood trauma on suicide risk and on severity of suicide attempt in suicide attempters.

Methods: A total of 181 suicide attempters were included. Family history of suicide was assessed with the Karolinska Suicide History Interview or through patient records. Childhood trauma was assessed with the Karolinska Interpersonal Violence Scale (KIVS) measuring exposure to violence and expressed violent behavior in childhood (between 6 and 14 years of age) and during adult life (15 years or older). Suicide intent was measured with the Freeman scale.

Results: Male suicide attempters with a positive family history of suicide made more serious and well planned suicide attempts and had a significantly higher suicide risk. In logistic regression, family history of suicide and exposure to interpersonal violence as a child were independent predictors of suicide in male suicide attempters.

Limitations: The information about family history of suicide and exposure to interpersonal violence as a child derives from the patients only. In the first part of the inclusion period the information was collected from patient records.

Conclusions: The results of this study imply that suicides among those at biological risk might be prevented with the early recognition of environmental risks.

A systematic review of school-based interventions aimed at preventing, treating, and responding to suicide- related behavior in young people

Robinson J, Cox G, Malone A, Williamson M, Baldwin G, Fletcher K, O'Brien M (Australia)
Crisis. Published online: 28 November 2012. doi: 10.1027/0227-5910/a000168, 2012

Background: Suicide, in particular among young people, is a major public health problem, although little is known regarding effective interventions for managing and preventing suicide-related behavior.

Aims: To review the empirical literature pertaining to suicide postvention, prevention, and early intervention, specifically in school settings.

Method: MEDLINE, PsycINFO, and the Cochrane Central Register of Controlled Trials (CCRCT) as well as citation lists of relevant articles using terms related to suicide and schools were searched in July 2011. School-based programs targeting suicide, attempted suicide, suicidal ideation, and self-harm where intent is not specified were included. No exclusion was placed on trial design. All studies had to include a suicide-related outcome.

Results: A total of 412 potentially relevant studies were identified, 43 of which met the inclusion criteria, as well as three secondary publications: 15 universal awareness programs, 23 selective interventions, 3 targeted interventions, and 2 postvention trials.

Limitations: Overall, the evidence was limited and hampered by methodological concerns, particularly a lack of RCTs.

Conclusions: The most promising interventions for schools appear to be gatekeeper training and screening programs. However, more research is needed.

The role of impulsivity in the relationship between anxiety and suicidal ideation

Schaefer KE, Esposito-Smythers C, Riskind JH (USA)
Journal of Affective Disorders 143, 95-101, 2012

Background: The purpose of the present study was to examine the degree to which trait and cognitive (looming cognitive style) measures of anxiety are associated with suicidal ideation (SI), as well as whether trait and cognitive (time misperception) measures of impulsivity moderate the association between these variables.

Methods: The sample included 100 undergraduate students (72% female) who completed the Spielberger State-Trait Anxiety Inventory, Looming Maladaptive Style Questionnaire, Barratt Impulsiveness Scale, Time Paradigm Version 1.0 Task,

Beck Scale for Suicidal Ideation, and the Brief Symptom Inventory.

Results: Trait anxiety and looming cognitive style were found to be positively associated with SI. Further, both trait impulsivity and time misperception moderated the association between these variables and SI, but in a different manner. Consistent with study hypotheses, among those high in trait anxiety, greater overestimation of time was associated with a higher likelihood of SI. Contrary to study hypotheses, among those low in trait anxiety, high trait impulsivity was associated with a greater likelihood of SI. The same pattern of results was found when looming cognitive style served as the independent variable.

Limitations: The use of a cross-sectional design limits the ability to determine the temporal relationship of the study variables. Further, the sample included predominantly Caucasian undergraduates and thus study results may not generalize to other populations.

Conclusions: Clinically, results suggest that high trait anxiety, looming cognitive style, time misperception, and trait impulsivity may be important risk factors for SI among college students and thus should be assessed when students present for treatment. Treatments that focus on problem solving, cognitive restructuring, and affect regulation strategies may help decrease anxiety and impulsivity, which in turn may help reduce the likelihood of suicidal thoughts.

Persistent mental health disturbances during the 10 years after a disaster: Four-wave longitudinal comparative study

van der Velden PG, Wong A, Boshuizen HC, Grievink L (Netherlands)
Psychiatry and the Clinical Neurosciences 67, 110-118, 2013

Aim: Although some studies have examined the long-term effects of disasters, very little is known about severe persistent symptoms following disasters. The aim of the present study was to examine persistent mental health problems and to what extent disaster exposure predicts long-term persistent disturbances.

Methods: Following a major disaster, a four-wave study was conducted (surveys 2-3 weeks, 18 months, 4 years and 10 years after the event) that examined severe post-traumatic stress disorder (PTSD) symptomatology (Impact of Event Scale), anxiety and depression symptoms and sleeping problems (Symptom Check List-90-R), and use of physician-prescribed tranquilizers. Participants were affected adult Dutch native residents (n = 1083). At wave 2 and 3, a control group participated (n = 694). At wave 1, severity of disaster exposure was examined. Multiple imputation was used to target the problem of missing data across surveys due to non-response such as in the fourth wave (61%).

Results: In total, 6.7% (95% confidence interval [CI]: 5.1-8.2) developed persistent PTSD symptoms during the 10years after the event. For anxiety, depression, sleeping problems these prevalences were 3.8% (95%CI: 2.7-5.0), 6.2% (95%CI: 4.7-7.6) and 4.8% (95%CI: 3.5-6.1) respectively. In total 1.3% (95%CI: 0.6-2.0) used tranquilizers at all waves. Approximately one out of 10 with severe symptoms

2-3 weeks after the event, developed persistent symptoms. Even in the long term, affected residents compared to controls had more often chronic anxiety symptoms and sleeping problems. High disaster exposure independently predicted persistent PTSD symptoms (adjusted odds ratio [adj. OR], 4.20; 95%CI: 2.02-8.74, P<0.001), anxiety (adj. OR, 3.43; 95%CI: 1.28-9.20, P<0.01), depression symptoms (adj. OR, 2.95; 95%CI: 1.26-6.93, P<0.01), and sleeping problems (adj. OR, 3.74; 95%CI: 1.56-8.95, P<0.001).

Conclusion: Post-disaster mental health care should (also) target persistent mental health disturbances in the long term, especially PTSD, anxiety, depression symptoms, and sleeping problems. High disaster exposure may be an early marker for risk of persistent symptoms.

Reducing suicidal ideation: Cost-effectiveness analysis of a randomized controlled trial of unguided web-based self-help

van Spijker BAJ, Majo MC, Smit F, van Straten A, Kerkhof AJFM (Netherlands)
Journal of Medical Internet Research 14, e141, 2012

Background: Suicidal ideation is highly prevalent, but often remains untreated. The Internet can be used to provide accessible interventions.

Objective: To evaluate the cost-effectiveness of an online, unguided, self-help intervention for reducing suicidal ideation.

Methods: A total of 236 adults with mild to moderate suicidal thoughts, defined as scores between 1-26 on the Beck Scale for Suicide Ideation (BSS), were recruited in the general population and randomized to the intervention (n = 116) or to a waitlist, information-only, control group (n = 120). The intervention aimed to decrease the frequency and intensity of suicidal ideation and consisted of 6 modules based on cognitive behavioral techniques. Participants in both groups had unrestricted access to care as usual. Assessments took place at baseline and 6 weeks later (post-test). All questionnaires were self-report and administered via the Internet. Treatment response was defined as a clinically significant decrease in suicidal ideation on the BSS. Total per-participant costs encompassed costs of health service uptake, participants' out-of-pocket expenses, costs stemming from production losses, and intervention costs. These were expressed in Euros (€) for the reference year 2009.

Results: At post-test, treatment response was 35.3% and 20.8% in the experimental and control conditions, respectively. The incremental effectiveness was 0.35 - 0.21 = 0.15 (SE 0.06, P = .01). The annualized incremental costs were -€5039 per participant. Therefore, the mean incremental cost-effectiveness ratio (ICER) was estimated to be -€5039/0.15 = -€34,727 after rounding (US -$41,325) for an additional treatment response, indicating annual cost savings per treatment responder.

Conclusions: This is the first trial to indicate that online self-help to reduce suicidal ideation is feasible, effective, and cost saving. Limitations included reliance on self-report and a short timeframe (6 weeks). Therefore, replication with a longer follow-up period is recommended.

When does depression become a disorder? Using recurrence rates to evaluate the validity of proposed changes in major depression diagnostic thresholds

Wakefield JC, Schmitz MF (USA)

World Psychiatry 12, 44-52, 2013

High community prevalence estimates of DSM-defined major depressive disorder (MDD) have led to proposals to raise MDD's diagnostic threshold to more validly distinguish pathology from normal-range distress. However, such proposals lack empirical validation. We used MDD recurrence rates in the longitudinal 2-wave Epidemiologic Catchment Area Study to test the predictive validity of three proposals to narrow MDD diagnosis: a) excluding "uncomplicated" episodes (i.e., episodes that last no longer than 2 months and do not include suicidal ideation, psychotic ideation, psychomotor retardation, or feelings of worthlessness); b) excluding mild episodes (i.e., episodes with only five to six symptoms); and c) excluding nonmelancholic episodes. For each proposal, we used lifetime MDD diagnoses at wave 1 to distinguish the group proposed for exclusion, other MDD, and those with no MDD history. We then compared these groups' 1-year MDD rates at wave 2. A proposal was considered strongly supported if at wave 2 the excluded group's MDD rate was not only significantly lower than the rate for other MDD but also not significantly greater than the no-MDD-history group. Results indicated that all three excluded groups had significantly lower recurrence rates than other MDD (uncomplicated vs. complicated, 3.4% vs. 14.6%; mild vs. severe, 9.6% vs. 20.7%; nonmelancholic vs. melancholic, 10.6% vs. 19.2%, respectively). However, only uncomplicated MDD's recurrence rate was also not significantly greater than the MDD occurrence rate for the no-MDD-history group (3.4% vs. 1.7%, respectively). This low recurrence rate resulted from an interaction between uncomplicated duration and symptom criteria. Multiple-episode uncomplicated MDD did not entail significantly elevated recurrence over single-episode cases (3.7% vs. 3.0%, respectively). Uncomplicated MDD's general-distress symptoms, transient duration, and lack of elevated recurrence suggest it may generally represent nonpathologic intense sadness that should be addressed in treatment guidelines and considered for exclusion from MDD diagnosis to increase the validity of the MDD/normal sadness boundary.

A systematic review process to evaluate suicide prevention programs: A sample case of community-based programs

York J, Lamis DA, Friedman L, Berman AL, Joiner TE, McIntosh JL, Silverman MM, Konick L, Gutierrez PM, Pearson J (USA)

Journal of Community Psychology 41, 35-51, 2013

The Guide to Community Preventive Services (Guide), one of the most rigorous methods of systematic reviews, was adopted to evaluate the effectiveness of 16 community, primarily youth, suicide prevention interventions, through a multi-sectoral collaboration. The Guide steps for obtaining and evaluating evidence on effectiveness include: forming a multidisciplinary team; developing a conceptual approach to organizing, grouping, selecting, and evaluating the interventions; selecting the interventions; searching for and retrieving evidence; assessing the quality of and summarizing the body of evidence; translating the evidence of effectiveness into recommendations; considering additional evidence; and identifying and summarizing research gaps. The intervention effects were calculated using Hedge's g-type (standardized mean differences) effect sizes. The strength of the body of evidence was characterized on the basis of suitability of the study design for assessing effectiveness and quality of study execution. Results indicated that student curriculum, combined curriculum and gatekeeper training, and competence programs have a positive effect on adolescent's knowledge and attitudes about suicide, but only a negligible effect on suicidal behaviors. Five of 7 studies with moderate to large effect sizes on outcomes were also those with both good quality of execution and the greatest suitability of the design. Policy recommendations are offered for the improved evaluation of the effectiveness of suicide prevention programs in youth.

Orphaned and abused youth are vulnerable to pregnancy and suicide risk

Zapata LB, Kissin DM, Bogoliubova O, Yorick RV, Kraft JM, Jamieson DJ, Marchbanks PA, Hillis SD (USA, Russia)

Child Abuse and Neglect. Published online: 4 January 2013. doi: 10.1016/j.chiabu.2012.10.005, 2013

Objective: Little is known about the magnitude and consequences of violence against children for those living outside family care. We sought to estimate the frequency of childhood abuse and examine its association with lifetime pregnancy involvement (LPI) and past year suicide ideation among orphaned youth. *Methods:* We analyzed data collected via cross-sectional interviewer-administered surveys completed by 293 orphaned youth aged 16-23 years living outside of family care in St. Petersburg, Russia. We used multivariable logistic regression to estimate adjusted odds ratios (AORs) of LPI and past year suicide ideation associated with childhood physical and sexual abuse. Other risk factors were also examined (e.g., social vulnerability, sexual and substance use behaviors), and characteristics of orphaned youth with LPI and past year suicide ideation were described.

Results: The prevalence of childhood abuse was higher among females than among males (23.3% versus 15.6% for physical abuse, and 20.3% versus 5.6% for sexual abuse), as was the prevalence of LPI and past year suicide ideation among those with histories of abuse. Experiences of childhood abuse were strong risk factors for both LPI and past year suicide ideation, with significant variation by gender. While both types of abuse were significantly associated with LPI and past year suicide ideation among females, physical abuse was significantly associated with LPI and sexual abuse was associated with suicide ideation for males. Of the other characteristics examined, strong modifiable risk factors included having no one to turn to for help and no involvement in activities outside of class. Among those with LPI (n = 36), nearly 20% had been pregnant or gotten someone pregnant ≥ 2 times, most (61.8%) reported at least one induced abortion, and current use of effective contraception was nearly non-existent. Among those with past year suicide ideation (n = 30), nearly half (44.8%) reported attempting suicide.

Conclusions: There is an urgent need for interventions to prevent and mitigate the negative influence of childhood abuse experiences. Programs providing services to orphaned youth should increase access to sexual education, effective contraceptives, and mental health counseling.

Body mass index and suicidal behaviors: A critical review of epidemiological evidence

Zhang J, Yan F, Li Y, McKeown RE (USA)

Journal of Affective Disorders. Published online: 20 September 2012. doi: 10.1016/j.jad.2012.05.048, 2012

Introduction: Obesity has been associated with an elevated risk of depression and other mental health symptoms. An increasing number of robust prospective studies, however, counter-intuitively and consistently suggested that body mass index (BMI) was inversely associated with the risk of completed suicide in a dose-response fashion. The current contribution appraised the epidemiological evidence and examined the nature of the purported relationship.

Method: We conducted a systematic review of English publications of original studies using the terms "obesity", "overweight", "body mass index", "BMI", "attempted suicide", "completed suicide", "suicide ideation", "suicidal behaviors" and "suicide". Data were extracted primarily through MEDLINE and PUBMED databases.

Results: Almost all cohort studies reported an inverse relationship between BMI and the risk of completed suicide irrespective of region of origin and the gender of study participants. Overall, among men, a high BMI was associated with a low risk of attempted or completed suicide. There was a paradox among women, namely, a high BMI was associated with an elevated risk of attempted suicide but a low risk of completed suicide.

Limitations: As a narrative review, the current report was interpretive and qualitative in nature.

Conclusion: Consideration of observational data, methodological issues stemmed from the rarity of deaths by suicide, homogeneity of study populations, heterogeneity of suicide methods, and the corresponding neurobiological changes made interpretation difficult. Intercultural cohort observations across countries may help to weigh the contributions from biological and socio-cultural factors. The purported association not only represents a scientific challenge, it's also an opportunity potentially leading to important insights into prevention of suicide death.

Citation List

FATAL SUICIDAL BEHAVIOR

Epidemiology

Abel WD, James K, Bridgelal-Nagassar R, Holder-Nevins D, Eldemire H, Thompson E, Sewell C (2012). The epidemiology of suicide in Jamaica 2002-2010: Rates and patterns. *West Indian Medical Journal* 61, 509-515.

Adinkrah M (2012). Homicide-suicide in Ghana: Perpetrators, victims, and incidence characteristics. *International Journal of Offender Therapy and Comparative Criminology*. Published online: 24 December 2012. doi: 10.1177/0306624X12470530.

Afroz B, Moniruzzaman S, Ekman DS, Andersson R (2012). The impact of economic crisis on injury mortality: The case of the 'Asian crisis'. *Public Health* 126, 836-838.

Ahlm K, Saveman BI, Björnstig U (2013). Drowning deaths in Sweden with emphasis on the presence of alcohol and drugs - A retrospective study, 1992-2009. *BMC Public Health* 13, 216.

Ahmad MZ, Hussain T, Kumar M (2012). Pattern of poisoning reported at BC Roy hospital, Haldia Purba Midnapur, West Bengal. *Medico-Legal Update* 12, 231-233.

Ahmadi A, Mohammadi R, Almasi A, Sadeghi-Bazargani H, Bazargan-Hejazi S (2012). Risk and protective factors of self-immolation: A population based case control study from Iran. *Injury Prevention* 18, A165.

Al-Zacko SM (2012). Self-inflicted burns in Mosul: A cross-sectional study. *Annals of Burns and Fire Disasters* 25, 121-125.

Albrand LE (2012). The psychosomatic consequences of life imprisonment. *Conséquences Psychosomatiques de la réclusion criminelle à perpétuité* 141, 33-35.

Amiri B, Pourreza A, Foroushani AR, Hosseini SM, Poorolajal J (2012). Suicide and associated risk factors in Hamadan province, west of Iran, in 2008 and 2009. *Journal of Research in Health Sciences* 12, 88-92.

Anestis MD, Bryan CJ (2012). Means and capacity for suicidal behavior: A comparison of the ratio of suicide attempts and deaths by suicide in the U.S. military and general population. *Journal of Affective Disorders*. Published online: 19 December 2012. doi: 10.1016/j.jad.2012.11.045.

Angst J, Hengartner MP, Gamma A, von Zerssen D, Angst F (2012). Mortality of 403 patients with mood disorders 48 to 52 years after their psychiatric hospitalisation. *European Archives of Psychiatry and Clinical Neuroscience*. Published online: 4 November 2012. doi: 10.1007/s00406-012-0380-1.

Anonymous (2012). CNE quiz. *Journal of Psychosocial Nursing & Mental Health Services* 50, 19-47.

Anonymous (2012). Understanding older men's perspectives on depression and suicide in primary care: Results from the men's health and aging study (MEHAS). *Gerontologist* 52, 271-271.

Anonymous (2013). Suicide in the UK: Questioning ourselves. *Lancet* 381, 348.

Anthony L, Kulkarni C (2012). Patterns of poisoning and drug overdosage and their outcome among in-patients admitted to the emergency medicine department of a tertiary care hospital. *Indian Journal of Critical Care Medicine* 16, 130-135.

Arendt M, Munk-Jørgensen P, Sher L, Jensen SOW (2012). Mortality following treatment for cannabis use disorders: Predictors and causes. *Journal of Substance Abuse Treatment* 44, 400-406.

Aunon-Martin I, Doussoux PC, Baltasar JL, Polentinos-Castro E, Mazzini JP, Erasun CR (2012). Correlation between pattern and mechanism of injury of free fall. *Strategies in Trauma and Limb Reconstruction* 7, 141-145.

Bando DH, Brunoni AR, Bensenor IM, Lotufo PA (2012). Suicide rates and income in Sao Paulo and Brazil: A temporal and spatial epidemiologic analysis from 1996 to 2008. *BMC Psychiatry* 12, 127.

Beautrais AL, Larkin GL, Fergusson DM, Horwood LJ, Mulder RT (2012). Mortality and non-fatal suicidal behaviour in the 20 years after a medically serious suicide attempt. *Injury Prevention* 18, A33.

Bella ME, Acosta L, Villace B, Lopez de Neira M, Enders J, Fernandez R (2013). Analysis of mortality from suicide in children, adolescents and youth. Argentina, 2005-2007. *Archivos Argentinos de Pediatria* 111, 16-21.

Bezo B, Maggi S, Roberts WL (2012). The rights and freedoms gradient of health: Evidence from a cross-national study. *Frontiers in Psychology* 3, 441.

Bodell LP, Joiner TE, Keel PK (2013). Comorbidity-independent risk for suicidality increases with bulimia nervosa but not with anorexia nervosa. *Journal of Psychiatric Research* 47, 617-621.

Boumba VA, Georgiadis M, Mirescu N, Vougiouklakis T (2012). Fatal intoxications in a forensic autopsy material from Epirus, Greece, during the period 1998-2010. *Journal of Forensic Sciences*. Published online: 26 October 2012. doi: 10.1111/1556-4029.12014.

Bourget D, Gagne P (2012). Women who kill their mates. *Behavioral Sciences and the Law* 30, 598-614.

Braubach M, Algoet A, Beaton M, Lauriou S, Héroux ME, Krzyzanowski M (2012). Mortality associated with exposure to carbon monoxide in WHO European member states. *Indoor Air* 23, 115-125.

Brice JH, Moss C, Purpura P, Delbridge TR (2012). Epidemiology of low-level bridge jumping in Pittsburgh: A 10-year study. *Prehospital Emergency Care* 17, 155-161.

Brittain J, Axelrod G, Venters H (2013). Deaths in New York City Jails, 2001-2009. *American Journal of Public Health* 103, 638-640.

Buchade D, Kukde H, Dere R, Savardekar R, Devraj N, Maiyyar A (2012). Autopsy study of cut throat cases brought to morgue of Sion hospital, Mumbai- A three year study. *Indian Journal of Forensic Medicine and Toxicology* 6, 44-46.

Bussu A, Detotto C, Sterzi V (2013). Social conformity and suicide. *Journal of Socio-Economics* 42, 67-78.

Caetano R, Kaplan MS, Huguet N, McFarland BH, Conner K, Giesbrecht N, Nolte KB (2013). Acute alcohol intoxication and suicide among United States ethnic/racial groups: Findings from the national violent death reporting system. *Alcoholism Clinical and Experimental Research*. Published online: 5 February 2013. doi: 10.1111/acer.12038.

Carroll R, Metcalfe C, Gunnell D, Mohamed F, Eddleston M (2012). Diurnal variation in probability of death following self-poisoning in Sri Lanka-Evidence for chronotoxicity in humans. *International Journal of Epidemiology* 41, 1821-1828.

Castagnini A, Foldager L, Bertelsen A (2013). Excess mortality of acute and transient psychotic disorders: Comparison with bipolar affective disorder and schizophrenia. *Acta Psychiatrica Scandinavica*. Published online: 20 January 2013. doi: 10.1111/acps.12077.

Chae MH, Boyle DJ (2013). Police suicide: Prevalence, risk, and protective factors. *Policing* 36, 91-118.

Chalya PL, Gilyoma JM (2012). The burden of intentional injuries in Mwanza city, North-Western Tanzania: A tertiary hospital survey. *Tanzania Journal of Health Research* 14, 1-10.

Chattopadhyay S, Sahu SK (2012). A predictive stressor-integrated model of suicide right from one's birth: A Bayesian approach. *Journal of Medical Imaging and Health Informatics* 2, 125-131.

Chen Y-Y, Bennewith O, Hawton K, Simkin S, Cooper J, Kapur N, Gunnell D (2012). Suicide by burning barbecue charcoal in England. *Journal of Public Health.* Published online: 23 November 2012. doi: 10.1093/pubmed/fds095.

Choi Y, Kim Y, Ko Y, Cha ES, Kim J, Lee WJ (2012). Economic burden of acute pesticide poisoning in South Korea. *Tropical Medicine & International Health* 17, 1534-1543.

Chon DS (2013). Economic development, change of age distribution, and stream analogy of homicide and suicide: A cross-national assessment. *Justice Quarterly* 30, 169-193.

Cizek Sajko M, Cizek N, Jareb B (2012). Suicide among childhood cancer survivors in Slovenia. *Acta Medica Academica* 41, 154-160.

Clarke MC, Tanskanen A, Huttunen MO, Cannon M (2012). Sudden death of father or sibling in early childhood increases risk for psychotic disorder. *Schizophrenia Research* 143, 363-366.

Clements C, Morriss R, Jones S, Peters S, Roberts C, Kapur N (2013). Suicide in bipolar disorder in a national English sample, 1996-2009: Frequency, trends and characteristics. *Psychological Medicine.* Published online: 19 March 2013. doi: 10.1017/S0033291713000329.

Cramer RJ, Garza MJ, Henderson CE, Ribeiro JD, Silva C, Smith AR, Joiner Jr TE, White J (2012). A trait-interpersonal perspective on suicide risk in criminal offenders. *Archives of Suicide Research* 16, 334-347.

Cros J, Alvarez J-C, Sbidian E, Charlier P, de la Grandmaison GL (2012). Homicidal deaths in the western suburbs of Paris a 15-year-study. *American Journal of Forensic Medicine and Pathology* 33, 404-409.

Daigle MS, Naud H (2012). Risk of dying by suicide inside or outside prison: The shortened lives of male offenders. *Canadian Journal of Criminology and Criminal Justice* 54, 511

Dailey NJ, Norwood T, Moore ZS, Fleischauer AT, Proescholdbell S (2012). Evaluation of the North Carolina violent death reporting system, 2009. *North Carolina Medical Journal* 73, 257-262.

Dalus D, Mathew AJ, Somarajan Pillai S (2012). Formic acid poisoning in a tertiary care center in South India: A 2-year retrospective analysis of clinical profile and predictors of mortality. *Journal of Emergency Medicine* 44, 373-380.

de Leo D, Too LS, Kõlves K, Milner A, Ide N (2013). Has the suicide rate risen with the 2011 Queensland floods? *Journal of Loss and Trauma* 18, 170-178.

Deasy C, Bray J, Smith K, Bernard S, Cameron P, Comm VS (2013). Hanging-associated out-of-hospital cardiac arrests in Melbourne, Australia. *Emergency Medicine Journal* 30, 38-42.

Ding D, Wang W, Wu J, Yang H, Li S, Dai X, Yang B, Wang T, Yuan C, Ma G, Bell GS, Kwan P, de Boer HM, Hong Z, Sander JW (2012). Premature mortality risk in people with convulsive epilepsy: Long follow-up of a cohort in rural China. *Epilepsia* 54, 512-517.

Edwards G (2013). Tarasoff, duty to warn laws, and suicide. *International Review of Law and Economics* 34, 1-8.

Emmanuel MK, Campbell MH (2012). Commentary: Homicide-suicide in the Caribbean. *Journal of the American Academy of Psychiatry and the Law* 40, 469-471.

Emmerova I (2012). Suicides and attempted suicides of children and adolescents in the Slovak Republic and possibilities of their prevention. *New Educational Review* 29, 81-89.

Erlangsen A, Conwell Y (2013). Age-related response to redeemed antidepressants measured by completed suicide in older adults: A nationwide cohort study. *American Journal of Geriatric Psychiatry.* Published online: 18 March 2013. doi: 10.1016/j.jagp.2012.08.008.

Esscher A, Hogberg U, Haglund B, Essen B (2013). Maternal mortality in Sweden 1988-2007: More deaths than officially reported. *Acta Obstetricia Et Gynecologica Scandinavica* 92, 40-46.

Feodor Nilsson S, Hjorthoj CR, Erlangsen A, Nordentoft M (2013). Suicide and unintentional injury mortality among homeless people: A Danish nationwide register-based cohort study. *European Journal of Public Health.* Published online: 12 March 2013. doi: 10.1093/eurpub/ckt025.

Flaig B, Zedler B, Ackermann H, Bratzke H, Parzeller M (2012). Anthropometrical differences between suicide and other non-natural death circumstances: An autopsy study. *International Journal of Legal Medicine.* Published online: 9 November 2012. doi: 10.1007/s00414-012-0776-5.

Fleegler EW, Lee LK, Monuteaux MC, Hemenway D, Mannix R (2013). Firearm legislation and firearm-related fatalities in the United States. *JAMA.* Published online: 6 March 2013. doi: 10.1001/jamainternmed.2013.1286.

Foo XY, Mohd Alwi MN, Ismail SI, Ibrahim N, Jamil Osman Z (2012). Religious commitment, attitudes toward suicide, and suicidal behaviors among college students of different ethnic and religious groups in Malaysia. *Journal of Religion and Health.* Published online: 30 November 2012. doi: 10.1007/s10943-012-9667-9.

Fowler KA, Crosby AE, Parks SE, Ivey AZ, Silverman PR (2013). Epidemiological investigation of a youth suicide cluster: Delaware 2012. *Delaware Medical Journal* 85, 15-19.

Foxhall K (2012). Suicide tops all causes of U.S. deaths from injury: U.S. surgeon general report seeks to integrate suicide prevention into health care reform. *Contemporary Pediatrics* 29, 13.

Francisco V, Silveira J, Zacarias A (2012). Suicide in Mozambique: Evidence from 10 years mortuary data from forensic services at Maputo Central hospital, Maputo City. *Injury Prevention* 18, A166.

Freire C, Koifman S (2013). Pesticides, depression and suicide: A systematic review of the epidemiological evidence. *International Journal of Hygiene and Environmental Health.* Published online: 17 February 2013. doi: 10.1016/j.ijheh.2012.12.003.

Frisch M, Simonsen J (2013). Marriage, cohabitation and mortality in Denmark: National cohort study of 6.5 million persons followed for up to three decades (1982-2011). *International Journal of Epidemiology.* Published online: 11 March 2013. doi: 10.1093/ije/dyt024.

Fu Kw, Chan CH (2013). A study of the impact of thirteen celebrity suicides on subsequent suicide rates in South Korea from 2005 to 2009. *PLoS ONE.* Published online: 16 January 2013. doi: 10.1371/journal.pone.0053870.

Fu TST, Lee CS, Gunnell D, Lee WC, Cheng ATA (2012). Changing trends in the prevalence of common mental disorders in Taiwan: A 20-year repeated cross-sectional survey. *Lancet* 381, 235-241.

Giupponi G, Pycha R, Innamorati M, Lamis DA, Schmidt E, Conca A, Kapfhammer HP, Lester D, Girardi P, Pompili M (2012). The association between suicide and the utilization of mental health services in South Tirol, Italy: A psychological autopsy study. *International Journal of Social Psychiatry.* Published online: 17 October 2012. doi: 10.1177/0020764012461209.

Goodin DS, Ebers GC, Cutter G, Cook SD, O'Donnell T, Reder AT, Kremenchutzky M, Oger J, Rametta M, Beckmann K, Knappertz V (2012). Cause of death in MS: Long-term follow-up of a randomised cohort, 21 years after the start of the pivotal ifnbeta-1b study. *BMJ Open.* Published online: 30 November 2012. doi: 10.1136/bmjopen-2012-001972.

Gouda HS, Rohith K, Mahadeshwara Prasad DR, Sasanka P (2012). A study of acute organophosphate poisoning at a tertiary hospital, Belgaum, Karnataka. *Medico-Legal Update* 12, 75-79.

Griffin MT (2012). At the end of life. Old age, death and suicide in antiquity. *Gnomon-Kritische Zeitschrift Fur Die Gesamte Klassische Altertumswissenschaft* 84, 472-473.

Griffith J (2012). Correlates of suicide among army national guard soldiers. *Military Psychology* 24, 568-591.

Grigoriev P, Doblhammer-Reiter G, Shkolnikov V (2012). Trends, patterns, and determinants of regional mortality in Belarus, 1990-2007. *Population Studies* 67, 61-68.

Guntheti BK, Singh UP (2011). The pattern of poisoning in Khammam. *Journal of Indian Academy of Forensic Medicine* 33, 296-300.

Habenstein A, Steffen T, Bartsch C, Michaud K, Reisch T (2013). Chances and limits of method restriction: A detailed analysis of suicide methods in Switzerland. *Archives of Suicide Research* 17, 75-87.

Hagaman AK, Wagenaar BH, McLean KE, Kaiser BN, Winskell K, Kohrt BA (2013). Suicide in rural Haiti: Clinical and community perceptions of prevalence, etiology, and prevention. *Social Science and Medicine* 83, 61-69.

Hanna VN, Ahmad A (2013). Corrected and republished: Suicide in the Kurdistan region of Iraq, state of the art*. *Nordic Journal of Psychiatry*. Published online: 21 January 2013. doi: 10.3109/08039488.2012.761401.

Healy D, Le Noury J, Harris M, Butt M, Linden S, Whitaker C, Zou L, Roberts AP (2012). Mortality in schizophrenia and related psychoses: Data from two cohorts, 1875-1924 and 1994-2010. *BMJ Open*. Published online: 8 October 2012. doi: 10.1136/bmjopen-2012-001810.

Hegerl U, Koburger N, Rummel-Kluge C, Gravert C, Walden M, Mergl R (2012). One followed by many?-long-term effects of a celebrity suicide on the number of suicidal acts on the German railway net. *Journal of Affective Disorders* 146, 39-44.

Hoang U, Goldacre Mj, Stewart R (2012). Avoidable mortality in people with schizophrenia or bipolar disorder in England. *Acta Psychiatrica Scandinavica* 127, 195-201.

Holder-Nevins D, James K, Bridgelal-Nagassar R, Bailey A, Thompson E, Eldemire H, Sewell C, Abel WD (2012). Suicide among adolescents in Jamaica: What do we know. *West Indian Medical Journal* 61, 516-520.

Hossain K (1946). Suicidal poisoning in Calcutta. *Indian Medical Gazette* 81, 418-422.

Hosseinian A, Pakravan N, Rafiei A, Feyzbakhsh S (2011). Aluminum phosphide poisoning known as rice tablet: A common toxicity in north Iran. *Indian Journal of Medical Sciences* 65, 143-150.

Ilgen MA, McCarthy JF, Ignacio RV (2012). Veterans who have served in the conflicts of Iraq and Afghanistan are at increased risk of suicide compared to other veterans if they have a psychiatric diagnosis. *Evidence Based Mental Health* 15, 99.

Innamorati M, Serafini G, Lester D, Amore M, Girardi P, Pompili M (2013). Violent deaths among Russian and EU male older adults. *International Journal of Social Psychiatry*. Published online: 1 January 2013. doi: 10.1177/0020764012467261.

Inoue K, Fukunaga T, Fujita Y, Okazaki Y (2012). Can the number of new housing starts serve as an indicator of suicide trends in Japan?: Exploring potential indicators to prevent suicides. *International Medical Journal* 19, 297-298.

Irwin JA, Austin EL (2013). Suicide ideation and suicide attempts among white southern lesbians. *Journal of Gay and Lesbian Mental Health* 17, 4-20.

Jagodic HK, Agius M, Pregelj P (2012). Inter-regional variations in suicide rates. *Psychiatria Danubina* 24, S82-S85.

Jess T, Frisch M, Simonsen J (2012). Trends in overall and cause-specific mortality among patients with inflammatory bowel disease from 1982 to 2010. *Clinical Gastroenterology and Hepatology* 11, 43-48.

Jia CX, Mehlum L, Qin P (2012). Aids/HIV infection, comorbid psychiatric illness, and risk for subsequent suicide: A nationwide register linkage study. *Journal of Clinical Psychiatry* 73, 1315-1321.

Jones CM, Mack KA, Paulozzi LJ (2013). Pharmaceutical overdose deaths, United States, 2010. *JAMA* 309, 657-659.

Jordal M, Wijewardena K, Olsson P (2013). Unmarried women's ways of facing single motherhood in Sri Lanka — A qualitative interview study. *BMC Womens Health* 13, 5.

Karch DL, Logan J, McDaniel D, Parks S, Patel N, Centers for Disease C, Prevention (2012). Surveillance for violent deaths—national violent death reporting system, 16 states, 2009. *Morbidity and Mortality Weekly Report Surveillance Summaries* 61, 1-43.

Katz IR, Kemp JE, Blow FC, McCarthy JF, Bossarte RM (2013). Changes in suicide rates and in mental health staffing in the veterans health administration, 2005-2009. *Psychiatric Services.* Published online: 15 March 2013. doi: 10.1176/appi.ps.201200253.

Kelen GD, Catlett CL, Kubit JG, Hsieh Y-H (2012). Hospital-based shootings in the United States: 2000 to 2011. *Annals of Emergency Medicine* 60, 790-798.

Khetran AK, Rehman S, Khan Z, Baloch M (2012). Incidence of deaths due to gunshot injuries at district Barkhan, Balochistan. *Journal of the Liaquat University of Medical and Health Sciences* 11, 90-92.

Khurana P, Dala JS, Multani AS, Tejpal HR (2011). The study of aluminium phosphide poisoning in a tertiary care hospital, Amritsar. *Journal of Indian Academy of Forensic Medicine* 33, 332-336.

Kielland KB, Skaug K, Amundsen EJ, Dalgard O (2012). All-cause and liver-related mortality in hepatitis C infected drug users followed for 33 years: A controlled study. *Journal of Hepatology* 58, 31-37.

Kisely S, Preston N, Xiao J, Lawrence D, Louise S, Crowe E (2012). Reducing all-cause mortality among patients with psychiatric disorders: A population-based study. *CMAJ* 185, E50-E56.

Kõlves K, Milner A, Värnik P (2013). Suicide rates and socioeconomic factors in Eastern European countries after the collapse of the Soviet Union: Trends between 1990 and 2008. *Sociology of Health and Illness.* Published online: 11 February 2013. doi: 10.1111/1467-9566.12011.

Krishnamurthy L, Rohini K, Shashikala P (2012). Socio-demographic profile of organophosphorous poisoning in a tertiary care hospital. *Indian Journal of Public Health Research and Development* 3, 169-171.

Kumral B, Büyük Y, Gündomu UN, ahin E, Feyzi ahin M (2012). Medico-legal evaluation of deaths due to decapitation. *Romanian Journal of Legal Medicine* 20, 251-254.

Lathrop SL (2013). Childhood fatalities in New Mexico: Medical examiner-investigated cases, 2000-2010. *Journal of Forensic Science.* Published online: 12 March 2013. doi: 10.1111/1556-4029.12106.

Lee SK, Rhee JS, Yum HS (2012). Cyanide poisoning deaths detected at the national forensic service headquarters in Seoul of Korea: A six year survey (2005~2010). *Toxicological Research* 28, 195-199.

Lester D, Haines J, Williams CL (2012). Firearm suicides among males in Australia: An analysis of Tasmanian coroners' inquest files. *International Journal of Men's Health* 11, 170-176.

Levav I (2012). Suicide in Israel. Suicides, 1981-2009. Suicide attempts, 2004-2010. *Israel Journal of Psychiatry and Related Sciences* 49, 235-236.

Li HW, Chang HF, Yu YM, Dai GX, Yin ZY (2012). Forensic medical study on morphology and formative mechanism of blunt head injury. *Chinese Journal of Traumatology* 15, 342-345.

Liu Y, Arai A, Obayashi Y, Kanda K, Boostrom E, Lee RB, Tamashiro H (2012). Trends of gender gaps in life expectancy in Japan, 1947-2010: Associations with gender mortality ratio and a social development index. *Geriatrics and Gerontology International.* Published online: 6 December 2012. doi: 10.1111/ggi.12001.

Loewenthal KM (2012). Mental health and mental health care for Jews in the Diaspora, with particular reference to the UK. *Israel Journal of Psychiatry and Related Sciences* 49, 159-166.

Macente LB, Zandonade E (2012). Spatial distribution of suicide incidence rates in municipalities in the state of Espirito Santo (Brazil), 2003-2007: Spatial analysis to identify risk areas. *Revista Brasileira De Psiquiatria* 34, 261-269.

Mackenzie DW (2013). Applying the Anderson-Darling test to suicide clusters. *Crisis.* Published online: 15 March 2013. doi: 10.1027/0227-5910/a000197.

Magagna G, de la Fuente EI, Vargas C, Lozano LM, Cabezas JL (2012). Bayesian estimation of the prevalence of suicide risk in institutionalized older people. *Omega* 66, 121.

Makara-Studzinska M, Sygit K, Sygit M, Gozdziewska M, Zubilewicz J, Krys-Noszczyk K (2012). Analysis of the phenomenon of attempted suicides in 1978-2010 in Poland, with particular emphasis on rural areas of Lublin province. *Annals of Agricultural and Environmental Medicine* 19, 762-769.

Malone Km, Quinlivan L, Grant T, Kelleher Cc (2012). Ageing towards 21 as a risk factor for young adult suicide in the UK and Ireland. *Epidemiology and Psychiatric Sciences.* Published online: 13 November 2012. doi: 10.1017/S2045796012000649.

Marín-León L, De Oliveira HB, Botega NJ (2012). Suicide in Brazil, 2004-2010: The importance of small counties. *Pan American Journal of Public Health* 32, 351-359.

McKay K, Milner A, Maple M (2013). Women and suicide: Beyond the gender paradox. *International Journal of Culture and Mental Health.* Published online: 18 February 2013. doi: 10.1080/17542863.2013.765495.

Meel BL (2012). Poverty and suicide in the Transkei region of South Africa. *South African Journal of Psychiatry* 18, 127.

Meera T, Bapin Kumar Singh M (2011). Pattern of neck findings in suicidal hanging a study in Manipur. *Journal of Indian Academy of Forensic Medicine* 33, 352-354.

Mehra AA, Gianakos D, Driscoll C (2012). Primer on suicide in older adults. *Clinical Geriatrics* 20, 22-27.

Milner A, Page A, LaMontagne AD (2012). Duration of unemployment and suicide in Australia over the period 1985-2006: An ecological investigation by sex and age during rising versus declining national unemployment rates. *Journal of Epidemiology and Community Health* 67, 237-244.

Minagawa Y (2013). The social consequences of postcommunist structural change: An analysis of suicide trends in Eastern Europe. *Social Forces* 91, 1035-1056.

Minayo MCdS, Cavalcante FG (2012). Anticipating the end: Suicide among the elderly in Brazil. *Ciencia e Saude Coletiva* 17, 1941.

Minelli N, Marchetti D (2013). Discrepancies in death certificates, public health registries, and judicial determinations in Italy. *Journal of Forensic Science.* Published online: 12 March 2013. doi: 10.1111/1556-4029.12114.

Miret M, Ayuso-Mateos JL, Sánchez-Moreno J, Vieta E (2013). Depressive disorders and suicide: Epidemiology, risk factors, and burden. *Neuroscience and Biobehavioral Reviews.* Published online: 11 January 2013. doi: 10.1016/j.neubiorev.2013.01.008.

Mitsui N, Asakura S, Inoue T, Shimizu Y, Fujii Y, Kako Y, Tanaka T, Kitagawa N, Kusumi I (2012). Temperament and character profiles of Japanese university student suicide completers. *Comprehensive Psychiatry.* Published online: 12 December 2012. doi: 10.1016/j.comppsych.2012.11.002

Mohammadi R, Sadeghi-Bazargani H, Fardiazar Z (2012). Victims of domestic injuries and suicide among women of reproductive age in Iran. *Injury Prevention* 18, A85-A86.

Mohanty S, Sen M, Sahu G (2012). Analysis of risk factors of dowry death - A South Indian study. *Journal of Forensic and Legal Medicine.* Published online: 15 November 2012. doi: 10.1016/j.jflm.2012.09.027.

Murphy O, Kelleher C, Malone K (2012). Trends in youth suicide in Ireland and the UK from 1980-2010. *Irish Journal of Medical Science* 181, S451-S452.

Nakash O, Liphshitz I, Keinan-Boker L, Levav I (2013). The effect of cancer on suicide among elderly Holocaust survivors. *Suicide and Life-Threatening Behavior.* Published online: 5 February 2013. doi: 10.1111/sltb.12015.

Nakimuli-Mpungu E (2013). Suicide: Global perspectives from the who world mental health surveys. *American Journal of Psychiatry* 170, 126-127.

Nazarzadeh M, Bidel Z, Ayubi E, Khirollah A, Carson KV, Sayehmiri K (2013). Determination of the social related factors of suicide in Iran: A systematic review and meta-analysis. *BMC Public Health* 13, 4.

Nickels KC, Grossardt BR, Wirrell EC (2012). Epilepsy-related mortality is low in children: A 30-year population-based study in Olmsted county, MN. *Epilepsia* 53, 2164-2171.

Njei B, Lim JK (2013). Suicide among U.S. Adults with hepatocellular carcinoma. *Gastrointestinal Cancer Research* 6, 31-32.

Nordentoft M, Wahlbeck K, Hallgren J, Westman J, Osby U, Alinaghizadeh H, Gissler M, Laursen TM (2013). Excess mortality, causes of death and life expectancy in 270,770 patients with recent onset of mental disorders in Denmark, Finland and Sweden. *PLoS ONE* 8, e55176.

Nordstrom DL, Yokoi-Shelton ML, Zosel A (2012). Using multiple cause-of-death data to improve surveillance of drug-related mortality. *Journal of Public Health Management and Practice.* Published online: 21 December 2012. doi: 10.1097/PHH.0b013e318271c622.

Norouzi K, Taghinejad H, Mohammadi F, Mohammadi E, Suhrabi Z (2012). What is missed in self-immolated patients' care?: A grounded theory study. *Journal of Clinical Nursing* 21, 3418.

Nuchhi UC, Gannur DG, Yoganarasimha K (2012). Evaluation of dowry related crimes in Bijapur City. *Indian Journal of Forensic Medicine and Toxicology* 6, 209-213.

O'Riley A, Van Orden KA, He H, Podgorski C, Conwell Y (2012). Suicide and death ideation in older adults obtaining aging services. *Gerontologist* 52, 246.

Olin B, Jayewardene AK, Bunker M, Moreno F (2012). Mortality and suicide risk in treatment-resistant depression: An observational study of the long-term impact of intervention. *PLoS ONE.* Published online: 25 October 2012. doi: 10.1371/journal.pone.0048002.

Oliver LN, Peters PA, Kohen DE (2012). Mortality rates among children and teenagers living in Inuit Nunangat, 1994 to 2008. *Health Reports* 23, 1-6.

Ortega FB, Silventoinen K, Tynelius P, Rasmussen F (2012). Muscular strength in male adolescents and premature death: Cohort study of one million participants. *British Medical Journal* 345, E7279.

Palimar Prof V, Vidhi, Gupta C (2012). Fatal deliberate self-harm in adolescents- A Manipal perspective. *Research Journal of Pharmaceutical, Biological and Chemical Sciences* 3, 401-406.

Panczak R, Spoerri A, Zwahlen M, Bopp M, Gutzwiller F, Egger M (2013). Religion and suicide in patients with mental illness or cancer. *Suicide and Life-Threatening Behavior.* Published online: 18 January 2013. doi: 10.1111/sltb.12009.

Panczak R, Zwahlen M, Spoerri A, Tal K, Killias M, Egger M (2013). Incidence and risk factors of homicide-suicide in Swiss households: National cohort study. *PLoS ONE* 8, e53714-e53714.

Park BCB, Lester D (2012). Rural and urban suicide in South Korea. *Psychological Reports* 111, 495-497.

Park S, Choi JW, Kyoung Yi K, Hong JP (2012). Suicide mortality and risk factors in the 12 months after discharge from psychiatric inpatient care in Korea: 1989-2006. *Psychiatry Research*. Published online: 8 October 2012. doi: 10.1016/j.psychres.2012.09.039.

Parry J (2012). Erratum to suicide in a Central Indian steel town. *Contributions to Indian Sociology* 46, 439.

Peiris-John R, Wainiqolo I, Kafoa B, McCaig E, Ameratunga S (2012). Population based characteristics of fatalities and hospital admissions for acute poisoning in Fiji. *Injury Prevention* 18, A87-A88.

Petaros A, Slaus M, Coklo M, Sosa I, Cengija M, Bosnar A (2013). Retrospective analysis of free-fall fractures with regard to height and cause of fall. *Forensic Science International* 226, 290-295.

Peterhansel C, Petroff D, Klinitzke G, Kersting A, Wagner B (2013). Risk of completed suicide after bariatric surgery: A systematic review. *Obesity Reviews*. Published online: 9 January 2013. doi: 10.1111/obr.12014.

Phillips JA (2012). Factors associated with temporal and spatial patterns in suicide rates across U.S. States, 1976-2000. *Demography* 50, 591-614.

Pompili M, Vichi M, Qin P, Innamorati M, De Leo D, Girardi P (2012). Does the level of education influence completed suicide? A nationwide register study. *Journal of Affective Disorders* 147, 437-440.

Ponte de Souza ML, Yamall Orellana JD (2012). Suicide among the Indigenous people in Brazil: A hidden public health issue. *Revista Brasileira De Psiquiatria* 34, 489-490.

Pritchett L, Viarengo M (2013). Why demographic suicide? The puzzles of European fertility. *Population and Development Review* 38, 55-71.

Rajendra KR, Srinivasa RP, Rudramurthy S (2012). A retrospective study of suicidal deaths at district hospital, Tumkur. *Medico-Legal Update* 12, 197-199.

Reeves A, Stuckler D, McKee M, Gunnell D, Chang S-S, Basu S (2012). Increase in state suicide rates in the USA during economic recession. *Lancet* 380, 1813-1814.

Remes H, Martikainen P (2012). Social determinants of mortality after leaving the parental home-childhood and current factors. *Advances in Life Course Research* 17, 199-209.

Rezaeian M (2013). Epidemiology of self-immolation. *Burns* 39, 184-186.

Sahoo S (2012). Suicides versus attempted suicides: What is the truth in the numbers? *Indian Journal of Community Medicine* 37, 202-203.

Salmerón D, Cirera L, Ballesta M, Navarro-Mateu F (2013). Time trends and geographical variations in mortality due to suicide and causes of undetermined intent in Spain, 1991-2008. *Journal of Public Health*. Published online: 4 January 2013. doi: 10.1093/pubmed/fds103.

Samanta Prof AK, Nayak SR (2012). Newer trends in hanging death. *Journal of Indian Academy of Forensic Medicine* 34, 37-39.

Satish NT, Harish S, Girish Chandra YP (2012). Study of pattern of injuries in fatal railway accidents. *Indian Journal of Forensic Medicine and Toxicology* 6, 257-261.

Sawalha AF (2012). Deliberate self-poisoning: A study from Nablus. *International Journal of Adolescent Medicine and Health* 24, 373-377.

Sayied NE, Mohamed HS, Thabet RAEA (2012). Feeling of depression and loneliness among elderly people attending geriatric clubs at Assiut city. *Life Science Journal* 9, 140-145.

Selek S (2013). Altitude, immigration and suicide rates: A study from Turkey. *Psychiatry Investigation* 10, 89-91.

Sonawane SS, Nanandkar SD (2012). Medico legal autopsies of custodial deaths in Mumbai region - A two years prospective study. *Indian Journal of Forensic Medicine and Toxicology* 6, 159-162.

Srinivas J, Chand Basha V, Sudhakar Reddy K (2012). A comprehensive medico-legal analysis of paediatric deaths at Osmania general hospital Hyderabad. *Indian Journal of Forensic Medicine and Toxicology* 6, 40-43.

Straif-Bourgeois S, Ratard R (2012). Suicide mortality rates in Louisiana, 1999-2010. *Journal of the Louisiana State Medical Society* 164, 274-276.

Talaie H, Owliaey H, Pajoumand A, Gholaminejad M, Mehrpour O (2012). Temperature changes among organophosphate poisoned patients, Tehran- Iran. *DARU* 20, 52.

Tennakoon DASS, Karunarathna Wdv, Udugampala Uss (2012). Carbofuran concentrations in blood, bile and tissues in fatal cases of homicide and suicide. *Forensic Science International.* Published online: 20 November 2012. doi: 10.1016/j.forsciint.2012.10.039.

Tichelli A, Labopin M, Rovó A, Badoglio M, Arat M, van Lint MT, Lawitschka A, Schwarze CP, Passweg J, Socié G (2013). Increase of suicide and accidental death after hematopoietic stem cell transplantation: A cohort study on behalf of the late effects working party of the European group for blood and marrow transplantation (EBMT). *Cancer.* Published online: 19 March 2013. doi: 10.1002/cncr.27987.

Titelman D, Oskarsson H, Wahlbeck K, Nordentoft M, Mehlum L, Jiang GX, Erlangsen A, Nrugham L, Wasserman D (2013). Suicide mortality trends in the Nordic countries 1980-2009. *Nordic Journal of Psychiatry.* Published online: 7 January 2013. doi: 10.3109/08039488.2012.752036.

Tozija F, Gjorgjev D, Kochubovski M (2012). Violence and maltreatment of elderly-Applied ecological model in risk assessment and policy intervention. *Journal of Environmental Protection and Ecology* 13, 2173-2185.

Tran TNL, Nguyen TTH, Luong MA, Do TD, Khieu TQT (2012). Suicide-related mortality in Vietnam in 2005-2010. *Injury Prevention* 18, A33.

Tripodi SJ, Pettus-Davis C (2012). Histories of childhood victimization and subsequent mental health problems, substance use, and sexual victimization for a sample of incarcerated women in the U.S. *International Journal of Law and Psychiatry* 36, 30-40.

Turner JC, Leno EV, Keller A (2013). Causes of mortality among American college students: A pilot study. *Journal of College Student Psychotherapy* 27, 31-42.

Ubeda C, Galante M, Perinetti A, Peltzer R (2012). What do we understand by undetermined intention deaths? Injuries patterns' intentionality identification. *Injury Prevention* 18, A242.

van Houwelingen C, Baumert J, Kerkhof A, Beersma D, Ladwig K-H (2013). Train suicide mortality and availability of trains: A tale of two countries. *Psychiatry Research.* Published online: 1 February 2013. doi: 10.1016/j.psychres.2012.12.026.

Varakina Z, Zhl V, Vyazmin AM, Sannikov AL, Grjibovski AM (2012). Epidemiology of child poisonings by chemical substances with suicidal purpose in Arkhangelsk, Russia. *European Journal of Public Health* 22, 219.

Varma NM, Kalele SD (2011). Study of profile of deaths due to poisoning in Bhavnagar region. *Journal of Indian Academy of Forensic Medicine* 33, 313-318

Wainiqolo I, Kafoa B, Kool B, Herman J, McCaig E, Ameratunga S (2012). A profile of injury in Fiji: Findings from a population-based injury surveillance system (TRIP-10). *BMC Public Health* 12, 1074.

Wakasugi M, Kazama JJ, Yamamoto S, Kawamura K, Narita I (2012). Cause-specific excess mortality among dialysis patients: Comparison with the general population in Japan. *Therapeutic Apheresis and Dialysis.* Published online: 11 December 2012. doi: 10.1111/j.1744-9987.2012.01144.x.

Wang M, Ching C-K (2012). Pattern of coroner's autopsies at health sciences authority, Singapore: A retrospective study (2009-2010). *Medicine, Science, and the Law*. Published online: 5 October 2012. doi: 10.1258/msl.2012.012058.

Weber R, Ruppik M, Rickenbach M, Spoerri A, Furrer H, Battegay M, Cavassini M, Calmy A, Bernasconi E, Schmid P, Flepp M, Kowalska J, Ledergerber B (2012). Decreasing mortality and changing patterns of causes of death in the Swiss HIV cohort study. *HIV Medicine* 14, 195-207.

Wiktorsson S, Akerblom O, Marlow T, Skoog I, Waern M (2012). Factors associated with suicide attempt in persons aged 80 and above: A comparison study. *Gerontologist* 52, 499.

Yang AC, Tsai S-J, Yang C-H, Shia B-C, Fuh J-L, Wang S-J, Peng C-K, Huang NE (2013). Suicide and media reporting: A longitudinal and spatial analysis. *Social Psychiatry and Psychiatric Epidemiology* 48, 427-435.

Yang S, Khang YH, Chun H, Harper S, Lynch J (2012). The changing gender differences in life expectancy in Korea 1970-2005. *Social Science and Medicine* 75, 1280-1287.

Yozwiak JA, Lentzsch-Parcells CM, Zapolski TCB (2012). Suicide and suicidal ideation among college students. *International Journal on Disability and Human Development* 11, 185-189.

Zamani G, Mehdizadeh M, Sadeghi P (2012). Attempt to suicide in young ages with epilepsy. *Iranian Journal of Pediatrics* 22, 404-407.

Risk and protective factors

Abdirahman HA, Bah TT, Shrestha HL, Jacobsen KH (2012). Bullying, mental health, and parental involvement among adolescents in the Caribbean. *West Indian Medical Journal* 61, 504-508.

Ali S, Nathani M, Jabeen S, Yazdani I, Mouton CD, Bailey RK, Mahr M, Pate RJ, Riley WJ (2013). Alcohol: The lubricant to suicidality. *Innovations in Clinical Neuroscience* 10, 20-29.

Allen B, Cramer RJ, Harris PB, Rufino KA (2013). Borderline personality symptomatology as a mediator of the link between child maltreatment and adult suicide potential. *Archives of Suicide Research* 17, 41-51.

Anonymous (2012). Varenicline and bupropion: Suicide. *Prescrire International* 21, 240.

Anonymous. (2012). Accelerating suicide rate linked to economic downturn in the U.S. *British Medical Journal* 345, e7638.

Badkur DS, Yadav Prof J, Arora A, Bajpayee Prof R, Dubey BP (2012). Nomenclature for knot position in hanging a study of 200 cases. *Journal of Indian Academy of Forensic Medicine* 34, 34-36.

Balhara YP, Verma R (2012). Schizophrenia and suicide. *East Asian Archives of Psychiatry* 22, 126-133.

Barbería E, Xifró A, Martin-Fumadó C, Suelves JM (2013). Suicides and violent forensic sources. *Suicidios Violentos y Fuentes Forenses* 25, 78.

Bartleman J (2012). Youth despair and suicide in Northern Ontario. *Paediatrics and Child Health* 17, 371-372.

Beland SG, Greenfield B, Lynd L, Brabant MJ, Tournier M, Abou Chakra CN, Moride Y (2012). Development and validation of an algorithm based on administrative claims data for the surveillance of suicide attempts in youth. *Drug Safety* 35, 896.

Ben Park BC, Lester D (2012). Rural and urban suicide in South Korea. *Psychological Reports* 111, 495-497.

Bjørngaard JH, Bjerkeset O, Vatten L, Janszky I, Gunnell D, Romundstad P (2013). Maternal age at child birth, birth order, and suicide at a young age: A sibling comparison. *American Journal of Epidemiology*. Published online: 10 March 2013. doi: 10.1093/aje/kwt014.

Black DW, Shaw MC, McCormick BA, Allen J (2012). Marital status, childhood maltreatment, and family dysfunction: A controlled study of pathological gambling. *The Journal of Clinical Psychiatry* 73, 1293-1297.

Bland P (2012). Suicides rise during economic recession. *Practitioner* 256, 12.

Blüml V, Regier MD, Hlavin G, Rockett IRH, König F, Vyssoki B, Bschor T, Kapusta ND (2013). Lithium in the public water supply and suicide mortality in Texas. *Journal of Psychiatric Research* 47, 407-411.

Borders A, McAndrew LM, Quigley KS, Chandler HK (2012). Rumination moderates the associations between PTSD and depressive symptoms and risky behaviors in U.S. Veterans. *Journal of Trauma and Stress* 25, 583-586.

Boyd MA, Bradshaw W, Robinson M (2013). Mental health issues of women deployed to Iraq and Afghanistan. *Archives of Psychiatric Nursing* 27, 10.

Bryan CJ, Hernandez AM, Allison S, Clemans T (2012). Combat exposure and suicide risk in two samples of military personnel. *Journal of Clinical Psychology* 69, 64-77.

Buoli M, Caldiroli A, Altamura AC (2013). Psychotic versus non-psychotic major depressive disorder: A comparative naturalistic study. *Asian Journal of Psychiatry*. Published online: 14 March 2013. doi: 10.1016/j.ajp.2013.02.003.

Burrows S, Perron S (2012). Policy analysis and evaluation of effectiveness of a suicide prevention initiative in Montreal. *Injury Prevention* 18, A165.

Cal SF, Santiago MB (2013). Resilience in systemic lupus erythematosus. *Psychology, Health and Medicine.* Published online: 28 January 2013. doi: 10.1080/13548506.2013.764457.

Calhoun L (2011). The silencing of soldiers. *Independent Review* 16, 247-270.

Carlsson S, Sandin F, Fall K, Lambe M, Adolfsson J, Stattin P, Bill-Axelson A (2013). Risk of suicide in men with low-risk prostate cancer. *European Journal of Cancer.* Published online: 18 January 2013. doi: 10.1016/j.ejca.2012.12.018.

Carroll BJ (2013). Suicide risk and efficacy of antidepressant drugs. *JAMA Psychiatry* 70, 123-125.

Chambers SK, Smith DP, Berry M, Lepore SJ, Foley E, Clutton S, McDowall R, Occhipinti S, Frydenberg M, Gardiner RA (2013). A randomised controlled trial of a mindfulness intervention for men with advanced prostate cancer. *BMC Cancer* 13, 89.

Chang EC, Yu EA, Lee JY, Hirsch JK, Kupfermann Y, Kahle ER (2012). An examination of optimism/pessimism and suicide risk in primary care patients: Does belief in a changeable future make a difference? *Cognitive Therapy and Research.* Published online: 16 December 2012. doi: 10.1007/s10608-012-9505-0.

Chen CC, Kuo CC, Wu TN, Yang CY (2012). Death of a son is associated with risk of suicide among parous women in Taiwan: A nested case-control study. *Journal of Epidemiology* 22, 532-536.

Chen YY, Yip PS, Tsai CW, Fan HF (2012). Media representation of gender patterns of suicide in Taiwan. *Crisis* 33, 144-150.

Cheng AW, Lee CS, Iwamoto DK (2012). Heavy drinking, poor mental health, and substance use among Asian Americans in the NLAAS: A gender-based comparison. *Asian American Journal of Psychology* 3, 160-167.

Cheung YTD, Spittal MJ, Williamson MK, Tung SJ, Pirkis J (2013). Application of scan statistics to detect suicide clusters in Australia. *PLoS ONE* 8, e54168.

Chistiakov DA, Kekelidze ZI, Chekhonin VP (2012). Endophenotypes as a measure of suicidality. *Journal of Applied Genetics* 53, 389-413.

Chowdhury A, Islam I, Lee D (2013). The great recession, jobs and social crises: Policies matter. *International Journal of Social Economics* 40, 220-245.

Çinar N, ah S, Batum K, Kar ida S (2012). Interictal psychiatric disorders in epilepsy. *Ep leps de nter ktal Ps k yatr k Bozukluklar* 6, 256-260.

Clayden Rc, Zaruk A, Meyre D, Thabane L, Samaan Z (2012). The association of attempted suicide with genetic variants in the slc6a4 and tph genes depends on the definition of suicidal behavior: A systematic review and meta-analysis. *Translational Psychiatry.* Published online: 2 October 2012. doi: 10.1038/tp.2012.96.

Congdon P (2012). Assessing the impact of socioeconomic variables on small area variations in suicide outcomes in England. *International Journal of Environmental Research and Public Health* 10, 158-177.

Conner KR, Bohnert AS, McCarthy JF, Valenstein M, Bossarte R, Ignacio R, Lu N, Ilgen MA (2012). Mental disorder comorbidity and suicide among 2.96 million men receiving care in the veterans health administration health system. *Journal of Abnormal Psychology* 122, 256-263.

Conner KR, McCarthy MD, Bajorska A, Caine ED, Tu XM, Knox KL (2012). Mood, anxiety, and substance-use disorders and suicide risk in a military population cohort. *Suicide and Life-Threatening Behavior* 42, 699-708.

Corbett R, Mazin N, Grimshaw R, Bebbington P (2012). Thinking of suicide: Understanding the risks associated with child institutional care. *Criminal Justice Matters* 90, 38-40.

Costanza A, D'Orta I, Perroud N, Burkhardt S, Malafosse A, Mangin P, La Harpe R (2013). Neurobiology of suicide: Do biomarkers exist? *International Journal of Legal Medicine.* Published online: 22 February 2013. doi: 10.1007/s00414-013-0835-6.

Cutcliffe J, Links P, Harder H, Bergmans Y, Balderson K, Eynan R, Ambreen M, Neibaum R (2012). Understanding the risks of recent discharge: The phenomenological experiences trying to survive while living under the proverbial "sword of damocles". *Crisis* 33, 265-272.

Cybulska B (2012). Immediate medical care after sexual assault. *Bailliere's Best Practice and Research in Clinical Obstetrics and Gynaecology* 27, 141-149.

D'Argenio A, Catania G, Marchetti M (2013). Murder followed by suicide: Filicide-suicide mothers in Italy from 1992 to 2010. *Journal of Forensic Sciences.* Published online: 14 January 2013. doi: 10.1111/1556-4029.12057.

de Portugal E, González N, Del Amo V, Haro JM, Díaz-Caneja CM, de Dios Luna del Castillo J, Cervilla JA (2012). Empirical redefinition of delusional disorder and its phenomenology: The Deliremp study. *Comprehensive Psychiatry* 54, 243-255.

de Souza Minayo MC, Cavalcante FG (2012). Anticipating the end: Suicide among the elderly in Brazil. *Ciencia & Saude Coletiva* 17, 1941.

De Vogli R, Marmot M, Stuckler D (2013). Strong evidence that the economic crisis caused a rise in suicides in Europe: The need for social protection. *Journal of Epidemiology and Community Health* 67, 378-379.

Deb AK (1946). Suicide and homicide in relation to sexual difficulties. *Indian Medical Record* 66, 134.

Dennington L (2012). Comprehensive guide to suicidal behaviours: Working with individuals at risk and their families. *Journal of Mental Health* 21, 614-616.

Dhakad U, Singh BP (2012). Re: Hepner et al.: Suicidal ideation among patients with bladder pain syndrome/interstitial cystitis. *Urology* 80, 957.

Dietz LJ, Stoyak S, Melhem N, Porta G, Matthews KA, Walker Payne M, Brent DA (2012). Cortisol response to social stress in parentally bereaved youth. *Biological Psychiatry* 73, 379-387.

Dome P, Gonda X, Rihmer Z (2012). Effects of smoking on health outcomes in bipolar disorder with a special focus on suicidal behavior. *Neuropsychiatry* 2, 429-441.

Draper B, Altendorf A, De Leo D, Snowdon J, Kõlves K (2012). Personality traits, suicide and psychiatric disorder: A controlled psychological autopsy study. *Gerontologist* 52, 499.

Du DT, Zhou EH, Goldsmith J, Nardinelli C, Hammad TA (2012). Atomoxetine use during a period of FDA actions. *Medical Care* 50, 987-992.

Duric V, Banasr M, Stockmeier CA, Simen AA, Newton SS, Overholser JC, Jurjus GJ, Dieter L, Duman RS (2013). Altered expression of synapse and glutamate related genes in post-mortem hippocampus of depressed subjects. *International Journal of Neuropsychopharmacology* 16, 69-82.

Edelstein A (2012). Intimate partner homicide and suicide among Ethiopian men in Israel. *Israel Journal of Psychiatry and Related Sciences* 49, 21.

Erhardt S, Lim CK, Linderholm KR, Janelidze S, Lindqvist D, Samuelsson M, Lundberg K, Postolache TT, Träskman-Bendz L, Guillemin GJ, Brundin L (2012). Connecting inflammation with glutamate agonism in suicidality. *Neuropsychopharmacology* 38, 743–752.

Fazel S, Wolf A, Geddes JR (2013). Suicide in prisoners with bipolar disorder and other psychiatric disorders: A systematic review. *Bipolar Disorders.* Published online: 26 February 2013. doi: 10.1111/bdi.12053.

Fountoulakis KN, Kontis D, Gonda X, Siamouli M, Yatham LN (2012). Treatment of mixed bipolar states. *International Journal of Neuropsychopharmacology* 15, 1015-1026.

Fountoulakis KN, Savopoulos C, Siamouli M, Zaggelidou E, Mageiria S, Iacovides A, Hatzitolios AI (2012). Trends in suicidality amid the economic crisis in Greece. *European Archives of Psychiatry and Clinical Neuroscience*. Published online: 26 December 2012. doi: 10.1007/s00406-012-0385-9.

Gandy M, Sharpe L, Perry KN, Miller L, Thayer Z, Boserio J, Mohamed A (2012). The psychosocial correlates of depressive disorders and suicide risk in people with epilepsy. *Journal of Psychosomatic Research* 74, 227-232.

Gandy M, Sharpe L, Perry KN, Miller L, Thayer Z, Boserio J, Mohamed A (2012). Rates of DSM-IV mood, anxiety disorders, and suicidality in Australian adult epilepsy outpatients: A comparison of well-controlled versus refractory epilepsy. *Epilepsy and Behavior* 26, 29-35.

Gibbons RD, Brown CH, Hur K, Davis JM, Mann JJ (2013). Suicide risk and efficacy of antidepressant drugs-reply. *JAMA Psychiatry* 70, 123-125.

Gibson SA, Korade Z, Shelton RC (2012). Oxidative stress and glutathione response in tissue cultures from persons with major depression. *Journal of Psychiatric Research* 46, 1326-1332.

Gold KJ, Sen A, Schwenk TL (2012). Details on suicide among U.S. physicians: Data from the National Violent Death Reporting System. *General Hospital Psychiatry* 35, 45-49.

Goldstein BI, Birmaher B (2012). Prevalence, clinical presentation and differential diagnosis of pediatric bipolar disorder. *Israel Journal of Psychiatry and Related Sciences* 49, 3-14.

Gotsens M, Marí-Dell'Olmo M, Pérez K, Palència L, Borrell C (2012). Trends in socio-economic inequalities in injury mortality among men in small areas of 26 Spanish cities, 1996-2007. *Accident Analysis and Prevention* 51, 120-128.

Gradus JL, Shipherd JC, Suvak MK, Giasson HL, Miller M (2012). Suicide attempts and suicide among Marines: A decade of follow-up. *Suicide and Life-Threatening Behavior* 43, 39-49.

Gregg JJ, Fiske A (2012). Hopelessness and suicidal behavior in later life: A critical review. *Gerontologist* 52, 245.

Gunn Iii JF, Lester D (2012). Using Google searches on the internet to monitor suicidal behavior. *Journal of Affective Disorders*. Published online: 22 November 2012. doi: 10.1016/j.jad.2012.11.004.

Gunn KM, Kettler LJ, Skaczkowski GL, Turnbull DA (2012). Farmers' stress and coping in a time of drought. *Rural and Remote Health* 12, 2071.

Hamazaki K, Hamazaki T, Inadera H (2012). Fatty acid composition in the postmortem amygdala of patients with schizophrenia, bipolar disorder, and major depressive disorder. *Journal of Psychiatric Research* 46, 1024-1028.

Hames JL, Hagan CR, Joiner TE (2013). Interpersonal processes in depression. *Annual Review of Clinical Psychology*. Published online: 3 January 2013. doi: 10.1146/annurev-clinpsy-050212-185553.

Hammarberg K, Kirkman M (2012). Infertility in resource-constrained settings: Moving towards amelioration. *Reproductive BioMedicine Online* 26, 189-195.

Haw C, Hawton K, Niedzwiedz C, Platt S (2012). Suicide clusters: A review of risk factors and mechanisms. *Suicide and Life-Threatening Behavior*. Published online: 5 November 2012. doi: 10.1111/j.1943-278x.2012.00130.x.

Hawton K, Casañas i Comabella C, Haw C, Saunders K (2013). Risk factors for suicide in individuals with depression: A systematic review. *Journal of Affective Disorders* 147, 17-28.

Henna E, Hatch JP, Nicoletti M, Swann AC, Zunta-Soares G, Soares JC (2013). Is impulsivity a common trait in bipolar and unipolar disorders? *Bipolar Disorders* 15, 223-227.

Herea S-G, Scripcaru C (2012). Statistical analysis of suicide characteristics in Iasi County. *Revista Medico-Chirurgical a Societ ii de Medici i Naturali ti din Ia i* 116, 674-680.

Hochberg MS, Berman RS, Kalet AL, Zabar SR, Gillespie C, Pachter HL (2012). The stress of residency: Recognizing the signs of depression and suicide in you and your fellow residents. *American Journal of Surgery* 205, 141-146.

Hooman S, Zahra H, Safa M, Hassan FM, Reza MM (2013). Association between cigarette smoking and suicide in psychiatric inpatients. *Tobacco Induced Diseases* 11, 5.

Hooven C, Snedker KA, Thompson EA (2012). Suicide risk at young adulthood: Continuities and discontinuities from adolescence. *Youth & Society* 44, 524-547.

Huang CLC, Chung-Wei L (2012). Factors associated with mortality among heroin users after seeking treatment with methadone: A population-based cohort study in Taiwan. *Journal of Substance Abuse Treatment* 44, 295-300.

Huang HT, Wan KS (2012). Heart rate variability in junior high school students with depression and anxiety in Taiwan. *Acta Neuropsychiatrica.* Published online: 26 September 2012. doi: 10.1111/acn.12010.

Hubbeling D (2012). Transfer of suicide risk versus looking at suicides outside hospital in general. *Psychological Medicine* 42, 2685.

Humber N, Webb R, Piper M, Appleby L, Shaw J (2012). A national case-control study of risk factors among prisoners in England and Wales. *Social Psychiatry and Psychiatric Epidemiology.* Published online: 12 December 2012. doi: 10.1007/s00127-012-0632-4.

Humpston CS, Wood CM, Robinson ES (2012). Investigating the roles of different monoamine transmitters and impulse control using the 5-choice serial reaction time task. *Journal of Psychopharmacology* 27, 213-221.

Hunter E (2012). Indicators of psychoses or psychoses as indicators: The relationship between Indigenous social disadvantage and serious mental illness. *Australas Psychiatry* 21, 22-26.

Iessa N, Star K, Murray ML, Wilton L, Curran S, Edwards R, Aronson JK, Besag F, Santosh P, Wong ICK (2012). An evaluation of the evidence of an association between montelukast and suicide: A publicity exacerbated signal? *Drug Safety* 35, 901.

Iliceto P, Pompili M, Candilera G, Borges G, Lamis DA, Serafini G, Girardi P (2012). Suicide risk and psychopathology in immigrants: A multi-group confirmatory factor analysis. *Social Psychiatry and Psychiatric Epidemiology.* Published online: 25 October 2012. doi: 10.1007/s00127-012-0608-4.

Innos J, Leidmaa E, Philips M-A, Suett S, Alttoa A, Harro J, Koks S, Vasar E (2013). Lsamp(-/-) mice display lower sensitivity to amphetamine and have elevated 5-ht turnover. *Biochemical and Biophysical Research Communications* 430, 413-418.

Inoue K, Nishimura Y, Fujita Y, Ono Y, Fukunaga T (2012). The relationship between suicide and five climate issues in a large-scale and long term study in Japan. *West Indian Medical Journal* 61, 532-537

Ireland CRR, Kress AM, Frost LZ (2012). Association between mental health conditions diagnosed during initial eligibility for military health care benefits and subsequent deployment, attrition, and death by suicide among active duty service members. *Military Medicine* 177, 1149-1156.

Ishii N, Terao T, Araki Y, Kohno K, Mizokami Y, Arasaki M, Iwata N (2012). Risk factors for suicide in Japan: A model of predicting suicide in 2008 by risk factors of 2007. *Journal of Affective Disorders* 147, 352-354.

Jonsson U, Alexanderson K, Kjeldgard L, Westerlund H, Mittendorfer-Rutz E (2012). Diagnosis-specific disability pension predicts suicidal behaviour and mortality in young adults: A nationwide cohort study. *European Journal of Public Health* 22, 118-119.

Keyes KM, Cerda M (2013). Racial/ethnic differences in alcohol-related suicide: A call for focus on unraveling paradoxes and understanding structural forces that shape alcohol-related health. *Alcoholism: Clinical and Experimental Research*. Published online: 26 February 2013. doi: 10.1111/acer.12083.

Khatiwada S, Tripathi M, Pokharel K, Acharya R, Subedi A (2012). Ambiguous phorote granules for sesame seeds linked to accidental organophosphate fatal poisoning. *Journal of the Nepal Medical Association* 52, 49-51.

Khudair I, Jassim Z, Hanssens Y, Alsaad W (2013). Characteristics and determinants of adult patients with acute poisoning attending the accident and emergency department of a teaching hospital in Qatar. *Human and Experimental Toxicology* . Published online: 8 March 2013. doi: 10.1177/0960327113479043.

Kim HM, Smith EG, Ganoczy D, Walters H, Stano CM, Ilgen MA, Bohnert ASB, Valenstein M (2012). Predictors of suicide in patient charts among patients with depression in the veterans health administration health system: Importance of prescription drug and alcohol abuse. *Journal of Clinical Psychiatry* 73, e1269-e1275.

Kiropoulos LA, Meredith I, Tonkin A, Clarke D, Antonis P, Plunkett J (2012). Psychometric properties of the cardiac depression scale in patients with coronary heart disease. *BMC Psychiatry* 12, 216.

Kizza D, Knizek BL, Kinyanda E, Hjelmeland H (2012). Men in despair: A qualitative psychological autopsy study of suicide in northern Uganda. *Transcultural Psychiatry* 49, 696-717.

Klein AR (2012). Lethality assessments and the law enforcement response to domestic violence. *Journal of Police Crisis Negotiations* 12, 87-102.

Kondilis E, Ierodiakonou I, Gavana M, Giannakopoulos S, Benos A (2013). Suicide mortality and economic crisis in Greece: Men's achilles' heel. *Journal of Epidemiology and Community Health* . Published online: 13 March 2013. doi: 10.1136/jech-2013-202499.

Kralovec K, Fartacek C, Fartacek R, Ploderl M (2012). Religion and suicide risk in lesbian, gay and bisexual Austrians. *Journal of Religious Health*. Published online: 9 October 2012. doi: 10.1007/s10943-012-9645-2.

Kuipers P, Appleton J, Pridmore S (2012). Thematic analysis of key factors associated with Indigenous and non-Indigenous suicide in the Northern Territory, Australia. *Rural and Remote Health* 12, 2235.

Kyaga S, Landen M, Boman M, Hultman CM, Langstrom N, Lichtenstein P (2013). Mental illness, suicide and creativity: 40-year prospective total population study. *Journal of Psychiatric Research* 47, 83-90.

Kyle J (2013). Spirituality: Its role as a mediating protective factor in youth at risk for suicide. *Journal of Spirituality in Mental Health* 15, 47-67.

Labonte B, Suderman M, Maussion G, Lopez JP, Navarro-Sanchez L, Yerko V, Mechawar N, Szyf M, Meaney MJ, Turecki G (2013). Genome-wide methylation changes in the brains of suicide completers. *American Journal of Psychiatry*. Published online: 20 March 2013. doi: 10.1176/appi.ajp.2012.12050627.

Laukkanen E, Rissanen M-L, Tolmunen T, Kylma J, Hintikka J (2013). Adolescent self-cutting elsewhere than on the arms reveals more serious psychiatric symptoms. *European Child and Adolescent Psychiatry*. Published online: 20 February 2013. doi: 10.1007/s00787-013-0390-1.

Lawford BR, Morris CP, Swagell CD, Hughes IP, Young RM, Voisey J (2012). Nos1ap is associated with increased severity of PTSD and depression in untreated combat veterans. *Journal of Affective Disorders* 147, 87-93.

Lester D (2012). Toxoplasma gondii and homicide. *Psychological Reports* 111, 196-197.

Lester D, White J (2012). Which serial killers commit suicide? An exploratory study. *Forensic Science International* 223, e56-e59.

Li Z, Zhang J (2012). Coping skills, mental disorders, and suicide among rural youths in China. *Journal of Nervous and Mental Disease* 200, 885-890.

Lindholm Carlström E, Saetre P, Rosengren A, Thygesen JH, Djurovic S, Melle I, Andreassen OA, Werge T, Agartz I, Hall H, Terenius L, Jönsson EG (2012). Association between a genetic variant in the serotonin transporter gene (slc6a4) and suicidal behavior in patients with schizophrenia. *Behavioral and Brain Functions* 8, 24.

Litwiller BJ, Brausch AM (2013). Cyber bullying and physical bullying in adolescent suicide: The role of violent behavior and substance use. *Journal of Youth and Adolescence*. Published online: 5 February 2013. doi: 10.1007/s10964-013-9925-5.

Loberiza FR, Jr., Cannon AJ (2013). Sounding the alarm on deaths from suicide and accidents after hematopoietic stem cell transplantation. *Cancer* . Published online: 19 March 2013. doi: 10.1002/cncr.27982.

Lord VB (2012). Factors influencing subjects' observed level of suicide by cop intent. *Criminal Justice and Behavior* 39, 1633-1646.

Mahram M, Hosseinkhani Z, Nedjat S, Aflatouni A (2013). Epidemiologic evaluation of child abuse and neglect in school-aged children of Qazvin Province, I.R. Iran, 2011. *Iranian Journal of Pediatrics* 23, 159-164.

Mahtani KR, Protheroe J, Slight SP, Demarzo MMP, Blakeman T, Barton CA, Brijnath B, Roberts N (2013). Can the London 2012 olympics 'inspire a generation' to do more physical or sporting activities? An overview of systematic reviews. *BMJ Open*. Published online: 7 January 2013. doi: 10.1136/bmjopen-2012-002058.

Matsubayashi T, Sawada Y, Ueda M (2012). Natural disasters and suicide: Evidence from Japan. *Social Science and Medicine* 82, 126-133.

Matsumoto T, Akazawa M, Katsumata Y, Takeshima T (2012). Association among alcohol use disorder, depression, and suicide. *Alcoholism-Clinical and Experimental Research* 36, 50A.

McCarthy JF, Ilgen MA, Austin K, Blow FC, Katz IR (2013). Associations between body mass index and suicide in the veterans affairs health system. *Obesity*. Published online: 20 March 2013. doi: 10.1002/oby.20422.

McNamara PM (2012). Adolescent suicide in Australia: Rates, risk and resilience. *Clinical Child Psychology and Psychiatry* . Published online: 30 October 2012. doi: 10.1177/ 1359104512455812.

Mihaljevic S, Aukst-Margetic B, Vuksan-Cusa B, Koic E, Milosevic M (2012). Hopelessness, suicidality and religious coping in Croatian war veterans with PTSD. *Psychiatria Danubina* 24, 292-297.

Milham S, Stetzer D (2013). Dirty electricity, chronic stress, neurotransmitters and disease. *Electromagnetic Biology and Medicine*. Published online: 16 January 2013. doi: 10.3109/ 15368378.2012.743909.

Milner A, Page A, Lamontagne AD (2013). Long-term unemployment and suicide: A systematic review and meta-analysis. *PLoS ONE* 8, e51333.

Mitchell JE, Crosby R, de Zwaan M, Engel S, Roerig J, Steffen K, Gordon KH, Karr T, Lavender J, Wonderlich S (2012). Possible risk factors for increased suicide following bariatric surgery. *Obesity*. Published online: 3 October 2012. doi: 10.1002/oby.20066.

Mitka M (2013). Suicides by veterans. *JAMA* 309, 973.

Mittoux A, Tanghoj P, Moore N (2012). Exploring the potential prognostic effect of various country-specific health service data on all-cause mortality using data from a large prospective study in schizophrenia. *Pharmacoepidemiology and Drug Safety*. Published online: 3 December 2012. doi: 10.1002/pds.3372.

Molina RT, Lechuga EN (2003). Risk factors associated with suicide and attempted suicide. *Factores de riesgo asociados al suicidio e intento de suicidio* 17, 19-28.

Monette M (2012). Senior suicide: The tricky task of treatment. *Canadian Medical Association Journal* 184, E887-E888.

Morley K, Haber P, Sitharthan G, Tucker P, Sitharthan R (2012). Clinical predictors of suicidal behaviour among patients with alcohol and/or substance abuse and suicide risk. *Drug and Alcohol Review* 31, 58.

Moustgaard H, Joutsenniemi K, Sihvo S, Martikainen P (2013). Alcohol-related deaths and social factors in depression mortality: A register-based follow-up of depressed in-patients and antidepressant users in Finland. *Journal of Affective Disorders*. Published online: 25 January 2013. doi: 10.1016/j.jad.2012.12.008.

Mugunthan N, Davoren P (2012). Danger of hypoglycemia due to acute tramadol poisoning. *Endocrine Practice* 18, e151-e152.

Muguruza C, Moreno JL, Umali A, Callado LF, Meana JJ, González-Maeso J (2012). Dysregulated 5-ht 2a receptor binding in postmortem frontal cortex of schizophrenic subjects. *European Neuropsychopharmacology*. Published online: 20 November 2012. doi: 10.1016/j.euroneuro.2012.10.006.

Na KS, Oh SJ, Jung HY, Irene Lee S, Kim YK, Han C, Ko YH, Paik JW, Kim SG (2012). Alexithymia and low cooperativeness are associated with suicide attempts in male military personnel with adjustment disorder: A case-control study. *Psychiatry Research* 205, 220-226.

Nair MKC, Russell PSS, Shankar SR, Subramaniam VS, Nazeema S, Mammen P, Chembagam N (2013). Adolescent suicide: Characterizing the need and identifying the predictive factors for preventive consultation or hospitalization in a rural community setting. *International Journal of Adolescent Medicine and Health* 25, 81-86.

Nakamura M, Yasunaga H, Toda A, Sugihara T, Imamura T (2012). The impact of media reports on the 2008 outbreak of hydrogen sulfide suicides in Japan. *International Journal of Psychiatry in Medicine* 44, 133-140.

Neto MLR, Reis AOA, de Almeida JC (2012). Bipolar disorder, suicide and vulnerable children in northeast Brazil. *HealthMED* 6, 3190-3193.

Nevoralova Z, Dvorakova D (2013). Mood changes, depression and suicide risk during isotretinoin treatment: A prospective study. *International Journal of Dermatology* 52, 163-168.

Nogué S, Cino J, Civeira E, Puiguriguer J, Burillo-Putze G, Dueñas A, Soy D, Aguilar R, Corominas N (2012). Digitalis poisoning: The basis for treatment with antidigoxin antibodies. *Tratamiento de la intoxicación digitálica Bases para el uso de los anticuerpos antidigital* 24, 462-475.

Nordentoft M, Wahlbeck K, Gissler M, Westman J, Hallstrom J, Laursen TM (2012). Suicide, high-risk behaviour and excess mortality in early psychosis. *Early Intervention in Psychiatry* 6, 22.

Ozdemir B, Celbis O, Kaya A (2012). Cut throat injuries and honor killings: Review of 15 cases in eastern Turkey. *Journal of Forensic and Legal Medicine*. Published online: 12 October 2012. doi: 10.1016/j.jflm.2012.09.011.

Ozdemir R, Bayrakci B, Teksam O, Yalcin B, Kale G (2012). Thirty-three-year experience on childhood poisoning. *The Turkish Journal of Pediatrics* 54, 251-259.

Paulozzi LJ (2012). Prescription drug overdoses: A review. *Journal of Safety Research* 43, 283-289.

Peonim V, Sujirachato K, Srisont S, Udnoon J (2012). Pathology of HIV seropositive: Forensic autopsy study in a tertiary care hospital, Bangkok, Thailand. *Journal of the Medical Association of Thailand* 95, 1059-1065.

Pfeiffer PN, Kim HM, Ganoczy D, Zivin K, Valenstein M (2013). Treatment-resistant depression and risk of suicide. *Suicide and Life-Threatening Behavior*. Published online: 20 March 2013. doi: 10.1111/sltb.12022.

Picardi A, Lega I, Tarolla E (2013). Suicide risk in skin disorders. *Clinics in Dermatology* 31, 47-56.

Pigeon WR, Cribbet MR (2012). The pathophysiology of insomnia: From models to molecules (and back). *Current Opinion in Pulmonary Medicine* 18, 546-553.

Pisani AR, Wyman PA, Petrova M, Schmeelk-Cone K, Goldston DB, Xia Y, Gould MS (2012). Emotion regulation difficulties, youth-adult relationships, and suicide attempts among high school students in underserved communities. *Journal of Youth and Adolescence*. Published online: 18 December 2012. doi: 10.1007/s10964-012-9884-2.

Pitts-Tucker T (2012). Pressure to keep up macho image might be behind rise in suicides among men. *British Medical Journal* 345, e6356.

Ploderl M, Wagenmakers EJ, Tremblay P, Ramsay R, Kralovec K, Fartacek C, Fartacek R (2013). Suicide risk and sexual orientation: A critical review. *Archives of Sexual Behavior*. Published online: 26 February 2013. doi: 10.1007/s10508-012-0056-y.

Pridmore S, Kuipers P, Appleton J (2013). The 'operationalized predicaments of suicide' (OPS) applied to Northern Territory coroners' reports. *Asian Journal of Psychiatry*. Published online: 17 January 2013. doi: 10.1016/j.ajp.2012.12.003.

Pridmore S, Walter G (2013). Suicide and forced marriage. *Malaysian Journal of Medical Sciences* 20, 48-52.

Raza K, Talwar V, Setia A, Katare OP (2012). Acne: An understanding of the disease and its impact on life. *International Journal of Drug Development and Research* 4, 14-20.

Rezaie L, Schwebel DC (2012). An ecological approach to explain suicide by self-immolation among women in rural Iran. *Neurosciences* 17, 309-313.

Rice Tr, Sher L (2012). Killing in combat and suicide risk. *European Psychiatry*. Published online: 23 November 2012. doi: 10.1016/j.eurpsy.2012.10.001.

Rihmer Z, Dome P, Gonda X (2012). The role of general practitioners in prevention of depression-related suicides. *Neuropsychopharmacologia Hungarica* 14, 245-251.

Rihmer Z, Gonda X (2012). Predisposition for self-destruction? Affective temperaments as a suicide risk factor in patients with mood disorders. *Crisis* 33, 309-312.

Ritchie EC (2012). Suicide and the United States army: Perspectives from the former psychiatry consultant to the army surgeon general. *Cerebrum* 2012, 1.

River J (2012). Suicidal masculinities: Understanding the gendered nature of male suicide. *Australian Nursing Journal* 20, 49.

Robbins MS (2013). The psychiatric comorbidities of cluster headache. *Current Pain and Headache Reports* 17, 1-8.

Roberts SE, Jaremin B, Lloyd K (2012). High-risk occupations for suicide. *Psychological Medicine*. Published online: 26 October 2012. doi: 10.1017/S0033291712002024.

Roma P, Pazzelli F, Pompili M, Lester D, Girardi P, Ferracuti S (2012). Mental illness in homicide-suicide: A review. *The Journal of the American Academy of Psychiatry and the Law* 40, 462-468.

Rosenberg N (2012). Moshe silman's suicide and Werther effect. *Harefuah* 151, 445-446.

Shah A, Zhinchin G, Zarate-Escudero S, Somyaji M (2012). The relationship between the prescription of psychotropic drugs and suicide rates in older people in England and Wales. *International Journal of Social Psychiatry*. Published online: 8 November 2012. doi: 10.1177/0020764012464322.

Shumilov O, Kasatkina EA, Novikova TB, Sutinen ML, Chramov AV (2012). On the relationship between geomagnetic disturbances and suicide in northwest of Russia and Finnish lapland. *European Journal of Public Health* 22, 277.

Sibson J, Porta N, Ogbeide SA (2012). Determining suicide risk in geriatric populations: A review of the current literature. *Gerontologist* 52, 46.

Silventoinen K, Moustgaard H, Peltonen R, Martikainen P (2012). Changing associations between partnership history and risk of accidents, violence and suicides. *Journal of Epidemiology and Community Health*. Published online: 29 September 2012. doi: 10.1136/jech-2012-201311.

Simmons A, Yoder L (2013). Military resilience: A concept analysis. *Nursing Forum* 48, 17-25.

Somasundaram D, Sivayokan S (2013). Rebuilding community resilience in a post-war context: Developing insight and recommendations - A qualitative study in northern Sri Lanka. *International Journal of Mental Health Systems* 7, 3.

Spallek J, Lehnhardt J, Nielsen SS, Razum O, Norredam M (2012). Risk of suicide among immigrants in Europe: A systematic review. *European Journal of Public Health* 22, 100-101.

Sparkes A (2012). Elevated suicide risks, cats and toxoplasmosis. *Veterinary Record* 171, 303.

Stack S, Lester D, Rosenberg JS (2012). Music and suicidality: A quantitative review and extension. *Suicide and Life-Threatening Behavior* 42, 654-671.

Stranieri G, Carabetta C (2012). Depression and suicidality in modern life. *Psychiatria Danubina* 24, S91-S94.

Stratta P, Rossi A (2012). Suicide in the aftermath of the L'aquila (Italy) earthquake. *Crisis* 34, 142-144.

Sugaya N, Yoshida E, Yasuda S, Tochigi M, Takei K, Otani T, Otowa T, Minato T, Umekage T, Konishi Y, Sakano Y, Chen J, Nomura S, Okazaki Y, Kaiya H, Sasaki T, Tanii H (2012). Prevalence of bipolar disorder in panic disorder patients in the Japanese population. *Journal of Affective Disorders* 147, 411-415.

Suhrabi Z, Delpisheh A, Taghinejad H (2012). Tragedy of women's self-immolation in Iran and developing communities: A review. *International Journal of Burns and Trauma* 2, 93-104.

Sun J, Guo X, Zhang J, Jia C, Xu A (2012). Suicide rates in Shandong, China, 1991-2010: Rapid decrease in rural rates and steady increase in male-female ratio. *Journal of Affective Disorders* 146, 361-368.

Suneetha K (2013). The impact of stressful conditions and prevalence of depression and suicides in adolescents. *Indian Journal of Public Health Research and Development* 4, 190-193.

Terranova C, Cardin F, Bruttocao A, Militello C (2012). Analysis of suicide in the elderly in Italy. Risk factors and prevention of suicidal behavior. *Aging Clinical and Experimental Research* 24, 20-23.

Tharp AT, Constans JI, Yin R, Sullivan G, Vasterling JJ, Rouse J, Schreiber MD, King M (2012). Service provision in disaster preparation, response, and recovery for individuals with predisaster mental illness. *American Journal of Disaster Medicine* 7, 171.

Thompson PM, Cruz DA, Olukotun DY, Delgado PL (2012). Serotonin receptor, SERT mRNA and correlations with symptoms in males with alcohol dependence and suicide. *Acta Psychiatrica Scandinavica* 126, 165-174.

Tormey WP, Srinivasan R, Moore T (2012). Biochemical toxicology and suicide in Ireland: A laboratory study. *Irish Journal of Medical Science* 182, 277-281.

Trofimovich L, Reger MA, Luxton DD, Oetjen-Gerdes LA (2013). Suicide risk by military occupation in the DoD active component population. *Suicide and Life-Threatening Behavior*. Published online: 24 January 2013. doi: 10.1111/sltb.12013.

Vijayakumari N (2011). Suicidal hanging: A prospective study. *Journal of Indian Academy of Forensic Medicine* 33, 355-357.

Violanti JM, Mnatsakanova A, Andrew ME (2012). Behind the blue shadow: A theoretical perspective for detecting police suicide. *International Journal of Emergency Mental Health* 14, 37-40.

Wahlbeck K, McDaid D (2012). Actions to alleviate the mental health impact of the economic crisis. *World Psychiatry* 11, 139-145.

Walter G, Pridmore S (2012). Suicide and the publicly exposed pedophile. *Malaysian Journal of Medical Sciences* 19, 51-57.

Wang M, Alexanderson K, Runeson B, Head J, Mittendorfer-Rutz E (2012). Does diagnosis-specific sickness absence predict suicidal behaviour?- A nationwide register-based study in Sweden. *European Journal of Public Health* 22, 269.

Ward KK, Roncancio AM, Plaxe SC (2012). Women with gynecologic malignancies have a greater incidence of suicide than women with other cancer types. *Suicide and Life-Threatening Behavior* 43, 109-115.

Weaver J, Munro D (2013). Austerity, neo-liberal economics, and youth suicide: The case of New Zealand, 1980-2000. *Journal of Social History* 46, 757-783.

Westen D, Malone JC, DeFife JA (2012). An empirically derived approach to the classification and diagnosis of mood disorders. *World Psychiatry* 11, 172-180.

Wexler L, Silveira ML, Bertone-Johnson E (2012). Factors associated with Alaska native fatal and nonfatal suicidal behaviors 2001-2009: Trends and implications for prevention. *Archives of Suicide Research* 16, 273-286.

Whaley AL, Noel LT (2012). Academic achievement and behavioral health among Asian American and African American adolescents: Testing the model minority and inferior minority assumptions. *Social Psychology of Education* 16, 23-43.

Whitlock J, Muehlenkamp J, Eckenrode J, Purington A, Baral Abrams G, Barreira P, Kress V (2012). Nonsuicidal self-injury as a gateway to suicide in young adults. *Journal of Adolescent Health* 52, 486-492.

Williams-Johnson J, Williams E, Gossell-Williams M, Sewell CA, Abel WD, Whitehorne-Smith PA (2012). Suicide attempt by self-poisoning: Characteristics of suicide attempters seen at the emergency room at the university hospital of the West Indies. *West Indian Medical Journal* 61, 526-531.

Yip PSF, Kwok SSM, Chen F, Xu X, Chen Y-Y (2012). A study on the mutual causation of suicide reporting and suicide incidences. *Journal of Affective Disorders*. Published online: 20 December 2012. doi: 10.1016/j.jad.2012.11.056.

Yoon J-H, Junger W, Kim B-W, Kim Y-J, Koh S-B (2012). Investigating the time lag effect between economic recession and suicide rates in agriculture, fisheries, and forestry workers in Korea. *Safety and Health at Work* 3, 294-297.

Zalsman G (2012). The official guidelines for suicide assessment in Israel *Israel Journal of Psychiatry and Related Sciences* 49, 39.

Zhang J, Yan F, Li Y, McKeown RE (2012). Body mass index and suicidal behaviors: A critical review of epidemiological evidence. *Journal of Affective Disorders*. Published online: 20 September 2012. doi: 10.1016/j.jad.2012.05.048.

Zlodre J, Fazel S (2012). All-cause and external mortality in released prisoners: Systematic review and meta-analysis. *American Journal of Public Health* 102, e67-75.

Prevention

Allen MH, Abar BW, McCormick M, Barnes DH, Haukoos J, Garmel GM, Boudreaux ED (2013). Screening for suicidal ideation and attempts among emergency department medical patients: Instrument and results from the psychiatric emergency research collaboration. *Suicide and Life-Threatening Behavior.* Published online: 16 February 2013. doi: 10.1111/sltb.12018.

Anonymous (2012). Action plan to reduce suicides in England. *Occupational Health* 64, 7.

Anonymous (2013). Youth suicide screening. *Journal of the American Medical Association* 309, 759.

Anstey KJ, Christensen H, Butterworth P, Easteal S, Mackinnon A, Jacomb T, Maxwell K, Rodgers B, Windsor T, Cherbuin N, Jorm AF (2012). Cohort profile: The path through life project. *International Journal of Epidemiology* 41, 951-960.

Atkins Whitmer D, Woods DL (2012). Analysis of the cost effectiveness of a suicide barrier on the Golden Gate Bridge. *Crisis* 34, 98-106.

Auzoult L, Abdellaoui S (2012). Perceptions of a peer suicide prevention program by inmates and professionals working in prisons. *Crisis.* Published online: 21 December 2012. doi: 10.1027/0227-5910/a000172.

Banerjee A, Zhou HY, Kelly KB, Downs BD, Como JJ, Claridge JA (2013). Anterior abdominal stab injury: A comparison of self-inflicted and intentional third-party stabbings. *American Journal of Surgery* 205, 274-279.

Bannink R, Joosten-van Zwanenburg E, van de Looij-Jansen P, van As E, Raat H (2012). Evaluation of computer-tailored health education ('e-health4uth') combined with personal counselling ('e-health4uth + counselling') on adolescents' behaviours and mental health status: Design of a three-armed cluster randomised controlled trial. *BMC Public Health* 12, 1083.

Bertolote JM (2012). Why is Brazil losing the race against youth suicide? *Revista Brasileira De Psiquiatria* 34, 245-246.

Betz ME, Miller M, Barber C, Miller I, Sullivan AF, Camargo CA, Jr., Boudreaux ED (2013). Lethal means restriction for suicide prevention: Beliefs and behaviors of emergency department providers. *Depression & Anxiety.* Published online: 14 March 2013. doi: 10.1002/da.22075.

Braithwaite R (2012). Can suicide be prevented? Suicide prevention and mental illness. *British Medical Journal* 345, e7557.

Braithwaite R (2012). Suicide prevention and mental illness. *British Medical Journal* 345, e8201.

Burke W, Colmer D, Johnson N, Leigh J, Key B, Parker C (2012). An organisational response to an increase in suicides: A case study. *Journal of Public Mental Health* 11, 98-105.

Burrows S, Perron S (2012). Policy analysis and evaluation of effectiveness of a suicide prevention initiative in Montreal. *Injury Prevention* 18, A165.

Caan W (2013). Urgent need for proactive leadership in local suicide prevention plans. *British Medical Journal* 346, f1529.

Caine E (2012). Suicide prevention: Confronting public health challenges. *Injury Prevention* 18, A51.

Caine ED (2013). Forging an agenda for suicide prevention in the United States. *American Public Health Association.* Published online: 16 September 2012. doi: 10.2105/AJPH.2012.301078.

Callanan C (2012). Emergency care staff receive guidance on suicide prevention. *Emergency Nurse: The Journal of the RCN Accident and Emergency Nursing Association* 20, 6-7.

Chakravarthy B, Hoonpongsimanont W, Anderson C, Habicht M, Bruckner T, Lotfipour S (2012). Depression, suicidal ideation, and suicidal attempt presenting to the emergency department; differences between these cohorts. *Injury Prevention* 18, A34.

Chiu H (2012). Suicide prevention in Asia. *Asia-Pacific Psychiatry* 4, 49.

Costello D, O'Brien M (2012). Grass roots suicide prevention in rural Western Australia (WA). *Injury Prevention* 18, A161.

Cover R (2012). Mediating suicide: Print journalism and the categorization of queer youth suicide discourses. *Archives of Sexual Behavior* 41, 1173-1183.

Cox GR, Owens C, Robinson J, Nicholas A, Lockley A, Williamson M, Cheung YT, Pirkis J (2013). Interventions to reduce suicides at suicide hotspots: A systematic review. *BMC Public Health* 13, 214.

Craig P, Cooper C, Gunnell D, Haw S, Lawson K, Macintyre S, Ogilvie D, Petticrew M, Reeves B, Sutton M, Thompson S (2012). Using natural experiments to evaluate population health interventions: New medical research council guidance. *Journal of Epidemiology and Community Health* 66, 1182-1186.

de Beurs DP, de Groot MH, de Keijser J, Verwey B, Mokkenstorm J, Twisk JW, van Duijn E, van Hemert AM, Verlinde L, Spijker J, van Luijn B, Vink J, Kerkhof AJ (2013). Improving the application of a practice guideline for the assessment and treatment of suicidal behavior by training the full staff of psychiatric departments via an e-learning supported train-the-trainer program: Study protocol for a randomized controlled trial. *Trials* 14, 9.

De Silva S, Parker A, Purcell R, Callahan P, Liu P, Hetrick S (2013). Mapping the evidence of prevention and intervention studies for suicidal and self-harming behaviors in young people. *Crisis.* Published online: 15 March 2013. doi: 10.1027/0227-5910/a000190.

Doarn CR, Shore J, Ferguson S, Jordan PJ, Saiki S, Poropatich RK (2012). Challenges, solutions, and best practices in telemental health service delivery across the Pacific Rim - A summary. *Telemedicine Journal and E-Health* 18, 654-660.

Dobscha SK, Corson K, Helmer DA, Bair MJ, Denneson LM, Brandt C, Beane A, Ganzini L (2013). Brief assessment for suicidal ideation in OEF/OIF veterans with positive depression screens. *General Hospital Psychiatry.* Published online: 23 January 2013. doi: 10.1016/j.genhosppsych.2012.12.001.

Evans RE, Price S (2012). Exploring organisational influences on the implementation of gatekeeper training: A qualitative study of the Applied Suicide Intervention Skills Training (ASIST) programme in Wales. *Critical Public Health.* Published online: 19 December 2012. doi: 10.1080/09581596.2012.752069.

Fisher LB, Overholser JC (2013). Refining the assessment of hopelessness: An improved way to look to the future. *Death Studies* 37, 212-227.

Fiske A (2012). Screening for suicide risk among older adult primary care patients. *Gerontologist* 52, 464.

Goldney RD, Davis AT, Scott V (2012). The International Association for Suicide Prevention. *Crisis* 34, 137-141.

Greenberg B, Strous RD (2012). Werther's syndrome: Copycat self-immolation in Israel with a call for responsible media response. *Israel Medical Association Journal* 14, 467-469.

Ham P, Allen C (2012). Adolescent health screening and counseling. *American Family Physician* 86, 1109-1116.

Harbauer G, Ring M, Schuetz C, Andreae A, Haas S (2013). Suicidality assessment with prism-s-simple, fast, and visual: A brief nonverbalmethod to assess suicidality in adolescent and adult patients. *Crisis* 34, 131-136.

Haring C, Sonneck G (2012). Suicide Prevention Austria (SUPRA): The implementation of a national suicide prevention program. *Neuropsychiatrie* 26, 91-94.

Harris FM, Maxwell M, O Connor RC, Coyne J, Arensman E, Szekely A, Gusmão R, Coffey C, Costa S, Cserháti Z, Koburger N, Van Audenhove C, McDaid D, Maloney J, Värnik P, Hegerl U (2013). Developing social capital in implementing a complex intervention: A process evaluation of the early implementation of a suicide prevention intervention in four European countries. *BMC Public Health* 13, 158.

Hatcher S, Pimentel A (2013). Do patients and clinicians differ in their assessment of suicidal intent after self-harm using the same suicide questionnaire scale? *International Emergency Nursing.* Published online: 5 January 2013. doi: 10.1016/j.ienj.2012.11.003.

Hawton K, Bergen H, Simkin S, Dodd S, Pocock P, Bernal W, Gunnell D, Kapur N (2013). Long term effect of reduced pack sizes of paracetamol on poisoning deaths and liver transplant activity in England and Wales: Interrupted time series analyses. *British Medical Journal* 346, f403.

Healy D, Naqvi S, Meagher D, Cullen W, Dunne C (2012). Primary care support for youth mental health: A preliminary evidence base for Ireland's mid-west. *Irish Journal of Medical Science* 182, 237-243.

Heilbron N, Goldston D, Walrath C, Rodi M, McKeon R (2012). Suicide risk protocols: Addressing the needs of high risk youths identified through suicide prevention efforts and in clinical settings. *Suicide and Life-Threatening Behavior* 43, 150-160.

Helama S, Holopainen J, Partonen T (2013). Temperature-associated suicide mortality: Contrasting roles of climatic warming and the suicide prevention program in Finland. *Environmental Health Preventative Medicine.* Published online: 5 February 2013. doi: 10.1007/s12199-013-0329-7.

Hendricks ML, Testa RJ (2012). A conceptual framework for clinical work with transgender and gender nonconforming clients: An adaptation of the minority stress model. *Professional Psychology-Research and Practice* 43, 460-467.

Hooven C (2013). Parents-CARE: A suicide prevention program for parents of at-risk youth. *Journal of Child Adolescent Psychiatric Nursing* 26, 85-95. Published online: 27 January 2013. doi: 10.1111/jcap.12025.

Horowitz LM, Bridge JA, Teach SJ, Ballard E, Klima J, Rosenstein DL, Wharff EA, Ginnis K, Cannon E, Joshi P, Pao M (2012). Ask Suicide-Screening Questions (ASQ) a brief instrument for the pediatric emergency department. *Archives of Pediatrics & Adolescent Medicine* 166, 1170-1176.

Inoue K, Fujita Y, Fukunaga T (2012). Investigation and discussion of specific and clear suicide prevention among women in Japan and South Korea. *International Medical Journal* 19, 286.

Inoue K, Fukunaga T (2012). A report on alcohol issue in relation to suicide prevention measures in Japan. *Alcoholism-Clinical and Experimental Research* 36, 132A.

Inoue K, Fukunaga T, Fujita Y, Okazaki Y (2012). The continued importance of suicide prevention among the elderly in Japan. *West Indian Medical Journal* 61, 556.

Inoue K, Fukunaga T, Ono Y (2012). Discussion of the need for seasonal strengthening of suicide prevention measures in Japan: Analysis of research nationally and in several Japanese prefectures over a long period. *International Medical Journal* 19, 215-217.

Inoue K, Okazaki Y, Kaiya H, Fujita Y (2012). An issue to keep in mind regarding specific suicide prevention measures focussing on bipolar disorder. *West Indian Medical Journal* 61, 555.

James LC (2012). Introduction to special section on suicide prevention. *Military Psychology* 24, 565-567.

Jobes DA, Lento R, Brazaitis K (2012). An evidence-based clinical approach to suicide prevention in the department of defense: The Collaborative Assessment and Management of Suicidality (CAMS). *Military Psychology* 24, 604-623.

Johnson LA, Parsons ME (2012). Adolescent suicide prevention in a school setting: Use of a gatekeeper program. *NASN School Nurse* 27, 312-317.

Kasckow J, Zickmund S, Rotondi A, Mrkva A, Gurklis J, Chinman M, Fox L, Loganathan M, Hanusa B, Haas G (2013). Development of telehealth dialogues for monitoring suicidal patients with schizophrenia: Consumer feedback. *Community Mental Health Journal*. Published online: 10 January 2013. doi: 10.1007/s10597-012-9589-8.

Kavakli M, Li M, Rudra T (2012). Towards the development of a virtual counselor to tackle students' exam stress. *Journal of Integrated Design and Process Science* 16, 5-26.

Kerr DCR, Reinke WM, Eddy JM (2012). Trajectories of depressive symptoms and externalizing behaviors across adolescence: Associations with histories of suicide attempt and ideation in early adulthood. *Suicide and Life-Threatening Behavior* 43, 50-66.

Kim SK, Kim NS (2013). The role of the pediatrician in youth violence prevention. *Korean Journal of Pediatrics* 56, 1-7.

Kleiman EM, Liu RT (2013). Social support as a protective factor in suicide: Findings from two nationally representative samples. *Journal of Affective Disorders*. Published online: 2013. doi: 10.1016/j.jad.2013.01.033i.

Klimes-Dougan B, Klingbeil DA, Meller SJ (2012). The impact of universal suicide-prevention programs on the help-seeking attitudes and behaviors of youths. *Crisis* 34, 82-97.

Kopacz MS (2013). Providing pastoral care services in a clinical setting to veterans at-risk of suicide. *Journal of Religion & Health*. Published online: 8 March 2013. doi: 10.1007/s10943-013-9693-2.

Kweon Y-S, Lee K-U, Yeon B, Lee H-K, Lee CT, Choi K-H, Oh Y-M, Lee K-S (2012). Characteristics of patients dropping out from the suicide prevention program. *Asia-Pacific Psychiatry* 4, 185.

Langford L, Litts D, Pearson JL (2012). Using science to improve communications about suicide among military and veteran populations: Looking for a few good messages. *American Journal of Public Health Association* 103, 31-38.

Large MM (2012). High-risk strategies v. universal precautions against suicide. *British Journal of Psychiatry* 201, 410-411.

Large MM, Nielssen OB (2012). Risk factors for inpatient suicide do not translate into meaningful risk categories—all psychiatric inpatients are high-risk. *The Journal of Clinical Psychiatry* 73, 1034-1035.

Lee CT, Lee K-U, Yeon B, Lee H-K, Kweon Y-S, Choi K-H, Oh Y-M (2012). Clinical and demographical characteristics of patients refusing to participate in the suicide prevention program. *Asia-Pacific Psychiatry* 4, 184-185.

Lewiecki EM, Miller SA (2013). Suicide, guns, and public policy. *American Journal of Public Health* 103, 27-31.

Limb M (2012). Low cost measures should be used to tackle high suicide rate in India. *British Medical Journal* 345, E6875-E687.

Lodge S (2012). 'A long journey starts with a single step'- Waimakariri's journey into suicide prevention. *Injury Prevention* 18, A166-A167.

MacLay T (2012). A suicide prevention protocol for critical care. *Nursing Critical Care* 7, 17-21.

Maniam T, Chinna K, Mariapun J (2013). Suicide prevention program for at-risk groups: Pointers from an epidemiological study. *Preventive Medicine*. Published online: 27 February 2013. doi: 10.1016/j.ypmed.2013.02.022.

Margolis GJ, Shtull PR (2012). The police response to mental illness on campus. *Journal of College Student Psychotherapy* 26, 307-321.

Mathieson JH, Ashton J (2012). Suicide and economic recession: Local efforts are paramount in preventing suicide during recession. *British Medical Journal* 345, E6387.

Matthieu MM, Hensley MA (2012). Gatekeeper training outcomes: Enhancing the capacity of staff in substance abuse treatment programs to prevent suicide in a high risk population. *Mental Health and Substance Use: Dual Diagnosis.* Published online: 29 November 2012. doi: 10.1080/17523281.2012.744342.

McLoughlin AB, Malone KM, Owens C, Kelleher C (2012). Suicide in the children of Ireland from 2003-2008: A mixed method study. *Irish Journal of Medical Science* 181, S446.

Mills PD, Watts BV, Huh TJ, Boar S, Kemp J (2013). Helping elderly patients to avoid suicide: A review of case reports from a national veterans affairs database. *Journal of Nervous Mental Disorders* 201, 12-16.

Monette M (2012). Senior suicide: The tricky task of treatment. *Canadian Medical Association Journal* 184, E887-E888.

Murphy HE (2012). Improving the lives of students, gay and straight alike: Gay-straight alliances and the role of school psychologists. *Psychology in the Schools* 49, 883-891.

Musil R, Zill P, Seemüller F, Bondy B, Meyer S, Spellmann I, Bender W, Adli M, Heuser I, Fisher R, Gaebel W, Maier W, Rietschel M, Rujescu D, Schennach R, Möller HJ, Riedel M (2012). Genetics of emergent suicidality during antidepressive treatment-data from a naturalistic study on a large sample of inpatients with a major depressive episode. *European Neuropsychopharmacology.* Published online: 11 October 2012. doi: 10.1016/j.euroneuro.2012.08.009.

Nada-Raja S, Knightbridge K (2012). Preliminary findings from the evaluation of an internet-based depression treatment programme (RID trial) in New Zealand. *Injury Prevention* 18, A33-A34.

Newland J (2012). Mental disorders in children and adolescents. *Nurse Practitioner* 37, 5.

Oh KS (2012). Newer issues related to suicide prevention in Korea. *Asia-Pacific Psychiatry* 4, 49.

Pirkis J, Spittal MJ, Cox G, Robinson J, Cheung YTD, Studdert D (2013). The effectiveness of structural interventions at suicide hotspots: A meta-analysis. *International Journal of Epidemiology* 42, 541-548.

Poteat VP, Sinclair KO, Digiovanni CD, Koenig BW, Russell ST (2012). Gay-straight alliances are associated with student health: A multischool comparison of LGBTQ and heterosexual youth. *Journal of Research on Adolescence.* Published online: 8 October 2012. doi: 10.1111/j.1532-7795.2012.00832.x.

Pringle B, Colpe LJ, Heinssen RK, Schoenbaum M, Sherrill JT, Claassen CA, Pearson JL (2013). A strategic approach for prioritizing research and action to prevent suicide. *Psychiatric Services* 64, 71-75.

Qian J (2012). Mental health care in China: Providing services for under-treated patients. *Journal of Mental Health Policy and Economics* 15, 179-186.

Radhakrishnan R, Andrade C (2012). Suicide: An Indian perspective. *Indian Journal of Psychiatry* 54, 304-319.

Robinson J, Cox G, Malone A, Williamson M, Baldwin G, Fletcher K, O'Brien M (2012). A systematic review of school-based interventions aimed at preventing, treating, and responding to suicide- related behavior in young people. *Crisis.* Published online: 28 November 2012. doi: 10.1027/0227-5910/a000168.

Rockett IRH, Regier MD, Kapusta ND, Coben J, Miller TR, Hanzlick RL, Todd KH, Sattin RW, Kennedy LW, Kleinig J, Smith GS (2012). Patterns and trends in leading causes of unintentional and violence-related injury mortality: United States, 2000-2009. *Injury Prevention* 18, A239.

Rosenman S (1998). Suicide prevention. *Australasian Journal on Ageing* 17, 151.

Roskar S (2012). Educational strategies for preventing suicide: Review of studies in Slovenia, Gotland and Germany. *International Journal of Psychiatry in Clinical Practice* 16, 6.

Rusu IR, Cosman D, Neme B (2012). Family - Protective factor to prevent suicidal behavior in adolescents. *Human and Veterinary Medicine* 4, 103-106.

Ruth BJ, McLaughlin D, Glanino M, Feldman BN, Muroff J (2012). You can't recover from suicide: Perspectives on suicide education in MSW programs. *Journal of Social Work Education* 48, 501-516.

Sanchez HG (2013). Suicide prevention in administrative segregation units: What is missing? *Journal of Correctional Health Care.* Published online: 11 February 2013. doi: 10.1177/1078345812474638.

Sanci L, Grabsch B, Chondros P, Shiell A, Pirkis J, Sawyer S, Hegarty K, Patterson E, Cahill H, Ozer E, Seymour J, Patton G (2012). The Prevention Access and Risk Taking in Young People (PARTY) project protocol: A cluster randomised controlled trial of health risk screening and motivational interviewing for young people presenting to general practice. *BMC Public Health* 12, 400.

Schlebusch L (2012). Suicide prevention: A proposed national strategy for South Africa. *African Journal of Psychiatry* 15, 436-440.

Shiraishi Y (2012). Impact of 'safe community' model in suicide prevention in Japan. *Injury Prevention* 18, A33.

Spiwak R, Elias B, Bolton JM, Martens PJ, Sareen J (2012). Suicide policy in Canada: Lessons from history. *Canadian Journal of Public Health* 103, 338-341.

Srinivasa Reddy P, Rajendra Kumar R, Rudramurthy (2012). Asphyxial deaths at district hospital, Tumkur a retrospective study. *Journal of Indian Academy of Forensic Medicine* 34, 146-147.

Stogner J, Khey DN, Griffin OH, Miller BL, Boman JH (2012). Regulating a novel drug: An evaluation of changes in use of salvia divinorum in the first year of Florida's ban. *International Journal of Drug Policy* 23, 512-521.

Stuber J, Quinnett P (2013). Making the case for primary care and mandated suicide prevention education. *Suicide and Life-Threatening Behavior* 43, 117-124.

Sveticic J, De Leo D (2012). The hypothesis of a continuum in suicidality: A discussion on its validity and practical implications. *Mental Illness* 4, 73-78.

Takeshima T (2012). Suicide and suicide prevention in Japan. *Asia-Pacific Psychiatry* 4, 49-50.

Tarren-Sweeney M (2013). The Assessment Checklist for Adolescents - ACA: A scale for measuring the mental health of young people in foster, kinship, residential and adoptive care. *Children and Youth Services Review* 35, 384-393.

Tatz C (2012). Aborigines, sport and suicide. *Sport in Society* 15, 922-935.

Tighe J, McKay K (2012). Alive and kicking goals!: Preliminary findings from a Kimberley suicide prevention program. *Advances in Mental Health* 10, 240-245.

Till B, Voracek M, Herberth A, Strauss M, Etzersdorfer E, Eisenwort B, Sonneck G, Niederkrotenthaler T (2013). The role of interviews with health professionals in the media in suicide prevention. *Archives of Suicide Research* 17, 88-89.

van Orden KA, Stone DM, Rowe J, McIntosh WL, Podgorski C, Conwell Y (2013). The senior connection: Design and rationale of a randomized trial of peer companionship to reduce suicide risk in later life. *Contemporary Clinical Trials.* Published online: 16 March 2013. doi: 10.1016/j.cct.2013.03.003.

Vannoy S, Park M, Unutzer J, Hinton L (2012). Older men's perspectives on what has stopped them from suicide and how to help others. *Gerontologist* 52, 271-272.

Viljoen JL, Cruise KR, Nicholls TL, Desmarais SL, Webster CD (2012). Taking stock and taking steps: The case for an adolescent version of the short-term assessment of risk and treatability. *International Journal of Forensic Mental Health* 11, 135-149.

Voss WD, Kaufman E, O'Connor SS, Comtois KA, Conner KR, Ries RK (2013). Preventing addiction related suicide: A pilot study. *Journal of Substance Abuse Treatment* 44, 565-569.

Waitzkin H, Englehart JDBA, Bossarte RMP (2012). AJPH supplement on military suicide/bossarte responds. *American Journal of Public Health* 102, E7-E8.

Walsh E, Hooven C, Kronick B (2013). School-wide staff and faculty training in suicide risk awareness: Successes and challenges. *Journal of Child Adolescent Psychiatric Nursing* 26, 53-61.

Wang M-C, Lightsey OR, Jr., Tran KK, Bonaparte TS (2013). Examining suicide protective factors among black college students. *Death Studies* 37, 228-247.

Weber T, Eberle J, Messelhauser U, Schiffmann L, Nies C, Schabram J, Zielke A, Holzer K, Rottler E, Henne-Bruns D, Keller M, von Wietersheim J (2012). Parathyroidectomy, elevated depression scores, and suicidal ideation in patients with primary hyperparathyroidism: Results of a prospective multicenter study. *Archives of Surgery.* Published online: 15 October 2012. doi: 10.1001/2013.jamasurg.316.

White J, Stoneman L (2012). Thinking and doing prevention: A critical analysis of contemporary youth crime and suicide prevention discourses. *Child and Youth Services* 33, 104-126.

Wilder H, Wilder J (2012). In the wake of don't ask don't tell: Suicide prevention and outreach for LGB service members. *Military Psychology* 24, 624-642.

Wilkins N, Thigpen S (2012). News from the CDC: Making evaluation findings actionable for suicide prevention practice. *Translational Behavioral Medicine* 2, 376-377.

Wiltsey Stirman S, Miller CJ, Toder K, Calloway A, Beck AT, Evans AC, Crits-Christoph P (2012). Perspectives on cognitive therapy training within community mental health settings: Implications for clinician satisfaction and skill development. *Depression Research and Treatment* 2012, 391084.

Wong GH, Hui CL, Wong DY, Tang JY, Chang WC, Chan SK, Lee EH, Xu JQ, Lin JJ, Lai DC, Tam W, Kok J, Chung DW, Hung SF, Chen EY (2012). Developments in early intervention for psychosis in Hong Kong. *East Asian Archives of Psychiatry* 22, 100-104.

Wong MC (2012). Case series of all completed suicide cases under the elderly suicide prevention programme of a mental hospital in Hong Kong from 2002-2010. *Asia-Pacific Psychiatry* 4, 97-98.

Xiang Y-T, Yu X, Sartorius N, Ungvari GS, Chiu HFK (2012). Mental health in China: Challenges and progress. *Lancet* 380, 1715-1716.

Yildiz M, Kara M, Bozdemir MN, Kara B, Goktekin MC, Gurbuz S, Ayranci M, Emet M (2012). Parasuicidal patients in the emergency department and their relationship with cannabinoid gene polymorphism. *Bulletin of Clinical Psychopharmacology* 22, 177-183.

York J, Lamis DA, Friedman L, Berman AL, Joiner TE, McIntosh JL, Silverman MM, Konick L, Gutierrez PM, Pearson J (2013). A systematic review process to evaluate suicide prevention programs: A sample case of community-based programs. *Journal of Community Psychology* 41, 35-51.

York JA, Lamis DA, Pope CA, Egede LE (2012). Veteran-specific suicide prevention. *The Psychiatric Quarterly.* Published online: 26 September 2012. doi: 10.1007/s11126-012-9241-3.

Yur'yev A, Varnik P, Yur'yeva L, Varnik A (2013). Alert for suicide prevention in Greece: Remember lessons from Eastern Europe! *International Journal of Social Psychiatry* 59, 101.

Zarghami M (2012). Selection of person of the year from public health perspective: Promotion of mass clusters of copycat self-immolation. *Iranian Journal of Psychiatry and Behavioral Sciences* 6, 1-11.

Postvention and Bereavement

Bartik W, Maple M, Edwards H, Kiernan M (2013). Adolescent survivors after suicide: Australian young people's bereavement narratives. *Crisis.* Published online: 28 January 2013. doi: 10.1027/0227-5910/a000185.

Bolton JM, Au W, Leslie WD, Martens PJ, Enns MW, Roos LL, Katz LY, Wilcox HC, Erlangsen A, Chateau D, Walld R, Spiwak R, Seguin M, Shear K, Sareen J (2012). Parents bereaved by offspring suicide: A population-based longitudinal case-control study. *Archives of General Psychiatry* 70, 158-167.

Brent DA, Melhem NM, Masten AS, Porta G, Payne MW (2012). Longitudinal effects of parental bereavement on adolescent developmental competence. *Journal of Clinical Child Adolescent Psychology* 41, 778-791.

Caleb R (2013). After the suicide: Helping the bereaved to find a path from grief to recovery. *British Journal of Guidance & Counselling* 41, 85-87.

Gill IJ (2012). An identity theory perspective on how trainee clinical psychologists experience the death of a client by suicide. *Training and Education in Professional Psychology* 6, 151-159.

Groos AD, Shakespeare-Finch J (2013). Positive experiences for participants in suicide bereavement groups: A grounded theory model. *Death Studies* 37, 1-24.

Hefren JE, Thyer BA (2012). The effectiveness of guided mourning for adults with complicated mourning. *Journal of Human Behavior in the Social Environment* 22, 988.

Lichtenthal WG, Neimeyer RA, Currier JM, Roberts K, Jordan N (2013). Cause of death and the quest for meaning after the loss of a child. *Death Studies* 37, 311-342.

Maple M, Edwards HE, Minichiello V, Plummer D (2012). Still part of the family: The importance of physical, emotional and spiritual memorial places and spaces for parents bereaved through the suicide death of their son or daughter. *Mortality* 18, 54-71.

Meier AM, Carr DR, Currier JM, Neimeyer RA (2013). Attachment anxiety and avoidance in coping with bereavement: Two studies. *Journal of Social and Clinical Psychology* 32, 315-334.

Nader IW, Niederkrotenthaler T, Schild AHE, Koller I, Tran US, Kapusta ND, Sonneck G, Voracek M (2013). Development of a scale to assess knowledge about suicide postvention using item response theory. *Suicide and Life-Threatening Behavior* 43, 174-184.

Sharpe TL, Joe S, Taylor KC (2012). Suicide and homicide bereavement among African Americans: Implications for survivor research and practice. *Omega* 66, 153-172.

Song JI, Shin DW, Choi J-Y, Kang J, Baek Y-J, Mo H-N, Seo M-J, Hwang YH, Lim Y-K, Lee OK (2012). Quality of life and mental health in the bereaved family members of patients with terminal cancer. *Psycho-Oncology* 21, 1158-1166.

Spuij M, Prinzie P, Zijderlaan J, Stikkelbroek Y, Dillen L, de Roos C, Boelen PA (2012). Psychometric properties of the Dutch Inventories of Prolonged Grief for Children and Adolescents. *Clinical Psychology & Psychotherapy* 19, 540-551.

Sun FK, Long A (2013). A suicidal recovery theory to guide individuals on their healing and recovering process following a suicide attempt. *Journal of Advanced Nursing.* Published online: 7 January 2013. doi: 10.1111/jan.12070.

Valente SM (2012). Devastating losses: How parents cope with the death of a child to suicide or drugs. *Choice* 50, 762.

Wagner B, Muller J, Maercker A (2012). Death by request in Switzerland: Posttraumatic stress disorder and complicated grief after witnessing assisted suicide. *European Psychiatry* 27, 542-546.

Wood L, Byram V, Gosling AS, Stokes J (2012). Continuing bonds after suicide bereavement in childhood. *Death Studies* 36, 873-898.

Young IT, Iglewicz A, Glorioso D, Lanouette N, Seay K, Ilapakurti M, Zisook S (2012). Suicide bereavement and complicated grief. *Dialogues in Clinical Neuroscience* 14, 177-186.

NON FATAL SUICIDAL BEHAVIOR

Epidemiology

Abdalla S, Kelleher CC, Quirke B, Daly L (2013). Disparities in fatal and non-fatal injuries between Irish travellers and the Irish general population are similar to those of other Indigenous minorities: A cross-sectional population-based comparative study. *BMJ Open.* Published online: 28 January 2013. doi: 10.1136/bmjopen-2012-002296.

Abou-Mrad F, Mourad C, Najem C (2012). Depressive symptoms among surrogate decision makers in Lebanese Icus. *Functional Neurology* 27, 95-99.

Aishvarya S, Maniam T, Sidi H, Oei Tps (2013). Suicide ideation and intent in Malaysia: A review of the literature. *Comprehensive Psychiatry.* Published online: 19 February 2013. doi: 10.1016/j.comppsych.2013.01.005.

Angelkovska A, Houghton S, Hopkins S (2012). Differential profiles of risk of self-harm among clinically referred primary school aged children. *School Psychology International* 33, 646-660.

Anonymous (2012). Risk factors for suicidal behavior in older adults: Charting global connections. *Gerontologist* 52, 498.

Anonymous (2012). Suicide risk and challenges of older adulthood. *Gerontologist* 52, 245.

Anstey KJ, Christensen H, Butterworth P, Easteal S, Mackinnon A, Jacomb T, Maxwell K, Rodgers B, Windsor T, Cherbuin N, Jorm AF (2012). Cohort profile: The path through life project. *International Journal of Epidemiology* 41, 951-960.

Armey MF, Nugent NR, Crowther JH (2012). An exploratory analysis of situational affect, early life stress, and nonsuicidal self-injury in college students. *Journal of Child & Adolescent Trauma* 5, 327-343.

Bell V, Mendez F, Martinez C, Palma PP, Bosch M (2012). Characteristics of the Colombian armed conflict and the mental health of civilians living in active conflict zones. *Conflict and Health* 6, 10.

Betancourt TS, Newnham EA, Layne CM, Kim S, Steinberg AM, Ellis H, Birman D (2012). Trauma history and psychopathology in war-affected refugee children referred for trauma-related mental health services in the United States. *Journal of Trauma and Stress* 25, 682-690.

Bjorkenstam C, Bjorkenstam E, Ljung R, Vinnerljung B, Tuvblad C (2013). Suicidal behavior among delinquent former child welfare clients. *European Child and Adolescent Psychiatry.* Published online: 8 January 2013. doi: 10.1007/s00787-012-0372-8.

Bonenberger M, Plener PL, Kirchner I, Keller F (2013). How I deal with stress (HIDS) - A screening instrument for the assessment of non-suicidal self-injury and coping strategies in adolescents. *Nervenheilkunde* 32, 11.

Bot M, Pouwer F, de Jonge P, Tack CJ, Geelhoed-Duijvestijn PH, Snoek FJ (2012). Differential associations between depressive symptoms and glycaemic control in outpatients with diabetes. *Diabetic Medicine* 30, e115-e122.

Brinkman TM, Zhang N, Recklitis CJ, Kimberg C, Zeltzer LK, Muriel AC, Stovall M, Srivastava DK, Robison LL, Krull KR (2012). Very late onset and recurrent suicide ideation in adult survivors of childhood cancer: A report from the childhood cancer survivor study. *Pediatric Blood & Cancer* 59, 1123.

Bryan CJ, Clemans TA, Hernandez AM, David Rudd M (2012). Loss of consciousness, depression, posttraumatic stress disorder, and suicide risk among deployed military personnel with mild traumatic brain injury. *Journal of Head Trauma Rehabilitation* 28, 13-20.

Bryan CJ, Ray-Sannerud B, Morrow CE, Etienne N (2012). Shame, pride, and suicidal ideation in a military clinical sample. *Journal of Affective Disorders* 147, 212-216.

Burton CM, Marshal MP, Chisolm DJ, Sucato GS, Friedman MS (2013). Sexual minority-related victimization as a mediator of mental health disparities in sexual minority youth: A longitudinal analysis. *Journal of Youth and Adolescence* 42, 394-402.

Callahan ST, Fuchs DC, Shelton RC, Balmer LS, Dudley JA, Gideon PS, Deranieri MM, Stratton SM, Williams CL, Ray WA, Cooper WO (2013). Identifying suicidal behavior among adolescents using administrative claims data. *Pharmacoepidemiology and Drug Safety.* Published online: 15 February 2013. doi: 10.1002/pds.3421.

Cao Y, Yang J, Ramirez M, Peek-Asa C (2012). Characteristics of workplace threats requiring response from a university threat assessment team. *Journal of Occupational and Environmental Medicine* 55, 45-51.

Caribe AC, Nunez R, Montal D, Ribeiro L, Sarmento S, Quarantini LC, Miranda-Scippa A (2012). Religiosity as a protective factor in suicidal behavior: A case-control study. *The Journal of Nervous and Mental Disease* 200, 863-867.

Carla Inzunza C, Felipe Navia G, Catalán P, Brehme C, Ventura T (2012). Features of adolescents hospitalized for a suicide attempt in a general hospital. *Conducta suicida en niños y adolescentes ingresados en un hospital general Análisis descriptivo* 140, 751-762.

Carlisle CE, Mamdani M, Schachar R, To T (2012). Predictors of psychiatric aftercare among formerly hospitalized adolescents. *Canadian Journal of Psychiatry* 57, 666-676.

Cash SJ, Thelwall M, Peck SN, Ferrell JZ, Bridge JA (2013). Adolescent suicide statements on myspace. *Cyberpsychology, Behavior and Social Networking* 16, 166-174.

Casiano H, Jolene Kinley D, Katz LY, Chartier MJ, Sareen J (2012). Media use and health outcomes in adolescents: Findings from a nationally representative survey. *Journal of the Canadian Academy of Child and Adolescent Psychiatry* 21, 296-301.

Ceretta LB, Réus GZ, Abelaira HM, Jornada LK, Schwalm MT, Hoepers NJ, Tomazzi CD, Gulbis KG, Ceretta RA, Quevedo J (2012). Increased prevalence of mood disorders and suicidal ideation in type 2 diabetic patients. *Acta Diabetologica* 49, S227-S234.

Cero I, Sifers S (2013). Moderating factors in the path from physical abuse to attempted suicide in adolescents: Application of the interpersonal-psychological theory of suicide. *Suicide and Life-Threatening Behavior.* Published online: 5 February 2013. doi: 10.1111/sltb.12016.

Ceschi A, Rauber-Luthy C, Kupferschmidt H, Banner NR, Ansari M, Krahenbuhl S, Taegtmeyer AB (2013). Acute calcineurin inhibitor overdose: Analysis of cases reported to a national poison center between 1995 and 2011. *American Journal of Transplantation* 13, 786-795.

Cheung YTD, Wong PWC, Lee AM, Lam TH, Fan YSS, Yip PSF (2012). Non-suicidal self-injury and suicidal behavior: Prevalence, co-occurrence, and correlates of suicide among adolescents in Hong Kong. *Social Psychiatry and Psychiatric Epidemiology.* Published online: 22 December 2012. doi: 10.1007/s00127-012-0640-4.

Chhetri Ud, Ansari I, Shrestha S (2012). Pattern of pediatric poisoning and accident in Patan hospital. *Kathmandu University Medical Journal* 10, 39-43.

Chiu HF, Dai J, Xiang YT, Chan SS, Leung T, Yu X, Hou ZJ, Ungvari GS, Caine ED (2012). Suicidal thoughts and behaviors in older adults in rural China: A preliminary study. *International Journal of Geriatric Psychiatry* 27, 1124-1130.

Chou CH, Ko HC, Wu JY, Cheng CP (2013). The prevalence of and psychosocial risks for suicide attempts in male and female college students in Taiwan. *Suicide and Life-Threatening Behavior.* Published online: 8 January 2013. doi: 10.1111/sltb.12007.

Christensen H, Batterham PJ, Soubelet A, Mackinnon AJ (2013). A test of the interpersonal theory of suicide in a large community-based cohort. *Journal of Affective Disorders* 144, 225-234.

Chung I (2012). Sociocultural study of immigrant suicide-attempters: An ecological perspective. *Journal of Social Work* 12, 614-629.

Coryell W, Fiedorowicz J, Leon AC, Endicott J, Keller MB (2012). Age of onset and the prospectively observed course of illness in bipolar disorder. *Journal of Affective Disorders* 146, 34-38.

Dalen JD (2012). The association between school class composition and suicidal ideation in late adolescence: Findings from the Young-Hunt 3 study. *Child and Adolescent Psychiatry and Mental Health* 6, 37.

Dell'Osso L, Casu G, Carlini M, Conversano C, Gremigni P, Carmassi C (2012). Sexual obsessions and suicidal behaviors in patients with mood disorders, panic disorders and schizophrenia. *Annals of General Psychiatry* 11, 27.

Dennis C-L, Heaman M, Vigod S (2012). Epidemiology of postpartum depressive symptoms among Canadian women: Regional and national results from a cross-sectional survey. *Canadian Journal of Psychiatry* 57, 537-546.

Ding L-J, Wang W-Q, Wen C, Liao Z-H, Wu S-Y (2012). Suicide attempters in people aged 18 and older in Xiamen, China. *Asia-Pacific Psychiatry* 4, 150.

Drapeau CW, DeBrule DS (2013). The relationship of hypomania, creativity, and suicidal ideation in undergraduates. *Creativity Research Journal* 25, 75-79.

Dutta D, Bharati S, Roy C, Das G (2013). Measurement of prevalence of 'major depressive syndrome' among Indian patients attending pain clinic with chronic pain using phq-9 scale. *Journal of Anaesthesiology Clinical Pharmacology* 29, 76-82.

Economou M, Madianos M, Peppou LE, Theleritis C, Patelakis A, Stefanis C (2013). Suicidal ideation and reported suicide attempts in Greece during the economic crisis. *World Psychiatry* 12, 53-59

Eisenberg D, Hunt J, Speer N (2013). Mental health in American colleges and universities: Variation across student subgroups and across campuses. *Journal of Nervous and Mental Disease* 201, 60.

Elisei S, Verdolini N, Anastasi S (2012). Suicidal attempts among emergency department patients: One-year of clinical experience. *Psychiatria Danubina* 24, S140-S142.

Erol A, Ersoy B, Mete L (2013). Association of suicide attempts with childhood traumatic experiences in patients with major depression. *Turkish Journal of Psychiatry* 24, 1-6.

Evren C, Cinar O, Evren B, Celik S (2012). Relationship of self-mutilative behaviours with severity of borderline personality, childhood trauma and impulsivity in male substance-dependent inpatients. *Psychiatry Research* 200, 20-25.

Fässberg MM, Ostling S, Börjesson-Hanson A, Skoog I, Wærn M (2013). Suicidal feelings in the twilight of life: A cross-sectional population-based study of 97-year-olds. *BMJ Open*. Published online: 1 February 2013. doi: 10.1136/bmjopen-2012-002260.

Ferreira Goncalves S, Martins C, Rosendo AP, Machado BC, Silva E (2012). Self-injurious behavior in Portuguese adolescents. *Psicothema* 24, 536-541.

Fisher HL, Caspi A, Poulton R, Meier MH, Houts R, Harrington H, Arseneault L, Moffitt TE (2013). Specificity of childhood psychotic symptoms for predicting schizophrenia by 38 years of age: A birth cohort study. *Psychological Medicine*. Published online: 10 January 2013. doi: 10.1017/S0033291712003091.

Forgeot d'Arc B, Dawson M, Soulieres I, Mottron L (2012). Self-injury in autism is largely unexplained: Now what? *Journal of Autism and Developmental Disorders* 42, 2513-2514.

Forrest G (2012). Evaluation of a prison based activities program on aggression, self harm and metabolic monitoring parameters. *International Journal of Mental Health Nursing* 21, 7.

Fragar L, Inder KJ, Kelly BJ, Coleman C, Perkins D, Lewin TJ (2013). Unintentional injury, psychological distress and depressive symptoms: Is there an association for rural Australians? *Journal of Rural Health* 29, 12-19.

Fu JJ, Bazazi AR, Altice FL, Mohamed MN, Kamarulzaman A (2012). Absence of antiretroviral therapy and other risk factors for morbidity and mortality in Malaysian compulsory drug detention and rehabilitation centers. *PLoS ONE.* Published online: 18 September 2012. doi: 10.1371/journal.pone.0044249.

Gadermann AM, Gilman SE, McLaughlin KA, Nock MK, Petukhova M, Sampson NA, Kessler RC (2012). Projected rates of psychological disorders and suicidality among soldiers based on simulations of matched general population data. *Military Medicine* 177, 1002-1010.

Gisle L, Van Oyen H (2012). Household composition and suicidal behaviour in the adult population of Belgium. *Social Psychiatry and Psychiatric Epidemiology.* Published online: 15 November 2012. doi: 10.1007/s00127-012-0621-7.

Glatstein M, Garcia-Bournissen F, Scolnik D, Koren G (2010). Sulfonylurea intoxication at a tertiary care paediatric hospital. *Journal of Population Therapeutics and Clinical Pharmacology* 17, e51-e56

Goldblum P, Testa RJ, Pflum S, Hendricks ML, Bradford J, Bongar B (2012). The relationship between gender-based victimization and suicide attempts in transgender people. *Professional Psychology: Research and Practice* 43, 468.

Greydanus DE (2012). Self-harm is common in adolescents in England. *Evidence-Based Mental Health* 16, 28.

Grupp-Phelan J, McGuire L, Husky MM, Olfson M (2012). A randomized controlled trial to engage in care of adolescent emergency department patients with mental health problems that increase suicide risk. *Pediatric Emergency Care* 28, 1263-1268.

Gurung CK, Dahal R, Khanal P, Nepal S, Jaiswal AK (2011). Pattern of poisoning cases in a hospital in a Terai district of central Nepal. *Nepal Medical College Journal* 13, 160-163.

Hamidian Jahromi A, Wigle R, Fitzgerald MJ, Pahilan ME, Youssef AM (2012). Rising self-inflicted injuries in the United States: A call for a comprehensive prevention plan and insurance coverage. *American Surgeon* 78, 1297-1298.

Han CS, Oliffe JL, Ogrodniczuk JS (2013). Suicide among East Asians in North America: A scoping review. *Journal of Mental Health.* Published online: 16 January 2013. doi: 10.3109/09638237.2012.734651.

Han L, Zhang Y, Zheng Y (2012). Responses over time of child and adolescent survivors to the 2008 Wenchuan, China earthquake. *Social Behavior and Personality* 40, 1147-1152.

Hanwella R, Senanayake SM, de Silva VA (2012). Geographical variation in admissions due to poisoning in Sri Lanka: A time series analysis. *The Ceylon Medical Journal* 57, 152-158.

Hefti S, In-Albon T, Schmeck K, Schmid M (2013). Temperament and character traits and non-suicidal self-injury in adolescents results of an epidemiological study in schools in Basel. *Nervenheilkunde* 32, 45.

Hendrix L, Verelst S, Desruelles D, Gillet J-B (2013). Deliberate self-poisoning: Characteristics of patients and impact on the emergency department of a large university hospital. *Emergency Medicine Journal* 30, E9.

Hernandez JF, Mantel-Teeuwisse AK, van Thiel GJMW, Belitser SV, Warmerdam J, de Valk V, Raaijmakers JAM, Pieters T (2012). A 10-year analysis of the effects of media coverage of regulatory warnings on antidepressant use in the Netherlands and UK. *PLoS ONE.* Published online: 20 September 2012. doi: 10.1371/journal.pone.0045515.

Jacobs-Kayam A, Lev-Wiesel R, Zohar G (2013). Self-mutilation as expressed in self-figure drawings in adolescent sexual abuse survivors. *Arts in Psychotherapy* 40, 120-129.

Jain A, Jain R, Menezes RG, Subba SH, Kotian MS, Nagesh KR (2012). Suicide ideation among medical students: A cross sectional study from South India. *Injury Prevention* 18, A166.

Jibran M (2012). Self-inflicted injuries in individuals older than 60 years of age. *Journal of General Medicine* 1, 1-2.

Jin H, Atkinson JH, Duarte NA, Yu X, Shi C, Riggs PK, Li J, Gupta S, Wolfson T, Knight A, Franklin D, Letendre S, Wu Z, Grant I, Heaton RK (2012). Risks and predictors of current suicidality in HIV-infected heroin users in treatment in Yunnan, China: A controlled study. *Journal of Acquired Immune Deficiency Syndromes* 62, 311-316.

Jonson M, Skoog I, Marlow T, Fassberg MM, Waern M (2012). Anxiety symptoms and suicidal feelings in a population sample of 70-year-olds without dementia. *International Psychogeriatrics* 24, 1865-1871.

Karakus A, Celik MM, Karcioglu M, Tuzcu K, Erden ES, Zeren C (2012). Cases of organophosphate poisoning treated with high-dose of atropine in intensive care unit and the novel treatment approaches. *Toxicology and Industrial Health*. Published online: 25 September 2012. doi: 10.1177/0748233712462478.

Kassiri H, Feiz-Haddad MH, Ghasemi F, Rezaei M, Ghanavati F (2012). An epidemiologic and demographic survey of poisoning in Southwest of Iran. *Middle East Journal of Scientific Research* 12, 990-996.

Kato K, Akama F, Yamada K, Maehara M, Kimoto K, Kimoto K, Takahashi Y, Sato R, Onishi Y, Matsumoto H (2013). Frequency and clinical features of patients who attempted suicide by charcoal burning in Japan. *Journal of Affective Disorders* 145, 133-135.

Kato K, Mikami K, Akama F, Yamada K, Maehara M, Kimoto K, Kimoto K, Sato R, Takahashi Y, Fukushima R, Ichimura A, Matsumoto H (2012). Clinical features of suicide attempts in adults with autism spectrum disorders. *General Hospital Psychiatry* 35, 50-53.

Kato K, Mikami K, Nishino R, Akama F, Yamada K, Maehara M, Saito M, Kimoto K, Kimoto K, Takahashi Y, Sato R, Onishi Y, Ohya A, Ichimura A, Matsumoto H (2012). Frequency and clinical features of borderline personality disorder in adolescent suicide attempts in Japan. *Asian Journal of Psychiatry* 5, 363-364.

Kazdin AE, French NH, Unis AS, Esveldt-Dawson K, Sherick RB (1983). Hopelessness, depression, and suicidal intent among psychiatrically disturbed inpatient children. *Journal of Consulting and Clinical Psychology* 51, 504-510.

Kenneson A, Funderburk JS, Maisto SA (2013). Risk factors for secondary substance use disorders in people with childhood and adolescent-onset bipolar disorder: Opportunities for prevention. *Comprehensive Psychiatry*. Published online: 15 January 2013. doi: 10.1016/j.comppsych.2012.12.008.

Kessler RC, Bromet EJ (2013). The epidemiology of depression across cultures. *Annual Review of Public Health* 34, 119-138.

Kilty JM (2012). Suicide and self-harm in prisons and jails. *Punishment & Society-International Journal of Penology* 14, 481-484.

Kim C-G (2012). Depression and suicide ideation among college students. *Asia-Pacific Psychiatry* 4, 118.

Kleiman EM, Riskind JH (2013). Utilized social support and self-esteem mediate the relationship between perceived social support and suicide ideation. *Crisis* 34, 42-49.

Kluetsch RC, Schmahl C, Niedtfeld I, Densmore M, Calhoun VD, Daniels J, Kraus A, Ludaescher P, Bohus M, Lanius RA (2012). Alterations in default mode network connectivity during pain processing in borderline personality disorder. *Archives of General Psychiatry* 69, 993-1002.

Kotrla Topic M, Perkovic Kovacevic M, Mlacic B (2012). Relations of the big-five personality dimensions to autodestructive behavior in clinical and non-clinical adolescent populations. *Croatian Medical Journal* 53, 450-460.

Kuehl S, Nelson K, Collings S (2012). Back so soon: Rapid re-presentations to the emergency department following intentional self-harm. *New Zealand Medical Journal* 125, 70-79.

Kweon YS, Hwang S, Yeon B, Choi KH, Oh Y, Lee HK, Lee CT, Lee KU (2012). Characteristics of drug overdose in young suicide attempters. *Clinical Psychopharmacology and Neuroscience* 10, 180-184.

Kwon OY, Park SP (2013). Frequency of affective symptoms and their psychosocial impact in Korean people with epilepsy: A survey at two tertiary care hospitals. *Epilepsy and Behavior* 26, 51-56.

Lamis DA, Jahn DR (2013). Parent-child conflict and suicide rumination in college students: The mediating roles of depressive symptoms and anxiety sensitivity. *Journal of American College Health* 61, 106-113

Lamis DA, Lester D (2013). Gender differences in risk and protective factors for suicidal ideation among college students. *Journal of College Student Psychotherapy* 27, 62-77.

Langille DB, Asbridge M, Kisely S, Rasic D (2012). Suicidal behaviours in adolescents in Nova Scotia, Canada: Protective associations with measures of social capital. *Social Psychiatry and Psychiatric Epidemiology* 47, 1549-1555.

Lindner R (2012). Suicidality in the elderly. *Suizidalität im Alter* 137, 2002-2004.

Loas G, Defelice E (2012). Absolute and relative short-term stability of interpersonal dependency in suicide attempters. *The Journal of Nervous and Mental Disease* 200, 904-907.

Logan JE, Walsh S, Patel N, Hall JE (2013). Homicide-followed-by-suicide incidents involving child victims. *American Journal of Health Behavior* 37, 531-542

Lucero NB, Beckstrand RL, Callister LC, Birkhead ACS (2012). Prevalence of postpartum depression among Hispanic immigrant women. *Journal of the American Academy of Nurse Practitioners* 24, 726-734.

Lueckhoff M, Jordaan E, Koen L, Niehaus DJH (2012). Suicidal behaviour in a schizophrenic xhosa population. *South African Journal of Psychiatry* 18, 125.

Luke JN, Anderson IP, Gee GJ, Thorpe R, Rowley KG, Reilly RE, Thorpe A, Stewart PJ (2013). Suicide ideation and attempt in a community cohort of urban Aboriginal youth: A cross-sectional study. *Crisis.* Published online: 28 January 2013. doi: 10.1027/0227-5910/a000187.

Lund C, Teige B, Drottning P, Stiksrud B, Rui TO, Lyngra M, Ekeberg O, Jacobsen D, Hovda KE (2012). A one-year observational study of all hospitalized and fatal acute poisonings in Oslo: Epidemiology, intention and follow-up. *BMC Public Health* 12, 858.

Luong MA, Khieu TQT, Tran TNL, Nguyen TTH, Pham LT (2012). Injury situation in Vietnam in 2005-2010 and preventive strategies in 2011-2015. *Injury Prevention* 18, A233-A234.

Lupu A, Stefanescu P, Panaitescu V, Rosu M, Hostiuc S (2012). Aggressivity in penitentiaries. A retrospective study conducted in Galati county between 2003-2008. *Romanian Journal of Legal Medicine* 20, 283-286.

Mallett CA, Quinn LM, Stoddard-Dare P (2012). Significant gender differences in factors related to the detention of youthful offenders. *Women and Criminal Justice* 22, 309-326.

Maniglio R (2013). The impact of child sexual abuse on the course of bipolar disorder: A systematic review. *Bipolar Disorders.* Published online: 24 January 2013. doi: 10.1111/bdi.12050.

Manikkam L, Burns JK (2012). Antenatal depression and its risk factors: An urban prevalence study in Kwazulu-natal. *Samj South African Medical Journal* 102, 940-944.

Mark L, Samm A, Tooding L-M, Sisask M, Aasvee K, Zaborskis A, Zemaitiene N, Vaernik A (2013). Suicidal ideation, risk factors, and communication with parents an HBSC study on school children in Estonia, Lithuania, and Luxembourg. *Crisis* 34, 3-12.

Marwaha S, Parsons N, Broome M (2013). Mood instability, mental illness and suicidal ideas: Results from a household survey. *Social Psychiatry and Psychiatric Epidemiology*. Published online: 24 January 2013. doi: 10.1007/s00127-013-0653-7.

Matsu CR, Goebert D, Chung-Do JJ, Carlton B, Sugimoto-Matsuda J, Nishimura S (2012). Disparities in psychiatric emergency department visits among youth in Hawai'i, 2000-2010. *Journal of Pediatrics* 162, 618-623.

Miyaoka T, Wake R, Furuya M, Liaury K, Ieda M, Kawakami K, Tsuchie K, Inagaki T, Horiguchi J (2012). Yokukansan (TJ-54) for treatment of pervasive developmental disorder not otherwise specified and asperger's disorder: A 12-week prospective, open-label study. *BMC Psychiatry* 12, 215.

Modi D, Bhalavat R, Patterson JC, 2nd (2013). Suicidal and homicidal behaviors related to dextromethorphan abuse in a middle-aged woman. *Journal of Addiction Medicine*. Published online: 5 February 2013. doi: 10.1097/ADM.0b013e318281a547.

Mok CC, Chan K, Yip P (2012). Suicidal ideation in patients with systemic lupus erythematosus: Incidence and relationship with anxiety/depression score, disease activity and organ damage. *Arthritis and Rheumatism* 64, S281-S282.

Moravej H, Haghighat M, Moatamedi M (2013). Epidemiology of pediatric acute poisoning in southern Iran: A hospital-based study. *Bulletin of Emergency and Trauma* 1, 28-33.

Mousavi SG, Keramatian K, Maracy MR, Fouladi M (2012). Suicidal ideation, depression, and aggression among students of three universities of Isfahan, Iran in 2008. *Iranian Journal of Psychiatry and Behavioral Sciences* 6, 47-52.

Nan H, Lee PH, McDowell I, Ni MY, Stewart SM, Lam TH (2012). Depressive symptoms in people with chronic physical conditions: Prevalence and risk factors in a Hong Kong community sample. *BMC Psychiatry* 12, 198.

Nasseri K, Mills PK, Mirshahidi HR, Moulton LH (2012). Suicide in cancer patients in California, 1997-2006. *Archives of Suicide Research* 16, 324-333.

Navines R, Gutierrez F, Arranz B, Moreno-Espana J, Luisa Imaz M, Soler V, Vazquez M, Carlos Pascual J, Martin-Santos R, Kahn DA (2013). Long-term and bizarre self-injurious behavior: An approach to underlying psychological mechanisms and management. *Journal of Psychiatric Practice* 19, 65-71.

Nazem S, Fiske A, Nadorff MR (2012). A critical examination of the research on cognitive impairment, dementia and suicidal behaviors. *Gerontologist* 52, 245.

Neilson Ze, Morrison W (2012). Childhood self-poisoning: A one-year review. *Scottish Medical Journal* 57, 196-199.

Nexoe J, Wilche JP, Niclasen B, Kjeldsen AB, Faergemann C, Munck A, Lauritsen JM (2013). Violence- and alcohol-related acute healthcare visits in Greenland. *Scandinavian Journal of Public Health* 41, 113-118.

Nigg J (2012). Attention-deficit/hyperactivity disorder and adverse health outcomes. *Clinical Psychology Review* 33, 215-228.

Nyberg C, Schyllander J, Ekman DS, Janson S (2012). Socio-economic risk factors for injuries in Swedish children and adolescents: A national study over 15 years. *Global Public Health* 7, 1170-1184.

Nyer M, Holt DJ, Pedrelli P, Fava M, Ameral V, Cassiello CF, Nock MK, Ross M, Hutchinson D, Farabaugh A (2013). Factors that distinguish college students with depressive symptoms with and without suicidal thoughts. *Annals of Clinical Psychiatry* 25, 41-49.

O'Dwyer ST, Moyle W, Van Wyk S (2012). Suicidal ideation in family carers of people with dementia: An Australian study. *Gerontologist* 52, 331.

O'Dwyer ST, Moyle W, Zimmer-Gembeck M, De Leo D (2013). Suicidal ideation in family carers of people with dementia: A pilot study. *International Journal of Geriatric Psychiatry*. Published online: 4 March 2013. doi: 10.1002/gps.3941.

Odlaug BL, Grant JE, Kim SW (2012). Suicide attempts in 107 adolescents and adults with kleptomania. *Archives of Suicide Research* 16, 348-359.

Omma L, Sandlund M, Jacobsson L (2013). Suicidal expressions in young Swedish Sami, a cross-sectional study. *International Journal of Circumpolar Health* 72, 19862.

Ouédraogo M, Yéré S, Traoré S, Guissou IP (2012). Acute intoxications in two university hospitals in Burkina Faso. *African Health Sciences* 12, 483-486.

Paholpak P, Rangseekajee P, Arunpongpaisal S, Piyavhatkul N, Thepsuthammarat K, Paholpak S (2012). Characteristics and burden of hospitalization because of intentional self-harm: Thai national, hospital-based data for 2010. *Journal of the Medical Association of Thailand* 95, S156-S162.

Pan LA, Hassel S, Segreti AM, Nau SA, Brent DA, Phillips ML (2013). Differential patterns of activity and functional connectivity in emotion processing neural circuitry to angry and happy faces in adolescents with and without suicide attempt. *Psychological Medicine*. Published online: 9 January 2013. doi: 10.1017/S0033291712002966.

Park CH, Kim GS (2013). A validation study on DAS in the prediction of suicidal risk for adolescents. *Arts in Psychotherapy* 40, 108-114.

Parker G, Fletcher K, McCraw S, Futeran S, Hong M (2012). Identifying antecedent and illness course variables differentiating bipolar I, bipolar II and unipolar disorders. *Journal of Affective Disorders*. Published online: 21 December 2012. doi: 10.1016/j.jad.2012.11.061.

Parmentier C, Etain B, Yon L, Misson H, Mathieu F, Lajnef M, Cochet B, Raust A, Kahn JP, Wajsbrot-Elgrabli O, Cohen R, Henry C, Leboyer M, Bellivier F (2012). Clinical and dimensional characteristics of euthymic bipolar patients with or without suicidal behavior. *European Psychiatry* 27, 570-576.

Patil VC, Patil HV, Agrawal V, Tryambake S, Kore S (2012). Clinical profile and outcome of organophosphorus poisoning at tertiary care centre in Western Maharashtra. *Indian Journal of Forensic Medicine and Toxicology* 6, 239-243.

Pawlak J, Dmitrzak-Weglarz M, Skibi ska M, Szczepankiewicz A, Leszczy ska-Rodziewicz A, Rajewska-Rager A, Maciukiewicz M, Czerski P, Hauser J (2013). Suicide attempts and psychological risk factors in patients with bipolar and unipolar affective disorder. *General Hospital Psychiatry*. Published online: 23 January 2013. doi: 10.1016/j.genhosppsych.2012.11.010.

Perlis RH, Ruderfer D, Hamilton SP, Ernst C (2012). Copy number variation in subjects with major depressive disorder who attempted suicide. *PLoS ONE*. Published online: 27 September 2012. doi: 10.1371/journal.pone.0046315.

Perry BL, Pullen EL, Oser CB (2012). Too much of a good thing? Psychosocial resources, gendered racism, and suicidal ideation among low socioeconomic status African American women. *Social Psychology Quarterly* 75, 334-359.

Plener PL, Fischer CJ, In-Albon T, Rollett B, Nixon MK, Groschwitz RC, Schmid M (2013). Adolescent non-suicidal self-injury (NSSI) in German-speaking countries: Comparing prevalence rates from three community samples. *Social Psychiatry and Psychiatric Epidemiology*. Published online: 5 January 2013. doi: 10.1007/s00127-012-0645-z.

Pompili M, Innamorati M, Lester D, Serafini G, Erbuto D, Battuello M, Tatarelli R, Oquendo MA, Girardi P (2012). Suicide attempts in acute psychiatric referrals with substance use disorders. *Rivista di Psichiatria* 47, 313-318.

Power J, Brown SL, Usher AM (2013). Prevalence and incidence of nonsuicidal self-injury among federally sentenced women in Canada. *Criminal Justice and Behavior* 40, 302-320.

Rabin F, Bhuiyan SI, Islam T, Haque MA, Islam MA (2012). Psychiatric and psychological comorbidities in patients with psoriasis- A review. *Mymensingh Medical Journal* 21, 780-786.

Ragolsky M, Shimon H, Shalev H, Weizman A, Rubin E (2013). Suicidal thoughts are associated with platelet counts in adolescent inpatients. *Journal of Child and Adolescent Psychopharmacology* 23, 49-53.

Rajalin M, Hirvikoski T, Jokinen J (2012). Family history of suicide and exposure to interpersonal violence in childhood predict suicide in male suicide attempters. *Journal of Affective Disorders.* Published online: 25 December 2012. doi: 10.1016/j.jad.2012.11.055.

Ramim T, Mobayen M, Shoar N, Naderan M, Shoar S (2013). Burnt wives in Tehran: A warm tragedy of self-injury. *International Journal of Burns and Trauma* 3, 66-71.

Rausch J, Hametz P, Zuckerbrot R, Rausch W, Soren K (2012). Screening for depression in urban Latino adolescents. *Clinical Pediatrics* 51, 964-971.

Reich M, Comet B, Le Rhun E, Ramirez C (2012). Cotard's syndrome with glioblastoma multiforme. *Palliative & Supportive Care* 10, 135-139.

Roaldset JO, Linaker OM, Bjørkly S (2012). Predictive validity of the mini suicidal scale for self-harm in acute psychiatry: A prospective study of the first year after discharge. *Archives of Suicide Research* 16, 287-302.

Robinson JP, Espelage DL (2012). Bullying explains only part of LGBTQ-heterosexual risk disparities: Implications for policy and practice. *Educational Researcher* 41, 309-319.

Rolim Neto ML, Advincula Reis AO, de Almeida JC (2012). Bipolar disorder, suicide and vulnerable children in northeast Brazil. *HealthMED* 6, 3190-3193.

Roy P, Tremblay G, Oliffe JL, Jbilou J, Robertson S (2013). Male farmers with mental health disorders: A scoping review. *Australian Journal of Rural Health* 21, 3-7.

Sachs-Ericsson N, Corsentino E, Rushing NC, Sheffler J (2013). Early childhood abuse and late-life suicidal ideation. *Aging and Mental Health.* Published online: 21 January 2013. doi: 10.1080/13607863.2012.758236.

Sansone RA, Kelley AR, Forbis JS (2013). The relationship between forgiveness and history of suicide attempt. *Mental Health, Religion & Culture* 16, 31.

Schwalbe CS, Gearing RE, MacKenzie MJ, Brewer KB, Ibrahim RW (2013). The impact of length of placement on self-reported mental health problems in detained Jordanian youth. *International Journal of Law and Psychiatry* 36, 107-112.

Shahpesandy H, van Heeswijk A (2012). Suicide on the Isle of Wight: A case-study of 35 suicides among mental health service users between 2006 and 2008. *Irish Journal of Psychological Medicine* 29, 80-84.

Sharif-Alhoseini M, Rasouli Mr, Saadat S, Haddadi M, Gooya Mm, Afsari M, Rahimi-Movaghar V (2012). Suicide attempts and suicide in Iran: Results of national hospital surveillance data. *Public Health* 126, 990-992.

Shim E-J, Park J-H (2012). Suicidality and its associated factors in cancer patients: Results of a multi-center study in Korea. *International Journal of Psychiatry in Medicine* 43, 381-403.

Singh A, Rajesh DR, Kaur B, Bhardwaj A (2012). Profile and pattern of suicidal and homicidal burn victims at a tertiary care hospital in Northern India. *Indian Journal of Forensic Medicine and Toxicology* 6, 6-9.

Sisek-Šprem M, Bari V, Herceg M, Juki V, Miloševi M, Petrovi Z (2012). Demographic characteristic of aggressive patients with schizophrenia. *Demografske osobine agresivnih bolesnika oboljelih od shizofrenije* 40, 213-220.

Sornberger MJ, Smith NG, Toste JR, Heath NL (2013). Nonsuicidal self-injury, coping strategies, and sexual orientation. *Journal of Clinical Psychology.* Published online: 4 February 2013. doi: 10.1002/jclp.21947.

Soylu N, Alpaslan AH (2013). Suicidal behavior and associated factors in sexually abused adolescents. *Children and Youth Services Review* 35, 253-257.

Stathis SL, Doolan I, Letters P, Arnett A, Cory S, Quinlan L (2012). Use of the Westerman Aboriginal Symptoms Checklist - Youth (WASC-Y) to screen for mental health problems in Indigenous youth in custody. *Advances in Mental Health* 10, 235-239.

Straiton ML, Hjelmeland H, Grimholt TK, Dieserud G (2013). Self-harm and conventional gender roles in women. *Suicide and Life-Threatening Behavior* 43, 161-173.

Strehlau V, Torchalla I, Kathy L, Schuetz C, Krausz M (2012). Mental health, concurrent disorders, and health care utilization in homeless women. *Journal of Psychiatric Practice* 18, 349-360.

Sugawara N, Yasui-Furukori N, Sasaki G, Tanaka O, Umeda T, Takahashi I, Danjo K, Matsuzaka M, Kaneko S, Nakaji S (2012). Gender differences in factors associated with suicidal ideation and depressive symptoms among middle-aged workers in Japan. *Industrial Health.* Published online: 26 December 2012. doi: 10.2486/indhealth.MS1354.

Swearer SM, Espelage DL, Koenig B, Berry B, Collins A, Lembeck P (2012). A social-ecological model for bullying prevention and intervention in early adolescence. *Handbook of School Violence and School Safety: International Research and Practice, 2nd Edition* 333-355.

Tang WK, Chen YK, Liang HJ, Chu WC, Mok VC, Ungvari GS, Wong KS (2012). Cerebral microbleeds and suicidality in stroke. *Psychosomatics* 53, 439-445.

Tavares D, Quevedo L, Jansen K, Souza L, Pinheiro R, Silva R (2012). Prevalence of suicide risk and comorbidities in postpartum women in Pelotas. *Revista Brasileira De Psiquiatria* 34, 270-276.

Ten Have M, Van Dorsselaer S, de Graaf R (2012). Prevalence and risk factors for first onset of suicidal behaviors in the Netherlands mental health survey and incidence study-2. *Journal of Affective Disorders* 147, 205-211.

Testa RJ, Sciacca LM, Wang F, Hendricks ML, Goldblum P, Bradford J, Bongar B (2012). Effects of violence on transgender people. *Professional Psychology: Research and Practice* 43, 452.

Upadhyaya SK, Gupta S, Sharma A, Joshi A (2012). A study of psycho-socio-demographic variables of suicide attempters in hilly areas of Uttarakhand. *Indian Journal of Community Health* 24, 222-226.

Valois RF, Kerr JC, Scott Huebner E (2012). Peer victimization and perceived life satisfaction among early adolescents in the United States. *American Journal of Health Education* 43, 258-268.

Van Orden KA, O'Riley A, Richardson T, Podgorski C, Conwell Y (2012). Racial differences in suicide ideation among older adults in the U.S. *Gerontologist* 52, 498-499.

Volkmann J, Wolters A, Kupsch A, Mueller J, Kuehn AA, Schneider G-H, Poewe W, Hering S, Eisner W, Mueller J-U, Deuschl G, Pinsker MO, Skogseid I-M, Roeste GK, Krause M, Tronnier V, Schnitzler A, Voges J, Nikkhah G, Vesper J, Classen J, Naumann M, Benecke R, Dystonia DBSSG (2012). Pallidal deep brain stimulation in patients with primary generalised or segmental dystonia: 5-year follow-up of a randomised trial. *Lancet Neurology* 11, 1029-1038

Wang L, Liu L, Shi S, Gao J, Liu Y, Li Y, Zhang Z, Wang G, Zhang K, Tao M, Gao C, Li K, Wang X, Lv L, Jiang G, Wang X, Jia H, Zhang J, Lu C, Li Y, Li K, Hu C, Ning Y, Li Y, Sun J, Liu T, Zhang Y, Ha B, Tian H, Meng H, Hu J, Chen Y, Deng H, Huang G, Wu W, Li G, Fang X, Pan J, Hong X, Gao S, Li X, Yang D, Chen G, Liu T, Cai M, Dong J, Mei Q, Shen Z, Pan R, Liu Z, Wang X, Tan Y, Flint J, Kendler KS (2013). Cognitive trio: Relationship with major depression and clinical predictors in Han Chinese women. *Psychological Medicine.* Published online: 21 February 2013. doi: 10.1017/S0033291713000160.

Way BB, Kaufman AR, Knoll JL, Chlebowski SM (2013). Suicidal ideation among inmate-patients in state prison: Prevalence, reluctance to report, and treatment preferences. *Behavioural Science and the Law.* Published online: 15 February 2013. doi: 10.1002/bsl.2055.

Wensley K, Campbell M (2012). Heterosexual and nonheterosexual young university students' involvement in traditional and cyber forms of bullying. *Cyberpsychology Behavior and Social Networking* 15, 649-654.

Wharff EA, Ginnis KM, Ross AM (2012). Family-based crisis intervention with suicidal adolescents in the emergency room: A pilot study. *Social Work* 57, 133-143.

White AM, Macinnes E, Hingson RW, Pan IJ (2013). Hospitalizations for suicide-related drug poisonings and co-occurring alcohol overdoses in adolescents (ages 12-17) and young adults (ages 18-24) in the United States, 1999-2008: Results from the nationwide inpatient sample. *Suicide and Life-Threatening Behavior* 43, 198-212.

Wiegand TJ, Wax PM, Schwartz T, Finkelstein Y, Gorodetsky R, Brent J (2012). The toxicology investigators consortium case registry: The 2011 experience. *Journal of Medical Toxicology* 8, 360-377.

Wiktorsson S, Berg AI, Billstedt E, Duberstein PR, Marlow T, Skoog I, Waern M (2013). Neuroticism and extroversion in suicide attempters aged 75 and above and a general population comparison group. *Aging and Mental Health.* Published online: 21 January 2103. doi: 10.1080/13607863.2012.749835.

Wilkowska-Chmielewska J, Szelenberger W, Wojnar M (2013). Age-dependent symptomatology of depression in hospitalized patients and its implications for DSM-5. *Journal of Affective Disorders.* Published online: 16 January 2013. doi: 10.1016/j.jad.2012.12.012.

Wilson M, Dunlavy A (2012). Suicidal ideation among adolescents in Dar es Salaam, Tanzania: Patterns, planning and significant associations. *Injury Prevention* 18, A34.

Wong Z, Ongür D, Cohen B, Ravichandran C, Noam G, Murphy B (2013). Command hallucinations and clinical characteristics of suicidality in patients with psychotic spectrum disorders. *Comprehensive Psychiatry.* Published online: 30 January 2013. doi: 10.1016/j.comppsych.2012.12.022.

Wortzel HS, Blatchford P, Conner L, Adler LE, Binswanger IA (2012). Risk of death for veterans on release from prison. *Journal of the American Academy of Psychiatry and the Law* 40, 348-354.

Youssef NA, Green KT, Beckham JC, Elbogen EB (2013). A 3-year longitudinal study examining the effect of resilience on suicidality in veterans. *Annals of Clinical Psychiatry* 25, 59-66.

Zakharov S, Navratil T, Pelclova D (2013). Non-fatal suicidal self-poisonings in children and adolescents over a 5-year period (2007-2011). *Basic and Clinical Pharmacology and Toxicology.* Published online: 11 January 2013. doi: 10.1111/bcpt.12047.

Zaletel LZ, Cizek-Sajko M, Jereb B (2012). Suicidal risk among childhood cancer survivors in Slovenia. *Pediatric Blood & Cancer* 59, 1109.

Zetterqvist M, Lundh LG, Dahlstrom O, Svedin CG (2013). Prevalence and function of non-suicidal self-injury (NSSI) in a community sample of adolescents, using suggested DSM-5 criteria for a potential NSSI disorder. *Journal of Abnormal Child Psychology.* Published online: 24 January 2013. doi: 10.1007/s10802-013-9712-5.

Zetterqvist M, Lundh LG, Svedin CG (2012). A comparison of adolescents engaging in self-injurious behaviors with and without suicidal intent: Self-reported experiences of adverse life events and trauma symptoms. *Journal of Youth and Adolescence.* Published online: 5 December 2012. doi: 10.1007/s10964-012-9872-6.

Zhang J, Wang C (2012). Factors in the neighborhood as risks of suicide in rural China: A multi-level analysis. *Community Mental Health Journal* 48, 627-633.

Zosel A, Bartelson BB, Bailey E, Lowenstein S, Dart R (2013). Characterization of adolescent prescription drug abuse and misuse using the researched abuse diversion and addiction-related surveillance (radars®) system. *Journal of the American Academy of Child and Adolescent Psychiatry* 52, 196-204.

Risk and protective factors

Abel WD, Sewell C, Martin JS, Bailey-Davidson Y, Fox K (2012). Suicide ideation in Jamaican youth: Sociodemographic prevalence, protective and risk factors. *West Indian Medical Journal* 61, 521-525.

Acosta FJ, Aguilar EJ, Cejas MR, Gracia R (2013). Beliefs about illness and their relationship with hopelessness, depression, insight and suicide attempts in schizophrenia. *Psychiatria Danubina* 25, 49-54.

Acton EK, Tatum WO (2013). Inpatient psychiatric consultation for newly-diagnosed patients with psychogenic non-epileptic seizures. *Epilepsy and Behavior* 27, 36-39.

Agrawal A, Constantino AM, Bucholz KK, Glowinski A, Madden PAF, Heath AC, Lynskey MT (2013). Characterizing alcohol use disorders and suicidal ideation in young women. *Journal of Studies on Alcohol and Drugs* 74, 406-412.

Akena D, Joska J, Obuku EA, Amos T, Musisi S, Stein DJ (2012). Comparing the accuracy of brief versus long depression screening instruments which have been validated in low and middle income countries: A systematic review. *BMC Psychiatry* 12, 187.

Alfonso ML, Kaur R (2012). Self-injury among early adolescents: Identifying segments protected and at risk. *The Journal of School Health* 82, 537-547.

Ali TS, Krantz G, Mogren I (2012). Violence permeating daily life: A qualitative study investigating perspectives on violence among women in Karachi, Pakistan. *International Journal of Women's Health* 4, 577-585.

Almeida OP, Draper B, Snowdon J, Lautenschlager NT, Pirkis J, Byrne G, Sim M, Stocks N, Flicker L, Pfaff JJ (2012). Factors associated with suicidal thoughts in a large community study of older adults. *British Journal of Psychiatry* 201, 466-472.

Anonymous. (2012). Understanding self-harm. *Lancet* 380, 1532.

Antypa N, Giegling I, Calati R, Schneider B, Hartmann AM, Friedl M, Konte B, Lia L, De Ronchi D, Serretti A, Rujescu D (2012). MAOA and MAOB polymorphisms and anger-related traits in suicidal participants and controls. *European Archives of Psychiatry and Clinical Neuroscience.* Published online: 31 October 2012. doi: 10.1007/s00406-012-0378-8.

Anyansi TE, Agyapong VI (2012). Factors predicting suicidal ideation in the preceding 12 months among patients attending a community psychiatric outpatient clinic. *International Journal of Psychiatry in Clinical Practice.* Published online: 23 October 2012. doi: 10.3109/13651501.2012.735243.

Areas U, Mojs E, Warchoł-Biedermann K, Głowacka MD, Strzelecki W, Ziemska B, Marcinkowski JT (2012). Social and health care needs of elderly people living in the countryside in Poland. *Annals of Agricultural and Environmental Medicine* 19, 770-774.

Assefa D, Shibre T, Asher L, Fekadu A (2012). Internalized stigma among patients with schizophrenia in Ethiopia: A cross-sectional facility-based study. BMC Psychiatry 12, 239.

Asarnow J, McArthur D, Hughes J, Barbery V, Berk M (2012). Suicide attempt risk in youths: Utility of the Harkavy-Asnis Suicide Scale for monitoring risk levels. *Suicide and Life-Threatening Behavior* 42, 684-698.

Badura Brack A, Huefner JC, Handwerk ML (2012). The impact of abuse and gender on psychopathology, behavioral disturbance, and psychotropic medication count for youth in residential treatment. *American Journal of Orthopsychiatry* 82, 562-572.

Bagge CL, Glenn CR, Lee H-J (2012). Quantifying the impact of recent negative life events on suicide attempts. *Journal of Abnormal Psychology.* Published online: 22 October 2012. doi: 10.1037/a0030371.

Baker A, Wright K, Hansen E (2012). A qualitative study exploring female patients' experiences of self-harm in a medium secure unit. *Journal of Psychiatric and Mental Health Nursing.* Published online: 7 December 2012. doi: 10.1111/jpm.12031.

Balazs J, Miklósi M, Keresztény A, Hoven CW, Carli V, Wasserman C, Apter A, Bobes J, Brunner R, Cosman D, Cotter P, Haring C, Iosue M, Kaess M, Kahn J-P, Keeley H, Marusic D, Postuvan V, Resch F, Sáiz PA, Sisask M, Snir A, Tubiana A, Varnik A, Sarchiapone M, Wasserman D (2013). Adolescent subthreshold-depression and anxiety: Psychopathology, functional impairment and increased suicide risk. *Journal of Child Psychology and Psychiatry.* Published online: 18 January 2013. doi: 10.1111/jcpp.12016.

Ball H, Dutta R, Sumathipala A, Siribaddana S, Hotopf M, McGuffin P (2012). P1 genetic and environmental contributions to suicidal ideation, and relationship with depression: A twin study in Sri Lanka. *Journal of Neurology Neurosurgery and Psychiatry* 83, e1.

Batterham PJ, Christensen H, Calear AL (2013). Anxiety symptoms as precursors of major depression and suicidal ideation. *Depression and Anxiety.* Published online: 14 March 2013. doi: 10.1002/da.22066.

Bauman S, Toomey RB, Walker JL (2013). Associations among bullying, cyberbullying, and suicide in high school students. *Journal of Adolescence* 36, 341-350.

Beatson JA, Rao S (2012). Depression and borderline personality disorder. *Medical Journal of Australia Open* 4, 24-27.

Belleville G, Foldes-Busque G, Dixon M, Marquis-Pelletier E, Barbeau S, Poitras J, Chauny JM, Diodati JG, Fleet R, Marchand A (2012). Impact of seasonal and lunar cycles on psychological symptoms in the ED: An empirical investigation of widely spread beliefs. *General Hospital Psychiatry.* Published online: 3 July 2012. doi: 10.1016/j.genhosppsych.2012.10.002.

Benitez-Borrego S, Guardia-Olmos J, Aliaga-Moore A (2012). Child homicide by parents in Chile: A gender-based study and analysis of post-filicide attempted suicide. *International Journal of Law and Psychiatry* 36, 55-64.

Ben-Efraim YJ, Wasserman D, Wasserman J, Sokolowski M (2013). Family-based study of AVPR1B association and interaction with stressful life events on depression and anxiety in suicide attempts. *Neuropsychopharmacology.* Published online: 19 February 2013. doi: 10.1038/npp.2013.49.

Bener A, Verjee M, Dafeeah EE, Falah O, Al-Juhaishi T, Schlogl J, Sedeeq A, Khan S (2013). Psychological factors: Anxiety, depression, and somatization symptoms in low back pain patients. *Journal of Pain Research* 6, 95-101.

Bergen H, Hawton K, Kapur N (2012). Following self-harm, there are shared and differing risk factors for subsequent suicide death or accidental death. *Evidence Based Mental Health* 15, 101.

Bhattacharya A, Bisui B, Das R, Saha D, Sen S, Thakurta R, Singh OP (2012). Rapid response with ketamine on suicidal cognition in resistant depression. *Indian Journal of Psychological Medicine* 34, 170-175.

Bhavsar AR (2013). Respect and rationality: The challenge of attempted suicide. *American Journal of Bioethics* 13, 24-25.

Bilén K, Ponzer S, Ottosson C, Castrén M, Owe-Larsson B, Ekdahl K, Pettersson H (2013). Can repetition of deliberate self-harm be predicted? A prospective multicenter study validating clinical decision rules. *Journal of Affective Disorders.* Published online: 28 February 2013. doi: 10.1016/j.jad.2013.01.037.

Bishop TM, Pigeon WR, Possemato K, Bruder TM (2012). Sleep disturbance as a risk factor for suicidal ideation in veterans. *Sleep* 35, A334.

Björkenstam E, Hjern A, Mittendorfer-Rutz E, Vinnerljung B, Hallqvist J, Ljung R (2013). Multi-exposure and clustering of adverse childhood experiences, socioeconomic differences and psychotropic medication in young adults. *PLoS ONE*. Published online: 16 January 2013. doi: 10.1371/journal.pone.0053551.s001.

Black EB, Mildred H (2013). Predicting impulsive self-injurious behavior in a sample of adult women. *Journal of Nervous and Mental Disease* 201, 72-75.

Black SW, Pössel P (2012). The combined effects of self-referent information processing and ruminative responses on adolescent depression. *Journal of Youth and Adolescence*. Published online: 7 October 2012. doi: 10.1007/s10964-012-9827-y.

Blosnich J, Bossarte R (2013). Suicide acceptability among U.S. Veterans with active duty experience: Results from the 2010 general social survey. *Archives of Suicide Research* 17, 52-57.

Bocker E, Glasser M, Nielsen K, Weidenbacher-Hoper V (2012). Rural older adults' mental health: Status and challenges in care delivery. *Rural and Remote Health* 12, 2199.

Boelen PA (2012). Symptoms of prolonged grief, depression, and adult separation anxiety: Distinctiveness and correlates. *Psychiatry Research*. Published online: 12 October 2012. doi: 10.1016/j.psychres.2012.09.021.

Boeninger DK, Masyn KE, Conger RD (2012). Testing alternative explanations for the associations between parenting and adolescent suicidal problems. *Journal of Research on Adolescence*. Published online: 21 December 2012. doi: 10.1111/jora.12015.

Bortolato M, Pivac N, Seler DM, Perkovic MN, Pessia M, Giovanni GD (2013). The role of serotonergic system at the interface of aggression and suicide. *Neuroscience* 236, 160-185.

Bowen R, Balbuena L, Leuschen C, Baetz M (2012). Mood instability is the distinctive feature of neuroticism. Results from the British Health and Lifestyle Study (HALS). *Personality and Individual Differences* 53, 896-900.

Brabant M-E, Hebert M, Chagnon F (2013). Identification of sexually abused female adolescents at risk for suicidal ideations: A classification and regression tree analysis. *Journal of Child Sexual Abuse* 22, 153-172.

Brack AB, Huefner JC, Handwerk ML (2012). The impact of abuse and gender on psychopathology, behavioral disturbance, and psychotropic medication count for youth in residential treatment. *American Journal of Orthopsychiatry* 82, 562.

Breen AV, Lewis SP, Sutherland O (2013). Brief report: Non-suicidal self-injury in the context of self and identity development. *Journal of Adult Development* 20, 57-62.

Bresin K, Carter DL, Gordon KH (2012). The relationship between trait impulsivity, negative affective states, and urge for nonsuicidal self-injury: A daily diary study. *Psychiatry Research* 205, 227-231.

Bresin K, Gordon KH (2013). Endogenous opioids and nonsuicidal self-injury: A mechanism of affect regulation. *Neuroscience and Biobehavioral Reviews* 37, 374-383.

Breuillaud L, Rossetti C, Meylan EM, Merinat C, Halfon O, Magistretti PJ, Cardinaux J-R (2012). Deletion of creb-regulated transcription coactivator 1 induces pathological aggression, depression-related behaviors, and neuroplasticity genes dysregulation in mice. *Biological Psychiatry* 72, 528-536.

Brown C, Dashjian LT, Acosta TJ, Mueller CT, Kizer BE, Transgrud HB (2013). Learning from the life experiences of male-to-female transsexuals. *Journal of GLBT Family Studies* 9, 105.

Bryan CJ, Morrow CE, Etienne N, Ray-Sannerud B (2012). Guilt, shame, and suicidal ideation in a military outpatient clinical sample. *Depression and Anxiety* 30, 55-60.

Bryan CJ, McNaugton-Cassill M, Osman A, Hernandez AM (2013). The associations of physical and sexual assault with suicide risk in nonclinical military and undergraduate samples. *Suicide and Life-Threatening Behavior* 43, 223-234.

Bu ET, Hellandsjø, Skutle A (2013). After the ban of slot machines in Norway: A new group of treatment-seeking pathological gamblers? *Journal of Gambling Studies* 29, 37-50.

Buerli M, Schmid M, In-Albon T (2013). Emotion regulation and interpersonal relationships in adolescents with NSSI - Emotion recognition and emotion expression. *Nervenheilkunde* 32, 24-29.

Bushe CJ, Savill NC (2013). Systematic review of atomoxetine data in childhood and adolescent attention-deficit hyperactivity disorder 2009-2011: Focus on clinical efficacy and safety. *Journal of Psychopharmacology*. Published online: 25 February 2013. doi: 10.1177/0269881113478475.

Bussing R, Murphy TK, Storch EA, McNamara JPH, Reid AM, Garvan CW, Goodman WK (2012). Psychometric properties of the treatment-emergent activation and suicidality assessment profile (TEASAP) in youth with OCD. *Psychiatry Research* 205, 253-261.

Buttar A, Clements-Nolle K, Haas J, Reese F (2013). Dating violence, psychological distress, and attempted suicide among female adolescents in the juvenile justice system. *Journal of Correctional Health Care*. Published online: 8 March 2013. doi: 10.1177/1078345812474639.

Buykx P, Ritter A, Loxley W, Dietze P (2012). Patients who attend the emergency department following medication overdose: Self-reported mental health history and intended outcomes of overdose. *International Journal of Mental Health and Addiction* 10, 501-511.

Castro TS, Osório A (2012). Online violence: Not beautiful enough... Not thin enough. Anorectic testimonials in the web. *PsychNology Journal* 10, 169-186.

Campos RC, Besser A, Blatt SJ (2013). Recollections of parental rejection, self-criticism and depression in suicidality. *Archives of Suicide Research* 17, 58-74.

Capron DW, Norr AM, Macatee RJ, Schmidt NB (2013). Distress tolerance and anxiety sensitivity cognitive concerns: Testing the incremental contributions of affect dysregulation constructs on suicidal ideation and suicide attempt. *Behavior Therapy*. Published online: 19 December 2012. doi: 10.1016/j.beth.2012.12.002.

Carli V, Mandelli L, Zaninotto L, Iosue M, Hadlaczky G, Wasserman D, Hegerl U, Varnik A, Reisch T, Serretti A, Sarchiapone M (2013). Serious suicidal behaviors: Socio-demographic and clinical features in a multinational, multicenter sample. *Nordic Journal of Psychiatry*. Published online: 19 February 2013. doi: 10.3109/08039488.2013.767934.

Copeland WE, Wolke D, Angold A, Costello EJ (2013). Adult psychiatric outcomes of bullying and being bullied by peers in childhood and adolescence. *JAMA Psychiatry* 70, 419-426.

Cortese S, Holtmann M, Banaschewski T, Buitelaar J, Coghill D, Danckaerts M, Dittmann RW, Graham J, Taylor E, Sergeant J (2013). Practitioner review: Current best practice in the management of AES during treatment with ADHD medications in children and adolescents. *Journal of Child Psychology and Psychiatry and Allied Disciplines* 54, 227-246.

Caron J, Fleury MJ, Perreault M, Crocker A, Tremblay J, Tousignant M, Kestens Y, Cargo M, Daniel M (2012). Prevalence of psychological distress and mental disorders, and use of mental health services in the epidemiological catchment area of Montreal south-west. *BMC Psychiatry* 12, 183.

Cepuch G, Debska G, Pawlik L, Mazurek H (2012). Patient's perception of the meaning of life in cystic fibrosis - Its evaluation with respect to the stage of the disease and treatment. *Postepy Higieny i Medycyny Doswiadczalnej* 66, 714-721.

Chan-Hyung K, Daeyoung R, Yoon-Young N (2012). Comorbid panic disorder and suicide attempts in major depressive disorder. *International Journal of Psychiatry in Clinical Practice* 16, 21.

Chang F-Y, Chen P-H, Wu T-C, Pan W-H, Chang H-Y, Wu S-J, Yeh N-H, Tang R-B, Wu L, James FEMD (2012). Prevalence of functional gastrointestinal disorders in Taiwan: Questionnaire-based survey for adults based on the Rome III criteria. *Asia Pacific Journal of Clinical Nutrition* 21, 594-600.

Chhabra GS, Sodhi MK (2012). Impact of family conflict on the psychosocial behaviour in male adolescents. *Journal of Nepal Paediatric Society* 32, 124-131.

Challis S, Nielssen O, Harris A, Large M (2013). Systematic meta-analysis of the risk factors for deliberate self-harm before and after treatment for first-episode psychosis. *Acta Psychiatrica Scandinavica*. Published online: 9 January 2013. doi: 10.1111/acps.12074.

Chamberlain SR, Odlaug BL, Schreiber LRN, Grant JE (2013). Clinical and neurocognitive markers of suicidality in young adults. *Journal of Psychiatric Research* 47, 586-591.

Chan KL (2013). Victimization and poly-victimization among school-aged Chinese adolescents: Prevalence and associations with health. *Preventive Medicine* 56, 207-210.

Charlton RA, Lamar M, Ajilore O, Kumar A (2013). Preliminary analysis of age of illness onset effects on symptom profiles in major depressive disorder. *International Journal of Geriatric Psychiatry*. Published online: 19 February 2013. doi: 10.1002/gps.3939.

Cheung CF, Wang WM, Leung ZCS (2013). A pilot study on a knowledge-based case library to support suicide risk assessment. *International Social Work* 56, 208-227.

Chopra A, Selim B, Silber MH, Krahn L (2013). Para-suicidal amnestic behavior associated with chronic zolpidem use: Implications for patient safety. *Psychosomatics*. Published online: 22 January 2013. doi: 10.1016/j.psym.2012.10.012.

Chou KL (2012). Childhood sexual abuse and psychiatric disorders in middle-aged and older adults: Evidence from the 2007 adult psychiatric morbidity survey. *Journal of Clinical Psychiatry* 73, e1365-e1371.

Christian Elledge L, Williford A, Boulton AJ, Depaolis KJ, Little TD, Salmivalli C (2013). Individual and contextual predictors of cyberbullying: The influence of children's provictim attitudes and teachers' ability to intervene. *Journal of Youth and Adolescence*. Published online: 31 October 2013. doi: 10.1007/s10964-013-9920-x.

Ciuhodaru T, Iorga M, Romedea S-N (2013). The profile of the prisoner with deliberate self-harm by substance abuse. *European Journal of Science and Theology* 9, 195-206.

Clarke D (2012). The moderating effect of impulsivity on the relationship between stressful life events and depression among college women. *International Journal of Mental Health and Addiction* 10, 152-161.

Connor DF, Doerfler LA (2012). Characteristics of children with juvenile bipolar disorder or disruptive behavior disorders and negative mood: Can they be distinguished in the clinical setting? *Annals of Clinical Psychiatry* 24, 261-270.

Consoli A, Peyre H, Speranza M, Hassler C, Falissard B, Touchette E, Cohen D, Moro MR, Révah-Lévy A (2013). Suicidal behaviors in depressed adolescents: Role of perceived relationships in the family. *Child and Adolescent Psychiatry and Mental Health* 7, 8.

Cooper J, Steeg S, Webb R, Stewart SLK, Applegate E, Hawton K, Bergen H, Waters K, Kapur N (2012). Risk factors associated with repetition of self-harm in Black and minority ethnic (BME) groups: A multi-centre cohort study. *Journal of Affective Disorders*. Published online: 8 December 2012. doi: 10.1016/j.jad.2012.11.018.

Danes-Brozek V (2012). Contemporary characteristics of the developmental age psychopathology. *Psychiatria Danubina* 24, 384-387.

Davakis R (2012). Adolescent neglect: Research, policy and practice. *Journal of Youth and Adolescence* 41, 1695-1698.

Davies L, Oliver C (2012). The age related prevalence of aggression and self-injury in persons with an intellectual disability: A review. *Research in Developmental Disabilities* 34, 764-775.

De Berardis D, Campanella D, Serroni N, Moschetta FS, Di Emidio F, Conti C, Carano A, Acciavatti T, Di Iorio G, Martinotti G, Siracusano A, Di Giannantonio M (2013). Alexithymia, suicide risk and serum lipid levels among adult outpatients with panic disorder. *Comprehensive Psychiatry*. Published online: 15 January 2013. doi: 10.1016/j.comppsych.2012.12.013.

De Deyn PP, Drenth AF, Kremer BP, Oude Voshaar RC, Van Dam D (2013). Aripiprazole in the treatment of alzheimer's disease. *Expert Opinion on Pharmacotherapy* 14, 459-474.

De Luca SM, Wyman P, Warren K (2012). Latina adolescent suicide ideations and attempts: Associations with connectedness to parents, peers, and teachers. *Suicide and Life-Threatening Behavior* 42, 672-683.

De Sanctis V, Filati G, Fiscina B, Marsciani A, Piacentini G, Timoncini G, Reggiani L, Zucchini A (2012). Adolescent health care in Italy: A mini-review. *Georgian Medical News* 210, 8-12.

Debnath AK, Hcramani Singh N, Lenin Singh RK, Hemachand Singh T, Roshan Singh L (2011). Evaluation of psychosocial variables in patient of attempted suicide in RIMS. *Journal of Medical Society* 25, 32-34.

Dell'Osso L, Carmassi C, Massimetti G, Conversano C, Di Emidio G, Stratta P, Rossi A (2012). Post-traumatic stress spectrum in young versus middle-aged L'aquila 2009 earthquake survivors. *Journal of Psychopathology* 18, 281-289.

Demiralp E, Thompson RJ, Mata J, Jaeggi SM, Buschkuehl M, Barrett LF, Ellsworth PC, Demiralp M, Hernandez-Garcia L, Deldin PJ, Gotlib IH, Jonides J (2012). Feeling blue or turquoise? Emotional differentiation in major depressive disorder. *Psychological Science*. Published online: 15 October 2012. doi: 10.1177/0956797612444903.

Desmarais SL, Sellers BG, Viljoen JL, Cruise KR, Nicholls TL, Dvoskin JA (2012). Pilot implementation and preliminary evaluation of START:AV assessments in secure juvenile correctional facilities. *International Journal of Forensic Mental Health* 11, 150-164.

Derreberry T, McDonough A, Batson N, Webster M, Joshi I, Farris S, Garza G, Boggs N, Ahmed M, McCall W (2012). A theoretical model for understanding how insomnia is a risk factor for suicidal ideation. *Sleep* 35, A326.

Deshpande S, Patil P, Kalmegh B, Ghate M (2013). Untreated major depressive disorder with and without atypical features: A clinical comparative study. *Asian Journal of Psychiatry*. Published online: 14 January 2013. doi: 10.1016/j.ajp.2012.12.002.

Dir AL, Karyadi K, Cyders MA (2013). The uniqueness of negative urgency as a common risk factor for self-harm behaviors, alcohol consumption, and eating problems. *Addictive Behaviors* 38, 2158-2162.

Do YK, Shin E, Bautista MA, Foo K (2013). The associations between self-reported sleep duration and adolescent health outcomes: What is the role of time spent on internet use? *Sleep Medicine* 14, 195-200.

Dolan M, Whitworth H (2013). Childhood sexual abuse, adult psychiatric morbidity, and criminal outcomes in women assessed by medium secure forensic service. *Journal of Child Sexual Abuse* 22, 191.

Dowdy E, Furlong MJ, Sharkey JD (2013). Using surveillance of mental health to increase understanding of youth involvement in high-risk behaviors: A value-added analysis. *Journal of Emotional and Behavioral Disorders* 21, 33-44.

Duggan JM, Toste JR, Heath NL (2012). An examination of the relationship between body image factors and non-suicidal self-injury in young adults: The mediating influence of emotion dysregulation. *Psychiatry Research* 206, 256-264.

Dutton GR, Bodell LP, Smith AR, Joiner TE (2013). Examination of the relationship between obesity and suicidal ideation. *International Journal of Obesity.* Published Online: 15 January 2013. doi: 10.1038/ijo.2012.224.

Dvorak RD, Lamis DA, Malone PS (2013). Alcohol use, depressive symptoms, and impulsivity as risk factors for suicide proneness among college students. *Journal of Affective Disorders.* Published online: 7 March 2013. doi: 10.1016/j.jad.2013.01.046.

Dyer KF, Dorahy MJ, Shannon M, Corry M (2013). Trauma typology as a risk factor for aggression and self-harm in a complex PTSD population: The mediating role of alterations in self-perception. *Journal of Trauma and Dissociation* 14, 56-68.

Easton SD, Renner LM (2013). Factors from Durkheim's family integration related to suicidal ideation among men with histories of child sexual abuse. *Suicide and Life-Threatening Behavior.* Published online: 15 February 2013. doi: 10.1111/sltb.12020.

Easton SD, Renner LM, O'Leary P (2013). Suicide attempts among men with histories of child sexual abuse: Examining abuse severity, mental health, and masculine norms. *Child Abuse and Neglect.* Published online: 11 January 2013. doi: 10.1016/j.chiabu.2012.11.007.

Engqvist I, Nilsson K (2013). Experiences of the first days of postpartum psychosis: An interview study with women and next of kin in Sweden. *Issues in Mental Health Nursing* 34, 82-89.

Etain B, Mathieu F, Liquet S, Raust A, Cochet B, Richard JR, Gard S, Zanouy L, Kahn JP, Cohen RF, Bougerol T, Henry C, Leboyer M, Bellivier F (2013). Clinical features associated with trait-impulsiveness in euthymic bipolar disorder patients. *Journal of Affective Disorders* 144, 240-247.

Evans SJ, Kamali M, Prossin AR, Harrington GJ, Ellingrod VL, McInnis MG, Burant CF (2012). Association of plasma omega-3 and omega-6 lipids with burden of disease measures in bipolar subjects. *Journal of Psychiatric Research* 46, 1435-1441.

Exner-Cortens D, Eckenrode J, Rothman E (2012). Longitudinal associations between teen dating violence victimization and adverse health outcomes. *Pediatrics.* Published online: 10 December 2012. doi: 10.1542/peds.2012-1029.

Forster M, Dyal SR, Baezconde-Garbanati L, Chou C-P, Soto DW, Unger JB (2013). Bullying victimization as a mediator of associations between cultural/familial variables, substance use, and depressive symptoms among Hispanic youth. *Ethnicity and Health.* Published online: 9 January 2013. doi: 10.1080/13557858.2012.754407.

Fan AP, Kosik RO, Mandell GA, Tran DT, Cheng HM, Chen CH, Su T-P, Chiu AW (2012). Suicidal ideation in medical students: Who is at risk? *Annals of the Academy of Medicine, Singapore* 41, 377-382.

Fan T, Wu X, Yao L, Dong J (2012). Abnormal baseline brain activity in suicidal and non-suicidal patients with major depressive disorder. *Neuroscience Letters* 534, 35-40.

Farren CK, Hill KP, Weiss RD (2012). Bipolar disorder and alcohol use disorder: A review. *Current Psychiatry Reports* 14, 659-666.

Fedyszyn IE, Harris MG, Robinson J, Paxton SJ (2012). Suicide-related behaviours during initial treatment for first-episode psychosis: Classification, temporal course of risk, characteristics and predictors. *Early Intervention in Psychiatry* 6, 22.

Fikke LT, Melinder A, Landrø NI (2013). The effects of acute tryptophan depletion on impulsivity and mood in adolescents engaging in non-suicidal self-injury. *Human Psychopharmacology* 28, 61-71.

Fink E, Bodell L, Smith A, Joiner T (2012). The joint influence of disordered eating and anxiety sensitivity on the acquired capability for suicide. *Cognitive Therapy and Research.* Published online: 22 November 2012. doi: 10.1007/s10608-012-9502-3.

Finseth PI, Morken G, Andreassen OA, Malt UF, Vaaler AE (2012). Risk factors related to lifetime suicide attempts in acutely admitted bipolar disorder inpatients. *Bipolar Disorders* 14, 727-734.

Fischer B, Ialomiteanu A, Boak A, Adlaf E, Rehm J, Mann RE (2013). Prevalence and key covariates of non-medical prescription opioid use among the general secondary student and adult populations in Ontario, Canada. *Drug and Alcohol Review*. Published online: 11 January 2013. doi: 10.1111/dar.12025.

Florescu S, Sasu C, Galaon M, Popovici G, Gheorghe I, Pintia CM (2012). Mental comorbidity as predictor of suicidal behaviour. *European Journal of Public Health* 22, 193-194.

Fowler JC, DeFife JA (2012). Quality of object representations related to service utilization in a long-term residential treatment center. *Psychotherapy* 49, 418-422.

Franic T, Kralj Z, Marcinko D, Knez R, Kardum G (2013). Suicidal ideations and sleep-related problems in early adolescence. *Early Intervention in Psychiatry*. 28 February 2013. doi: 10.1111/eip.12035.

Fried LE, Williams S, Cabral H, Hacker K (2012). Differences in risk factors for suicide attempts among 9th and 11th grade youth: A longitudinal perspective. *Journal of School Nursing*. Published online: 24 September 2012. doi: 10.1177/1059840512461010.

Friestad C, Ase-Bente R, Kjelsberg E (2012). Adverse childhood experiences among women prisoners: Relationships to suicide attempts and drug abuse. *The International Journal of Social Psychiatry*. Published online: 8 October 2012. doi: 10.1177/0020764012461235.

Gage AJ (2013). Association of child marriage with suicidal thoughts and attempts among adolescent girls in Ethiopia. *Journal of Adolescent Health*. Published online: 20 February 2013. doi: 10.1016/j.jadohealth.2012.12.007.

Gorlyn M, Keilp JG, Oquendo MA, Burke AK, John Mann J (2013). Iowa gambling task performance in currently depressed suicide attempters. *Psychiatry Research*. Published online: 13 March 2013. doi: 10.1016/j.psychres.2013.01.030.

Gahr M, Plener PL, Kölle MA, Freudenmann RW, Schönfeldt-Lecuona C (2012). Self-mutilation induced by psychotropic substances: A systematic review. *Psychiatry Research* 200, 977-983.

Galatzer-Levy IR, Nickerson A, Litz BT, Marmar CR (2012). Patterns of lifetime PTSD comorbidity: A latent class analysis. *Depression and Anxiety*. Published online: 28 December 2012. doi: 10.1002/da.22048.

Gao K, Wang Z, Chen J, Kemp DE, Chan PK, Conroy CM, Serrano MB, Ganocy SJ, Calabrese JR (2012). Should an assessment of axis I comorbidity be included in the initial diagnostic assessment of mood disorders? Role of QIDS-16-SR total score in predicting number of axis I comorbidity. *Journal of Affective Disorders*. Published online: 28 December 2012. doi: 10.1016/j.jad.2012.12.004.

Gardner HG, Quinlan KP, Ewald MB, Ebel BE, Lichenstein R, Melzer-Lange MD, O'Neil J, Pomerantz WJ, Powell EC, Scholer SJ, Smith GA (2012). Firearm-related injuries affecting the pediatric population. *Pediatrics* 130, e1416-e1423.

Gelernter J, Xie P, Anton R, Zhao H, Almasy L, Farrer LA, Kranzler HR (2012). Alcohol dependence in two populations with consideration of suicide-related traits. *Alcoholism-Clinical and Experimental Research* 36, 48A.

Gere MK, Hagen KA, Villabø MA, Arnberg K, Neumer S-P, Torgersen S (2012). Fathers' mental health as a protective factor in the relationship between maternal and child depressive symptoms. *Depression and Anxiety* 30, 31-38.

Geulayov G, Metcalfe C, Gunnell DJ (2012). OP64 Parental suicide attempt and offspring self-harm and suicidal thoughts: Results from the Alspac birth cohort. *Journal of Epidemiology and Community Health* 66, A25.

Gieler U, Consoli SG, Tomas-Aragones L, Linder DM, Jemec GBE, Poot F, Szepietowski JC, De Korte J, Taube KM, Lvov A, Consoli SM (2013). Self-inflicted lesions in dermatology: Terminology and classification - A position paper from the European society for dermatology and psychiatry (ESDaP). *Acta Dermato-Venereologica* 93, 4-12.

Goel S, Goel S (2012). Clinico-Psychological profile of acne vulgaris among professional students. *Indian Journal of Public Health Research and Development* 3, 175-178.

Gonzalez VM (2012). Association of solitary binge drinking and suicidal behavior among emerging adult college students. *Psychology of Addictive Behaviors* 26, 609-614.

Goodwin RD, Prescott MR, Tamburrino M, Calabrese JR, Liberzon I, Galea S (2012). Cigarette smoking and subsequent risk of suicidal ideation among national guard soldiers. *Journal of Affective Disorders* 145, 111-114.

Goodwin RD, Mocarski M, Marusic A, Beautrais A (2013). Thoughts of self-harm and help-seeking behavior among youth in the community. *Suicide and Life-Threatening Behavior.* Published online: 5 February 2013. doi: 10.1111/sltb.12017.

Grano N, Karjalainen M, Edlund V, Saari E, Itkonen A, Anto J, Roine M (2013). Depression symptoms in help-seeking adolescents: A comparison between subjects at-risk for psychosis and other help-seekers. *Journal of Mental Health.* Published online: 16 January 2013. doi: 10.3109/09638237.2012.734654.

Grano N, Karjalainen M, Edlund V, Saari E, Itkonen A, Anto J, Roine M (2012). Adolescents at risk of psychosis have higher level of hopelessness than adolescents not at risk of psychosis. *Nordic Journal of Psychiatry.* Published online: 6 November 2012. doi: 10.3109/08039488.2012.735253.

Grenklo TB, Kreicbergs U, Hauksdóttir A, Valdimarsdóttir UA, Nyberg T, Steineck G, Fürst CJ (2013). Self-injury in teenagers who lost a parent to cancer: A nationwide, population-based, long-term follow-up. *JAMA Pediatrics* 167, 133-140.

Gyekis JP, Yu W, Dong S, Wang H, Qian J, Kota P, Yang J (2013). No association of genetic variants in BBDNF with major depression: A meta- and gene-based analysis. *American Journal of Medical Genetics Part B-Neuropsychiatric Genetics* 162B, 61-70

Guillaume S, Perroud N, Jollant F, Jaussent I, Olie E, Malafosse A, Courtet P (2013). HPA axis genes may modulate the effect of childhood adversities on decision-making in suicide attempters. *Journal of Psychiatric Research* 47, 259-265.

Guilloux JP, Douillard-Guilloux G, Kota R, Wang X, Gardier AM, Martinowich K, Tseng GC, Lewis DA, Sibille E (2012). Molecular evidence for BNDF- and GABA- related dysfunctions in the amygdala of female subjects with major depression. *Molecular Psychiatry* 17, 1130-1142.

Gupta MA, Gupta AK (2013). Cutaneous body image dissatisfaction and suicidal ideation: Mediation by interpersonal sensitivity. *Journal of Psychosomatic Research.* Published online: 28 June 2012. doi: 10.1016/j.jpsychores.2013.01.015.

Gupta MA, Gupta AD, Vujcic B (2012). Increased frequency of attention deficit hyperactivity disorder (ADHD) in acne versus dermatologic controls: Analysis of an epidemiologic database from the U.S. *Journal of Dermatological Treatment.* Published online: 8 December 2012. doi: 10.3109/09546634.2012.736021.

Gvion Y, Apter A (2012). Suicide and suicidal behavior. *Public Health Reviews* 34, 1-20.

Halady SW (2013). Attempted suicide, LGBT identity, and heightened scrutiny. *American Journal of Bioethics* 13, 20-22.

Hilt LM, Pollak SD (2013). Characterizing the ruminative process in young adolescents. *Journal of Clinical Child & Adolescent Psychology.* Published online: 11 March 2013. doi: 10.1080/15374416.2013.764825.

Hunt JI, Case BG, Birmaher B, Stout RL, Dickstein DP, Yen S, Goldstein TR, Goldstein BI, Axelson DA, Hower H, Strober M, Ryan N, Swenson L, Topor DR, Gill MK, Weinstock LM, Keller MB (2013). Irritability and elation in a large bipolar youth sample: Relative symptom severity and clinical outcomes over 4 years. *The Journal of Clinical Psychiatry* 74, e110-117.

Halfon N, Labelle R, Cohen D, Guilé JM, Breton JJ (2012). Juvenile bipolar disorder and suicidality: A review of the last 10 years of literature. *European Child and Adolescent Psychiatry* 22, 139-151.

Halstead RO, Pavkov TW, Hecker LL, Seliner MM (2012). Family dynamics and self-injury behaviors: A correlation analysis. *Journal of Marital and Family Therapy*. Published online: 29 September 2012. doi: 10.1111/j.1752-0606.2012.00336.x.

Han S, Lee H-S (2012). Factors associated with suicidal ideation: The role of context. *Journal of Public Health*. Published online: 13 December 2012. doi: 10.1093/pubmed/fds097.

Harder DW, Strauss JS, Kokes RF, Ritzler BA, Gift TE (1980). Life events and psychopathology severity among first psychiatric admissions. *Journal of Abnormal Psychology* 89, 165-180.

Harford TC, Yi Hy, Freeman RC (2012). A typology of violence against self and others and its associations with drinking and other drug use among high school students in a U.S. general population survey. *Journal of Child and Adolescent Substance Abuse* 21, 349-366.

Harr CR, Horn-Johnson TC, Williams NJ, Jones M, Riley K (2013). Personal trauma and risk behaviors among youth entering residential treatment. *Child and Adolescent Social Work Journal*. Published online: 13 February 2013. doi: 10.1007/s10560-013-0297-1.

Harvey K, Brown B (2012). Health communication and psychological distress: Exploring the language of self-harm. *Canadian Modern Language Review* 68, 316-340.

Hasking P, Andrews T, Martin G (2013). The role of exposure to self-injury among peers in predicting later self-injury. *Journal of Youth and Adolescence*. Published online: 24 February 2013. doi: 10.1007/s10964-013-9931-7.

Hassija CM, Jakupcak M, Gray MJ (2012). Numbing and dysphoria symptoms of posttraumatic stress disorder among Iraq and Afghanistan war veterans: A review of findings and implications for treatment. *Behavior Modification* 36, 834-856.

Hayashi N, Igarashi M, Imai A, Yoshizawa Y, Utsumi K, Ishikawa Y, Tokunaga T, Ishimoto K, Harima H, Tatebayashi Y, Kumagai N, Nozu M, Ishii H, Okazaki Y (2012). Post-hospitalization course and predictive signs of suicidal behavior of suicidal patients admitted to a psychiatric hospital: A 2-year prospective follow-up study. *BMC Psychiatry* 12, 186.

Hedeland RL, Jorgensen MH, Teilmann G, Thiesen LR, Valentiner M, Iskandar A, Morthorst B, Andersen J (2013). Childhood suicide attempts with acetaminophen in Denmark: Characteristics, social behaviour, trends and risk factors. *Scandinavian Journal of Public Health*. Published online: 28 January 2013. doi: 10.1177/1403494812474122.

Heikkilä HK, Väänänen J, Helminen M, Fröjd S, Marttunen M, Kaltiala-Heino R (2012). Involvement in bullying and suicidal ideation in middle adolescence: A 2-year follow-up study. *European Child and Adolescent Psychiatry* 22, 95-102.

Hellmuth JC, Stappenbeck CA, Hoerster KD, Jakupcak M (2012). Modeling PTSD symptom clusters, alcohol misuse, anger, and depression as they relate to aggression and suicidality in returning U.S. Veterans. *Journal of Trauma and Stress* 25, 527-534.

Hesdorffer DC, French JA, Posner K, Diventura B, Pollard JR, Sperling MR, Harden CL, Krauss GL, Kanner AM (2013). Suicidal ideation and behavior screening in intractable focal epilepsy eligible for drug trials. *Epilepsia*. Published online: 28 February 2013. doi: 10.1111/epi.12128.

Heslin KC, Stein JA, Dobalian A, Simon B, Lanto AB, Yano EM, Rubenstein LV (2012). Alcohol problems as a risk factor for postdisaster depressed mood among U.S. Veterans. *Psychology of Addictive Behaviors* 27, 207-213.

Hesselbrock M, Hesselbrock V, Chan G (2012). Alcohol dependence and suicide attempts among Alaska Natives. *Alcoholism-Clinical and Experimental Research* 36, 50A.

Hill MN, Hellemans KGC, Verma P, Gorzalka BB, Weinberg J (2012). Neurobiology of chronic mild stress: Parallels to major depression. *Neuroscience and Biobehavioral Reviews* 36, 2085-2117.

Hirsch JK, Chang EC, Jeglic EL (2012). Social problem solving and suicidal behavior: Ethnic differences in the moderating effects of loneliness and life stress. *Archives of Suicide Research* 16, 303-315.

Ho CSH, Mak K-K, Ho RCM, Chua V (2012). Ethnicity differences in patterns, risk and protective factors of suicidal behaviors in Singapore. *Asia-Pacific Psychiatry* 4, 96-97.

Höfer P, Schosser A, Calati R, Serretti A, Massat I, Kocabas NA, Konstantinidis A, Linotte S, Mendlewicz J, Souery D, Zohar J, Juven-Wetzler A, Montgomery S, Kasper S (2012). The impact of cytochrome P450 CYP2C9, CYP2C19 and CYP2D6 genes on suicide attempt and suicide risk-A European multicentre study on treatment-resistant major depressive disorder. *European Archives of Psychiatry and Clinical Neuroscience*. Published online: 19 October 2012. doi: 10.1007/s00406-012-0375-y.

Hoffman S, Marsiglia FF (2012). The impact of religiosity on suicidal ideation among youth in central Mexico. *Journal of Religion and Health*. Published online: 6 October 2012. doi: 10.1007/s10943-012-9654-1.

Homaifar BY, Brenner LA, Forster JE, Nagamoto H (2012). Traumatic brain injury, executive functioning, and suicidal behavior: A brief report. *Rehabilitation Psychology* 57, 337-341.

Hong N, Jon D-I, Hong HJ, Jung MH (2012). Factors affecting suicidal thoughts and depression among community dwelling elderly. *Asia-Pacific Psychiatry* 4, 176.

Hurtig T, Taanila A, Moilanen I, Nordstrom T, Ebeling H (2012). Suicidal and self-harm behaviour associated with adolescent attention deficit hyperactivity disorder- A study in the northern Finland birth cohort 1986. *Nordic Journal of Psychiatry* 66, 320-328.

Huntley Z, Maltezos S, Williams C, Morinan A, Hammon A, Ball D, Marshall EJ, Keaney F, Young S, Bolton P, Glaser K, Howe-Forbes R, Kuntsi J, Xenitidis K, Murphy D, J Asherson P (2012). Rates of undiagnosed attention deficit hyperactivity disorder in London drug and alcohol detoxification units. *BMC Psychiatry* 12, 223.

Iacoviello BM, Alloy LB, Abramson LY, Choi JY, Morgan JE (2013). Patterns of symptom onset and remission in episodes of hopelessness depression. *Depression and Anxiety*. Published online: 11 March 2013. doi: 10.1002/da.22085.

Iannaccone M, Cella S, Manzi SA, Visconti L, Manzi F, Cotrufo P (2013). My body and me: Self-injurious behaviors and body modifications in eating disorders-preliminary results. *Eating Disorders* 21, 130-139.

In-Albon T, Bürli M, Ruf C, Schmid M (2013). Non-suicidal self-injury and emotion regulation: A review on facial emotion recognition and facial mimicry. *Child and Adolescent Psychiatry and Mental Health* 7, 5.

Iqbal MM, Basil MJ, Kaplan J, Iqbal T (2012). Overview of serotonin syndrome. *Annals of Clinical Psychiatry* 24, 310-318.

Irwig MS (2012). Depressive symptoms and suicidal thoughts among former users of finasteride with persistent sexual side effects. *Journal of Clinical Psychiatry* 73, 1220-1223.

Iverson KM, Follette VM, Pistorello J, Fruzzetti AE (2012). An investigation of experiential avoidance, emotion dysregulation, and distress tolerance in young adult outpatients with borderline personality disorder symptoms. *Personality Disorders* 3, 415-422.

Jarvi S, Jackson B, Swenson L, Crawford H (2013). The impact of social contagion on non-suicidal self-injury: A review of the literature. *Archives of Suicide Research* 17, 1-19.

Jeon HJ, Peng D, Chua HC, Srisurapanont M, Fava M, Bae JN, Man Chang S, Hong JP (2013). Melancholic features and hostility are associated with suicidality risk in Asian patients with major depressive disorder. *Journal of Affective Disorders*. Published online: 13 February 2013. doi: 10.1016/j.jad.2013.01.001.

Joge US, Deo DS, Choudhari SG, Malkar VR, Ughade HM (2013). "Human immunodeficiency virus serostatus disclosure-rate, reactions, and discrimination": A cross-sectional study at a rural tertiary care hospital. *Indian Journal of Dermatology and Venereology and Leprology* 79, 135.

Jahn DR, Poindexter EK, Graham RD, Cukrowicz KC (2012). The moderating effect of the negative impact of recent life events on the relation between intrinsic religiosity and death ideation in older adults. *Suicide and Life-Threatening Behavior* 42, 589-601.

Jantzer V, Parzer P, Lehmkuhl U, Resch F (2012). Recent developments in the diagnosis of mental disorders in adolescence. *Kindheit Und Entwicklung* 21, 198-207.

Jaquier V, Hellmuth JC, Sullivan TP (2012). Posttraumatic stress and depression symptoms as correlates of deliberate self-harm among community women experiencing intimate partner violence. *Psychiatry Research* 206, 37-42.

Javidi H, Yadollahie M (2012). Post-traumatic stress disorder. *International Journal of Occupational and Environmental Medicine* 3, 2-9.

Jayakrishnan B, Al Asmi A, Al Qassabi A, Nandhagopal R, Mohammed I (2012). Acute drug overdose: Clinical profile, etiologic spectrum and determinants of duration of intensive medical treatment. *Oman Medical Journal* 27, 501-504.

Jones S (2012). Common parasite might lead to suicidal behavior. *Neuropsychiatry* 2, 375-376.

Juszczak GRP, Swiergiel AHP (2013). Recreational use of d-lysergamide from the seeds of argyreia nervosa, ipomoea tricolor, ipomoea violacea, and ipomoea purpurea in Poland. *Journal of Psychoactive Drugs* 45, 79.

Kaess M, Parzer P, Mattern M, Plener PL, Bifulco A, Resch F, Brunner R (2012). Adverse childhood experiences and their impact on frequency, severity, and the individual function of nonsuicidal self-injury in youth. *Psychiatry Research* 206, 265-272.

Kane MN, Jacobs RJ, Hawkins WE (2013). Attributions of autonomy and competence of older and younger homeless mentally ill. *Social Work in Health Care* 52, 78-98.

Kanwar A, Malik S, Prokop LJ, Sim LA, Feldstein D, Wang Z, Murad MH (2013). The association between anxiety disorders and suicidal behaviors: A systematic review and meta-analysis. *Depression and Anxiety*. Published online: 13 February 2013. doi: 10.1002/da.22074.

Kaplow JB, Gipson PY, Horwitz AG, Burch BN, King CA (2013). Emotional suppression mediates the relation between adverse life events and adolescent suicide: Implications for prevention. *Prevention Science*. Published online: 15 February 2013. doi: 10.1007/s11121-013-0367-9.

Kavakci O, Semiz M, Kartal A, Dikici A, Kugu N (2013). Prevalence of post-traumatic stress disorder among the inpatients in a tertiary clinic and relationship with suicidal attempts. *Neurology Psychiatry and Brain Research*. Published online: 13 March 2013. doi: 10.1016/j.npbr.2013.01.003.

Kawashima Y, Ito T, Narishige R, Saito T, Okubo Y (2012). The characteristics of serious suicide attempters in Japanese adolescents- Comparison study between adolescents and adults. *BMC Psychiatry* 12, 191.

Kelleher I, Lynch F, Harley M, Molloy C, Roddy S, Fitzpatrick C, Cannon M (2012). Psychotic symptoms in adolescence index risk for suicidal behavior: Findings from 2 population-based case-control clinical interview studies. *Archives of General Psychiatry* 69, 1277-1283.

Kennedy AP, Binder EB, Bowman D, Harenski K, Ely T, Cisler JM, Tripathi SP, VanNess S, Kilts CD (2012). A common TPH2 haplotype regulates the neural processing of a cognitive control demand. *American Journal of Medical Genetics Part B-Neuropsychiatric Genetics* 159B, 829-840.

Khan TM, Sulaiman SAS, Hassali MA (2012). Factors associated with suicidal behaviour among depressed patients in Penang, Malaysia. *Archives of Medical Science* 8, 697-703.

Khurana A, Romer D (2012). Modeling the distinct pathways of influence of coping strategies on youth suicidal ideation: A national longitudinal study. *Prevention Science* 13, 644-654.

Kim SW, Kang HJ, Kim SY, Kim JM, Yoon JS, Jung SW, Lee MS, Yim HW, Jun TY (2013). Impact of childhood adversity on the course and suicidality of depressive disorders: The Crescend study. *Depression and Anxiety.* Published online: 11 March 2013. doi: 10.1002/da.22088.

Kim J-H, Kwon J-W (2012). The impact of health-related quality of life on suicidal ideation and suicide attempts among Korean older adults. *Journal of Gerontology Nursing* 38, 48-59.

Kim HM, Smith EG, Ganoczy D, Walters H, Stano CM, Ilgen MA, Bohnert ASB, Valenstein M (2012). Predictors of suicide in patient charts among patients with depression in the veterans health administration health system: Importance of prescription drug and alcohol abuse. *Journal of Clinical Psychiatry* 73, e1269-e1275.

King J, Agius M, Zaman R (2012). The Kraepelinian Dichotomy in terms of suicidal behaviour. *Psychiatria Danubina* 24, S117-S118.

Kishi T, Yoshimura R, Fukuo Y, Okochi T, Matsunaga S, Umene-Nakano W, Nakamura J, Serretti A, Correll CU, Kane JM, Iwata N (2013). The serotonin 1a receptor gene confer susceptibility to mood disorders: Results from an extended meta-analysis of patients with major depression and bipolar disorder. *European Archives of Psychiatry and Clinical Neuroscience* 263, 105-118.

Klonsky ED, May AM, Glenn CR (2012). The relationship between nonsuicidal self-injury and attempted suicide: Converging evidence from four samples. *Journal of Abnormal Psychology* 122, 231-237.

Knowles S, Townsend E, Anderson M (2012). 'In two minds' - Socially motivated self-harm is perceived as less serious than internally motivated: A qualitative study of youth justice staff. *Journal of Health Psychology.* Published online: 5 November 2012. doi: 10.1177/1359105312459874.

Koch-Stoecker S, Schmitz B, Kanner AM (2013). Treatment of postsurgical psychiatric complications. *Epilepsia* 54, 46-52.

Koeda A, Otsuka K, Nakamura H, Yambe T, Fukumoto K, Onuma Y, Saga Y, Yoshioka Y, Mita T, Mizugai A, Sakai A, Endo S (2012). Characteristics of suicide attempts in patients diagnosed with schizophrenia in comparison with depression: A study of emergency room visit cases in Japan. *Schizophrenia Research* 142, 31-39.

Kohno K, Hoaki N, Inoue T, Nakai Y, Toyomaki A, Araki Y, Hatano K, Terao T (2012). Latitude effect on bipolar temperaments. *Journal of Affective Disorders* 142, 53-56.

Kosidou K, Hellner-Gumpert C, Fredlund P, Dalman C, Hallqvist J, Isacsson G, Magnusson C (2012). Immigration, transition into adult life and social adversity in relation to psychological distress and suicide attempts among young adults. *PLoS ONE* 7, E46284.

Kumar PNS, George B (2013). Life events, social support, coping strategies, and quality of life in attempted suicide: A case-control study. *Indian Journal of Psychiatry* 55, 46-51.

Kuramoto SJ, Runeson B, Stuart EA, Lichtenstein P, Wilcox HC (2012). Time to hospitalization for suicide attempt by the timing of parental suicide during offspring early development. *Archives of General Psychiatry* 70, 149-157.

Kuroki Y, Tilley JL (2012). Recursive partitioning analysis of lifetime suicidal behaviors in Asian Americans. *Asian American Journal of Psychology* 3, 17-28.

Labelle R, Breton JJ, Pouliot L, Dufresne MJ, Berthiaume C (2012). Cognitive correlates of serious suicidal ideation in a community sample of adolescents. *Journal of Affective Disorders* 145, 370-377.

Laimou D (2012). An epistemological and methodological approach to drives and diffusion of instincts through the clinical assessment of suicidal adolescents: The contribution of the Rorschach test. *Rorschachiana* 33, 108-124.

Lakhan SE, Kirchgessner A (2012). Chronic traumatic encephalopathy: The dangers of getting "dinged". *SpringerPlus* 1, 1-14.

Langevin R, Curnoe S (2013). Psychological profile of sex offenders using weapons in their crimes. *Journal of Sexual Aggression*. Published online: 25 February 2013. doi: 10.1080/13552600.2013.769636.

Lanza HI, Echols L, Graham S (2012). Deviating from the norm: Body mass index (BMI) differences and psychosocial adjustment among early adolescent girls. *Journal of Pediatric Psychology*. Published online: 17 December 2012. doi: 10.1093/jpepsy/jss130.

Lande RG (2012). Troublesome triad: Trauma, insomnia, and alcohol. *Journal of Addictive Diseases* 31, 376-381.

Lavdaniti M, Barbas G, Fratzana A, Zyga S (2012). Evaluation of depression in colon cancer patients. *Health Science Journal* 6, 681-692.

Lee J, Hahm HC (2012). HIV risk, substance use, and suicidal behaviors among Asian American lesbian and bisexual women. *AIDS Education and Prevention* 24, 549-563.

Lee YJ, Lim WJ, Kim SJ (2012). The relationship of sleep duration with suicide idea in depressed individuals. *Journal of Sleep Research* 21, 23.

Lemstra M, Rogers M, Moraros J, Grant E (2013). Risk indicators of suicide ideation among on-reserve first nations youth. *Paediatrics and Child Health* 18, 15-20.

Leontieva L, Gregory R (2013). Characteristics of patients with borderline personality disorder in a state psychiatric hospital. *Journal of Personality Disorders* 27, 222-232.

Lerner JS, Li Y, Weber EU (2012). The financial costs of sadness. *Psychological Science* 24, 72-79.

Lester D (2012). Defeat and entrapment as predictors of depression and suicidal ideation versus hopelessness and helplessness. *Psychological Reports* 111, 498-501.

Levi Y, Horesh N, Fischel T, Treves I, Or E, Bleich A, Weiser M, David HS, Konas S, Hermesh H, Givon Y, Apter AMD (2012). The 'impossible situation': Communication and mental pain in medically serious suicidal behavior. *Israel Journal of Psychiatry and Related Sciences* 49, 57-58.

Levi Y, Horesh N, Fischel TMD, Treves IMD, Or EMD, Bleich AMD, Weiser M, David HS, Konas S, Hermesh H, Gvion Y, Apter AMD (2012). Suicide intent of medically serious suicide attempts and its relationship with clinical and interpersonal characteristics. *Israel Journal of Psychiatry and Related Sciences* 49, 58.

Li Z, Qi D, Chen J, Zhang C, Yi Z, Yuan C, Wang Z, Hong W, Yu S, Cui D, Fang Y (2013). Venlafaxine inhibits the upregulation of plasma tumor necrosis factor-alpha (TNF-ALPHA) in the Chinese patients with major depressive disorder: A prospective longitudinal study. *Psychoneuroendocrinology* 38, 107-114.

Limeres J, Feijoo JF, Baluja F, Seoane JM, Diniz M, Diz P (2013). Oral self-injury: An update. *Dental Traumatology* 29, 8-14.

Links PS, Kolla NJ, Guimond T, McMain S (2013). Prospective risk factors for suicide attempts in a treated sample of patients with borderline personality disorder. *Canadian Journal of Psychiatry* 58, 99-106.

Longo J, Walls NE, Wisneski H (2013). Religion and religiosity: Protective or harmful factors for sexual minority youth? *Mental Health, Religion and Culture* 16, 273-290.

Lopez-Morinigo JD, Wiffen B, O'Connor J, Dutta R, Di Forti M, Murray RM, David AS (2013). Insight and suicidality in first-episode psychosis: Understanding the influence of suicidal history on insight dimensions at first presentation. *Early Intervention in Psychiatry*. Published online: 14 March 2013. doi: 10.1111/eip.12042.

Lopez R, Jaussent I, Scholz S, Bayard S, Montplaisir J, Dauvilliers Y (2013). Functional impairment in adult sleepwalkers: A case-control study. *Sleep* 36, 345-351.

Lyons-Ruth K, Bureau JF, Holmes B, Easterbrooks A, Brooks NH (2012). Borderline symptoms and suicidality/self-injury in late adolescence: Prospectively observed relationship correlates in infancy and childhood. *Psychiatry Research* 206, 273-281.

Mackenzie JM, Borrill J, Dewart H (2013). Researching suicide, attempted suicide and near-lethal self-harm by offenders in community settings: Challenges for future research. *International Journal of Forensic Mental Health* 12, 26-32.

MacKay L (2012). Trauma and Bowen family systems theory: Working with adults who were abused as children. *Australian and New Zealand Journal of Family Therapy* 33, 232-241.

Mak ADP, Lam LCW (2013). Neurocognitive profiles of people with borderline personality disorder. *Current Opinion in Psychiatry* 26, 90-96.

Mandal E, Zalewska K (2012). Attachment styles, childhood and adult traumatic experiences, mental states and methods of suicide attempts among psychiatrically treated women. *Psychiatria Polska* 46, 75-84.

Manrique-Garcia E, Zammit S, Dalman C, Hemmingsson T, Allebeck P (2012). Cannabis use and depression: A longitudinal study of a national cohort of Swedish conscripts. *BMC Psychiatry* 12, 112.

Marshall BD, Hadland SE (2012). The immediate and lasting effects of adolescent homelessness on suicidal ideation and behavior. *Journal of Adolescent Health* 51, 407-408.

Marusich JA, Grant KR, Blough BE, Wiley JL (2012). Effects of synthetic cathinones contained in "bath salts" on motor behavior and a functional observational battery in mice. *NeuroToxicology* 33, 1305-1313.

Marwaha S, Parsons N, Flanagan S, Broome M (2012). The prevalence and clinical associations of mood instability in adults living in England: Results from the adult psychiatric morbidity survey 2007. *Psychiatry Research* 205, 262-266.

Mata AD, van Dulmen MHM, Schinka KC, Swahn MH, Bossarte RM, Flannery DJ (2012). Extracurricular activity involvement is associated with adolescent suicidality through school belongingness. *Vulnerable Children and Youth Studies* 7, 347-356.

Matsumoto T (2012). Understanding and treating self-injury. *Psychiatria et Neurologia Japonica* 114, 983-989.

Margetic BA, Jakovljevic M, Ivanec D, Marcinko D, Margetic B, Jaksic N (2012). Current suicidality and previous suicidal attempts in patients with schizophrenia are associated with different dimensions of temperament and character. *Psychiatry Research* 200, 120-125.

Mazurek MO, Kanne SM, Wodka EL (2013). Physical aggression in children and adolescents with autism spectrum disorders. *Research in Autism Spectrum Disorders* 7, 455-465.

Mbakwem A, Aina OF, Amadi CE, Akinbode A, Mokwunye J (2012). Evaluation of psychological pain, a measure of suicidal tendencies, among heart failure patients at an academic hospital in West Africa. *European Heart Journal* 33, 336-433.

McCabe K, Blucker R, Gillaspy JA, Jr., Cherry A, Mignogna M, Roddenberry A, McCaffree MA, Gillaspy SR (2012). Reliability of the postpartum depression screening scale in the neonatal intensive care unit. *Nursing Research* 61, 441-445.

McClean JM, Anspikian A, Winters BN, Tsuang JW (2012). Factors that affect treatment initiation among individuals with serious mental illness and substance abuse disorder. *Addictive Disorders and Their Treatment*. Published online: 3 December 2012. doi: 10.1097/ADT.0b013e31827914b3.

McLaughlin J, O'Carroll RE, O'Connor RC (2012). Intimate partner abuse and suicidality: A systematic review. *Clinical Psychology Review* 32, 677-689.

Melle I, Johannessen JO, Joa I, Haahr U, Rossberg JI, Evensen J, Hegelstad WtV, Simonsen E, Larsen TK, Vaglum P, McGlashan TH, Friis S (2012). Suicide and accidental death in first-episode schizophrenia spectrum psychosis. *Early Intervention in Psychiatry* 6, 23.

Min S, Park S, Noh H, Kim M, Kim H, Shin J, Ahn J, Jang Y, Shin E (2012). The influence of alcohol use on suicide attempts. *Alcoholism-Clinical and Experimental Research* 36, 49A.

Marshall SK, Tilton-Weaver LC, Stattin H (2013). Non-suicidal self-injury and depressive symptoms during middle adolescence: A longitudinal analysis. *Journal of Youth and Adolescence*. Published online: 1 February 2013. doi: 10.1007/s10964-013-9919-3.

McCall WV, Batson N, Webster M, Case LD, Joshi I, Derreberry T, McDonough A, Farris SR (2013). Nightmares and dysfunctional beliefs about sleep mediate the effect of insomnia symptoms on suicidal ideation. *Journal of Clinical Sleep and Medicine* 9, 135-140.

McIntyre L, Williams JVA, Lavorato DH, Patten S (2012). Depression and suicide ideation in late adolescence and early adulthood are an outcome of child hunger. *Journal of Affective Disorders*. Published online: 29 December 2012. doi: 0.1016/j.jad.2012.11.029.

McMahon EM, Corcoran P, McAuliffe C, Keeley H, Perry IJ, Arensman E (2013). Mediating effects of coping style on associations between mental health factors and self-harm among adolescents. *Crisis*. Published online: 28 January 2013. doi: 10.1027/0227-5910/a000188.

Mills R, Scott J, Alati R, O'Callaghan M, Najman JM, Strathearn L (2013). Child maltreatment and adolescent mental health problems in a large birth cohort. *Child Abuse and Neglect*. Published online: 4 February 2013. doi: 10.1016/j.chiabu.2012.11.008.

Miranda R, Tsypes A, Gallagher M, Rajappa K (2013). Rumination and hopelessness as mediators of the relation between perceived emotion dysregulation and suicidal ideation. *Cognitive Therapy and Research*. Published online: 22 January 2013. doi: 10.1007/s10608- 013-9524-5.

Mittendorfer-Rutz E, Kjeldgard L, Runeson B, Perski A, Melchior M, Head J, Alexanderson K (2012). Sickness absence due to specific mental diagnoses and all-cause and cause-specific mortality: A cohort study of 4.9 million inhabitants of Sweden. *PLoS ONE* 7, E45788.

Mittendorfer-Rutz E, Rasmussen F, Lange T (2012). A life-course study on effects of parental markers of morbidity and mortality on offspring's suicide attempt. *PLoS ONE* 7, E51585.

Miyagawa K, Tsuji M, Takeda H (2012). Possible involvement of histone acetylation in the development of emotional resistance to stress stimuli in mice. *Behavioural Brain Research* 235, 318-325.

Mocking RJ, Patrick Pflanz C, Pringle A, Parsons E, McTavish SF, Cowen PJ, Harmer CJ (2012). Effects of short-term varenicline administration on emotional and cognitive processing in healthy, non-smoking adults: A randomized, double-blind, study. *Neuropsychopharmacology* 38, 476-484.

Mojs E, Warchol-Biedermann K, Danuta Glowacka MD, Strzelecki W, Ziemska B, Marcinkowski JT (2012). Are students prone to depression and suicidal thoughts? Assessment of the risk of depression in university students from rural and urban areas. *Annals of Agricultural and Environmental Medicine* 19, 770-774.

Moreira L, Bins H, Toressan R, Ferro C, Harttmann T, Petribú K, Juruena MF, do Rosário MC, Ferrão YA (2012). An exploratory dimensional approach to premenstrual manifestation of obsessive-compulsive disorder symptoms: A multicentre study. *Journal of Psychosomatic Research* 74, 313-319.

Muehlenkamp J, Brausch A, Quigley K, Whitlock J (2012). Interpersonal features and functions of nonsuicidal self-injury. *Suicide and Life-Threatening Behavior*. Published online: 19 October 2012. doi: 10.1111/j.1943-278X.2012.00128.x.

Murphy TM, Mullins N, Ryan M, Foster T, Kelly C, McClelland R, O'Grady J, Corcoran E, Brady J, Reilly M, Jeffers A, Brown K, Maher A, Bannan N, Casement A, Lynch D, Bolger S, Buckley A, Quinlivan L, Daly L, Kelleher C, Malone KM (2012). Genetic variation in DNMT3B and increased global DNA methylation is associated with suicide attempts in psychiatric patients. *Genes, Brain and Behavior* 12, 125-132.

Mustanski B, Liu RT (2012). A longitudinal study of predictors of suicide attempts among lesbian, gay, bisexual, and transgender youth. *Archives of Sexual Behavior* 42, 437-448.

Myrick AC, Brand BL, McNary SW, Classen CC, Lanius R, Loewenstein RJ, Pain C, Putnam FW (2012). An exploration of young adults' progress in treatment for dissociative disorder. *Journal of Trauma & Dissociation* 13, 582-595.

Nehlin C, Fredriksson A, Öster C (2013). Young female psychiatric patients' reasons for excessive alcohol use: A qualitative interview study. *Mental Health and Substance Use*. Published online: 6 March 2013. doi: 10.1080/17523281.2012.755559.

Neilson Ze, Morrison W (2012). Childhood self-poisoning: A one-year review. *Scottish Medical Journal* 57, 196-199.

Neria Y, Wickramaratne P, Olfson M, Gameroff MJ, Pilowsky DJ, Lantigua R, Shea S, Weissman MM (2013). Mental and physical health consequences of the September 11, 2001 (9/11) attacks in primary care: A longitudinal study. *Journal of Traumatic Stress* 26, 45-55.

Nickel JC, Tripp DA (2012). Suicidal ideation among patients with bladder pain syndrome/interstitial cystitis comment. *Urology* 80, 285.

Niezen R (2013). Internet suicide: Communities of affirmation and the lethality of communication. *Transcultural Psychiatry*. Published online: 11 January 2013. doi: 10.1177/1363461512473733.

Norman RE, Byambaa M, De R, Butchart A, Scott J, Vos T (2012). The long-term health consequences of child physical abuse, emotional abuse, and neglect: A systematic review and meta-analysis. *PLoS Medicine* 9, 1349.

Novaco RW, Swanson RD, Gonzalez OI, Gahm GA, Reger MD (2012). Anger and postcombat mental health: Validation of a brief anger measure with U.S. soldiers postdeployed from Iraq and Afghanistan. *Psychological Assessment* 24, 661-675.

Nsamenang SA, Webb JR, Cukrowicz KC, Hirsch JK (2013). Depressive symptoms and interpersonal needs as mediators of forgiveness and suicidal behavior among rural primary care patients. *Journal of Affective Disorders*. Published online: 28 February 2013. doi: 10.1016/j.jad.2013.01.042.

Nyamathi A, Branson C, Idemundia F, Reback C, Shoptaw S, Marfisee M, Keenan C, Khalilifard F, Liu Y, Yadav K (2012). Correlates of depressed mood among young stimulant-using homeless gay and bisexual men. *Issues in Mental Health Nursing* 33, 641-649.

Ojagbemi A, Oladeji B, Abiona T, Gureje O (2013). Suicidal behaviour in old age - Results from the IBADAN study of ageing. *BMC Psychiatry* 13, 80.

Orbach I, Carlson G, Feshbach S, Glaubman H, Gross Y (1983). Attraction and repulsion by life and death in suicidal and in normal children. *Journal of Consulting and Clinical Psychology* 51, 661-670.

Ousey C, Ousey K (2012). Management of self-harm wounds. *Nursing Standard* 27, 58-64.

Ouzir M (2013). Impulsivity in schizophrenia: A comprehensive update. *Aggression and Violent Behavior* 18, 247-254.

Pap D, Gonda X, Molnar E, Lazary J, Benko A, Downey D, Thomas E, Chase D, Toth ZG, Mekli K, Platt H, Payton A, Elliott R, Anderson IM, Deakin JFW, Bagdy G, Juhasz G (2012). Genetic variants in the catechol-o-methyltransferase gene are associated with impulsivity and executive function: Relevance for major depression. *American Journal of Medical Genetics Part B-Neuropsychiatric Genetics* 159B, 928-940.

Paris J, Lis E (2012). Can sociocultural and historical mechanisms influence the development of borderline personality disorder? *Transcultural Psychiatry*. Published online: 5 December 2012. doi: 10.1177/1363461512468105.

Park JY, Han JW, Jeong H, Jeong HG, Kim TH, Yoon IY, Kim KW (2013). Suicidal behaviors in elderly Koreans: One-month-point prevalence and factors related to suicidality. *Journal of Affective Disorders*. Published online: 13 March 2013. doi: 10.1016/j.jad.2013.02.025.

Park JH, Yoo J-H, Kim SH (2012). Associations between non-restorative sleep, short sleep duration and suicidality: Findings from a representative sample of Korean adolescents. *Psychiatry and the Clinical Neurosciences* 67, 28-34.

Park S, Hong KE, Park EJ, Ha KS, Yoo HJ (2012). The association between problematic internet use and depression, suicidal ideation and bipolar disorder symptoms in Korean adolescents. *The Australian and New Zealand Journal of Psychiatry* 47, 153-159.

Patorno E, Hernandez-Diaz S, Glynn RJ, Avorn J, Mogun H, Schneeweiss S (2012). Risk of suicidal acts in new anticonvulsant or antidepressant drug users with chronic pain conditions. *Pharmacoepidemiology and Drug Safety* 21, 444.

Pechtel P, Pizzagalli DA (2013). Disrupted reinforcement learning and maladaptive behavior in women with a history of childhood sexual abuse: A high-density event-related potential study. *JAMA Psychiatry* 13, 1-9.

Peñas-Lledó EM, Naranjo MEG, Llerena A (2013). Impact of cytochrome P450 genes on suicide attempt and risk. *European Archives of Psychiatry and Clinical Neuroscience*. Published online: 19 October 2012. doi: 10.1007/s00406-012-0375-y.

Peltzer K, Naidoo P, Matseke G, Louw J, McHunu G, Tutshana B (2012). Prevalence of post-traumatic stress symptoms and associated factors in tuberculosis (TB), TB retreatment and/or TB-HIV co-infected primary public health-care patients in three districts in South Africa. *Psychology Health Medicine*. Published online: 15 October 2012. doi: 10.1080/13548506.2012.726364.

Perroud N, Baud P, Ardu S, Krejci I, Mouthon D, Vessaz M, Guillaume S, Jaussent I, Olié E, Malafosse A, Courtet P (2012). Temperament personality profiles in suicidal behaviour: An investigation of associated demographic, clinical and genetic factors. *Journal of Affective Disorders* 146, 246-253.

Perry BL, Stevens-Watkins D, Oser CB (2013). The moderating effects of skin color and ethnic identity affirmation on suicide risk among low-SES African American women. *Race and Social Problems* 5, 1-14.

Perugi G, Angst J, Azorin JM, Bowden C, Vieta E, Young AH (2013). The bipolar-borderline personality disorders connection in major depressive patients. *Acta Psychiatrica Scandinavica*. Published online: 4 February 2013. doi: 10.1111/acps.12083.

Peterson CM, Fischer S (2012). A prospective study of the influence of the upps model of impulsivity on the co-occurrence of bulimic symptoms and non-suicidal self-injury. *Eating Behaviors* 13, 335-341.

Phillips R, Stallard P, Spears M, Montgomery AA, Sayal K, Millings A (2012). Using a brief assessment of negative emotions to screen for self-harm behaviour in adolescents (aged 11-16); A prospective cohort analysis of data from eight UK schools. *European Journal of Public Health* 22, 220-221.

Phuong TB, Huong NT, Tien TQ, Chi HK, Dunne MP (2013). Factors associated with health risk behavior among school children in urban Vietnam. *Global Health Action* 6, 1-9.

Picardi A, Viroli C, Tarsitani L, Miglio R, de Girolamo G, Dell'acqua G, Biondi M (2012). Heterogeneity and symptom structure of schizophrenia. *Psychiatry Research* 198, 386-394.

Pluck G, Anderson M, Armstrong S, Armstrong M, Nadkarni A (2013). Repeat self-harm among children and adolescents referred to a specialist service. *Journal of Child and Adolescent Trauma* 6, 57-73.

Palmier-Claus J, Shryane N, Taylor P, Lewis S, Drake R (2012). Mood variability predicts the course of suicidal ideation in individuals with first and second episode psychosis. *Psychiatry Research*. Published online: 9 December 2012. doi: 10.1016/j.psychres.2012.11.014.

Pluck G, Lekka NP, Sarkar S, Lee KH, Bath PA, Sharif O, Woodruff PWR (2012). Clinical and neuropsychological aspects of non-fatal self-harm in schizophrenia. *European Psychiatry*. Published online: 9 October 2012. doi: 10.1016/j.eurpsy.2012.08.003.

Pompili M, Forte A, Palermo M, Stefani H, Lamis DA, Serafini G, Amore M, Girardi P (2012). Suicide risk in multiple sclerosis: A systematic review of current literature. *Journal of Psychosomatic Research* 73, 411-417.

Pompili M, Gibiino S, Innamorati M, Serafini G, Del Casale A, De Risio L, Palermo M, Montebovi F, Campi S, De Luca V, Sher L, Tatarelli R, Biondi M, Duval F, Serretti A, Girardi P (2012). Prolactin and thyroid hormone levels are associated with suicide attempts in psychiatric patients. *Psychiatry Research* 200, 389-394.

Pratt L (2013). Screening for depression and its relationship to thoughts of self-harm. *Comprehensive Psychiatry* 54, E8.

Pressley JC, Dawson P, Carpenter DJ (2012). Injury-related hospital admissions of military dependents compared with similarly aged nonmilitary insured infants, children, and adolescents. *Journal of Trauma and Acute Care Surgery* 73, S236-S242.

Preyde M, Watkins H, Csuzdi N, Carter J, Lazure K, White S, Penney R, Ashbourne G, Cameron G, Frensch K (2012). Non-suicidal self-injury and suicidal behaviour in children and adolescents accessing residential or intensive home-based mental health services. *Journal of the Canadian Academy of Child and Adolescent Psychiatry* 21, 270-281.

Pugh MJ, Copeland LA, Zeber JE, Wang CP, Amuan ME, Mortensen EM, Tabares JV, Van Cott AC, Cooper TL, Cramer JA (2012). Antiepileptic drug monotherapy exposure and suicide-related behavior in older veterans. *Journal of American Geriatrics Society* 60, 2042-2047.

Pukay-Martin ND, Pontoski KE, Maxwell MA, Calhoun PS, Dutton CE, Clancy CP, Hertzberg MA, Collie CF, Beckham JC (2012). The influence of depressive symptoms on suicidal ideation among U.S. Vietnam-era and Afghanistan/Iraq-era veterans with posttraumatic stress disorder. *Journal of Traumatic Stress* 25, 578-582.

Roberts RE, Hao DT (2013). Obesity has few effects on future psychosocial functioning of adolescents. *Eating Behaviors* 14, 128-136.

Rasic D, Weerasinghe S, Asbridge M, Langille DB (2012). Longitudinal associations of cannabis and illicit drug use with depression, suicidal ideation and suicidal attempts among Nova Scotia high school students. *Drug and Alcohol Dependence* 129, 49-53.

Radovic S, Hasking P (2013). The relationship between portrayals of nonsuicidal self-injury, attitudes, knowledge, and behavior. *Crisis*. Published online: 15 March 2013. doi: 10.1027/0227-5910/a000199.

Raudino A, Fergusson DM, Horwood LJ (2013). The quality of parent/child relationships in adolescence is associated with poor adult psychosocial adjustment. *Journal of Adolescence* 36, 331-340.

Reneflot A, Evensen M (2012). Unemployment and psychological distress among young adults in the Nordic countries: A review of the literature. *International Journal of Social Welfare.* Published online: 6 November 2012. doi: 10.1111/ijsw.12000.

Rhodes AE, Bethell J, Newton AS, Antony J, Tonmyr L, Bhanji F, Chaulk D, Curtis S, Gouin S, Joubert GI, Porter R, Silver N, Spruyt J, Thompson GC, Turner TW (2012). Developing measures of quality for the emergency department management of pediatric suicide-related behaviors. *Pediatric Emergency Care* 28, 1124-1128.

Rhodes AE, Boyle MH, Bethell J, Wekerle C, Tonmyr L, Goodman D, Leslie B, Lam K, Manion I (2012). Child maltreatment and repeat presentations to the emergency department for suicide-related behaviors. *Child Abuse and Neglect* 36, 542-551.

Richard-Devantoy S, Guillaume S, Olié E, Courtet P, Jollant F (2013). Altered explicit recognition of facial disgust associated with predisposition to suicidal behavior but not depression. *Journal of Affective Disorders.* Published online: 13 March 2013. doi: 10.1016/j.jad.2013.01.049.

Richer I, Bertrand K, Vandermeerschen J, Roy E (2012). A prospective cohort study of non-fatal accidental overdose among street youth: The link with suicidal ideation. *Drug and Alcohol Review.* Published online: 7 November 2012. doi: 10.1111/dar.12003.

Rihmer Z, Gonda X, Torzsa P, Kalabay L, Akiskal HS, Eory A (2013). Affective temperament, history of suicide attempt and family history of suicide in general practice patients. *Journal of Affective Disorders.* Published online: 7 March 2013. doi: 10.1016/j.jad.2013.02.010.

Rieck T, Jackson A, Martin S, Petrie T, Greenleaf C (2012). Health-related fitness, body mass index, and risk of depression among adolescents. *Medicine and Science in Sports and Exercise.* Published online: 27 December 2012. doi: 10.1249/MSS.0b013e3182831db1.

Rihmer Z, Gonda X (2012). Pharmacological prevention of suicide in patients with major mood disorders. *Neuroscience and Biobehavioral Reviews.* Published online: 27 September 2012. doi: 10.1016/j.neubiorev.2012.09.009.

Rivera-Ledesma A, Montero-Lopez Lena M, Sandoval-Avila R (2012). Psychological maladjustment, quality of life and coping in diabetic patients with chronic renal failure in peritoneal dialysis. *Salud Mental* 35, 329-337.

Rojahn J, Zaja RH, Turygin N, Moore L, van Ingen DJ (2012). Functions of maladaptive behavior in intellectual and developmental disabilities: Behavior categories and topographies. *Research in Developmental Disabilities* 33, 2020-2027.

Romito P, Beltramini L, Escriba-Aguir V (2013). Intimate partner violence and mental health among Italian adolescents: Gender similarities and differences. *Violence Against Women.* Published online: 29 January 2013. doi: 10.1177/1077801212475339.

Rosmarin DH, Bigda-Peyton JS, Kertz SJ, Smith N, Rauch SL, Björgvinsson T (2012). A test of faith in God and treatment: The relationship of belief in God to psychiatric treatment outcomes. *Journal of Affective Disorders* 149, 441-446.

Rudorfer MV, Hillefors M (2012). Assessing psychiatric adverse effects during clinical drug development. *Pharmaceutical Medicine* 26, 363-394.

Ruggiero S, Rafaniello C, Bravaccio C, Grimaldi G, Granato R, Pascotto A, Sportiello L, Parretta E, Rinaldi B, Panei P, Rossi F, Capuano A (2012). Safety of attention-deficit/hyperactivity disorder medications in children: An intensive pharmacosurveillance monitoring study. *Journal of Child and Adolescent Psychopharmacology* 22, 415-422.

Rushing NC, Corsentino E, Hames JL, Sachs-Ericsson N, Steffens DC (2012). The relationship of religious involvement indicators and social support to current and past suicidality among depressed older adults. *Aging and Mental Health* 17, 366-374.

Saez-Francas N, Alegre J, Calvo N, Antonio Ramos-Quiroga J, Ruiz E, Hernandez-Vara J, Casas M (2012). Attention-deficit hyperactivity disorder in chronic fatigue syndrome patients. *Psychiatry Research* 200, 748-753.

Saha I, Paul B, Das DK, Dinda J, Mukherjee A, Basu S (2012). Repeated abuse during childhood and adolescence leading to suicidal behavior in an adolescent: A case report. *Journal of Family Violence* 28, 213-217.

Saias T, Beck F, Bodard J, Guignard R, du Roscoaet E (2012). Social participation, social environment and death ideations in later life. *PLoS ONE* 7, e46723.

Saingam D, Assanangkornchai S, Geater A (2012). Drinking-smoking status and health risk behaviors among high school students in Thailand. *Journal of Drug Education* 42, 177-193.

Sanchez-Gistau V, Baeza I, Arango C, Gonzalez-Pinto A, de la Serna E, Parellada M, Graell M, Paya B, Llorente C, Castro-Fornieles J (2012). Predictors of suicide attempt in early-onset, first-episode psychoses: A longitudinal 24-month follow-up study. *Journal of Clinical Psychiatry* 74, 59-66.

Sansone RA, Hahn HS, Dittoe N, Wiederman MW (2012). The relationship between borderline personality symptoms and body mass index in a consecutive sample of cardiac stress test patients. *Eating and Weight Disorders* 17, e128-e131.

Santorelli N, Woods A, Carlin E, Marsic A, Kaslow NJ (2012). Attachment mediates the childhood maltreatment-daily hassles link in low-income, suicidal African American women. *Journal of Aggression, Maltreatment and Trauma* 21, 739-757.

Sarin E, Singh B, Samson L, Sweat M (2013). Suicidal ideation and HIV risk behaviors among a cohort of injecting drug users in New Delhi, India. *Substance Abuse, Treatmeant, Prevention and Policy* 8, 2.

Schadé A, van Grootheest G, Smit JH (2013). HIV-infected mental health patients: Characteristics and comparison with HIV-infected patients from the general population and non-infected mental health patients. *BMC Psychiatry* 13, 35.

Schaefer KE, Esposito-Smythers C, Riskind JH (2012). The role of impulsivity in the relationship between anxiety and suicidal ideation. *Journal of Affective Disorders* 143, 95-101.

Scott BG, Weems CF (2013). Natural disasters and existential concerns: A test of tillich's theory of existential anxiety. *Journal of Humanistic Psychology* 53, 114-128.

Selby EA, Franklin J, Carson-Wong A, Rizvi SL (2013). Emotional cascades and self-injury: Investigating instability of rumination and negative emotion. *Journal of Clinical Psychology*. Published online: 4 February 2013. doi: 10.1002/jclp.21966.

Selby EA, Yen S, Spirito A (2012). Time varying prediction of thoughts of death and suicidal ideation in adolescents: Weekly ratings over 6-month follow-up. *Journal of Clinical and Child Adolescent Psychology*. Published online: 13 November 2012. doi: 10.1080/15374416.2012.736356.

Seminog O, Goldacre M (2012). Risk of intentional self-harm in young people with selected mental and chronic physical conditions in England. *Journal of Epidemiology and Community Health* 66, A59-A60.

Seok J-H, Lee K-U, Kim W, Lee S-H, Kang E-H, Ham B-J, Yang J-C, Chae J-H (2012). Impact of early-life stress and resilience on patients with major depressive disorder. *Yonsei Medical Journal* 53, 1093-1098.

Serretti A, Souery D, Antypa N, Calati R, Sentissi O, Amital D, Moser U, Kasper S, Zohar J, Mendlewicz J (2013). The impact of adverse life events on clinical features and interaction with gene variants in mood disorder patients. *Psychopathology*. Published online: 13 February 2013. doi: 10.1159/000345358.

Shahani L (2013). Tetrabenazine and suicidal ideation. *Journal of Neuropsychiatry Clinical Neurosciences* 25, E30.

Shanafelt TD, Boone S, Tan L, Dyrbye LN, Sotile W, Satele D, West CP, Sloan J, Oreskovich MR (2012). Burnout and satisfaction with work-life balance among U.S. physicians relative to the general U.S. population. *Archives of Internal Medicine* 172, 1377-1385.

Sharp C, Green KL, Yaroslavsky I, Venta A, Zanarini MC, Pettit J (2012). The incremental validity of borderline personality disorder relative to major depressive disorder for suicidal ideation and deliberate self-harm in adolescents. *Journal of Personality Disorders* 26, 927-938.

Sher L (2012). High and low testosterone levels may be associated with suicidal behavior in young and older men, respectively. *The Australian and New Zealand Journal of Psychiatry*. Published online: 9 October 2012. doi: 10.1177/0004867412463976.

Singareddy R, Vgontzas AN, Meyer R, Calhoun S, Fernandez-Mendoza J, Shaffer M, Bixler EO (2012). Sleep and suicidal ideation and/or attempts in young children: Poor sleep, higher REM percent sleep and impulsivity are associated with increased risk of suicidal ideation and/or attempts. *Sleep* 35, A321.

Singh M, Kumar A, Verma AK, Kumar S, Singh AK (2012). Abdominal organ involvement in blunt injuries. *Journal of Indian Academy of Forensic Medicine* 34, 24-26.

Smith AR, Fink EL, Anestis MD, Ribeiro JD, Gordon KH, Davis H, Keel PK, Bardone-Cone AM, Peterson CB, Klein MH, Crow S, Mitchell JE, Crosby RD, Wonderlich SA, Grange Dl, Joiner TE (2012). Exercise caution: Over-exercise is associated with suicidality among individuals with disordered eating. *Psychiatry Research* 206, 246-255.

Song JY, Yu HY, Kim SH, Hwang SSH, Cho H-S, Kim YS, Ha K, Ahn YM (2012). Assessment of risk factors related to suicide attempts in patients with bipolar disorder. *Journal of Nervous and Mental Disease* 200, 978-984.

Spooner S, Rastle M, Elmore K (2012). Maternal depression screening during prenatal and postpartum care at a Navy and Marine Corps military treatment facility. *Military Medicine* 177, 1208-1211.

St. Germain SA, Hooley JM (2013). Aberrant pain perception in direct and indirect non-suicidal self-injury: An empirical test of Joiner's interpersonal theory. *Comprehensive Psychiatry*. Published online: 29 January 2013. doi: 10.1016/j.comppsych.2012.12.029.

Starling J, Williams LM, Hainsworth C, Harris AW (2012). The presentation of early-onset psychotic disorders. *Australian and New Zealand Journal of Psychiatry*. Published online: 9 October 2012. doi: 10.1177/0004867412463615.

Stewart-Evans JL, Sharman A, Isaac J (2012). A narrative review of secondary hazards in hospitals from cases of chemical self-poisoning and chemical exposure. *European Journal of Emergency Medicine*. Published online: 20 December 2012. doi: 10.1097/MEJ.0b013e32835d002c.

Steyn R, Vawda N, Wyatt GE, Williams JK, Madu SN (2013). Posttraumatic stress disorder diagnostic criteria and suicidal ideation in a South African police sample. *African Journal of Psychiatry* 16, 19-22.

Støen Grotmol K, Gude T, Moum T, Vaglum P, Tyssen R (2012). Risk factors at medical school for later severe depression: A 15-year longitudinal, nationwide study (NORDOC). *Journal of Affective Disorders* 146, 106-111.

Storch EA, Sulkowski ML, Nadeau J, Lewin AB, Arnold EB, Mutch PJ, Jones AM, Murphy TK (2013). The phenomenology and clinical correlates of suicidal thoughts and behaviors in youth with autism spectrum disorders. *Journal of Autism and Developmental Disorders*. Published online: 28 February 2013. doi: 10.1007/s10803-013-1795-x.

Straiton M, Roen K, Dieserud G, Hjelmeland H (2012). Pushing the boundaries: Understanding self-harm in a non-clinical population. *Archives of Psychiatric Nursing* 27, 78-83.

Subhi N, Geelan D (2012). When Christianity and Homosexuality collide: Understanding the potential intrapersonal conflict. *Journal of Homosexuality* 59, 1382-1402.

Sue S, Cheng JKY, Saad CS, Chu JP (2012). Asian American mental health a call to action. *American Psychologist* 67, 532-544.

Suh S, Kim H, Yang HC, Cho ER, Lee SK, Shin C (2013). Longitudinal course of depression scores with and without insomnia in non-depressed individuals: A 6-year follow-up longitudinal study in a Korean cohort. *Sleep* 36, 369-376.

Suliman S, Troeman Z, Stein DJ, Seedat S (2013). Predictors of acute stress disorder severity. *Journal of Affective Disorders.* Published online: 4 March 2013. doi: 10.1016/j.jad.2013.01.041.

Sullivan D, Landau MJ, Branscombe NR, Rothschild ZK, Cronin TJ (2013). Self-harm focus leads to greater collective guilt: The case of the U.S.-Iraq conflict. *Political Psychology.* Published online: 24 January 2013. doi: 10.1111/pops.12010.

Sung SC, Wisniewski SR, Balasubramani GK, Zisook S, Kurian B, Warden D, Trivedi MH, Rush AJ (2012). Does early-onset chronic or recurrent major depression impact outcomes with antidepressant medications? A CO-MED trial report. *Psychological Medicine.* Published online: 11 December 2012. doi: 10.1017/S0033291712001742.

Suresh Kumar P, George B (2013). Life events, social support, coping strategies, and quality of life in attempted suicide: A case control study. *Indian Journal of Psychiatry* 55, 46-51.

Svaldi J, Dorn C, Matthies S, Philipsen A (2012). Effects of suppression and acceptance of sadness on the urge for non-suicidal self-injury and self-punishment. *Psychiatry Research* 200, 404-416.

Synofzik M, Biskup S, Leyhe T, Reimold M, Fallgatter AJ, Metzger F (2012). Suicide attempt as the presenting symptom of C9ORF72 dementia. *American Journal of Psychiatry* 169, 1211-1213.

Tadokoro Y, Oshima T, Fukuchi T, Kanner AM, Kanemoto K (2012). Screening for major depressive episodes in Japanese patients with epilepsy: Validation and translation of the Japanese version of neurological disorders depression inventory for epilepsy (NDDI-E). *Epilepsy & Behavior* 25, 18-22.

Tan AC, Rehfuss MC, Suarez EC, Parks-Savage A (2012). Nonsuicidal self-injury in an adolescent population in Singapore. *Clinical Child Psychology and Psychiatry.* Published online: 3 December 2012. doi: 10.1177/1359104512467273.

Tandon SD, Dariotis JK, Tucker MG, Sonenstein FL (2012). Coping, stress, and social support associations with internalizing and externalizing behavior among urban adolescents and young adults: Revelations from a cluster analysis. *Journal of Adolescent Health.* Published online: 29 November 2012. doi: 10.1016/j.jadohealth.2012.10.001.

Tang J, Wu S, Miao D (2013). Experimental test of escape theory: Accessibility to implicit suicidal mind. *Suicide and Life-Threatening Behavior.* Published online: 1 March 2013. doi: 10.1111/sltb.12021.

Tate L, Feeney A (2012). The principles of risk assessment. *Medicine* 40, 574-576.

Taverner T, Closs SJ, Briggs M (2013). The journey to chronic pain: A grounded theory of older adults' experiences of pain associated with leg ulceration. *Pain Management Nursing.* Published online: 9 February 2013. doi: 10.1016/j.pmn.2012.08.002.

Tay L, Tan K, Diener E, Gonzalez E (2013). Social relations, health behaviors, and health outcomes: A survey and synthesis. *Applied Psychology: Health and Well-Being* 5, 28-78.

Taylor RJ, Nguyen AW, Sinkewicz M, Joe S, Chatters LM (2012). Comorbid mood and anxiety disorders, suicidal behavior, and substance abuse among Black Caribbeans in the U.S.A. *Journal of African American Studies.* Published online: 7 November 2012. doi: 10.1007/s12111-012-9237-y.

Thomas ML, Brown GG, Gur RC, Hansen JA, Nock MK, Heeringa S, Ursano RJ, Stein MB (2013). Parallel psychometric and cognitive modeling analyses of the Penn face memory test in the army study to assess risk and resilience in service members. *Journal of Clinical Experimental Neuropsychology* 35, 225-245.

Thomas S, Bliss S, Malik M (2012). Suicidal ideation and self-harm following K2 use. *Journal - Oklahoma State Medical Association* 105, 430-433.

Thompson EA, Connelly CD, Thomas-Jones D, Eggert LL (2013). School difficulties and co-occurring health risk factors: Substance use, aggression, depression, and suicidal behaviors. *Journal of Child and Adolescent Psychiatric Nursing* 26, 74-84.

Thompson R, Litrownik AJ, Isbell P, Everson MD, English DJ, Dubowitz H, Proctor LJ, Flaherty EG (2012). Adverse experiences and suicidal ideation in adolescence: Exploring the link using the longscan samples. *Psychology of Violence* 2, 211-225.

Tobler AL, Maldonado-Molina MM, Staras SA, O'Mara RJ, Livingston MD, Komro KA (2012). Perceived racial/ethnic discrimination, problem behaviors, and mental health among minority urban youth. *Ethnicity & Health*. Published online: 9 October 2012. doi: 10.1080/13557858.2012.730609.

Toovey S, Prinssen EP, Rayner CR, Thakrar BT, Dutkowski R, Koerner A, Chu T, Sirzen-Zelenskaya A, Britschgi M, Bansod S, Donner B (2012). Post-marketing assessment of neuropsychiatric adverse events in influenza patients treated with Oseltamivir: An updated review. *Advances in Therapy* 29, 826-848.

Tran Bich P, Nguyen Thanh H, Truong Quang T, Hoang Khanh C, Dunne MP (2013). Factors associated with health risk behavior among school children in urban Vietnam. *Global Health Action* 6, 1-9.

Tresno F, Ito Y, Mearns J (2012). Risk factors for nonsuicidal self-injury in Japanese college students: The moderating role of mood regulation expectancies. *International Journal of Psychology*. Published online: 22 October 2012. doi: 10.1080/00207594.2012.733399.

Tripodi SJ, Onifade E, Pettus-Davis C (2013). Nonfatal suicidal behavior among women prisoners: The predictive roles of childhood victimization, childhood neglect, and childhood positive support. *International Journal of Offender Therapy and Comparative Criminology*. Published online: 11 January 2013. doi: 10.1177/0306624X12472879.

Tripp A, Oh H, Guilloux J-P, Martinowich K, Lewis DA, Sibille E (2012). Brain-derived neurotrophic factor signaling and subgenual anterior cingulate cortex dysfunction in major depressive disorder. *American Journal of Psychiatry* 169, 1194-1202.

Trivedi MH, Morris DW, Wisniewski SR, Nierenberg AA, Gaynes BN, Kurian BT, Warden D, Stegman D, Shores-Wilson K, Rush AJ (2013). Clinical and sociodemographic characteristics associated with suicidal ideation in depressed outpatients. *Canadian Journal of Psychiatry* 58, 113-122.

Tsirigotis K, Gruszczynski W, Lewik-Tsirigotis M (2012). Manifestations of indirect self-destructiveness and methods of suicide attempts. *Psychiatric Quarterly*. Published online: 4 October 2012. doi: 10.1007/s11126-012-9239-x.

Tufik SB, Bennedsen L, Andersen ML, Tufik S (2013). Potential role of sleep in bipolar disorder. *Journal of Psychiatric Research* 47, 133-134.

Tuisku V, Pelkonen M, Kiviruusu O, Karlsson L, Marttunen M (2012). Alcohol use and psychiatric comorbid disorders predict deliberate self-harm behaviour and other suicidality among depressed adolescent outpatients in 1-year follow-up. *Nordic Journal of Psychiatry* 66, 268-275.

Turnbull DL, Cox BJ, Oleski J, Katz LY (2013). The effects of borderline personality disorder and panic disorder on suicide attempts and the associated influence of affective dysregulation in the general population. *Journal of Nervour Mental Disoders* 201, 130-135.

Turner HA, Finkelhor D, Shattuck A, Hamby S (2012). Recent victimization exposure and suicidal ideation in adolescents. *Archives of Pediatrics and Adolescent Medicine* 166, 1149-1154.

Turner MG, Exum ML, Brame R, Holt TJ (2013). Bullying victimization and adolescent mental health: General and typological effects across sex. *Journal of Criminal Justice* 41, 53-59.

Uebelacker LA, Weisberg R, Millman M, Yen S, Keller M (2012). Prospective study of risk factors for suicidal behavior in individuals with anxiety disorders. *Psychological Medicine*. Published online: 9 November 2012. doi: 10.1017/S0033291712002504.

Umhau JC, George DT, Heaney RP, Lewis MD, Ursano RJ, Heilig M, Hibbeln JR, Schwandt ML (2013). Low vitamin D status and suicide: A case-control study of active duty military service members. *PLoS ONE* 8, e51543.

Undheim AM (2013). Involvement in bullying as predictor of suicidal ideation among 12- to 15-year-old Norwegian adolescents. *European Child and Adolescent Psychiatry*. Published online: 10 January 2013. doi: 10.1007/s00787-012-0373-7.

van der Velden PG, Wong A, Boshuizen HC, Grievink L (2013). Persistent mental health disturbances during the 10 years after a disaster: Four-wave longitudinal comparative study. *Psychiatry and the Clinical Neurosciences* 67, 110-118.

Valtolina GG, Colombo C (2012). Psychological well-being, family relations, and developmental isues of children left behind. *Psychological Reports* 111, 905-928.

van Bergen DD, Bos HM, van Lisdonk J, Keuzenkamp S, Sandfort TG (2012). Victimization and suicidality among Dutch lesbian, gay, and bisexual youths. *American Journal of Public Health* 103, 70-72.

Vanderoost F, van der Wielen S, van Nunen K, Louckx F, Van Hal G (2012). Job loss and suicidal thoughts in Belgium. *European Journal of Public Health* 22, 37.

Vansteelandt K, Claes L, Muehlenkamp J, De Cuyper K, Lemmens J, Probst M, Vanderlinden J, Pieters G (2012). Variability in affective activation predicts non-suicidal self-injury in eating disorders. *European Eating Disorder Review* 21, 143-147.

Vidal CEL, Gontijo ECDM, Lima LA (2013). Attempted suicide: Prognostic factors and estimated excess mortality. *Cadernos de Saude Publica* 29, 175-187.

Vignarajah B, Links PS (2009). The clinical significance of co-morbid posttraumatic stress disorder and borderline personality disorder: Case study and literature review. *Personality and Mental Health* 3, 217-224 .

Vinokur D, Levine SZ, Roe D, Krivoy A, Fischel T (2013). Age of onset group characteristics in forensic patients with schizophrenia. *European Psychiatry*. Published online: 8 February 2013. doi: 10.1016/j.eurpsy.2012.11.006.

Vitiello B, Brent DA, Greenhill LL, Emslie G, Wells K, Walkup JT, Stanley B, Bukstein O, Kennard BD, Compton S, Coffey B, Cwik MF, Posner K, Wagner A, March JS, Riddle M, Goldstein T, Curry J, Capasso L, Mayes T, Shen S, Gugga SS, Turner JB, Barnett S, Zelazny J (2009). Depressive symptoms and clinical status during the treatment of adolescent suicide attempters (TASA) study. *Journal of the American Academy of Child and Adolescent Psychiatry* 48, 997-1004.

Wai-Kwong T, Huajun L, Vincent M, Gabor S U, Ka-Sing W (2012). Is pain associated with suicidality in stroke? *Archives of Physical Medicine and Rehabilitation*. Published online: 19 December 2012. doi: 10.1016/j.apmr.2012.11.044.

Walker T (2012). Former finasteride users with sexual side effects at increased risk for depressive symptoms, suicidal thoughts. *Formulary* 47, 341.

Wang M-C, Nyutu PN, Tran KK (2012). Coping, reasons for living, and suicide in Black college students. *Journal of Counseling and Development* 90, 459-466.

Wei S, Liu L, Bi B, Li H, Hou J, Chen W, Tan S, Chen X, Jia X, Dong G, Qin X (2012). Comparison of impulsive and nonimpulsive suicide attempt patients treated in the emergency departments of four general hospitals in Shenyang, China. *General Hospital Psychiatry* 35, 186-191.

Wei S, Liu L, Bi B, Li H, Hou J, Tan S, Chen X, Chen W, Jia X, Dong G, Qin X, Liu Y (2012). An intervention and follow-up study following a suicide attempt in the emergency departments of four general hospitals in Shenyang, China. *Crisis* 24, 107-115.

Wei S, Yan H, Chen W, Liu L, Bi B, Li H, Hou J, Tan S, Chen X, Dong G, Qin X (2012). Gender-specific differences among patients treated for suicide attempts in the emergency departments of four general hospitals in Shenyang, China. *General Hospital Psychiatry* 35, 54-58.

West CP, Dyrbye LN, Satele DV, Sloan JA, Shanafelt TD (2012). Concurrent validity of single-item measures of emotional exhaustion and depersonalization in burnout assessment. *Journal of General Internal Medicine* 27, 1445-1452.

Westermeyer J, Canive J (2012). Posttraumatic stress disorder and its comorbidities among American Indian veterans. *Community Mental Health Journal.* Published online: 13 November 2012. doi: 10.1007/s10597-012-9565-3.

Wiborg JF, Gieseler D, Löwe B (2013). Suicidal ideation in German primary care. *General Hospital Psychiatry.* Published online: 6 March 2013. doi: 10.1016/j.genhosppsych.2013.02.001.

Wilson ML, Dunlavy AC, Viswanathan B, Bovet P (2012). Suicidal expression among school-attending adolescents in a middle-income Sub-Saharan country. *International Journal of Environmental Research and Public Health* 9, 4122-4134.

Wilson KG, Kowal J, Henderson PR, McWilliams LA, Péloquin K (2013). Chronic pain and the interpersonal theory of suicide. *Rehabilitation Psychology* 58, 111-115.

Wisner KL, Sit DK, McShea MC, Rizzo DM, Zoretich RA, Hughes CL, Eng HF, Luther JF, Wisniewski SR, Costantino ML, Confer AL, Moses-Kolko EL, Famy CS, Hanusa BH (2013). Onset timing, thoughts of self-harm, and diagnoses in postpartum women with screen-positive depression findings. *JAMA Psychiatry.* Published online: 13 March 2013. doi: 10.1001/jamapsychiatry.2013.87.

Wojnar M, Jakubczyk A, Klimkiewicz A, Wrzosek M, Lukaszkiewicz J, Burmeister M, Brower KJ (2012). Association of genetic and environmental factors with suicide risk in alcohol-dependent patients. *Alcoholism-Clinical and Experimental Research* 36, 78A.

Wong PW, Fu KW, Yau RS, Ma HH, Law YW, Chang SS, Yip PS (2013). Accessing suicide-related information on the internet: A retrospective observational study of search behavior. *Journal of Medical Internet Research* 15, e3.

Yackerson NS, Zilberman A, Todder D, Kaplan Z (2013). The influence of air-suspended particulate concentration on the incidence of suicide attempts and exacerbation of schizophrenia. *International Journal of Biometeorology.* Published online: 16 January 2013. doi: 10.1007/s00484-012-0624-9.

Yanes PK, Morse G, Hsiao C-B, Simms L, Roberts JE (2012). Autobiographical memory specificity and the persistence of depressive symptoms in HIV-positive patients: Rumination and social problem-solving skills as mediators. *Cognition & Emotion* 26, 1496-1507.

Yarmuth M, Patterson J, Burton T, Douglas C, Taylor T, Boyle M (2012). Using research to understand youth in high-risk urban communities. *Social Marketing Quarterly* 18, 187.

Yaseen ZS, Chartrand H, Mojtabai R, Bolton J, Galynker II (2012). Fear of dying in panic attacks predicts suicide attempt in comorbid depressive illness: Prospective evidence from the national epidemiological survey on alcohol and related conditions. *Depression and Anxiety.* Published online: 20 December 2012. doi: 10.1002/da.22039.

Yee HA, Loh HS, Ng CG (2013). The prevalence and correlates of alcohol use disorder amongst bipolar patients in a hospital setting, Malaysia. *International Journal of Psychiatry and Clinical Practice*. Published online: 29 January 2013. doi: 10.3109/13651501.2012.752012.

Yeh HH, Lin YC, Huang N, Tsai HJ, Chen CY (2013). Differential factors predicting first and repetitive suicide attempts among youth in Taiwan: A population-based study. *Comprehensive Psychiatry* 54, e13.

Yen S, Gagnon K, Spirito A (2012). Borderline personality disorder in suicidal adolescents. *Personality and Mental Health*. Published online: 28 September 2012. doi: 10.1002/pmh.1216.

You J, Lin MP, Fu K, Leung F (2013). The best friend and friendship group influence on adolescent nonsuicidal self-injury. *Journal of Abnormal Child Psychology*. Published online: 10 March 2013. doi: 10.1007/s10802-013-9734-z.

Yun YH, Choi YN, Kim YA, Choi EJ (2012). The suicide ideation of stomach cancer survivors and its correlates in Korea. *Annals of Oncology* 23, 512.

Zapata LB, Kissin DM, Bogoliubova O, Yorick RV, Kraft JM, Jamieson DJ, Marchbanks PA, Hillis SD (2013). Orphaned and abused youth are vulnerable to pregnancy and suicide risk. *Child Abuse and Neglect*. Published online: 4 January 2013. doi: 10.1016/j.chiabu.2012.10.005.

Zayas LH, Gulbas LE (2012). Are suicide attempts by young Latinas a cultural idiom of distress? *Transcultural Psychiatry*. 49, 718-734.

Zhang J, Fang L, Wu YW, Wieczorek WF (2013). Depression, anxiety, and suicidal ideation among Chinese Americans: A study of immigration-related factors. *Journal of Nervous Mental Disorders* 201, 17-22.

Zhou X, Yan Z, Therese H (2012). Depression and aggression in never-married men in China: A growing problem. *Social Psychiatry and Psychiatric Epidemiology*. Published online: 12 December 2012. doi: 10.1007/s00127-012-0638-y

Prevention

Andersson G, Sarkohi A, Karlsson J, Bjarehed J, Hesser H (2013). Effects of two forms of internet-delivered cognitive behaviour therapy for depression on future thinking. *Cognitive Therapy and Research* 37, 29-34.

Callahan P, Liu P, Purcell R, Parker AG, Hetrick SE (2012). Evidence map of prevention and treatment interventions for depression in young people. *Depression Research and Treatment.* Published online: 15 March 2012. doi: 10.1155/2012/820735.

Hegerl U, Rummel-Kluge C, Varnik A, Arensman E, Koburger N (2013). Alliances against depression-A community based approach to target depression and to prevent suicidal behaviour. *Neuroscience and Biobehavioral Reviews.* Published online: 21 February 2013. doi: 10.1016/j.neubiorev.2013.02.009.

Hirata M, Kawanishi C, Oyama N, Miyake Y, Otsuka K, Yamada T, Kishi Y, Ito H, Arakawa R (2013). Training workshop on caring for suicide attempters implemented by the ministry of health, labour and welfare, Japan. *Psychiatry and the Clinical Neurosciences* 67, 64.

Jacob KS (2012). Depression: A major public health problem in need of a multi-sectoral response. *Indian Journal of Medical Research* 136, 537-539.

Jonsson U, Alexanderson K, Kjeldgard L, Westerlund H, Mittendorfer-Rutz E (2013). Diagnosis-specific disability pension predicts suicidal behaviour and mortality in young adults: A nationwide prospective cohort study. *BMJ Open.* Published online: 8 February 2013. doi: 10.1136/bmjopen-2012-002286.

Morgan VA, Waterreus A, Jablensky A, Mackinnon A, McGrath JJ, Carr V, Bush R, Castle D, Cohen M, Harvey C, Galletly C, Stain HJ, Neil AL, McGorry P, Hocking B, Shah S, Saw S (2012). People living with psychotic illness in 2010: The second Australian national survey of psychosis. *Australia and New Zealand Journal of Psychiatry* 46, 735-752.

Noblin JL, Venta A, Sharp C (2013). The validity of the MSI-BPD among inpatient adolescents. *Assessment.* Published online: 23 January 2013. doi: 10.1177/1073191112473177.

Nock MK, Green JG, Hwang I, McLaughlin KA, Sampson NA, Zaslavsky AM, Kessler RC (2013). Prevalence, correlates, and treatment of lifetime suicidal behavior among adolescents: Results from the national comorbidity survey replication adolescent supplement. *JAMA Psychiatry* 70, 300-310.

Nordenskjold A, von Knorring L, Ljung T, Carlborg A, Brus O, Engstrom I (2013). Continuation electroconvulsive therapy with pharmacotherapy versus pharmacotherapy alone for prevention of relapse of depression: A randomized controlled trial. *Journal of ECT.* Published online: 8 January 2013. doi: 10.1097/YCT.0b013e318276591f.

Petkus A, Wetherell J, Stein MB, Craske M, Chavira D, Sherbourne C, Sullivan G, Roy-Byrne P (2012). Suicidal ideation and response to treatment in older adults with social anxiety disorder. *Gerontologist* 52, 475-476.

Shahid M (2013). Deliberate self harm prevention in Pakistan. *Journal of the College of Physicians and Surgeons Pakistan* 23, 101-102.

Szymanski BR, Bohnert KM, Zivin K, McCarthy JF (2013). Integrated care: Treatment initiation following positive depression screens. *Journal of General Internal Medicine* 28, 346-352.

Ward J, Bailey D (2013). A participatory action research methodology in the management of self-harm in prison. *Journal of Mental Health.* Published online: 16 January 2013. doi: 10.3109/09638237.2012.734645.

Care and support

Abbasi A (2012). 'A very dangerous conversation': The patient's internal conflicts elaborated through the use of ethnic and religious differences between analyst and patient. *The International Journal of Psycho-Analysis* 93, 515-534.

Ahmed AIA, Ali ANA, Kramers C, Härmark LVD, Burger DM, Verhoeven WMA (2012). Neuropsychiatric adverse events of varenicline: A systematic review of published reports. *Journal of Clinical Psychopharmacology* 33, 55-62.

Akechi T (2012). Psychotherapy for depression among patients with advanced cancer. *Japanese Journal of Clinical Oncology* 42, 1113-1119.

Almeida OP, Pirkis J, Kerse N, Sim M (2012). Targeted education for general practitioners reduces risk of depression or suicide ideation or attempts in older primary care patients. *Evidence-Based Mental Health* 16, 8.

Angeletti G, Pompili M, Innamorati M, Santucci C, Savoja V, Goldblatt M, Girardi P (2013). Short-term psychodynamic psychotherapy in patients with "male depression" syndrome, hopelessness, and suicide risk: A pilot study. *Depression Research and Treatment* 2013, 408983.

Anonymous (2012). New NICE guidance for the longer-term management of self-harm. *Community Practitioner* 85, 13.

Anonymous. (2012). Accelerating suicide rate linked to economic downturn in the U.S. *British Medical Journal* 345, e7638.

Attard A (2012). Antidepressants. *Medicine* 40, 681-683.

Babakhanian M, Sadeghi M, Mansoori N, Mehrjerdi ZA, Tabatabai M (2012). Nonmedical abuse of benzodiazepines in opiate-dependent patients in Tehran, Iran. *Iranian Journal of Psychiatry and Behavioral Sciences* 6, 62-67.

Ballon J, Stroup TS (2013). Polypharmacy for schizophrenia. *Current Opinion in Psychiatry* 26, 208-213.

Barton AL, Hirsch JK, Lovejoy MC (2012). Peer response to messages of distress. *Crisis*. Published online: 28 November 2012. doi: 10.1027/0227-5910/a000169, 2012.

Bedics JD (2013). Similar benefits with dialectical behaviour therapy or general psychiatric management for people with borderline personality disorder. *Evidence Based Mentel Health* 16, 16.

Bellino S, Rinaldi C, Brunetti C, Bogetto F (2012). Interpersonal psychotherapy: Recent indications beyond major depression. *Journal of Psychopathology* 18, 359-375.

Berk M, Berk L, Davey CG, Moylan S, Giorlando F, Singh AB, Katra H, Dodd S, Malhi GS (2012). Treatment of bipolar depression. *Medical Journal of Australia* 198, 138-139.

Berry RS, Aurelius MB, Barickman N, Lathrop SL (2012). Utility of a grief services program for medical examiners' offices. *Journal of Forensic Sciences*. Published online: 27 December 2012. doi: 10.1111/1556-4029.12043.

Betz ME, Sullivan AF, Manton AP, Espinola JA, Miller I, Camargo CA, Boudreaux ED (2013). Knowledge, attitudes, and practices of emergency department providers in the care of suicidal patients. *Depression and Anxiety*. Published online: 20 February 2013. doi: 10.1002/da.22071.

Thome A, Smith PO, Cook-Wiens G, Yeh HW, Gaffney GR, Hellings JA (2012). A retrospective study of amitriptyline in youth with autism spectrum disorders. *Journal of Autism and Developmental Disorders*. Published online: 8 November 2012. doi: 10.1007/s10803-012-1647-0.

Black DW, Blum N, McCormick B, Allen J (2013). Systems training for emotional predictability and problem solving (STEPPS) group treatment for offenders with borderline personality disorder. *Journal of Nervour Mental Disoders* 201, 124-129.

Blackall GF, Volpe RL, Green MJ (2013). After the suicide attempt: Offering patients another chance. *American Journal of Bioethics* 13, 14-16.

Booth R, Keogh K, Doyle J, Owens T (2012). Living through distress: A skills training group for reducing deliberate self-harm. *Behavioural and Cognitive Psychotherapy*. Published online: 7 December 2012. doi: 10.1017/S1352465812001002.

Bryan CJ, Corso KA, Corso ML, Kanzler KE, Ray-Sannerud B, Morrow CE (2012). Therapeutic alliance and change in suicidal ideation during treatment in integrated primary care settings. *Archives of Suicide Research* 16, 316-323.

Butler J (2012). Self-harm. *Medicine* 40, 650-653.

Carter A, Hall W (2013). Managing suicide risk in experimental treatments of treatment-resistant depression. *AJOB Neuroscience* 4, 38-39.

Carter GL, Clover K, Whyte IM, Dawson AH, D'Este C (2013). Postcards from the edge: 5-year outcomes of a randomised controlled trial for hospital-treated self-poisoning. *British Journal of Psychiatry*. Published online: 21 March 2013. doi: 10.1192/bjp.bp.112.112664.

Cebrià AI, Parra I, Pàmias M, Escayola A, García-Parés G, Puntí J, Laredo A, Vallès V, Cavero M, Oliva JC, Hegerl U, Pérez-Solà V, Palao DJ (2012). Effectiveness of a telephone management programme for patients discharged from an emergency department after a suicide attempt: Controlled study in a Spanish population. *Journal of Affective Disorders*. Published online: 6 December 2012. doi: 10.1016/j.jad.2012.11.016.

Clark MS, Jansen KL, Anthony Cloy J (2012). Treatment of childhood and adolescent depression. *American Family Physician* 86, 442-448.

Cooke L, Gotto J, Mayorga L, Grant M, Lynn R (2013). What do I say? Suicide assessment and management. *Clinical Journal of Oncology Nursing* 17, E1-E7.

Cox GR, Callahan P, Churchill R, Hunot V, Merry SN, Parker AG, Hetrick SE (2012). Psychological therapies versus antidepressant medication, alone and in combination for depression in children and adolescents. *Cochrane Database of Systematic Reviews* 11, CD008324.

Cox GR, Fisher CA, De Silva S, Phelan M, Akinwale OP, Simmons MB, Hetrick SE (2012). Interventions for preventing relapse and recurrence of a depressive disorder in children and adolescents. *Cochrane Database of Systematic Reviews*. Published online: 14 November 2012. doi: 10.1002/14651858.CD007504.pub2.

Dabaghzadeh F, Ghaeli P, Khalili H, Alimadadi A, Jafari S, Akhondzadeh S, Khazaeipour Z (2013). Cyproheptadine for prevention of neuropsychiatric adverse effects of efavirenz: A randomized clinical trial. *AIDS Patient Care STDS* 27, 146-154.

de Kernier N, Marty F, Devouche E (2012). Restoring psychic containers of identity after a suicide attempt in adolescence. *Bulletin of the Menninger Clinic* 76, 365-392.

Decou CR, Skewes MC, López EDS, Skanis ML (2012). The benefits of discussing suicide with Alaska native college students: Qualitative analysis of in-depth interviews. *Cultural Diversity and Ethnic Minority Psychology* 19, 67-75.

Deuschl G, Schupbach M, Knudsen K, Pinsker MO, Cornu P, Rau J, Agid Y, Schade-Brittinger C (2013). Stimulation of the subthalamic nucleus at an earlier disease stage of parkinson's disease: Concept and standards of the Earlystim-study. *Parkinsonism Related Disorders* 19, 56-61.

Deuter K, Procter N, Rogers J (2013). The emergency telephone conversation in the context of the older person in suicidal crisis. *Crisis*. Published online: 28 January 2013. doi: 10.1027/0227-5910/a000189.

Diamond GS, O'Malley A, Wintersteen MB, Peters S, Yunghans S, Biddle V, O'Brien C, Schrand S (2012). Attitudes, practices, and barriers to adolescent suicide and mental health screening: A survey of Pennsylvania primary care providers. *Journal of Primary Care and Community Health* 3, 29-35.

Donley E (2013). Suicide risk of your client: Initial identification and management for the allied health professional. *Journal of Allied Health* 42, 56-61.

Eisenzimmer RK (2012). Code-51: Keeping suicidal veterans safe in the emergency department. *Journal of Psychosocial Nursing and Mental Health Services* 50, 30-35.

Ellis LA, Collin P, Davenport TA, Hurley PJ, Burns JM, Hickie IB (2012). Young men, mental health, and technology: Implications for service design and delivery in the digital age. *Journal of Medical Internet Research* 14, e160.

Fagiolini A, Comandini A, Dell'osso MC, Kasper S (2012). Rediscovering trazodone for the treatment of major depressive disorder. *CNS Drugs* 26, 1033-1049.

Federici A, Wisniewski L (2013). An intensive DBT program for patients with multidiagnostic eating disorder presentations: A case series analysis. *International Journal of Eating Disorders*. Published online: 5 February 2013. doi: 10.1002/eat.22112.

Gega L, Swift L, Barton G, Todd G, Reeve N, Bird K, Holland R, Howe A, Wilson J, Molle J (2012). Computerised therapy for depression with clinician vs. assistant and brief vs. extended phone support: Study protocol for a randomised controlled trial. *Trials* 13, 151.

Ghaemi SN, Vohringer PA, Whitham EA (2013). Antidepressants from a public health perspective: Re-examining effectiveness, suicide, and carcinogenicity. *Acta Psychiatrica Scandinavica* 127, 89-93.

Gilbert F (2013). Deep brain stimulation and postoperative suicidality among treatment resistant depression patients: Should eligibility protocols exclude patients with a history of suicide attempts and anger/impulsivity? *AJOB Neuroscience* 4, 28-35.

Gilbert F (2013). Deep brain stimulation for treatment resistant depression: Postoperative feelings of self-estrangement, suicide attempt and impulsive-aggressive behaviours. *Neuroethics*. Published online: 31 January 2013. doi: 10.1007/s12152-013-9178-8.

Gilman SE, Fitzmaurice GM, Bruce ML, ten Have T, Glymour MM, Carliner H, Alexopoulos GS, Mulsant BH, Reynolds CF, Cohen A (2013). Economic inequalities in the effectiveness of a primary care intervention for depression and suicidal ideation. *Epidemiology* 24, 14-22.

Grant JE, Odlaug BL, Schreiber LRN, Chamberlain SR, Won Kim S (2013). Memantine reduces stealing behavior and impulsivity in kleptomania: A pilot study. *International Clinical Psychopharmacology* 28, 106-111.

Gravell RE, Davison H (2012). Responding to suicidal ideation after stroke: An evaluation of the impact on staff of introducing a service based protocol. *International Journal of Stroke* 7, 69-70.

Groschwitz RC, Plener PL (2013). Psychotherapeutic interventions for non-suicidal self-injury. *Nervenheilkunde* 32, 30-36.

Han C, Park GY, Wang SM, Lee SY, Lee SJ, Bahk WM, Pae CU (2012). Can botulinum toxin improve mood in depressed patients? *Expert Review of Neurotherapeutics* 12, 1049-1051.

Harada K, Eto N, Nishimura R (2012). Features of the intervention system for suicidal patients admitted to the emergency unit of Fukuoka University Hospital. *Asia-Pacific Psychiatry* 4, 70-71.

Harned MS, Tkachuck MA, Youngberg KA (2013). Treatment preference among suicidal and self-injuring women with borderline personality disorder and PTSD. *Journal of Clinical Psychology*. Published online: 26 February 2013. doi: 10.1002/jclp.21943.

Heinzerling KG, Gadzhyan J, van Oudheusden H, Rodriguez F, McCracken J, Shoptaw S (2013). Pilot randomized trial of bupropion for adolescent methamphetamine abuse/dependence. *Journal of Adolescent Health* 52, 502-505.

Hong S, Jang Y, Kim H, Kim M-H, Min S (2012). Predicting factors for the utilization of community mental health centers following suicide attempt. *International Journal of Psychiatry in Clinical Practice* 16, 34.

Horgan Á (2013). Review: Service user involvement in the evaluation of psycho-social intervention for self-harm: A systematic literature review. *Journal of Research in Nursing* 18, 131-132.

Howe E (2013). Five ethical and clinical challenges psychiatrists may face when treating patients with borderline personality disorder who are or may become suicidal. *Innovations in Clinical Neuroscience* 10, 14-19.

Howland RH (2013). Ketamine for the treatment of depression. *Journal of Psychosocial Nursing & Mental Health Services* 51, 11-14.

Jacobson CM, Mufson L (2012). Interpersonal psychotherapy for depressed adolescents adapted for self-injury (IPT-ASI): Rationale, overview, and case summary. *American Journal of Psychotherapy* 66, 349-374.

Jones I (2012). Perinatal psychiatry. *Medicine* 40, 654-657.

Jones S, McGrath E, Hampshire K, Owen R, Riste L, Roberts C, Davies L, Mayes D (2013). A randomised controlled trial of time limited cbt informed psychological therapy for anxiety in bipolar disorder. *BMC Psychiatry* 13, 54.

Kaliora SC, Braga RJ, Petrides G, Chatzimanolis J, Papadimitriou GN, Zervas IM (2013). The practice of electroconvulsive therapy in Greece. *Journal of ECT*. Published online: 4 January 2013. doi: 10.1097/YCT.0b013e31827e0d49.

Kant S, Liebelt E (2012). Recognizing serotonin toxicity in the pediatric emergency department. *Pediatric Emergency Care* 28, 817-821.

Kato K, Yamada K, Akama F, Saito M, Kimito K, Kimoto K, Sato R, Ishida N, Ichimura A, Matsumoto H (2012). Tandospirone combination therapy for the treatment of major depressive disorder in patients admitted to an emergency medical center following suicide attempts: A retrospective study. *International Medical Journal* 19, 208-210.

Kishi Y (2012). Can education change nursing attitudes of Japanese nursing personnel toward patients who have attempted suicide? *Asia-Pacific Psychiatry* 4, 14-15.

Konradt B, Hirsch RD, Jonitz MF, Junglas K (2012). Evaluation of a standardized humor group in a clinical setting: A feasibility study for older patients with depression. *International Journal of Geriatric Psychiatry*. Published online: 7 November 2012. doi: 10.1002/gps.3893.

Kruse JA (2012). Methanol and ethylene glycol intoxication. *Critical Care Clinics* 28, 661-711.

Kupferberg I, Gilat I (2012). The discursive self-construction of suicidal help seekers in computer-mediated discourse. *Communication and Medicine* 9, 23-35.

Laugharne R, Flynn A (2013). Personality disorders in consultation-liaison psychiatry. *Current Opinion in Psychiatry* 26, 84.

Levy Y, Austin MP, Halliday G (2012). Use of ultra-brief pulse electroconvulsive therapy to treat severe postnatal mood disorder. *Australasian Psychiatry* 20, 429-432.

Logan G, Oken T, Simons L, Garcia G (2012). Depression, anxiety, and suicide screening in cystic fibrosis: Patient accessibility to mental health treatment. *Pediatric Pulmonology* 47, 441.

Lozano R, Naghavi M, Foreman K, Lim S, Shibuya K, Aboyans V, Abraham J, Adair T, Aggarwal R, Ahn SY, Alvarado M, Anderson HR, Anderson LM, Andrews KG, Atkinson C, Baddour LM, Barker-Collo S, Bartels DH, Bell ML, Benjamin EJ, Bennett D, Bhalla K, Bikbov B, Bin Abdulhak A, Birbeck G, Blyth F, Bolliger I, Boufous SA, Bucello C, Burch M, Burney P, Carapetis J, Chen H, Chou D, Chugh SS, Coffeng LE, Colan SD, Colquhoun S, Colson KE, Condon J, Connor MD, Cooper LT, Corriere M, Cortinovis M, de Vaccaro KC, Couser W, Cowie BC, Criqui MH, Cross M, Dabhadkar KC, Dahodwala N, De Leo D, Degenhardt L, Delossantos A, Denenberg J, Des Jarlais DC, Dharmaratne SD, Dorsey ER, Driscoll T, Duber H, Ebel B, Erwin PJ, Espindola P, Ezzati M, Feigin V, Flaxman AD, Forouzanfar MH, Fowkes FGR, Franklin R, Fransen M, Freeman MK, Gabriel SE, Gakidou E, Gaspari F, Gillum RF,

Gonzalez-Medina D, Halasa YA, Haring D, Harrison JE, Havmoeller R, Hay RJ, Hoen B, Hotez PJ, Hoy D, Jacobsen KH, James SL, Jasrasaria R, Jayaraman S, Johns N, Karthikeyan G, Kassebaum N, Keren A, Khoo J-P, Knowlton LM, Kobusingye O, Koranteng A, Krishna-murthi R, Lipnick M, Lipshultz SE, Ohno SL, Mabweijano J, MacIntyre MF, Mallinger L, March L, Marks GB, Marks R, Matsumori A, Matzopoulos R, Mayosi BM, McAnulty JH, McDermott MM, McGrath J, Mensah GA, Merriman TR, Michaud C, Miller M, Miller TR, Mock C, Mocumbi AO, Mokdad AA, Moran A, Mulholland K, Nair MN, Naldi L, Narayan KMV, Nasseri K, Norman P, O'Donnell M, Omer SB, Ortblad K, Osborne R, Ozgediz D, Pahari B, Pandian JD, Rivero AP, Padilla RP, Perez-Ruiz F, Perico N, Phillips D, Pierce K, Pope CA, III, Porrini E, Pourmalek F, Raju M, Ranganathan D, Rehm JT, Rein DB, Remuzzi G, Rivara FP, Roberts T, De Leon FR, Rosenfeld LC, Rushton L, Sacco RL, Salomon JA, Sampson U, Sanman E, Schwebel DC, Segui-Gomez M, Shepard DS, Singh D, Singleton J, Sliwa K, Smith E, Steer A, Taylor JA, Thomas B, Tleyjeh IM, Towbin JA, Truelsen T, Undurraga EA, Venketasubramanian N, Vijayakumar L, Vos T, Wagner GR, Wang M, Wang W, Watt K, Wein-stock MA, Weintraub R, Wilkinson JD, Woolf AD, Wulf S, Yeh P-H, Yip P, Zabetian A, Zheng Z-J, Lopez AD, Murray CJL (2012). Global and regional mortality from 235 causes of death for 20 age groups in 1990 and 2010: A systematic analysis for the global burden of disease study 2010. *Lancet* 380, 2095-2128.

Lu DY, Lu TR, Zhu PP (2012). Genetics in neural toxicities of drugs. *Central Nervous System Agents in Medicinal Chemistry* 12, 250-253.

Lucas-Carrasco R (2012). Reliability and validity of the Spanish version of the World Health Organization-five well-being index in elderly. *Psychiatry and Clinical Neurosciences* 66, 508-513.

Lundh A, Forsman M, Serlachius E, Lichtenstein P, Landen M (2012). Outcomes of child psychi-atric treatment. *Acta Psychiatrica Scandinavica.* Published online: 22 November 2012. doi: 10.1111/acps.12043.

Lutfiyya MN, Bianco JA, Quinlan SK, Hall C, Waring SC (2012). Mental health and mental health care in rural America: The hope of redesigned primary care. *Disease-a-Month* 58, 629-638.

MacPherson HA, Cheavens JS, Fristad MA (2012). Dialectical behavior therapy for adolescents: Theory, treatment adaptations, and empirical outcomes. *Clinical Child and Family Psychology Review* 16, 59-80.

Maheshwari R, Joshi P (2012). Assessment, referral, and treatment of suicidal adolescents. *Pedi-atric Annals* 41, 516-521.

Malhi GS, Tanious M, Das P, Coulston CM, Berk M (2013). Potential mechanisms of action of lithium in bipolar disorder : Current understanding. *CNS Drugs* 27, 135-153.

Marchand WR, Lee JN, Johnson S, Gale P, Thatcher J (2013). Differences in functional connec-tivity in major depression versus bipolar II depression. *Journal of Affective Disorders.* Published online: 20 February 2013. doi: 10.1016/j.jad.2013.01.028.

Marciano R, Mullis DM, Jauch EC, Carr CM, Raney L, Martin RH, Walker BJ, Saef SH (2012). Does targeted education of emergency physicians improve their comfort level in treating psy-chiatric patients? *Western Journal of Emergency Medicine* 13, 453-457.

Maxwell M (2013). Targeted education for general practitioners reduces risk of depression or suicide ideation or attempts in older primary care patients. *Evidence Based Mental Health* 16, 8.

McCauley JL, Killeen T, Gros DF, Brady KT, Back SE (2012). Posttraumatic stress disorder and co-occurring substance use disorders: Advances in assessment and treatment. *Clinical Psychology: Science and Practice* 19, 283-304.

McGarvey EL, Leon-Verdin M, Wanchek TN, Bonnie RJ (2013). Decisions to initiate involuntary commitment: The role of intensive community services and other factors. *Psychiatric Services* 64, 120-126

Meltzer HY (2012). Clozapine. *Clinical Schizophrenia & Related Psychoses* 6, 134-144.

Meltzer HY (2013). Update on typical and atypical antipsychotic drugs. *Annul Review of Medicine* 64, 393-406.

Memel B (2012). A quality improvement project to decrease the length of stay on a psychiatric adolescent partial hospital program. *Journal of Child and Adolescent Psychiatric Nursing* 25, 207-218.

Monteggia LM, Gideons E, Kavalali ET (2012). The role of eukaryotic elongation factor 2 kinase in rapid antidepressant action of ketamine. *Biological Psychiatry*. Published online: 10 October 2012. doi: 10.1016/j.biopsych.2012.09.006.

Morris C, Simpson J, Sampson M, Beesley F (2013). Cultivating positive emotions: A useful adjunct when working with people who self-harm? *Clinical Psychology and Psychotherapy*. Published online: 11 March 2013. doi: 10.1002/cpp.1836.

Morthorst B, Krogh J, Erlangsen A (2012). An assertive outreach intervention does not reduce repeat suicide attempts compared with usual care. *Evidence-Based Mental Health*. Published online: 8 December 2012. doi: 10.1136/eb-2012-101042

Nassir Ghaemi S, Vohringer PA, Whitham EA (2013). Antidepressants from a public health perspective: Re-examining effectiveness, suicide, and carcinogenicity. *Acta Psychiatrica Scandinavica* 127, 89-93.

Neacsiu AD, Ward-Ciesielski EF, Linehan MM (2012). Emerging approaches to counseling intervention: Dialectical Behavior Therapy. *Counseling Psychologist* 40, 1003-1032.

Nordentoft M (2012). Saving young lives: Early intervention in psychosis and the risk of suicide. *Early Intervention in Psychiatry* 6, 65.

Norman RMG, Manchanda R, Windell D, Hassall L, Harricharan R, Northcott S (2012). Predicting suicidal thoughts in patients of an early intervention program. *Early Intervention in Psychiatry* 6, 74.

Norrie J, Davidson K, Tata P, Gumley A (2013). Influence of therapist competence and quantity of cognitive behavioural therapy on suicidal behaviour and inpatient hospitalisation in a randomised controlled trial in borderline personality disorder: Further analyses of treatment effects in the boscot study. *Psychology and Psychotherapy*. Published online: 19 February 2013. doi: 10.1111/papt.12004.

Novakovic V, Sher L (2012). The use of clozapine for the treatment of schizophrenia and implications for suicide prevention. *International Journal on Disability and Human Development* 11, 5-8.

Okamoto M, Kawakami N, Kido Y, Sakurai K (2012). Social capital and suicide: An ecological study in Tokyo, Japan. *Environmental Health and Preventive Medicine*. Published online: 23 November 2012. doi: 10.1007/s12199-012-0321-7.

Panagioti M, Gooding PA, Tarrier N (2012). An empirical investigation of the effectiveness of the broad-minded affective coping procedure (BMAC) to boost mood among individuals with posttraumatic stress disorder (PTSD). *Behaviour Research and Therapy* 50, 589-595.

Pane HT, White RS, Nadorff MR, Grills-Taquechel A, Stanley MA (2013). Multisystemic therapy for child non-externalizing psychological and health problems: A preliminary review. *Clinical Child and Family Psychology Review* 16, 81-99.

Peterson AL, Roache JD, Raj J, Young-McCaughan S (2013). The need for expanded monitoring of adverse events in behavioral health clinical trials. *Contemporary Clincal Trials* 34, 152-154.

Pil L, Annemans L, Pauwels K, Muijzers E, Portzky G (2012). Cost-effectiveness analysis of a helpline for suicide prevention. *Value in Health* 15, A524.

Plener PL, Libal G, Fegert JM, Koelch MG (2013). Psychopharmacological treatment of non-suicidal self-injury. *Nervenheilkunde* 32, 38.

Pompili M, Lester D, Dominici G, Longo L, Marconi G, Forte A, Serafini G, Amore M, Girardi P (2013). Indications for electroconvulsive treatment in schizophrenia: A systematic review. *Schizophrenia Research*. Published online: 15 March 2013. doi: 10.1016/j.schres.2013.02.005.

Pompili M, Rihmer Z, Gonda X, Serafini G, Sher L, Girardi P (2012). Early onset of action and sleep-improving effect are crucial in decreasing suicide risk: The role of quetiapine xr in the treatment of unipolar and bipolar depression. *Rivista di Psichiatria* 47, 489-497.

Preuss UW, Zimmermann J, Schultz G, Watzke A, Schmidt P, Loehnert B, Soyka M (2012). Does a history of suicide attempts predict treatment non-completion and outcome in alcohol-dependent individuals? *Alcoholism-Clinical and Experimental Research* 36, 50A.

Ralston L, Schuermeyer I, Fraiman J, Datta-Barua I (2013). A national review of cancer centers: Caregiver protocol for patient suicide. *Psycho-Oncology* 22, 85.

Rissanen I, Jaaskelainen E, Isohanni M, Koponen H, Joukamaa M, Alaraisanen A, Miettunen J (2012). Use of antipsychotic medication and suicidality-The Northern Finland birth cohort 1966. *Human Psychopharmacology* 27, 476-485.

Rosenthal JZ, Boyer P, Vialet C, Hwang E, Tourian KA (2013). Efficacy and safety of desvenlafax-ine 50mg/d for prevention of relapse in major depressive disorder: A randomized controlled trial. *Journal of Clinical Psychiatry* 74, 158-166.

Rossouw TI, Fonagy P (2012). Mentalization-based treatment for self-harm in adolescents: A ran-domized controlledtrial. *Journal of the American Academy of Child and Adolescent Psychiatry* 51, 1304-1313.e1303.

Rudd MD (2012). Brief cognitive behavioral therapy (BCBT) for suicidality in military popula-tions. *Military Psychology* 24, 592-603.

Scanavino MdT, Ventuneac A, Abdo CHN, Tavares H, Amaral MLSd, Messina B, Reis SCd, Martins JPLB, Parsons JT (2013). Compulsive sexual behavior and psychopathology among treatment-seeking men in São Paulo, Brazil. *Psychiatry Research*. Published online: 14 Febru-ary 2013. doi: 10.1016/j.psychres.2013.01.02.

Schade LC (2013). Non-suicidal self-injury (NSSI): A case for using emotionally focused family therapy. *Contemporary Family Therapy*. Published online: 29 January 2013. doi: 10.1007/s10591-013-9236-8.

Schiavone FL, Links PS (2012). Common elements for the psychotherapeutic management of patients with self injurious behavior. *Child Abuse and Neglect* 37, 133-138.

Scott EM, Hermens DF, Naismith SL, White D, Whitwell B, Guastella AJ, Glozier N, Hickie IB (2012). Thoughts of death or suicidal ideation are common in young people aged 12 to 30 years presenting for mental health care. *BMC Psychiatry* 12, 234.

Sharkey S, Smithson J, Hewis E, Jones R, Emmens T, Ford T, Owens C (2012). Supportive inter-changes and face-work as 'protective talk' in an online self-harm support forum. *Communica-tion and Medicine* 9, 71-82.

Shoyinka S, Lauriello J (2012). Mental health access to care in Missouri. *Missouri Medicine* 109, 470-474.

Siefert CJ (2012). A goal-oriented limited-duration approach for borderline personality disorder during brief inpatient hospitalizations. *Psychotherapy* 49, 502-518.

Siegel LS (2012). Confessions and reflections of the black sheep of the learning disabilities field. *Australian Journal of Learning Difficulties* 17, 63-77.

Stringer B, van Meijel B, Eikelenboom M, Koekkoek B, Verhaak PFM, Kerkhof AJMF, Penninx BWJH, Beekman ATF (2012). Perceived need for care and health care utilization among depressed and anxious patients with and without suicidal ideation. *Crisis*. Published online: 21 December 2012. doi: 10.1027/0227-5910/a000182.

Sudhir Kumar CT, Tharayil HM, Anil Kumar TV, Ranjith G (2012). A survey of psychiatric services for people who attempt suicide in South India. *Indian Journal of Psychiatry* 54, 352-355.

Swales MA, Taylor B, Hibbs RAB (2012). Implementing Dialectical Behaviour Therapy: Programme survival in routine healthcare settings. *Journal of Mental Health* 21, 548.

Swanson SA, Stuermer T, Pate V, Azrael D, Miller M (2012). The association between class and dose level of antidepressant medication with suicidal behaviors. *Pharmacoepidemiology and Drug Safety* 21, 453.

Symonds C, Anderson IM (2012). Unipolar depression and dysthymia. *Medicine* 40, 591-595.

Taliaferro LA, Muehlenkamp JJ, Hetler J, Edwall G, Wright C, Borowsky IW (2013). Non-suicidal self-injury among adolescents: A training priority for primary care providers. *Journal of Adolescent Health* 52, S79.

Tamburello AC, Lieberman JA, Baum RM, Reeves R (2012). Successful removal of quetiapine from a correctional formulary. *Journal of the American Academy of Psychiatry and the Law* 40, 502-508.

Tan SY, Qin XX, Li Y, Deng GH (2009). Analysis of features for suicide attempters at emergency departments in general hospitals. *National Medical Journal of China* 89, 3332-3336.

Tohen M, Katagiri H, Fujikoshi S, Kanba S (2013). Efficacy of olanzapine monotherapy in acute bipolar depression: A pooled analysis of controlled studies. *Journal of Affective Disorders*. Published online: 26 February 2013. doi: doi.org/10.1016/j.jad.2013.01.022.

Van Noorden MS, Van Fenema EM, Van Der Wee NJA, Van Rood YR, Carlier IVE, Zitman FG, Giltay EJ (2012). Predicting outcomes of mood, anxiety and somatoform disorders: The leiden routine outcome monitoring study. *Journal of Affective Disorders* 142, 122-131.

Van Orden KA, Talbot N, King D (2012). Using the interpersonal theory of suicide to inform interpersonal psychotherapy with a suicidal older adult. *Clinical Case Studies* 11, 333-347.

van Spijker BAJ, Majo MC, Smit F, van Straten A, Kerkhof AJFM (2012). Reducing suicidal ideation: Cost-effectiveness analysis of a randomized controlled trial of unguided web-based self-help. *Journal of Medical Internet Research* 14, e141.

Vasiliadis H-M, Gagne S, Jozwiak N, Preville M (2013). Gender differences in health service use for mental health reasons in community dwelling older adults with suicidal ideation. *International Psychogeriatrics* 25, 374-381.

Ward-Ciesielski EF (2013). An open pilot feasibility study of a brief dialectical behavior therapy skills-based intervention for suicidal individuals. *Suicide and Life-Threatening Behavior*. Published online: 15 February 2013. doi: 10.1111/sltb.12019.

Ward J, de Motte C, Bailey D (2013). Service user involvement in the evaluation of psycho-social intervention for self-harm: A systematic literature review. *Journal of Research in Nursing* 18, 114-130.

Watanabe N, Nishida A, Shimodera S, Inoue K, Oshima N, Sasaki T, Inoue S, Akechi T, Furukawa TA, Okazaki Y (2012). Help-seeking behavior among Japanese school students who self-harm: Results from a self-report survey of 18,104 adolescents. *Neuropsychiatric Disease and Treatment* 8, 561-569.

Westerlund M, Hadlaczky G, Wasserman D (2012). The representation of suicide on the internet: Implications for clinicians. *Journal of Medical Internet Research* 14, e122.

Wigal SB, Childress AC, Belden HW, Berry SA (2013). NWP06, an extended-release oral suspension of methylphenidate, improved attention-deficit/hyperactivity disorder symptoms compared with placebo in a laboratory classroom study. *Journal of Child and Adolescent Psychopharmacology* 23, 3-10.

Williams DE, McAdam D (2012). Assessment, behavioral treatment, and prevention of Pica: Clinical guidelines and recommendations for practitioners. *Research in Developmental for Disabilities* 33, 2050-2057.

Winter D, Bradshaw S, Bunn F, Wellsted D (2013). A systematic review of the literature on counselling and psychotherapy for the prevention of suicide: Quantitative outcome and process studies. *Counselling and Psychotherapy Research.* Published online: 31 October 2012. doi: 10.1080/14733145.2012.737004.

Wu P, Li LP, Jin J, Yuan XH, Liu X, Fan B, Fuller C, Lu YG, Hoven CW (2012). Need for mental health services and service use among high school students in China. *Psychiatric Services* 63, 1026-1031.

Yamaguchi T, Fujii C, Nemoto T, Tsujino N, Takeshi K, Mizuno M (2012). A clinical study on suicidal behavior and its prevention in people with untreated schizophrenia. *Early Intervention in Psychiatry* 6, 76.

Yap MB, Reavley NJ, Jorm AF (2013). The associations between psychiatric label use and young people's help-seeking preferences: Results from an Australian national survey. *Epidemiology and Psychiatric Science.* Published online: 25 February 2013. doi: 10.1017/S2045796013000073.

Yap MBH, Reavley N, Jorm AF (2012). Where would young people seek help for mental disorders and what stops them? Findings from an Australian national survey. *Journal of Affective Disorders* 147, 255-261.

Zamani N, Jamshidi F (2012). How frequent is complete recovery after suicidal hanging? *Medicine, Science and the Law* 52, 246.

Zemishlany Z (2012). Boundaries of responsibility in the management of suicidal patients. *Israel Journal of Psychiatry and Related Sciences* 49, 28.

CASE REPORTS

Abdelraheem MB, Elbushra M, Ali E-T, Ellidir RA, Bushara AI, Abdelraheem WB, Zijlstra EE (2012). Filicide and suicide in a family by paraphenylene diamine poisoning: A mother who committed suicide and poisoned her four children of which one died. *Toxicology and Industrial Health.* Published online: 6 December 2012. doi: 10.1177/0748233712448118.

Aggarwal N, Kupfer Y, Seneviratne C, Tessler S (2013). Methylene blue reverses recalcitrant shock in beta-blocker and calcium channel blocker overdose. *BMJ Case Reports.* Published online: 18 January 2013. doi: 10.1136/bcr-2012-007402.

Al B, Subasi M, Karsli B, Yarbil P, Zengin S (2012). Compartment syndrome on a patient's forearm related to carbon monoxide poisoning. *The American Journal of Emergency Medicine* 30, e2101-2104.

Altay S, Cakmak HA, Boz GC, Koca S, Velibey Y (2012). Prolonged coagulopathy related to coumarin rodenticide in a young patient: Superwarfarin poisoning. *Cardiovascular Journal of Africa* 23, E9-E11.

Amir LH, Ryan KM, Jordan SE (2012). Avoiding risk at what cost? Putting use of medicines for breastfeeding women into perspective. *International Journal of Breastfeeding* 7, 14.

Anderson D, Mount C, Roth B (2012). Care of a suicidal patient following an intentional morphine overdose: An ethical dilemma. *Critical Care Medicine* 40, U242-U243.

Austin AE, Guddat SS, Tsokos M, Gilbert JD, Byard RW (2013). Multiple injuries in suicide simulating homicide: Report of three cases. *Journal of Forensic Legal Medicine.* Published online: 26 February 2013. doi:10.1016/j.jflm.2013.02.005

Avci A, Yilmaz A, Celik M, Demir K, Keles F (2013). Successful treatment of suicide attempt by megadose of propafenone and captopril. *Cardiovascular Toxicology.* Published online: 9 February 2013. doi: 10.1007/s12012-013-9201-7.

Bansude ME, Kachare RV, Dode CR (2012). Case report - Unusual cases of late deaths in hanging. *Indian Journal of Forensic Medicine and Toxicology* 6, 83-85.

Bartlett VL, Killu C, Finder S, Hackner D (2010). Clinical ethics in the ICU: A case of attempted suicide. *ICU Director* 1, 312-317.

Battefort F, Dehours E, Vallé B, Hamdaoui A, Bounes V, Ducassé J-L (2012). Suicide attempt by intravenous potassium self-poisoning: A case report. *Case Reports in Emergency Medicine* 2012, 323818.

Baum AL (2012). Concussive injury, suicidal ideation in a 16-year-old female athlete. *Psychiatric Annals* 42, 361-363.

Bayir PT, Demirkan B, Duyuler S, Güray U, Kisacik HL (2012). Water intoxication resulting in ventricular arrythmias. *Turkiye Acil Tip Dergisi* 12, 188-190.

Bebarta VS, Shiner DC, Varney SM (2012). A case of moderate liver enzyme elevation after acute acetaminophen overdose despite undetectable acetaminophen level and normal initial liver enzymes. *Americal Journal of Therapy.* Published online: 24 September 2012. doi: 10.1097/MJT.0b013e31824714a8.

Benali L, Abalan F, Christin E, Abriat F, Liguoro D, Gromb S (2012). An unusual case of attempted suicide by a depressive woman: Self-inflicted intracranial stabbing. *Forensic Science International* 226, E9-E11.

Bergler-Czop B, Brzezinska-Wcislo L (2012). Psychodermatologic disorders: Case reports and review of literature. *Postepy Dermatologii I Alergologii* 29, 401-406.

Blacha C, Schmid MM, Gahr M, Freudenmann RW, Plener PL, Finter F, Connemann BJ, Schonfeldt-Lecuona C (2012). Self-inflicted testicular amputation in first lysergic acid diethylamide use. *Journal of Addiction Medicine* 1, 83-84.

Borkar JL, Meshram SK, Ambade VN, Dixit PG (2011). Worn jeans trouser: An unusual ligature material for hanging. *Journal of Forensic Medicine and Toxicology* 28, 42-44.

Bott E, Dodd M (2013). Suicide by hydrogen sulfide inhalation. *American Journal of Forensic Medical Pathology* 34, 23-25.

Butchard K, Bagaoisan K, Collas D (2012). Multiple thrombolysis in munchausen's syndrome - A failed attempt at suicide. *International Journal of Stroke* 7, 16.

Byrne M, Zumberg M (2012). Intentional low-molecular-weight heparin overdose: A case report and review. *Blood Coagulation and Fibrinolysis* 23, 772-774.

Chandrakanth HV, Arun M, Manjunatha B, Pramod Kumar GN, Hemanth Kumar RG, Balaraj BM (2012). Unplanned complex suicide- A case report. *Medico-Legal Update* 12, 19-21.

Chao SL, Wang TL, Chong CF, Lin LW (2012). Steroid psychosis in an adrenal insufficiency and hypothyroidism patient. *Journal of Acute Medicine* 2, 121-124.

Chaudhary S, Kashani K, Williams AW, El-Zoghby ZM, Albright RC, Qian Q (2013). Rapid self-infusion of tap water. *Iranian Journal of Kidney Diseases* 7, 156-159.

Chen H-W, Chen K-C, Chen J-S (2012). Colchicine and nsaid combination causing acute kidney injury. *Journal of the College of Physicians and Surgeons* 22, 737-739.

Cinar N, Sahin S, Bozdemir M, Simsek S, Karsidag S (2012). Hanging-induced burst suppression pattern in EEG. *Journal of Emergencies, Trauma, and Shock* 5, 347-349.

Colucci AP, Gagliano-Candela R, Aventaggiato L, De Donno A, Leonardi S, Strisciullo G, Introna F (2013). Suicide by self-administration of a drug mixture (propofol, midazolam, and zolpidem) in an anesthesiologist: The first case report in Italy. *Journal of Forensic Science.* Published online: 13 February 2012. doi: 10.1111/1556-4029.12053.

Das S, Patra AP, Shaha KK, Sistla SC, Jena MK (2013). High-voltage suicidal electrocution with multiple exit wounds. *American Journal of Forensic Medical Pathology* 34, 34-37.

Davis TN, Dacus S, Strickland E, Machalicek W, Coviello L (2013). Reduction of automatically maintained self-injurious behavior utilizing noncontingent matched stimuli. *Developmental Neurorehabilitation.* Published online: 11 March 2013. doi: 10.3109/17518423.2013.766819.

Dickerson EM, Jones P, Wilkins D, Regnier J, Prahlow JA (2013). Complicated suicide versus autoeroticism?: A case involving multiple drugs and a porta-potty. *Americal Journal of Forensic Medicine & Pathology* 34, 29-33.

Dogan S, Regeer Ej, Mol Emm, Braam Aw (2013). Compulsory admission after threatened infanticide and suicide by a patient with a feigned psychosis. *Tijdschrift voor Psychiatrie* 55, 209-213.

Droste J, Hundia V, Pettit A, Narayan N, Nejim A (2012). Excision of injection site substantially reduced serum insulin concentration in a potentially life-threatening insulin analogue overdose. *Practical Diabetes* 29, 243-245.

Eren B, Turkmen N, Erkol Z (2012). Bilateral long styloid process detected at autopsy (Case report). *Georgian Medical News* 206, 49-51.

Fingeret M (2013). Remote suicidal ideation in a cancer patient with a poor prognosis: A case report. *Psycho-Oncology* 22, 57.

Fischer CA, Licht EA, Mendez MF (2012). The neuropsychiatric manifestations of Huntington's Disease-Like 2. *Journal of Neuropsychiatry Clinical Neuroscience* 24, 489-492.

Gerace E, Ciccotelli V, Rapetti P, Salomone A, Vincenti M (2012). Distribution of chloralose in a fatal intoxication. *Journal of Analytical Toxicology* 36, 452-456.

Gómez A, Bórquez P (2012). Suicide by interruption of hemodialysis, in a patient with chronic renal failure. Analisis of one case. *Revista Medica de Chile* 140, 771-774.

Greenfield RM (2012). The attachment function of acute and chronic suicidal illness in the psychotherapy of an adult female incest survivor. *Clinical Social Work Journal.* Published online: 29 December 2012. doi: 10.1007/s10615-012-0429-7.

Große Perdekamp M, Braunwarth R, Kromeier J, Nadjem H, Pollak S, Thierauf A (2012). Muzzle-loading weapons discharging spherical lead bullets: Two case studies and experimental simulation using a skin-soap composite model. *International Journal of Legal Medicine.* Published online: 19 December 2012. doi: 10.1007/s00414-012-0808-1.

Gupta M, Kharb V (2012). MRKH syndrome: Psychological disturbances and suicide. *Journal of Indian Academy of Forensic Medicine* 34, 86-88.

Haj Salem N, Aissaoui A, Boughattas M, Chadly A (2013). An unusual case of smothering by a medical nebulizer. *Journal of Forensic Legal Medcine.* Published online: 28 February 2013. doi: 10.1016/j.jflm.2013.02.006.

Hamelin EI, Johnson RC, Osterloh JD, Howard DJ, Thomas JD (2012). Evaluation of ricinine, a ricin biomarker, from a non-lethal castor bean ingestion. *Journal of Analytical Toxicology* 26, 660-662.

Hardoy MC, Zamboni F, Mameli L, Calabrese JR (2012). Self-injurious and aggressive behavior associated with a tacrolimus overdose. *Psychosomatics* 53, 602-603.

Healey C, Morriss R, Henshaw C, Wadoo O, Sajjad A, Scholefield H, Kinderman P (2013). Self-harm in postpartum depression and referrals to a perinatal mental health team: An audit study. *Archives of Women's Mental Health.* Published online: 6 March 2013. doi: 10.1007/s00737-013-0335-1.

Hejna P (2012). Comments on complete post-mortem decapitation in suicidal hanging. *Forensic Science, Medicine, and Pathology* 8, 484-485.

Hejna P, Zatopkova L, Safr M, Straka L (2013). Circular saw-associated fatality mimicking gunshot injury. *Journal of Forensic Science* 58, S267-S269.

Hiromine Y, Kawabata Y, Yamauchi T, Noso S, Babaya N, Harada T, Ito H, Ikegami H (2012). Prolonged hyperinsulinemia after subcutaneous injection of 2400 U regular insulin in a suicide attempt: Time course of serum insulin with frequent measurements. *Journal of Diabetes Investigation* 3, 468-470 .

Hutchinson V, Wheatley R (2012). A mental health professional's personal experience of suicide (part 1). *International Journal of Mental Health Nursing* 21, 12.

Jarwani BS, Motiani P, Divetia R, Thakkar G (2012). Rare combination of bilateral putaminal necrosis, optic neuritis, and polyneuropathy in a case of acute methanol intoxication among patients met with hooch tragedy in Gujarat, India. *Journal of Emergencies, Trauma, and Shock* 5, 356-359.

Jornil J, Nielsen TS, Rosendal I, Ahlner J, Zackrisson AL, Boel LWT, Brock B (2013). A poor metabolizer of both CYP2C19 and CYP2D identified by mechanistic pharmacokinetic simulation in a fatal drug poisoning case involving venlafaxine. *Forensic Science International* 226, e26-e31.

Kai K, Kono M, Karakida S, Sasaki T, Nasu K, Narahara H (2012). Depression and pregnancy-associated death by suicide after spinal cord injury: A case report. *Clinical and Experimental Obstetrics and Gynecology* 39, 532-534.

Korkmaz HA, Dizdarer C, Hazan F, Karaarslan U (2013). Attempted suicide with levothyroxine in an adolescent girl. *Journal of Pediatric Endocrinology* 26, 129-131.

Kumar GNP, Arun M, Manjunatha B, Balaraj BM, Verghese AJ (2013). Suicidal strangulation by plastic lock tie. *Journal of Forensic Legal Medicine* 20, 60-62.

Kunz SN, Brandtner H, Meyer H (2013). Unusual blood spatter patterns on the firearm and hand: A backspatter analysis to reconstruct the position and orientation of a firearm. *Forensic Science International* 24, 132-140.

Kuramochi M, Kato S, Okajima Y, Yamaga K (2012). Factitious disorder mixed with somatoform disorder in a patient treated with a psychotherapeutic approach: Psychopathology and treatment. *Psychiatria et Neurologia Japonica* 114, 906-914.

Langrand J, Moesch C, Le Grand R, Bloch V, Garnier R, Baud Fj, Megarbane B (2013). A life-threatening dichlorophen poisoning case: Clinical features and kinetics study. *Clinical Toxicology* 51, 178-181.

Lankford A (2012). A psychological autopsy of 9/11 ringleader Mohamed Atta. *Journal of Police and Criminal Psychology* 27, 150.

Laurent PE, Coulange M, Desfeux J, Bartoli C, Coquart B, Vidal V, Gorincour G (2013). Post-mortem computed tomography in a case of suicide by air embolism. *Diagnostic and Interventional Imaging*. Published online: 1 March 2013. doi: 10.1016/j.diii.2013.01.014.

Le JF, Lohr WD (2012). Aggression and self-injury in a patient with severe autism. *Pediatric Annals* 41, 1-3.

Lehavot K, Ben-Zeev D, Neville REL (2012). Ethical considerations and social media: A case of suicidal postings on Facebook. *Journal of Dual Diagnosis* 8, 341.

Lev-Ran S, Balchand K (2013). New onset non-suicidal self-injury in a 57-year-old woman with co-morbid depression and alcohol dependence: Case report. *The American Journal on Addictions* 22, 178-179.

Mahmoodpoor A, Hamishehkar H, Soleimanpour H (2012). Multi organ failure following intravenous gasoline for suicide: A case report. *Acta Medica Iranica* 50, 846-848.

Mehrpour O, Aghabiklooei A, Abdollahi M, Singh S (2012). Severe hypoglycemia following acute aluminum phosphide (rice tablet) poisoning: A case report and review of the literature. *Acta Medica Iranica* 50, 568-571.

Miyazato T, Ishikawa T, Michiue T, Oritani S, Maeda H (2012). Pathological and toxicological findings in four cases of fatal hydrogen sulfide inhalation. *Forensic Toxicology* 31, 172-179.

Modelli MES, Rodrigues MS, Castro BZM, Corrêa RS (2013). Self-induced fatal air embolism: Accidental autoerotic death or suicide? *Journal of Forensic Sciences* 58, S261-S263.

Moudi S, Alijanpour E, Manouchehri AA, Jafarian H (2012). A case report of prolonged apnea during ect in a patient with suicidal attempt by organophosphorus poison. *Iranian Journal of Psychiatry and Behavioral Sciences* 6, 68-71.

Musshoff F, Hagemeier L, Kirschbaum K, Madea B (2012). Two cases of suicide by asphyxiation due to helium and argon. *Forensic Science International* 223, E27-E30.

Musshoff F, Kirschbaum KM, Madea B (2013). Another suicide using the veterinary drug T61 and distribution of drugs in the body. *Journal of Analytical Toxicology* 37, 186.

Nakanishi R, Hirose T, Tamura Y, Fujitani Y, Watada H (2012). Attempted suicide with liraglutide overdose did not induce hypoglycemia. *Diabetes Research and Clinical Practice* 99, e3-e4.

Neukamm MA, Vogt S, Hermanns-Clausen M, Naue J, Thierauf A, Auwärter V (2012). Fatal doxepin intoxication - Suicide or slow gradual intoxication? *Forensic Science International* 227, 82-84.

Niitsu H, Fujita Y, Fujita S, Kumagai R, Takamiya M, Aoki Y, Dewa K (2012). Distribution of aconitum alkaloids in autopsy cases of aconite poisoning. *Forensic Science International* 227, 111-117.

Ong Yl, Yap Hl (2013). Do intercultural factors play a role in exacerbating psychiatric symptoms? *Singapore Medical Journal* 54, e16-e17.

Petrich CE, Bui MP, Farrell HM (2013). A case of a suicide attempt associated with hyperthyroidism. *General Hospital Psychiatry*. Published online: 19 Janurary 2013. doi: 10.1016/j.genhosppsych.2012.12.006.

Prado LG, Huber J, Huber CG, Mogler C, Ehrenheim J, Nyarangi-Dix J, Pahernik S, Hohenfellner M (2012). Penile methadone injection in suicidal intent: Life-threatening and fatal for erectile function. *Journal of Andrology* 33, 801-804.

Proença P, Franco JM, Mustra C, Monteiro C, Costa J, Corte-Real F, Vieira DN (2012). UPLC-MS/MS determination in blood of a mixed-drug fatal intoxication: A case report. *Forensic Science International* 227, 85-89.

Rajpal S, Beedupalli J, Reddy P (2012). Recrudescent digoxin toxicity treated with plasma exchange: A case report and review of literature. *Cardiovascular Toxicology* 12, 363-368.

Rapp M, Spiegler J, Haertel C, Gillessen-Kaesbach G, Kaiser MM (2013). Severe complications in wound healing and fracture treatment in two brothers with congenital insensitivity to pain with anhidrosis. *Journal of Pediatric Orthopaedics-Part B* 22, 76-80.

Rojek S, Klys M, Strona M, Maciow M, Kula K (2012). "Legal highs"- Toxicity in the clinical and medico-legal aspect as exemplified by suicide with bk-mbdb administration. *Forensic Science International* 222, E1-E6.

Roka YB, Thapa R, Puri PR, Aryal S (2011). Van Gogh Syndrome. *Journal of Nepal Health Research Council* 9, 79-81.

Roma P, Pazzelli F, Pompili M, Girardi P, Ferracuti S (2012). Shibari: Double hanging during consensual sexual asphyxia. *Archives of Sexual Behavior.* Published online: 28 November 2012. doi: 10.1007/s10508-012-0035-3.

Ronquillo L, Minassian A, Vilke GM, Wilson MP (2012). Literature-based recommendations for suicide assessment in the emergency department: A review. *Journal of Emergency Medicine* 43, 836-842.

Rudhran V, Thippeswamy H, Chaturvedi SK (2012). Phallicide: A case of auto penile amputation as a mode of suicide. *The Australian and New Zealand Journal of Psychiatry.* Published online: 11 October 2012. doi: 10.1177/0004867412463092.

Ryoo S, Sohn C, Kim H, Kwak M, Oh B, Lim K (2013). Intracardiac thrombus formation induced by carbon monoxide poisoning. *Humuan & Experimental Toxicology.* Published online: 28 January 2013. doi: 10.1177/0960327112472991.

Sacks Z, Vaidya A, Sharma N, Gottlieb B (2012). Interactive medical case. A patient found unresponsive. *New England Journal of Medicine* 367, e36.

Sandage SJ (2012). The tragic-ironic self: A qualitative case study of suicide. *Psychoanalytic Psychology* 29, 17-33.

Santhosh CS, Vishwanthan KG, Selvakumar C, Nawaz B (2012). An unusual form of complex suicide - Case report. *Medico-Legal Update* 12, 160-162.

Scholten HA, Nap A, Bouwman RA, Biermann H (2012). Intralipid as antidote for tricyclic antidepressants and SSRI's: A case report. *Anaesthesia and Intensive Care* 40, 1076-1077.

Seavey A, Moore TM (2012). Schema-focused therapy for major depressive disorder and personality disorder: A case study. *Clinical Case Studies* 11, 457-473.

Sein Anand J, Barwina M, Zajac M, Kaletha K (2012). Suicidal intoxication with potassium chlorate successfully treated with renal replacement therapy and extracorporeal liver support. *Przegląd Lekarski* 69, 585-586.

Sharma SK, Singh K (2011). Case of suicidal hanging in danger of being considered as a homicidal death: Case report. *Journal of Forensic Medicine and Toxicology* 28, 58-60.

Simonse E, Valk-Swinkels CG, van 't Veer NE, Ermens AA, Veldkamp EJ (2012). Iron autointoxication in a 16-year-old girl: A protective role for hepcidin? *Annals of Clinical Biochemistry* 50, 76-79.

Singh LK, Praharaj SK, Sahu M (2012). Nonfatal suicidal overdose of olanzapine in an adolescent. *Current Drug Safety* 7, 328-329.

Soleimani L, Burdick KE, Goldberg JF, Simon AB (2013). The intersection of symptomatology in adult ADHD and bipolar disorder. *Psychiatric Annals* 43, 20-25.

Sood S, Howell J, Sundararajan V, Angus P, Gow P (2013). Paracetamol overdose in Victoria remains a significant health care burden. *Journal of Gastroenterology and Hepatology*. Published online: 11 March 2013. doi: 10.1111/jgh.12196.

Sridhar A, Sandeep Y, Krishnakishore C, Sriramnaveen P, Manjusha Y, Sivakumar V (2012). Fatal poisoning by isoniazid and rifampicin. *Indian Journal of Nephrology* 22, 385-387.

Stojanovi I, Mili M, Antovi A, Todorovi S, Jovanovi I (2013). Unusual suicide with a chainsaw. *Forensic Science International*. Published online: 26 February 2013. doi: 10.1016/j.forsciint.2013.02.011.

Strajina V, Zivkovic V, Nikolic S (2013). Anomalous anterior papillary muscle as an autopsy finding in two cases. *Journal of Forensic Sciences* 58, 544-547.

Straka L, Novomesky F, Stuller F, Janik M, Krajcovic J, Hejna P (2013). A planned complex suicide by gunshot and vehicular crash. *Forensic Science International*. Published online: 4 March 2013. doi: 10.1016/j.forsciint.2013.02.016.

Sukumar S, Das UB (2012). Sodium dichromate poisoning - A case report. *Indian Journal of Forensic Medicine and Toxicology* 6, 171-173.

Suzuki T, Wada T, Funaki S, Abe H, Seki I, Imaki S, Nakazawa A (2012). Traumatic left ventricular free-wall laceration by a gunshot: Report of a case. *Surgery Today*. Published online: 6 April 2012. doi: 10.1007/s00595-012-0457-5.

Szpak A, Allen D (2012). A case of acute suicidality following excessive caffeine intake. *Journal of Psychopharmacology* 26, 1502-1510.

Taherinia A, Heidarpour A (2012). St elevation in tricyclic antidepressants toxicity: A case report. *Iranian Heart Journal* 13, 43-45.

Tominaga K, Izumi M, Suzukawa M, Shinjo T, Izawa Y, Yonekawa C, Ano M, Yamashita K, Muronoi T, Mochiduki R (2012). Takotsubo cardiomyopathy as a delayed complication with a herbicide containing glufosinate ammonium in a suicide attempt: A case report. *Case Reports in Medicine* 2012, 630468.

Turkmen N, Eren B, Uyaniker ZD, Ergonen AT (2012). An uncommon suicide method: Self-strangulation. *Medicinski Arhiv* 66, 423-424.

Verma SK, Kapoor N, Bhaskar R, Upadhyay R (2012). Pyopneumothorax following suicidal kerosene ingestion. *BMJ Case Reports*. Published online: 18 December 2012. doi: 10.1136/bcr-2012-007795.

Waldman W, Kabata P, Sein Anand J (2012). Double, suicidal intoxication with hydroxycarbamide-A case report. *Przegląd Lekarski* 69, 587-588.

Wasserscheid K, Backendorf A, Michna D, Mallmann R, Hoffmann B (2013). Long-term outcome after suicidal colchicine intoxication in a 14-year-old girl: Case report and review of literature. *Pediatric Emergency Care* 29, 89-92.

Weymann A, Sebening C (2013). A rare, combined cardiac and hepatic crossbow injury. *Annals of Thoracic Cardiovascular Surgery*. Published online: 31 January 2013. doi: 10.5761/atcs.cr.12.02083.

Wilson CM (1945). An unusual suicide. *The Journal of Criminal Law and Criminology* 36, 220.

Woo JS, Kapadia N, Phanco SE, Lynch CA (2012). Positive outcome after intentional overdose of dabigatran. *Journal of Medical Toxicology*. Published online: 5 December 2012. doi:10.1007/s13181-012-0276-5.

Xu K, Li W (2012). An ethical stakeholder approach to crisis communication: A case study of Foxconn's 2010 employee suicide crisis. *Journal of Business Ethics*. Published online: 26 October 2012. doi: 10.1007/s10551-012-1522-0.

Yakubo S, Ueda Y, Tanekura N, Arashima Y, Nakayama T, Komiya T, Kato K (2012). The first case of a patient suffering from coxiella burnetii infection attempting suicide arising from a state of depression. *International Medical Journal* 19, 312-313.

Zanifé D, Schmitt C, Balzani C, Ichai C, Lavrut T, Tichadou L, De Haro L (2012). A case report of a veterinary surgeon's suicide with pentobarbital and dexmedetomidine. *Une Observation de Suicide d'un Vétérinaire par Pentobarbital et Dexmédétomidine* 24, 149-151.

Zigman D, Blier P (2013). Urgent ketamine infusion rapidly eliminated suicidal ideation for a patient with major depressive disorder: A case report. *Journal of Clinical Psychopharmacology* 33, 270-272.

MISCELLANEOUS

Aasland OG (2012). Physician suicide-why? *General Hospital Psychiatry* 35, 1-2.

Albert PR, Benkelfat C (2013). The neurobiology of depression—revisiting the serotonin hypothesis. II. Genetic, epigenetic and clinical studies. *Philosophical Transactions of the Royal Society B: Biological Sciences* 368, 20120535.

Amiri B, Pourreza A, Rahimi Foroushani A, Hosseini SM, Poorolajal J (2012). Suicide and associated risk factors in Hamadan Province, west of Iran, in 2008 and 2009. *Journal of Research in Health Sciences* 12, 88-92.

Anderson AH (2012). Heaven's gate. Postmodernity and popular culture in a suicide group. *Journal of Ecclesiastical History* 63, 859.

Anonymous (2012). People who self harm have a high mortality from natural causes. *British Medical Journal* 345, e6447.

Anonymous (2012). Suicide. *Psychologist* 25, 802-803.

Anonymous (2008). Suicide after childhood cancer. *Journal of Clinical Oncology* 26, 1192.

Anonymous (2012). Toolkit explains that suicide is not the answer. *Journal of Psychosocial Nursing and Mental Health Services* 50, 6.

Aragam N, Wang KS, Anderson JL, Liu X (2012). Tmprss9 and grin2b are associated with neuroticism: A genome-wide association study in a European sample. *Journal of Molecular Neuroscience*. Published online: 11 December 2012. doi: 10.1007/s12031-012-9931-1.

Baptiste L (2012). Talking self-harm in young people. *Community Practitioner* 85, 16.

Bähr A (2013). Between "self-murder" and "suicide" the modern etymology of self-killing. *Journal of Social History* 46, 620-632.

Barberia E, Xifro A, Martin-Fumado C, Maria Suelves J (2013). Violent suicides and forensic information sources. *Emergencias* 25, 78.

Barzilay-Levkowitz S, Apter A (2012). Prospective predictors of adolescent suicidal behaviour as viewed through the interpersonal theory of suicide. *Israel Journal of Psychiatry and Related Sciences* 49, 50.

Beaton SJ, Forster PM, Maple M (2012). The language of suicide. *Psychologist* 25, 731.

Beautrais AL, Fergusson DM (2012). Media reporting of suicide in New Zealand: "More matter with less art" (Hamlet, Shakespeare). *New Zealand Medical Journal* 125, 5-10.

Bee D (2012). Suicide and attitudes to animal euthanasia. *Veterinary Record* 171, 279.

Bell R (2012). Slave suicide, abolition and the problem of resistance. *Slavery and Abolition* 33, 525-549.

Benkabbou A, Castaing D, Salloum C, Adam R, Azoulay D, Vibert E (2013). Treatment of failed roux-en-y hepaticojejunostomy after post-cholecystectomy bile ducts injuries. *Surgery* 153, 95-102.

Bennett MH, Trytko B, Jonker B (2012). Hyperbaric oxygen therapy for the adjunctive treatment of traumatic brain injury. *Cochrane Database of Systematic Reviews* 18, CD004609.

Bertsch K, Schmidinger I, Neumann ID, Herpertz SC (2012). Reduced plasma oxytocin levels in female patients with borderline personality disorder. *Hormones and Behavior* 63, 424-429.

Bethel J, Samata A (2013). Dear Emily; survive or die - The burden of suicide. *International Emergency Nursing*. Published online: 8 March 2013. doi: 10.1016/j.ienj.2013.01.002.

Biddle L, Cooper J, Owen-Smith A, Klineberg E, Bennewith O, Hawton K, Kapur N, Donovan J, Gunnell D (2012). Qualitative interviewing with vulnerable populations: Individuals' experiences of participating in suicide and self-harm based research. *Journal of Affective Disorders* 145, 356-362.

Birchwood M, Jackson C, Brunet K, Holden J, Barton K (2012). Personal beliefs about illness questionnaire-revised (PBIQ-R): Reliability and validation in a first episode sample. *British Journal of Clinical Psychology* 51, 448-458.

Blasco-Fontecilla H, Penas-Lledo E, Vaquero-Lorenzo C, Dorado P, Saiz-Ruiz J, Llerena A, Baca-Garcia E (2013). Cyp2d6 polymorphism and mental and personality disorders in suicide attempters. *Journal of Personality Disorders.* Published online: 11 February 2013. doi: 10.1521/pedi_2013_27_080.

Bohnert AS, McCarthy JF, Ignacio RV, Ilgen MA, Eisenberg A, Blow FC (2013). Misclassification of suicide deaths: Examining the psychiatric history of overdose decedents. *Injury Prevention.* Published online: 15 January 2013. doi: 10.1136/injuryprev-2012-040631.

Bolo A, Ciubară AM, Chiri ă R (2012). Moral and ethical aspects of the relationship between depression and suicide. *Aspecte Morale i etice ale Rela iei Depresie-Suicid* 10, 71-79.

Botha F (2012). The economics of suicide in South Africa. *South African Journal of Economics* 80, 526.

BPS (2013). The experience of suicide. *Psychologist* 26, 82.

Brown SD (2012). A case-based toxicology module on agricultural-and mining-related occupational exposures. *American Journal of Pharmaceutical Education* 76, 136.

Brown SM, Elliott CG, Paine R (2013). Withdrawal of nonfutile life support after attempted suicide. *American Journal of Bioethics* 13, 3-12.

Brym RJ, Araj B (2012). Suicidality and suicide bombing revisited: A rejoinder to Merari. *Studies in Conflict and Terrorism* 35, 733-739.

Caponnetto P, Auditore R, Russo C, Cappello GC, Polosa R (2013). Impact of an electronic cigarette on smoking reduction and cessation in schizophrenic smokers: A prospective 12-month pilot study. *International Journal of Environmental Research and Public Health* 10, 446-461.

Carmona-Navarro MC, Pichardo-Martinez MC (2012). Attitudes of nursing professionals towards suicidal behavior: Influence of emotional intelligence. *Revista Latino-Americana de Enfermagem* 20, 1161-1168.

Carpenter RW, Tomko RL, Trull TJ, Boomsma DI (2013). Gene-environment studies and borderline personality disorder: A review. *Current Psychiatry Reports* 15, 1-7.

Cesur R, Sabia JJ, Tekin E (2013). The psychological costs of war: Military combat and mental health. *Journal of Health Economics* 32, 51-65.

Chandler A (2012). Inviting pain? Pain, dualism and embodiment in narratives of self-injury. *Sociology of Health & Illness.* Published online: 26 September 2012. doi: 10.1111/j.1467-9566.2012.01523.x.

Chapple A, Ziebland S, Simkin S, Hawton K (2013). How people bereaved by suicide perceive newspaper reporting: Qualitative study. *British Journal of Psychiatry.* Published online: 7 February 2013. doi: 10.1192/bjp.bp.112.114116.

Chatzittofis A, Nordström P, Hellström C, Arver S, Åsberg M, Jokinen J (2013). Csf 5-hiaa, cortisol and dheas levels in suicide attempters. *European Neuropsychopharmacology.* Published online: 28 February 2013. doi: 10.1016/j.euroneuro.2013.02.002.

Chen Y-Y, Chen F, Gunnell D, Yip PSF (2013). The impact of media reporting on the emergence of charcoal burning suicide in Taiwan. *PLoS ONE* 8, e55000.

Chojnicka I, Gajos K, Strawa K, Broda G, Fudalej S, Fudalej M, Stawinski P, Pawlak A, Krajewski P, Wojnar M, Ploski R (2013). Possible association between suicide committed under influence of ethanol and a variant in the auts2 gene. *PLoS ONE* 8, e57199.

Chu J, Floyd R, Diep H, Pardo S, Goldblum P, Bongar B (2013). A tool for the culturally competent assessment of suicide: The cultural assessment of risk for suicide (CARS) measure. *Psychological Assessment.* Published online: 28 January 2013. doi: 10.1037/a0031264.

Clarke LH, Korotchenko A, Bundon A (2012). 'The calendar is just about up': Older adults with multiple chronic conditions reflect on death and dying. *Ageing and Society* 32, 1399-1417.

Cohen G (2012). Circumvention tourism. *Cornell Law Review* 97, 1309-1398.

Colman E, Golden J, Roberts M, Egan A, Weaver J, Rosebraugh C (2012). The FDA's assessment of two drugs for chronic weight management. *New England Journal of Medicine* 367, 1577-1579.

Colvin JC (2013). Myths about suicide. *Journal of Loss & Trauma* 18, 378-381.

da Rocha NS, Chachamovich E, de Almeida Fleck MP, Tennant A (2012). An introduction to rasch analysis for psychiatric practice and research. *Journal of Psychiatric Research* 47, 141-148.

Darke S, Torok M, Duflou J (2012). Contributory and incidental blood concentrations in deaths involving citalopram. *Journal of Forensic Sciences*. Published online: 27 December 2012. doi: 10.1111/1556-4029.12046.

Darracq MA, Clark A, Qian L, Cantrell FL (2013). A retrospective review of isolated duloxetine-exposure cases. *Clinical Toxicology* 51, 106-110.

Davidson D, Harrington KV (2012). Workplace bullying: It's not just about lunch money anymore. *Southern Journal of Business and Ethics* 4, 93-99.

de Achaval S, Feudtner C, Palla S, Suarez-Almazor ME (2013). Validation of icd-9-cm codes for identification of acetaminophen-related emergency department visits in a large pediatric hospital. *BMC Health Services Research* 13, 72.

De Panfilis C, Marchesi C, Cabrino C, Monici A, Politi V, Rossi M, Maggini C (2012). Patient factors predicting early dropout from psychiatric outpatient care for borderline personality disorder. *Psychiatry Research* 200, 422-429.

Delgado-Gomez D, Lopez-Castroman J, de Leon-Martinez V, Baca-Garcia E, Cabanas-Arrate ML, Sanchez-Gonzalez A, Aguado D (2012). Psychometrical assessment and item analysis of the general health questionnaire in victims of terrorism. *Psychological Assessment* 25, 279-287.

Diaz JH (2012). The syndromic classification, differential diagnosis, management, and prevention of potentially fatal plant poisonings in Louisiana and the Gulf South. *The Journal of the Louisiana State Medical Society* 164, 207-215.

Dipoce J, Guelfguat M (2012). Radiologic findings in cases of attempted suicide and other self-injurious behavior. *Radiographics* 32, 2005-2024.

Dyrbye LN, Satele D, Sloan J, Shanafelt TD (2012). Utility of a brief screening tool to identify physicians in distress. *Journal of General Internal Medicine* 28, 421-427.

Eckes L, Tsokos M, Herre S, Gapert R, Hartwig S (2012). Toxicological identification of diphenhydramine (DPH) in suicide. *Forensic Science, Medicine, and Pathology*. Published online: 12 October 2012. doi: 10.1007/s12024-012-9383-5.

Elliott A, Katagiri M, Sawai A (2012). The new individualism and contemporary Japan: Theoretical avenues and the Japanese new individualist path. *Journal for the Theory of Social Behaviour* 42, 425-443.

Ellis TE (2012). Comment on "inevitable suicide". *Journal of Psychiatric Practice* 18, 318-319.

Faay MD, van de Sande R, Gooskens F, Hafsteinsdottir TB (2012). Kennedy axis V: Clinimetric properties assessed by mental health nurses. *International Journal of Mental Health Nursing*. Published online: 5 December 2012. doi: 10.1111/j.1447-0349.2012.00887.

Favara DM (2013). The burden of deliberate self-harm on the critical care unit of a peri-urban referral hospital in the Eastern cape: A 5-year review of 419 patients. *South African Medical Journal* 103, 40-43.

Ferriere R, Legendre S (2013). Eco-evolutionary feedbacks, adaptive dynamics and evolutionary rescue theory. *Philosophical Transactions of the Royal Society of London Series B, Biological Sciences* 368, 20120081-20120081.

Figueroa S, Dalack GW (2013). Exploring the impact of suicide on clinicians: A multidisciplinary retreat model. *Journal of Psychiatric Practice* 19, 72-77.

Fleet D, Mintz R (2013). Counsellors' perceptions of client progression when working with clients who intentionally self-harm and the impact such work has on the therapist. *Counselling and Psychotherapy Research* 13, 44-52.

Flegr J (2013). How and why toxoplasma makes us crazy. *Trends in Parasitology* 29, 156-163.

Fleury MJ, Grenier G, Bamvita JM, Piat M, Tremblay J (2013). Adequacy of help received among individuals with severe mental disorders. *Administration and Policy in Mental Health and Mental Health Services Research.* Published online: 19 January 2013. doi: 10.1007/s10488-013-0466-8.

Fosbol EL (2012). Importance of increasing the awareness of psychiatric consequences among caregivers in a cardiology setting. *Neuropsychiatry* 2, 463-465.

Frances A (2012). The epidemic of military suicide. *Psychiatric Times* 29, 1.

Freemantle E, Chen GG, Cruceanu C, Mechawar N, Turecki G (2013). Analysis of oxysterols and cholesterol in prefrontal cortex of suicides. *International Journal of Neuropsychopharmacology.* Published online: 1 February 2013. doi: 10.1017/S1461145712001587.

Freemantle E, Mechawar N, Turecki G (2012). Cholesterol and phospholipids in frontal cortex and synaptosomes of suicide completers: Relationship with endosomal lipid trafficking genes. *Journal of Psychiatric Research* 47, 272-279.

Frost J, Slordal L, Vege A, Nordrum IS (2012). Forensic autopsies in a naturalistic setting in Norway: Autopsy rates and toxicological findings. *Forensic Science International* 223, 353-358.

Gallagher LM, Kappatos D, Tisch C, Ellis PM (2012). Suicide by poisoning in New Zealand- A toxicological analysis. *The New Zealand Medical Journal* 125, 15-25.

Garcia-Nieto R, Blasco-Fontecilla H, Paz Yepes M, Baca-Garcia E (2012). Translation and validation of the "self-injurious thoughts and behaviors interview" in a Spanish population with suicidal behaviour. *Revista de Psiquiatría y Salud Mental.* Published online: 28 August 2012. doi: 10.1016/j.rpsm.2012.07.001.

Gavaghan C, King M (2013). Reporting suicide: Safety isn't everything. *Journal of Primary Health Care* 5, 82-85.

Ghoge H, Guyer M (2012). Jailer's special duty of care in inmate's suicide negligence-based claims. *Journal of the American Academy of Psychiatry and the Law* 40, 579-581.

Gilchrist P (2012). Beyond the brink: Beachy head as a climbing landscape. *International Journal of the History of Sport* 29, 1383-1404.

Gilman SL (2012). How new is self-harm? *Journal of Nervous and Mental Disease* 200, 1008-1016.

Glaizal M, Gazin V, Aymard I, Messina-Gourlot C, Richard N, Mallaret M, Saviuc P, de Haro L (2012). Suicidal poisonings with methadone in France: Results of a two year national survey by the toxicovigilance network. *Clinical Toxicology* 50, 841-846.

Goldblatt MJ, Schechter M, Maltsberger JT, Ronningstam E (2012). Comparison of journals of suicidology: A bibliometric study from 2006-2010. *Crisis* 33, 301-305.

Gonsaga RAT, Rimoli CF, Pires EA, Zogheib FS, Fujino MVT, Cunha MB (2012). Evaluation of the mortality due to external causes. *Revista do Colegio Brasileiro de Cirurgioes* 39, 263-267.

González-Castro TB, Tovilla-Zárate C, Juárez-Rojop I, Pool García S, Velázquez-Sánchez MP, Genis A, Nicolini H, López Narváez L (2013). Association of the 5htr2a gene with suicidal behavior: Case-control study and updated meta-analysis. *BMC Psychiatry* 13, 25.

Gross JA, Fiori LM, Labonté B, Lopez JP, Turecki G (2012). Effects of promoter methylation on increased expression of polyamine biosynthetic genes in suicide. *Journal of Psychiatric Research* 47, 513-519.

Gu H, Liu C, Chen M, Zhang Q, Zhai J, Wang K, Ji F, Xu Z, Shen Q, Bao X, Chen X, Li J, Dong Q, Chen C (2012). The combined effects of the 5- httlpr and htr1a rs6295 polymorphisms modulate decision making in schizophrenia patients. *Genes, Brain and Behavior* 12, 133-139.

Gunn 3rd JF, Lester D, Haines J, Williams CL (2012). Thwarted belongingness and perceived burdensomeness in suicide notes. *Crisis* 33, 178-181.

Gunnell D, Bennewith O, Simkin S, Cooper J, Klineberg E, Rodway C, Sutton L, Steeg S, Wells C, Hawton K, Kapur N (2012). Time trends in coroners' use of different verdicts for possible suicides and their impact on officially reported incidence of suicide in England: 1990-2005. *Psychological Medicine*. Published online: 1 November 2012. doi: 10.1017/S0033291712002401.

Gupta M, Kumar K (2012). Social dichotomy versus gender dichotomy: A case report of gender identity disorder. *Indian Journal of Psychological Medicine* 34, 190-192.

Gupta MA, Gupta AK (2013). Evaluation of cutaneous body image dissatisfaction in the dermatology patient. *Clinical Dermatology* 31, 72-79.

Gupta MA, Gupta AK (2013). A practical approach to the assessment of psychosocial and psychiatric comorbidity in the dermatology patient. *Clinics in Dermatology* 31, 57-61.

Gutteling BM, Montagne B, Nijs M, van den Bosch LMC (2012). Dialectical Behavior Therapy: Is outpatient group psychotherapy an effective alternative to individual psychotherapy? Preliminary conclusions. *Comprehensive Psychiatry* 53, 1161-1168.

Hampson NB, Bodwin D (2012). Toxic co-ingestions in intentional carbon monoxide poisoning. *Journal of Emergency Medicine* 44, 625-630.

Han H, Ahn DH, Song J, Hwang TY, Roh S (2012). Development of mental health indicators in Korea. *Psychiatry Investigation* 9, 311-318.

Hassanzadeh L, Erfani M, Najafi R, Shafiei M, Amini M, Shafiee A, Ebrahimi SES (2012). Synthesis, radiolabeling and bioevaluation of a novel arylpiperazine derivative containing triazole as a 5-ht 1a receptor imaging agents. *Nuclear Medicine and Biology* 40, 227-232.

Hauck JL, Harrison BE, Montecalvo AL (2013). Psychiatric nurses' attitude toward patients with borderline personality discorber experiencing deliberate self-harm. *Journal of Psychosocial Nursing and Mental Health Services* 51, 20-29.

He Q, Xue G, Chen C, Lu Z-L, Chen C, Lei X, Liu Y, Li J, Zhu B, Moyzis RK, Dong Q, Bechara A (2012). Comt val(158)met polymorphism interacts with stressful life events and parental warmth to influence decision making. *Scientific Reports* 2, 677.

Hejna P, Bohnert M (2012). Decapitation in suicidal hanging - Vital reaction patterns. *Journal of Forensic Sciences* 58, S270-S277.

Hempstead K, Nguyen T, David-Rus R, Jacquemin B (2012). Health problems and male firearm suicide. *Suicide and Life-Threatening Behavior* 43, 1-16.

Henry C, Luquiens A, Lançon C, Sapin H, Zins-Ritter M, Gerard S, Perrin E, Falissard B, Lukasiewicz M (2013). Inhibition/activation in bipolar disorder: Validation of the multidimensional assessment of thymic states scale (MATHYS). *BMC Psychiatry* 13, 79.

Hesselgrave N, Parsey RV (2013). Imaging the serotonin 1a receptor using [11c]way100635 in healthy controls and major depression. *Philosophical Transactions of the Royal Society B: Biological Sciences* 368, 20120004.

Hopper SM, Woo JW, Sharwood LN, Babl FE, Long EJ (2012). Prevalence of suicidality in asymptomatic adolescents in the paediatric emergency department and utility of a screening tool. *Emergency Medicine Australasia* 24, 540-546.

Horon R, McManus T, Schmollinger J, Barr T, Jimenez M (2012). A study of the use and interpretation of standardized suicide risk assessment: Measures within a psychiatrically hospitalized correctional population. *Suicide and Life-Threatening Behavior*. Published online: 30 October 2012. doi: 10.1111/j.1943-278x.2012.00124.

Horowitz L, Bridge J, Pao M (2013). Screening adolescent and young adult cancer patients for suicide risk: Ask (ASQ) and they will tell. *Psycho-Oncology* 22, 92-93.

Horowitz LM, Bridge JA, Teach SJ, Ballard E, Klima J, Rosenstein DL, Wharff EA, Ginnis K, Cannon E, Joshi P, Pao M (2012). Ask suicide-screening questions (ASQ) a brief instrument for the pediatric emergency department. *Archives of Pediatrics & Adolescent Medicine* 166, 1170-1176.

Horowitz LM, Snyder D, Ludi E, Rosenstein DL, Kohn-Godbout J, Lee L, Cartledge T, Farrar A, Pao M (2013). Ask suicide-screening questions to everyone in medical settings: The ASQ'em quality improvement project. *Psychosomatics.* Published online: 8 February 2013. doi: 10.1016/j.psym.2013.01.002.

Hoytema van Konijnenburg EM, Sieswerda-Hoogendoorn T, Brilleslijper-Kater SN, van der Lee JH, Teeuw AH (2012). New hospital-based policy for children whose parents present at the ER due to domestic violence, substance abuse and/or a suicide attempt. *European Journal of Pediatrics* 172, 207-214.

Hsu CF, Tsai MJ, Chen KC, Wu RC, Hu SC (2013). Can mortality from agricultural pesticide poisoning be predicted in the emergency department? Findings from a hospital-based study in Eastern Taiwan. *Tzu Chi Medical Journal.* Published online: 9 January 2013. doi: 10.1016/j.tcmj.2012.12.002.

Hubbeling D (2012). Letter to the editor: Transfer of suicide risk versus looking at suicides outside hospital in general. *Psychological Medicine* 42, 2685.

Huisman A, Robben PB, Kerkhof AJ (2013). Mental health reforms in Europe: Further evaluation of the Dutch supervision system for suicides of mental health care users. *Psychiatric Services* 64, 10-12.

Hurley C (2012). Language and suicide. *Psychologist* 25, 866.

Irani SR, Vincent A, Jacobson L, Logsdail S, Butterworth RJ (2013). Organic neuropsychiatry: A treatable cause of suicidal behaviour. *Practical Neurology* 13, 44-48.

Isung J, Aeinehband S, Mobarrez F, Martensson B, Nordstrom P, Asberg M, Piehl F, Jokinen J (2012). Low vascular endothelial growth factor and interleukin-8 in cerebrospinal fluid of suicide attempters. *Translational Psychiatry* 2, e196.

Jacob J, Albert D, Heard K (2012). Single-agent duloxetine ingestions. *Human and Experimental Toxicology.* Published online: 30 October 2012. doi: 10.1177/0960327112462726.

Jacobson JM, Osteen P, Jones A, Berman A (2012). Evaluation of the recognizing and responding to suicide risk training. *Suicide and Life-Threatening Behavior* 42, 471-485.

Jain SS, Karande VB, Ramteke KB, Raparti GT (2011). Rimonabant: Boom to ban. *Journal of Pharmaceutical Negative Results* 2, 45-50.

Janelidze S, Ventorp F, Erhardt S, Hansson O, Minthon L, Flax J, Samuelsson M, Traskman-Bendz L, Brundin L (2012). Altered chemokine levels in the cerebrospinal fluid and plasma of suicide attempters. *Psychoneuroendocrinology.* Published online: 9 October 2012. doi: 10.1016/j.psyneuen.2012.09.010.

Jankowski J, Campo-Engelstein L (2013). Suicide in the context of terminal illness. *American Journal of Bioethics* 13, 13-14.

Janssens R, van Delden JJM, Widdershoven GAM (2012). Palliative sedation: Not just normal medical practice. Ethical reflections on the royal Dutch medical association's guideline on palliative sedation. *Journal of Medical Ethics* 38, 664-668.

Jiménez E, Arias B, Mitjans M, Goikolea JM, Roda E, Sáiz PA, García-Portilla MP, Burón P, Bobes J, Oquendo MA, Vieta E, Benabarre A (2013). Genetic variability at impa2, inpp1 and gsk3 increases the risk of suicidal behavior in bipolar patients. *European Neuropsychopharmacology.* Published online: 1 March 2013. doi: 10.1016/j.euroneuro.2013.01.007.

Johnson K (2012). 'How very dare you!' Shame, insult and contemporary representations of queer subjectivities. *Subjectivity* 5, 416-437.

Joiner TE, Ribeiro JD, Silva C (2012). Nonsuicidal self-injury, suicidal behavior, and their co-occurrence as viewed through the lens of the interpersonal theory of suicide. *Current Directions in Psychological Science* 21, 342-347.

Kadouf HA (2012). The role of the Shari'ah in contemporary moral and social development. *Australian Journal of Basic and Applied Sciences* 6, 206-213.

Kamolz L-P (2012). Self-inflicted burn: Things we should keep in mind. *Journal of Burn Care and Research*. Published online: 17 October 2012. doi: 10.1097/BCR.0b013e3182685b72.

Kaplow JB, Layne CM, Pynoos RS, Cohen JA, Lieberman A (2012). DSM-V diagnostic criteria for bereavement-related disorders in children and adolescents: Developmental considerations. *Psychiatry-Interpersonal and Biological Processes* 75, 243-266.

Kawashima D, Kawano K (2012). Development of a short version of the suicide intervention response inventory. *Shinrigaku Kenkyu* 83, 330-336.

Kékesi KA, Juhász G, Simor A, Gulyássy P, Szego ÉM, Hunyadi-Gulyás É, Darula Z, Medzihradszky KF, Palkovits M, Penke B, Czurkó A (2012). Altered functional protein networks in the prefrontal cortex and amygdala of victims of suicide. *PLoS ONE*. Published online: 6 December 2012. doi: 10.1371/journal.pone.0050532.

Kellinghaus C (2013). Reversible suicidal ideation after exposure to lacosamide. *Seizure*. Published online: 25 January 2013. doi: 10.1016/j.seizure.2013.01.007.

Kernier ND (2012). Suicide attempt during adolescence: A way of killing the "infans" and a quest for individuation-separation. *Crisis* 33, 290-300.

Kervégant M, Merigot L, Glaizal M, Schmitt C, Tichadou L, de Haro L (2013). Paraquat poisonings in France during the European ban: Experience of the poison control center in Marseille. *Journal of Medical Toxicology*. Published online: 23 February 2013. doi: 10.1007/s13181-012-0283-6.

Kim DH, Park YM (2013). The association between suicidality and serotonergic dysfunction in depressed patients. *Journal of Affective Disorders*. Published online: 8 January 2013. doi: 10.1016/j.jad.2012.11.051.

Kim S-W, Yoon J-S (2013). Suicide, an urgent health issue in Korea. *Journal of Korean Medical Science* 28, 345-347.

Klein CA (2012). Live deaths online: Internet suicide and lethality. *The Journal of the American Academy of Psychiatry and the Law* 40, 530-536.

Klineberg E, Stansfeld SA, Bhui KS (2013). How do adolescents talk about self-harm? Findings from a qualitative school-based study in England. *Journal of Adolescent Health* 52, S78-S79.

Koenigsberg HW, Yuan P, Diaz GA, Guerreri S, Dorantes C, Mayson S, Zamfirescu C, New AS, Goodman M, Manji HK, Siever LJ (2012). Platelet protein kinase c and brain-derived neurotrophic factor levels in borderline personality disorder patients. *Psychiatry Research* 199, 92-97.

Kolar K, Erickson PG, Stewart D (2012). Coping strategies of street-involved youth: Exploring contexts of resilience. *Journal of Youth Studies* 15, 744-760.

Kovandzic T, Schaffer ME, Kleck G (2012). Estimating the causal effect of gun prevalence on homicide rates: A local average treatment effect approach. *Journal of Quantitative Criminology*. Published online: 11 October 2012. doi: 10.1007/s10940-012-9185-7.

Koycheva F, Korukov B, Hristova R, Yankov E, Karadimov D, Tzenev I, Popov R (2012). Analysis of the cases of trauma and suicide attempts serviced by university general hospital 'Tsaritsa Yoanna—isul', Sofia over 1 year period. *Injury Prevention* 18, A166.

Kukde HG, Ambade VN, Batra AK, Keoliya AN (2012). Significance of serum cholinesterase level in organophosphate poisoning. *Medico-Legal Update* 12, 70-74.

Kumar A, Kumar S (2013). Karma yoga: A path towards work in positive psychology. *Indian Journal of Psychiatry* 55, S150-S152.

Lang M (2013). Firearm background checks and suicide. *Economic Journal.* Published online: 7 January 2013. doi: 10.1111/ecoj.12007.

Lara F (2012). Movie review: It's kind of a funny story. *Journal of Creativity in Mental Health* 7, 304-307.

Large M (2013). Maudsley debate does the emphasis on risk in psychiatry serve the interests of patients or the public? No. *British Medical Journal* 346. f857.

Large M, Nielssen O (2012). Suicide is preventable but not predictable. *Australasian Psychiatry* 20, 532-533.

Latimer S, Meade T, Tennant A (2013). Measuring engagement in deliberate self-harm behaviours: Psychometric evaluation of six scales. *BMC Psychiatry* 13, 4.

Lehavot K, Ben-Zeev D, Neville REL (2012). Ethical considerations and social media: A case of suicidal postings on Facebook. *Journal of Dual Diagnosis* 8, 341.

Lester D, Gunn Iii JF (2012). Perceived burdensomeness and thwarted belonging: An investigation of the interpersonal theory of suicide. *Clinical Neuropsychiatry* 9, 221-224.

Liebling-Boccio DE, Jennings HR (2012). The current status of graduate training in suicide risk assessment. *Psychology in the Schools* 50, 72-86.

Lietu A, Saavala H, Hakko H, Joukama M, Rasanen P (2012). Weapons used in serious violence against a parent: Retrospective comparative register study. *Scandinavian Journal of Public Health* 40, 563-570.

Lippi G, Favaloro EJ, Cervellin G (2012). Massive posttraumatic bleeding: Epidemiology, causes, clinical features, and therapeutic management. *Seminars in Thrombosis & Hemostasis* 39, 83-93.

Liu W, Kuramoto SJ, Stuart EA (2013). An introduction to sensitivity analysis for unobserved confounding in nonexperimental prevention research. *Prevention Science.* Published online: 14 February 2013. doi: 10.1007/s11121-012-0339-5.

Lotrich FE, Albusaysi S, Ferrell RE (2012). Brain-derived neurotrophic factor serum levels and genotype: Association with depression during interferon- treatment. *Neuropsychopharmacology.* Published online: 18 December 2012. doi: 10.1038/npp.2012.263.

Lu CF, Jia CX, Xu AQ, Dai AY, Qin P (2012). Psychometric characteristics of Chinese version of barratt impulsiveness scale-11 in suicides and living controls of rural China. *Omega* 66, 215-229.

Luef E (2013). Low morals at a high latitude? Suicide in nineteenth-century Scandinavia. *Journal of Social History* 46, 668-683.

Madan I, Henderson M, Hashtroudi A, Hope V, Harvey SB (2013). Prospective evaluation of mental health training for occupational health practitioners. *Occupational Medicine.* Published online: 17 February 2013. doi: 10.1093/occmed/kqt008.

Maggioni F, Maggioni G, Mainardi F, Zanchin G (2013). Headache and suicide. A historical note. *Headache* 53, 388-389.

Maheu ME, Davoli MA, Turecki G, Mechawar N (2012). Amygdalar expression of proteins associated with neuroplasticity in major depression and suicide. *Journal of Psychiatric Research* 47, 384-390.

Maity T, Adhikari A, Bhattacharya K, Biswas S, Debnath PK, Maharana CS (2011). A study on evalution of antidepressant effect of imipramine adjunct with Aswagandha and Bramhi. *Nepal Medical College Journal* 13, 250-253.

Mallett CA, Fukushima M, Stoddard-Dare P, Quinn L (2013). Factors related to recidivism for youthful offenders. *Criminal Justice Studies* 26, 84-98.

Maniam T (2012). Consequences of "inevitable suicide". *Journal of Psychiatric Practice* 18, 319-320.

Maniam T, Chan LF (2013). Half a century of suicide studies - A plea for new directions in research and prevention. *Sains Malaysiana* 42, 399-402.

Mann JJ (2013). The serotonergic system in mood disorders and suicidal behaviour. *Philosophical Transactions of the Royal Society B: Biological Sciences* 368, 20120537.

Marinetti LJ, Antonides HM (2013). Analysis of synthetic cathinones commonly found in bath salts in human performance and postmortem toxicology: Method development, drug distribution and interpretation of results. *Journal of Analytical Toxicology* 37, 135-146.

Marsh I (2013). The uses of history in the unmaking of modern suicide. *Journal of Social History* 46, 744-756.

Matarazzo BB, Clemans TA, Silverman MM, Brenner LA (2012). The self-directed violence classification system and the columbia classification algorithm for suicide assessment: A crosswalk. *Suicide and Life-Threatening Behavior.* Published online: 12 November 2012. doi: 10.1111/j.1943-278x.2012.00131.

May S, Kinnison T, Ogden U (2012). Mental wellbeing suicide and attitudes to animal euthanasia. *Veterinary Record* 171, 279.

McClure M (2012). The athletes who self-harm to win. *New Scientist* 215, 10-11.

McGuinness TM (2012). Screening for pediatric bipolar disorder in primary care. *Journal of Psychosocial Nursing and Mental Health Services* 50, 17-20.

Medina CO, Jegannathan B, Dahlblom K, Kullgren G (2012). Suicidal expressions among young people in Nicaragua and Cambodia: A cross-cultural study. *BMC Psychiatry* 12, 28.

Mewton L, Slade T, Memedovic S, Teesson M (2012). Alcohol use in hazardous situations: Implications for DSM-IV and DSM-5 alcohol use disorders. *Alcoholism: Clinical and Experimental Research* 37, E228-E236.

Mikaszewska-Sokolewicz M, Zatorski P, Lazowski T, Jankowski K, Piotrowski M (2012). Multiple organ failure after a fall from heights complicated by cardiac rupture and subacute cardiac tamponade. *Anaesthesiology Intensive Therapy* 44, 154-157.

Millard C (2012). Reinventing intention: 'Self-harm' and the 'cry for help' in postwar Britain. *Current Opinion in Psychiatry* 25, 503-507.

Miller JM, Hesselgrave N, Ogden RT, Sullivan GM, Oquendo MA, Mann JJ, Parsey RV (2013). Positron emission tomography quantification of serotonin transporter in suicide attempters with major depressive disorder. *Biological Psychiatry.* Published online: 28 February 2013. doi: 10.1016/j.biopsych.2013.01.024.

Miller V (2012). A crisis of presence: On-line culture and being in the world. *Space & Polity* 16, 265.

Moghadamnia AA (2012). An update on toxicology of aluminum phosphide. *DARU* 20, 25.

Mood NE, Sabzghabaee AM, Ghodousi A, Yaraghi A, AteghehMousavi, Massoumi G, Shemshaki HR (2013). Histo-pathological findings and their relationship with age, gender and toxin amounts in paraquat intoxication. *Pakistan Journal of Medical Sciences* 29, 403-408.

Mooney JJ, Samson JA, McHale NL, Pappalarado KM, Alpert JE, Schildkraut JJ (2013). Increased gs within blood cell membrane lipid microdomains in some depressive disorders: An exploratory study. *Journal of Psychiatric Research.* Published online: 13 March 2013. doi: 10.1016/j.jpsychires.2013.02.005.

Morimoto K, Nagami T, Matsumoto N, Wada S, Kano T, Kakinuma C, Ogihara T (2012). Developmental changes of brain distribution and localization of oseltamivir and its active metabolite RO 64-0802 in rats. *Journal of Toxicological Sciences* 37, 1217-1223.

Munafò MR (2012). The serotonin transporter gene and depression. *Depression and Anxiety* 29, 915-917.

Narrow WE, Clarke DE, Kuramoto SJ, Kraemer HC, Kupfer DJ, Greiner L, Regier DA (2013). DSM-5 field trials in the United States and Canada, part lll: Development and reliability testing of a cross-cutting symptom assessment for DSM-5. *American Journal of Psychiatry* 170, 71-82.

Nechifor M, Ciubotariu D (2012). Behavioral involvement of imidazoline system. *Revista Medico-Chirurgicala a Societatii de Medici si Naturalisti din Iasi* 116, 552-556.

Nedic G, Nikolac Perkovic M, Nenadic Sviglin K, Muck-Seler D, Borovecki F, Pivac N (2012). Brain-derived neurotrophic factor val 66met polymorphism and alcohol-related phenotypes. *Progress in Neuro-Psychopharmacology and Biological Psychiatry* 40, 193-198.

Neto MLR, de Almeida JC, Reis AOA, de Abreu LC (2012). Narratives of suicide. *HealthMED* 6, 3565-3570.

Neville K, Roan NM (2012). Suicide in hospitalized medical-surgical patients: Exploring nurses' attitudes. *Journal of Psychosocial Nursing and Mental Health Services* 51, 35-43.

Newman WJ (2012). Psychopharmacologic management of aggression. *Psychiatric Clinics of North America* 35, 957-972.

Newton C, Bale C (2012). A qualitative analysis of perceptions of self-harm in members of the general public. *Journal of Public Mental Health* 11, 106-116.

Norheim AB, Grimholt TK, Ekeberg O (2013). Attitudes towards suicidal behaviour in outpatient clinics among mental health professionals in Oslo. *BMC Psychiatry* 13, 90.

Omar HA, Merrick J (2013). The young and suicide. *International Journal of Adolescent Medicine and Health* 25, 1-2.

Ogasawara K, Ozaki N (2012). Review of the new treatment guideline for major depressive disorder by the Japanese society of mood disorders. *Brain and Nerve* 64, 1159-1165.

Ordway GA, Szebeni A, Chandley MJ, Stockmeier CA, Xiang L, Newton SS, Turecki G, Duffourc MM, Zhu M-Y, Zhu H, Szebeni K (2012). Low gene expression of bone morphogenetic protein 7 in brainstem astrocytes in major depression. *International Journal of Neuropsychopharmacology* 15, 855-868.

Ougrin D, Boege I (2012). The self harm questionnaire: A new tool designed to improve identification of self harm in adolescents. *Journal of Adolescence* 36, 221-225.

Ougrin D, Zundel T, Ng AV, Habel B, Latif S (2013). Teaching therapeutic assessment for self-harm in adolescents: Training outcomes. *Psychology and Psychotherapy* 86, 70-85

Outwater AH, Ismail H, Mgalilwa L, Justin Temu M, Mbembati NA (2013). Burns in Tanzania: Morbidity and mortality, causes and risk factors: A review. *International Journal of Burns and Trauma* 3, 18-29.

Ouzouni C, Nakakis K (2012). Doctors' attitudes towards attempted suicide. *Health Science Journal* 6, 663-680.

Owens C, Sharkey S, Smithson J, Hewis E, Emmens T, Ford T, Jones R (2012). Building an online community to promote communication and collaborative learning between health professionals and young people who self-harm: An exploratory study. *Health Expectations*. Published online: 18 October 2012. doi: 10.1111/hex.12011.

Pan L, Segreti A, Almeida J, Jollant F, Lawrence N, Brent D, Phillips M (2012). Preserved hippocampal function during learning in the context of risk in adolescent suicide attempt. *Psychiatry Research* 211, 112-118.

Pao M (2013). Suicide by security blanket and other stories from the child psychiatry emergency service: What happens to children with acute mental illness. *Psychosomatics* 54, 100.

Papadopoulou A, Markianos M, Christodoulou C, Lykouras L (2012). Plasma total cholesterol in psychiatric patients after a suicide attempt and in follow-up. *Journal of Affective Disorders.* Published online: 10 December 2012. doi: 10.1016/j.jad.2012.11.032.

Park BCB, Lester D (2012). Suicides by fire in South Korea. *Burns.* Published online: 1 November 2012. doi: 10.1016/j.burns.2012.10.01.

Parvinen K (2013). Joint evolution of altruistic cooperation and dispersal in a metapopulation of small local populations. *Theoretical Population Biology* 85, 12-19.

Parker R (2012). Flesh wounds? New ways of understanding self-injury. *Qualitative Research* 12, 606.

Pecoraro A, Royer-Malvestuto C, Rosenwasser B, Moore K, Howell A, Ma M, Woody GE (2013). Factors contributing to dropping out from and returning to HIV treatment in an inner city primary care HIV clinic in the United States. *AIDS Care.* Published online: 21 February 2013. doi: 10.1080/09540121.2013.772273.

Penven JC, Janosik SM (2012). Threat assessment teams: A model for coordinating the institutional response and reducing legal liability when college students threaten suicide. *Journal of Student Affairs Research and Practice* 49, 299-314.

Pérez-Ortiz JM, García-Gutiérrez MS, Navarrete F, Giner S, Manzanares J (2012). Gene and protein alterations of fkbp5 and glucocorticoid receptor in the amygdala of suicide victims. *Psychoneuroendocrinology.* Published online: 4 December 2012. doi: 10.1016/j.psyneuen.2012.11.008.

Perlis RH, Ruderfer D, Maussion G, Chambert K, Gallagher P, Turecki G, Ernst C (2012). Bipolar disorder and a history of suicide attempts with a duplication in 5htr1a. *American Journal of Psychiatry* 169, 1213-1214.

Pestian JP, Matykiewicz P, Linn-Gust M (2012). What's in a note: Construction of a suicide note corpus. *Biomedical Informatics Insights* 5, 1-6.

Phillips E (2012). United States V-Washington: Why counsel's advice and presence at presentence interviews is necessary to prevent sentencing suicide. *Denver University Law Review* 89, 477-498.

Phutane V, Kruse M, Tek C, Srihari V (2012). How can we assess 'suicidality' in first-episode psychosis? Use of columbia suicide severity rating scale. *Early Intervention in Psychiatry* 6, 23.

Pigeon WR, Moynihan J, Matteson-Rusby S, Jungquist CR, Xia Y, Tu X, Perlis ML (2012). Comparative effectiveness of cbt interventions for co-morbid chronic pain & insomnia: A pilot study. *Behavioural Research and Therapy* 50, 685-689.

Pregelj P (2012). Single nucleotide polymorphisms and suicidal behaviour. *Psychiatria Danubina* 24, S61-S64.

Preuss UW, Ridinger M, Fehr C, Koller G, Bondy B, Wodarz N, Soyka M, Zill P (2012). Influence of 5-HT and da candidate gene variants on suicidal behavior in alcohol-dependent subjects. *Alcoholism-Clinical and Experimental Research* 36, 48A.

Pridmore S, Walter G (2012). Does art imitate death? Depictions of suicide in fiction. *Australas Psychiatry* 21, 65-72.

Pridmore S, Walter G (2012). Protest suicide. *Australasian Psychiatry* 20, 533-534.

Pun SS (2013). The politics of hope and cynicism in the realization of the vision of the 334 education reform in Hong Kong. *Asia Pacific Education Review* 14, 55-65.

Purkayastha M, Mukherjee KK (2012). Three cases of near death experience: Is it physiology, physics or philosophy? *Annals of Neurosciences* 19, 104-106.

Ramesh KV, Jayashankar V (2012). An analytical study of causes of death in fall from height cases from Gandhi medical college & hospital mortuary, Hyderabad from 2006 to 2008 year. *Indian Journal of Forensic Medicine and Toxicology* 6, 51-52.

Randall JM, Voth R, Burnett E, Bazhenova L, Bardwell WA (2013). Clinic-based depression screening in lung cancer patients using the phq-2 and phq-9 depression questionnaires: A pilot study. *Support Care Cancer.* Published online: 17 January 2013. doi: 10.1007/s00520-012-1712-4.

Rangaswamy T, Sujit J (2012). Psychosocial rehabilitation in developing countries. *International Review of Psychiatry* 24, 499-503.

Rao BR, Chand Basha V, Sudhakar Reddy K (2012). An analytical study of deaths due to hanging in Warangal area, Andhra Pradesh. *Indian Journal of Forensic Medicine and Toxicology* 6, 16-19.

Razykov I, Hudson M, Baron M, Thombs BD (2012). The utility of the patient health questionnaire-9 to assess suicide risk in patients with systemic sclerosis. *Arthritis and Rheumatism* 64, S1112-S1113.

Read J, Velldal E, Øvrelid L (2012). Topic classification for suicidology. *Journal of Computing Science and Engineering* 6, 143-150.

Rivero G, Gabilondo AM, García-Sevilla JA, Callado LF, La Harpe R, Morentin B, Meana JJ (2012). Brain rgs4 and rgs10 protein expression in schizophrenia and depression. Effect of drug treatment. *Psychopharmacology* 226, 177-188.

Robertson CD, Miskey H, Mitchell J, Nelson-Gray R (2013). Variety of self-injury: Is the number of different methods of non-suicidal self-injury related to personality, psychopathology, or functions of self-injury? *Archives of Suicide Research* 17, 33-40.

Rossetti J (2013). A vision for change: Lessons learned from Ireland's mental health care system. *Journal of Psychosocial Nursing & Mental Health Services* 51, 4-5.

Ruggiero S, Moro PA, Davanzo F, Capuano A, Rossi F, Sautebin L (2012). Evaluation of cosmetic product exposures reported to the milan poison control centre, Italy from 2005 to 2010. *Clinical Toxicology* 50, 902-910.

Sadjadi S (2013). The endocrinologist's office-puberty suppression: Saving children from a natural disaster? *Journal of Medical Humanities.* Published online: 14 March 2013. doi: 10.1007/s10912-013-9228-6.

Sand PG (2012). Negligible impact of a HTR1A gene promoter variant on suicidal behavior. *Revista Brasileira de Psiquiatria* 34, 360-361.

Sansone RA, Wiederman MW (2012). Spending too much: Relationships with borderline personality symptomatology. *International Journal of Psychiatry in Clinical Practice* 16, 316-318.

Sansone RA, Wiederman MW (2013). Distancing oneself from God: Relationships with borderline personality symptomatology. *Mental Health, Religion and Culture* 16, 210-214.

Sariola S, Simpson B (2013). Precarious ethics: Toxicology research among self-poisoning hospital admissions in Sri Lanka. *BioSocieties* 8, 41-57.

Saternus KS, Maxeiner H, Kernbach-Wighton G, Koebke J (2012). Traumatology of the superior thyroid horns in suicidal hanging - An injury analysis. *Legal Medicine.* Published online: 19 December 2012. doi: 10.1016/j.legalmed.2012.10.008.

Sawhney V (2012). Chaos theory and suicide. *Australasian Psychiatry* 20, 533.

Schmidlin K, Clough-Gorr KM, Spoerri A, Egger M, Zwahlen M (2013). Impact of unlinked deaths and coding changes on mortality trends in the Swiss national cohort. *BMC Medical Informatics and Decision Making* 13, 1.

Schmidt JD, Huete JM, Fodstad JC, Chin MD, Kurtz PF (2013). An evaluation of the aberrant behavior checklist for children under age 5. *Research in Developmental Disabilites* 34, 1190-1197.

Serafini G, Pompili M, Innamorati M, Gentile G, Borro M, Lamis DA, Lala N, Negro A, Simmaco M, Girardi P, Martelletti P (2012). Gene variants with suicidal risk in a sample of subjects with chronic migraine and affective temperamental dysregulation. *European Review for Medical and Pharmacological Sciences* 16, 1389-1398.

Serafini G, Pompili M, Innamorati M, Negro A, Fiorillo M, Lamis DA, Erbuto D, Marsibilio F, Romano A, Amore M, D'Alonzo L, Bozzao A, Girardi P, Martelletti P (2012). White matter hyperintensities and self-reported depression in a sample of patients with chronic headache. *Journal of Headache and Pain* 13, 661-667.

Sharkey EJ, Cassidy M, Brady J, Gilchrist MD, NicDaeid N (2012). Investigation of the force associated with the formation of lacerations and skull fractures. *International Journal of Legal Medicine* 126, 835-844.

Sheehan CM, Rogers RG, Williams Gt, Boardman JD (2012). Gender differences in the presence of drugs in violent deaths. *Addiction* 108, 547-555.

Sim SC, Kacevska M, Ingelman-Sundberg M (2012). Pharmacogenomics of drug-metabolizing enzymes: A recent update on clinical implications and endogenous effects. *Pharmacogenomics Journal* 13, 1-11.

Simó-Pinatella D, Alomar-Kurz E, Font-Roura J, Giné C, Matson JL, Cifre I (2013). Questions about behavioral function (QABF): Adaptation and validation of the Spanish version. *Research in Developmental Disabilities* 34, 1248-1255.

Sisask M (2012). Suicidal behaviors: A multidisciplinary issue. *Neuropsychiatry* 2, 477-480.

Slavin-Mulford J, Sinclair SJ, Malone J, Stein M, Bello I, Blais MA (2013). External correlates of the personality assessment inventory higher order structures. *Journal of Personality Assessment.* Published online: 25 February 2013. doi: 10.1080/00223891.2013.767820.

Smith AR, Silva C, Covington DW, Joiner TE (2013). An assessment of suicide-related knowledge and skills among health professionals. *Health Psychology.* Published online: 4 February 2013. doi: 10.1037/a0031062.

Smith JA, Frueh BC (2013). Further considerations on suicides among Union forces during the U.S. Civil War. *Journal of Anxiety Disorders.* Published online: 18 February 2013. doi: 10.1016/j.janxdis.2013.02.002.

Smith PN, Wolford-Clevenger C, Mandracchia JT, Jahn DR (2012). An exploratory factor analysis of the acquired capability for suicide scale in male prison inmates. *Psychological Services* 10, 97-105.

Sniegocki JH (2012). Catholic bioethics for a new millennium. *Choice* 50, 491.

Snyder D, Horowitz L, Kohn-Godbout J, Pao M (2013). Just ASQ'em: Screening for suicide risk on an inpatient oncology unit. *Psycho-Oncology* 22, 86.

Sohn JH, Ahn SH, Seong SJ, Ryu JM, Cho MJ (2013). Prevalence, work-loss days and quality of life of community dwelling subjects with depressive symptoms. *Journal of Korean Medical Science* 28, 280-286.

Spein AR, Pedersen CP, Silviken AC, Melhus M, Kvernmo SE, Bjerregaard P (2013). Self-rated health among Greenlandic Inuit and Norwegian Sami adolescents: Associated risk and protective correlates. *International Journal of Circumpolar Health* 2013, 72.

Spike JP (2013). The distinction between completing a suicide and assisting one: Why treating a suicide attempt does not require closing the "window of opportunity". *American Journal of Bioethics* 13, 26-27.

Stack S (2013). Citation classics in deviant behavior: A research note. *Deviant Behavior* 34, 85.

Stoica MV, Felthous AR (2013). Acute psychosis induced by bath salts: A case report with clinical and forensic implications. *Journal of Forensic Sciences* 58, 530-533.

Strakowski SM (2012). The complexities of depression. *Current Psychiatry Reports* 14, 608-609.

Strong SS, Lockyer BE (2012). Violent suicide in South Hampshire. *Journal of Pathology* 228, S32.

Suchankova P, Holm G, Träskman-Bendz L, Brundin L, Ekman A (2012). The +1444c>t polymorphism in the CRP gene: A study on personality traits and suicidal behaviour. *Psychiatric Genetics* 23, 70-76.

Tanner CM (2013). A second honeymoon for parkinson's disease? *New England Journal of Medicine* 368, 675-676.

Tarolla E, Biondi M, Fabi E, Gaviano I, Gigantesco A, Tarsitani L, Picardi A (2012). Measuring depression with questions about well-being: A study on psychiatric outpatients. *Rivista di Psichiatria* 47, 304-308.

Taye H, Magnus D (2013). Suicide and the sufficiency of surrogate decision makers. *American Journal of Bioethics* 13, 1-2.

Terman SA (2013). Is the principle of proportionality sufficient to guide physicians' decisions regarding withholding/withdrawing life-sustaining treatment after suicide attempts? *American Journal of Bioethics* 13, 22-24.

Terranova C, Sartore D (2012). Suicide and psychiatrist's liability in Italian law cases. *Journal of Forensic Sciences* 58, 523-526.

Terrones-Gonzalez A, Estrada-Martinez S, Maria Lechuga-Quinones A, Salvador-Moysen J, Martinez-Lopez Y, La-Llave-Leon O (2012). Psychometric properties of CES-D/is in university population in Durango city, Mexico. *Salud Mental* 35, 305-313.

Till B, Vitouch P, Herberth A, Sonneck G, Niederkrotenthaler T (2013). Personal suicidality in reception and identification with suicidal film characters. *Death Studies* 37, 383-392.

Tørmoen AJ, Rossow I, Larsson B, Mehlum L (2012). Nonsuicidal self-harm and suicide attempts in adolescents: Differences in kind or in degree? *Social Psychiatry and Psychiatric Epidemiology*. Published online: 27 December 2012. doi: 10.1007/s00127-012-0646-y.

Tosi D, Mendogni P, Rosso L, Palleschi A, Filippi N, Reda M, Santambrogio L, Nosotti M (2012). Early lung retransplantation in a patient affected by cystic fibrosis correlated with donor cause of death: A case report. *Transplantation Proceedings* 44, 2041-2042.

Tremoliere B, De Neys W, Bonnefon J-F (2012). Mortality salience and morality: Thinking about death makes people less utilitarian. *Cognition* 124, 379-384.

Troister T, Holden RR (2013). Factorial differentiation among depression, hopelessness, and psychache in statistically predicting suicidality. *Measurement and Evaluation in Counseling and Development* 46, 50-63.

Tsoi DT, Porwal M, Webster AC (2013). Interventions for smoking cessation and reduction in individuals with schizophrenia. *Cochrane Database of Systematic Reviews* 2, CD007253.

Tucker RP, Wingate LR, O'Keefe VM, Slish ML, Judah MR, Rhoades-Kerswill S (2012). The moderating effect of humor style on the relationship between interpersonal predictors of suicide and suicidal ideation. *Personality and Individual Differences* 54, 610-615.

Uyeji LL, Sauder CL, Derbidge CM, Beauchaine TP (2012). Neuroanatomical correlates of self-inflicted injury in female adolescents. *Psychophysiology* 49, S108.

Vaernik P, Sisask M, Vaernik A, Arensman E, Van Audenhove C, van der Feltz-Cornelis CM, Hegerl U (2012). Validity of suicide statistics in Europe in relation to undetermined deaths: Developing the 2-20 benchmark. *Injury Prevention* 18, 321-325.

Van Den Bulck H, Claessens N (2013). Celebrity suicide and the search for the moral high ground: Comparing frames in media and audience discussions of the death of a Flemish celebrity. *Critical Studies in Media Communication* 30, 69-84.

van Konijnenburg EMMH, Sieswerda-Hoogendoorn T, Brilleslijper-Kater SN, van der Lee JH, Teeuw AH (2013). New hospital-based policy for children whose parents present at the ER due to domestic violence, substance abuse and/or a suicide attempt. *European Journal of Pediatrics* 172, 207-214.

Viana AG, Trent L, Tull MT, Heiden L, Damon JD, Hight TL, Young J (2012). Non-medical use of prescription drugs among Mississippi youth: Constitutional, psychological, and family factors. *Addictive Behaviors* 37, 1382-1388.

Vousoura E, Verdeli H, Warner V, Wickramaratne P, Baily CDR (2012). Parental divorce, familial risk for depression, and psychopathology in offspring: A three-generation study. *Journal of Child and Family Studies* 21, 718-725.

Wada K, Sairenchi T, Haruyama Y, Taneichi H, Ishikawa Y, Muto T (2013). Relationship between the onset of depression and stress response measured by the brief job stress questionnaire among Japanese employees: A cohort study. *PLoS ONE* 8, e56319.

Wakefield JC, Schmitz MF (2013). When does depression become a disorder? Using recurrence rates to evaluate the validity of proposed changes in major depression diagnostic thresholds. *World Psychiatry: Official Journal of the World Psychiatric Association* 12, 44-52.

Wang AG, Koefoed P, Jacoby AS, Woldbye D, Rasmussen HB, Timm S, Dam H, Jakobsen KD, Nordentoft M, Jurgens G, Sorensen HJ, Garsdal O, Hvid M, Werge T (2013). Neuropeptide Y genes and suicidal behaviour among schizophrenic patients. *Psychiatric Genetics*. Published online: 12 February 2013. doi: 10.1097/YPG.0b013e32835d70ed.

Wang M, Yi J, Cai L, Hu M, Zhu X, Yao S, Auerbach RP (2012). Development and psychometric properties of the health-risk behavior inventory for Chinese adolescents. *BMC Medical Research Methodology* 12, 94.

Wang SM, Chou YC, Yeh MY, Chen CH, Tzeng WC (2013). Factors associated with quality of life after attempted suicide: A cross-sectional study. *Journal of Clinical Nursing*. Published online: 27 February 2013. doi: 10.1111/jocn.12148.

Weingarten K (2012). Sorrow: A therapist's reflection on the inevitable and the unknowable. *Family Process* 51, 440-455.

Wells TS, Horton JL, LeardMann CA, Jacobson IG, Boyko EJ (2012). A comparison of the prime-md phq-9 and phq-8 in a large military prospective study, the millennium cohort study. *Journal of Affective Disorders*. Published online: 13 December 2012. doi: 10.1016/j.jad.2012.11.052.

Whitlock J, Pietrusza C, Purington A (2013). Young adult respondent experiences of disclosing self-injury, suicide-related behavior, and psychological distress in a web-based survey. *Archives of Suicide Research* 17, 20-32.

Woodall MN, Alleyne CH (2012). Nail-gun head trauma: A comprehensive review of the literature. *Journal of Trauma and Acute Care Surgery* 73, 993-996.

Wright A, Rickards H, Cavanna AE (2012). Impulse-control disorders in gilles de la tourette syndrome. *Journal of Neuropsychiatry and Clinical Neurosciences* 24, 16-27.

Wright D (2012). Punishing the dead? Suicide, lordship, and community in Britain, 1500-1830. *The American Historical Review* 117, 1292.

Xu H-B, Zhang R-F, Luo D, Zhou Y, Wang Y, Fang L, Li W-J, Mu J, Zhang L, Zhang Y, Xie P (2012). Comparative proteomic analysis of plasma from major depressive patients: Identification of proteins associated with lipid metabolism and immunoregulation. *The International Journal of Neuropsychopharmacology* 15, 1413-1425.

Xu Y, Lam KF, Zhou F, Yip PSF, Watson R (2012). A study of suicide risk using a cox cure model via a retrospective sampling and multiple imputation. *Communications in Statistics - Theory and Methods* 41, 3389-3402.

Yap MBH, Reavley N, Mackinnon AJ, Jorm AF (2013). Psychiatric labels and other influences on young people's stigmatizing attitudes: Findings from an Australian national survey. *Journal of Affective Disorders*. Published online: 17 January 2013. doi: 10.1016/j.jad.2012.12.015.

Yaseen ZS, Gilmer E, Modi J, Cohen LJ, Galynker II (2012). Emergency room validation of the revised suicide trigger scale (STS-3): A measure of a hypothesized suicide trigger state. *PLoS ONE* 7, e45157.

Yip PS, Chang SS (2013). Providing quality care for the body and mind. *Journal of International Medicine* 273, 42-43.

Zacarias AE, Macassa G, Soares JJ, Svanström L, Antai D (2012). Symptoms of depression, anxiety, and somatization in female victims and perpetrators of intimate partner violence in Maputo City, Mozambique. *International Journal of Women's Health* 4, 491-503.

Zeng W (2012). The different views on life between Daoism and destructive cult. *Asian Social Science* 8, 264-268.

Zhang J, Tan J, Lester D (2013). Psychological strains found in the suicides of 72 celebrities. *Journal of Affective Disorders.* Published online: 22 February 2013. doi: 10.1016/j.jad.2013.01.031.

Zheng P, Gao HC, Qi ZG, Jia JM, Li FF, Chen JJ, Wang Y, Guo J, Melgiri ND, Xie P (2012). Peripheral metabolic abnormalities of lipids and amino acids implicated in increased risk of suicidal behavior in major depressive disorder. *Metabolomics.* Published online: 30 October 2012. doi: 10.1007/s11306-012-0474-9.

Zhurov V, Stead JDH, Merali Z, Palkovits M, Faludi G, Schild-Poulter C, Anisman H, Poulter MO (2012). Molecular pathway reconstruction and analysis of disturbed gene expression in depressed individuals who died by suicide. *PLoS ONE.* Published online: 22 October 2012. doi:10.1371/journal.pone.0047581.

Zouaoui K, Dulaurent S, Gaulier JM, Moesch C, Lachâtre G (2013). Determination of glyphosate and ampa in blood and urine from humans: About 13 cases of acute intoxication. *Forensic Science International* 226, e20-e25.

www.ingramcontent.com/pod-product-compliance
Lightning Source LLC
Chambersburg PA
CBHW080420270326

41929CB00018B/3099